Worship in the
New Testament

In Gratitude to the Triune God
for
My Colleague and Friend
The late Robert E. Webber
and
His Dynamic Dreams
of
"Ancient Future Worship"
and
The Institute for Worship Studies

Worship in the New Testament

Divine Mystery and Human Response

GERALD L. BORCHERT

CHALICE
PRESS
ST. LOUIS, MISSOURI

Cover image: FotoSearch
Cover and interior design: Elizabeth Wright

www.chalicepress.com

Print: 9780827225145   EPUB: 9780827242944   EPDF: 9780827242951

Library of Congress Cataloging–in–Publication Data

Borchert, Gerald L.
  Worship in the New Testament : divine mystery and human response / by Gerald L. Borchert.
     p. cm.
  ISBN 978-0-8272-2514-5
  1. Bible. N.T.–Criticism, interpretation, etc. 2. Worship–Biblical teaching. I. Title.

  BS2361.3.B67 2008
  264.009'015–dc22   2008012070

Contents

Abbreviations

Abbreviations for Biblical Books

Gen	Genesis	Jonah	Jonah
Exod	Exodus	Mic	Micah
Lev	Leviticus	Nah	Nahum
Num	Numbers	Hab	Habakkuk
Deut	Deuteronomy	Zeph	Zephaniah
Josh	Joshua	Hag	Haggai
Judg	Judges	Zech	Zechariah
Ruth	Ruth	Mal	Malachi
1, 2 Sam	1, 2 Samuel	Matt	Matthew
1, 2 Kgs	1, 2 Kings	Mark	Mark
1, 2 Chr	1, 2 Chronicles	Luke	Luke
Ezra	Ezra	John	John
Neh	Nehemiah	Acts	Acts
Esth	Esther	Rom	Romans
Job	Job	1, 2 Cor	1, 2 Corinthians
Ps, Pss	Psalm(s)	Gal	Galatians
Prov	Proverbs	Eph	Ephesians
Eccl	Ecclesiastes / Qoheleth	Phil	Philippians
Song	Song of Songs /Song of Solomon /Canticles	Col	Colossians
		1, 2 Thess	1, 2 Thessalonians
Isa	Isaiah	1, 2 Tim	1, 2 Timothy
Jer	Jeremiah	Titus	Titus
Lam	Lamentations	Phlm	Philemon
Ezek	Ezekiel	Heb	Hebrews
Dan	Daniel	Jas	James
Hos	Hosea	1, 2 Pet	1, 2 Peter
Joel	Joel	1, 2, 3 John	1, 2, 3 John
Amos	Amos	Jude	Jude
Obad	Obadiah	Rev	Revelation

Modern Abbreviations

AB	*Anchor Bible*
BrazTC	*Brazos Theological Commentary*
CBQ	*Catholic Biblical Quarterly*
EBC	*Expositor's Bible Commentary*
Herm	*Hermeneia*
IB	*The Interpreter's Bible*
IDB	*The Interpreter's Dictionary of the Bible*
ICC	*International Critical Commentary*

Int	*Interpretation*
ISBE	*International Standard Bible Encyclopedia*
NAC	*New American Commentary*
NICNT	*New International Commentary on the New Testament*
NIGNTC	*New International Greek New Testament Commentary*
NIB	*New Interpreter's Bible*
NIVAC	*New International Version Application Commentary*
NTL	*New Testament Library*
NTS	*New Testament Studies*
R&E	*Review and Expositor*
SHBC	*Smyth & Helwys Bible Commentary*
SBL	Society of Biblical Literature
SPag	*Sacra Pagina*
TDNT	*Theological Dictionary of the New Testament*
WBC	*Word Biblical Commentary*

Abbreviations of Modern Translations

KJV	King James Version
NIV	New International Version
NLT	New Living Translation
NRSV	New Revised Standard Version
RSV	Revised Standard Version

Commentaries and Other Works

MATTHEW

Some helpful commentaries on Matthew include: Craig L. Blomberg, *Matthew* in *NAC* (Nashville: Broadman, 1992); M. Eugene Boring, "Matthew," in *NIB* (Nashville: Abingdon, 1995); F. Dale Bruner, *The Christbook: Matthew 1–12* (Waco, Tex.: Word Books, 1987); W. D. Davies and D. Allison, *Matthew* in *ICC* (Edinburgh: T. & T. Clark, 1988); Robert H. Gundry, *Matthew* (Grand Rapids: Eerdmans, 1981); Donald A. Hagner, *Matthew 1–13* and *Matthew 14–28* in *WBC* (Dallas: Word Books, 1993, 1995); Douglas R. A. Hare, *Matthew* in *Int* (Louisville: John Knox, 1993); Daniel Harrington, *The Gospel of Matthew* in *SPag* (Collegeville, Minn.: Liturgical Press, 1991); Stanley Hauerwas, *Matthew* in *BrazTC* (Grand Rapids: Brazos, 2006); Ulrich Luz, *Studies in Matthew* (Grand Rapids: Eerdmans, 2005); Frank Stagg, "Matthew," in Vol. 6, *BBC* (Nashville: Broadman, 1972); Matthew J. Wilkens, *Matthew* in *NIVAC* (Grand Rapids: Zondervan, 2004), Ben Witherington III, *Matthew* in *SHBC* (Macon, Ga.: Smyth & Helwys, 2006). See also Craig L. Blomberg, *Jesus and the Gospels* (Nashville: Broadman & Holman, 1997).

MARK

For various treatments on Mark, see: Ernest Best, *Following Jesus: Discipleship in the Gospel of Mark* (Sheffield: University Press, 1981); M. Eugene Boring, *Mark* in *NTL* (Louisville: Westminster/John Knox, 2006); Rudolf Bultmann, *The History of the Synoptic Tradition* (New York: Harper & Row, 1963); Bruce Chilton, ed., *The Kingdom of God in the Teaching of Jesus* (Philadelphia: Fortress, 1984); C. E. B. Cranfield, *The Gospel According to Saint Mark* (Cambridge: University Press, 1963); C. H. Dodd, *The Parables of the Kingdom* (New York: Scribners, 1961); David E. Garland, *Mark* in *NIVAC* (Grand Rapids: Zondervan, 1996); Robert A. Guelich, *Mark 1–8:26* in *WBC* (Dallas: Word Books, 1989); Martin Hengel, *Studies in the Gospel of Mark* (Philadelphia: Fortress, 1985); David Rhoades and D. Michie, *Mark as Story: An Introduction to the Narrative of a Gospel* (Philadelphia: Fortress, 1982); Werner Kelber, *The Kingdom in Mark* (Philadelphia: Fortress, 1974); Robert Meye, *Jesus and the Twelve* (Grand Rapids: Eerdmans, 1968); Pheme Perkins, "Mark," in *NIB* (Nashville:Abingdon, 1995); Eduard Schweizer, *The Good News According to Mark* (Richmond, Va.:John Knox Press, 1970); Vincent Taylor, *The Gospel According to Mark* (New York: St. Martin's Press, 1966); Lamar Williamson Jr., *Mark* in *Int* (Louisville: John Knox, 1983); Ben Witherington III, *The Gospel of Mark: A Socio-Rhetorical Commentary* (Grand Rapids: Eerdmans, 2001).

LUKE

For commentaries on Luke, see: Darrell L. Block, *Luke* in *NIVAC* (Grand Rapids: Zondervan, 1996); Francois Bovon, *Luke 1* [1:1–9:50] in *Herm* (Minneapolis: Augsburg/Fortress, 2002); id., *Luke the Theologian,* 2d ed. (Waco, Tex.: Baylor U. Press, 2006); R. Alan Culpepper, "Luke," in *NIB* (Nashville: Abingdon, 1996); Hans Conzelmann, *The Theology of St. Luke* (New York: Harper & Brothers, 1990); Fred Craddock, *Luke* (Louisville: John Knox, 1990); Joseph A. Fitzmyer, *The Gospel According to Luke I–IX; The Gospel According to Luke X–XXIV* (Garden City, N.Y.: Doubleday, 1981; 1985); I. Howard Marshall, *The Gospel of Luke: A Commentary on the Greek Text* (Grand Rapids: Eerdmans, 1979); John Noland, *Luke 1–9:20; Luke 9:21–18:34; Luke 18:35–24:53* in *WBC* (Dallas: Word Books, 1989–1993); Mikeal Parsons, *Luke: Storyteller, Interpreter, Evangelist* (Peabody, Mass.: Hedrickson, 2007); Alfred Plummer, *A Critical and Exegetical Commentary on the Gospel of St. Luke* in *ICC* (Edinburgh: T. & Y. Clark, 1922); Eduard Schweizer, *The Good News According to Luke* (Atlanta: John Knox, 1984)

JOHN

For information among the many works on John, see, for example: George Beasley- Murrary, *John* in *WBC* (Waco, Tex.: Word Books, 1987); Gerald Borchert, *John 1–11* and *John 12–21* in *NAC* (Nashville: Broadman & Holman, 1996, 2002); Raymond E. Brown, *John i–xii* and *John xiii–xxi* in *AB* (Garden City, N.Y.: Doubleday, 1966, 1970); D. A. Carson, *The Gospel According to John* (Grand Rapids: Eerdmans, 1991); R. Alan Culpepper, *Anatomy of the Fourth Gospel* (Philadelphia: Fortress, 1983); C. H. Dodd, *The Interpretation of the Fourth Gospel* (Cambridge: University Press, 1958); Ernst Haenchen, *John 1* and *John 2* in *Herm* (Philadelphia: Fortress, 1984); Leon Morris, *The Gospel According to John* (Grand Rapids: Eerdmans, 1971); Gail R. O'Day, "John," in *NIB* (Nashville: Abingdon, 1995); Rudolf Schnackenburg, *The Gospel According to John,* 3 vols. (New York: Crossroad, 1987); Sandra M. Schneiders, *Written That You May Believe: Encountering Jesus in the Fourth Gospel* (New York: Crossroad [Herder & Herder], 1999); Brooke Foss Westcott, *The Gospel According to St. John* (Grand Rapids: Eerdmans, [1954]).

ACTS

For works on Acts, see: F. F. Bruce, *The Acts of the Apostles: The Greek Text with Introduction and Commentary,* 3d ed. (Grand Rapids: Eerdmans, 1990); C. H. Dodd, *The Apostolic Preaching and Its Development* (London: Hodder & Stoughton, 1936); Joseph A. Fitzmyer, *The Acts of the Apostles* in *AB* (Garden City, N.Y.: Doubleday, 1998); Ward Gasque, *A History of the Criticism of the Acts of the Apostles* (Grand Rapids: Eerdmans, 1975); David W. Gill and Conrad Gempf, *The Book of Acts in Its First Century Setting: Greco-Roman Setting* (Grand Rapids: Eerdmans, 1994); Enrst Haenchen, *The Acts of the Apostles: A Commentary* (Philadelphia: Westminster Press, 1971); Colin Hemer, *The Book of Acts in the Setting of Hellenistic History* (Tüebingen: Mohr/Siebeck, 1989); Martin Hengel, *Acts and the History of Early Christianity* (Philadelphia: Fortress, 1979); Luke Timothy Johnson, *The Acts of the Apostles* in *SPag* (Collegeville, Minn.: Liturgical Press, 1992); Richard N. Longenecker, *Acts* in *EBC,* Vol. 9 (Grand Rapids: Zondervan, 1981), 207–573; Jerome H. Neyrey, ed., *The Social World of Luke-Acts: Models of Interpretation* (Peabody, Mass.: Hendrickson, 1991); John B. Polhill, *Acts* in *NAC* (Nashville: Broadman Press, 1992); William H. Willimon, *Acts* in *Int* (Louisville: John Knox, 1988). See also works under the Gospel of Luke.

ROMANS

For information on the Epistle to the Romans, see: Paul Achtemeier, *Romans* in *Int* (Atlanta: John Knox, 1985); Gerald Borchert, "Romans, Letter to," in *Mercer Dictionary of the Bible,* ed. Watson E. Mills (Macon, Ga.: Mercer University Press, 1990), 772–74; id., "Romans, Pastoral Counseling, and the Introspective Conscience of the West," *R&E* 83.1 (Winter 1986): 81–92; Charles Cranfield, *A Critical and Exegetical Commentary on the Epistle to the Romans,* 2 vols. in *ICC* (Edinburgh: T. & T. Clark, 1980); James D. G. Dunn, *Romans 1–8* and *Romans 9–16* in *WBC* (Dallas: Word Books, 1988); Joseph A. Fitzmyer, *Romans* in *AB* (New York: Doubleday, 1993); Ernst Kasemann, *Commentary on Romans* (Grand Rapids: Eerdmans, 1980); Robert Jewett, *Romans* in *Herm* (Minneapolis: Fortress, 2007); Franz Leenhardt, *The Epistle to the Romans* (London: Lutterworth, 1961); Martin Luther, *Lectures on Romans,* ed. Hilton Oswald; Jacob Preus, vol. 25, *Luther's Works* (St. Louis: Concordia, 1972); Douglas J. Moo, *Romans* in *NIVAC* (Grand Rapids: Zondervan, 2000); John Stott, *Romans: God's Good News for the World* (Downers Grove, Ill.: InterVarsity Press, 1994); Charles H. Talbert, *Romans* in *SHBC* (Macon, Ga.: Smyth & Helwys, 2002).

1 & 2 CORINTHIANS

Among the many helpful works on the Corinthian letters are: Ernest Best, *Second Corinthians* in *Int* (Louisville: John Knox, 1987); C. K. Barrett, *The First Epistle to the Corinthians* (New York: Harper, 1968); id., *The Second Epistle to the Corinthians* (New York: Harper, 1973); Craig L. Blomberg, *1 Corinthians* in *NIVAC* (Grand Rapids: Zondervan, 1994); Gerald L. Borchert, "Assurance and Warning in 1 Corinthians," in *Assurance and Warning* (Nashville: Broadman, 1987), 19–85; F. F. Bruce, "I Corinthians," in *New Century Bible* (Grand Rapids: Eerdmans, 1971); Raymond F. Collins, *First Corinthians* in *SPag* (Collegeville, Minn.: Liturgical Press, 1999); Hans Conzelmann, *1 Corinthians* in *Herm* (Philadelphia: Fortress, 1975); C. T. Evans, "1 Corinthians," in *IB* (Nashville: Abingdon, 1953); Gordon D. Fee, *The First Epistle to the Corinthians* in *NICNT* (Grand Rapids: Eerdmans, 1987, 1994); Victor Paul Furnish, *II Corinthians* in *AB* (New York: Doubleday, 1984); David E. Garland, *2 Corinthians* in *NAC* (Nashville: Broadman & Holman, 1999); F. W. Grosieide, *Commentary on the First Epistle to the Corinthians* in *NICNT* (Grand

Rapids: Eerdmans, 1953); Murray J. Harris, *The Second Epistle to the Corinthians* in *NIGNTC* (Grand Rapids: Eerdmans, 2005); Richard B. Hays, *First Corinthians* in *Int* (Louisville: John Knox, 1997); J. Hering, *The First Epistle of Saint Paul to the Corinthians* (London: Epworth, 1937); Jan Lambrecht, *Second Corinthians* in *SPag* (Collegeville, Minn.: Liturgical Press, 1999); R. C. Lenski, *The Interpretation of I and II Corinthians* (Minneapolis: Augsburg, 1937); Frank J. Matera, *II Corinthians* in *NTL* (Louisville: Westminster/John Knox, 2003); Wayne E. Meeks, *The First Urban Christians: The Social World of the Apostle Paul* (New Haven: Yale University Press, 1983); J. M. O'Connor, *St. Paul's Corinth: Texts and Archaeology* (Wilmington, Del.: Michael Glazier, 1983); Walter Schmithals, *Gnosticism in Corinth* (Nashville: Abingdon, 1971); Charles H. Talbert, *Reading Corinthians: A Literary and Theological Commentary on 1 and 2 Corinthians* (New York: Crossroad, 1987); Ben Witherington III, *Conflict and Community in Corinth: A Socio-Rhetorical Commentary on 1 and 2 Corinthians* (Grand Rapids: Eerdmans, 1995).

GALATIANS

For some helpful works on Galatians, see: C. K. Barrett, *Freedom and Obligation: A Study of the Epistle to the Galatians* (London: SPCK, 1985); Hans D. Betz, *Galatians* in *Herm* (Philadelphia: Fortress, 1979); Gerald L. Borchert, "A Key to Pauline Thinking: Galatians 3:23–29," *R&E* 91 (1994): 145–51; id., "Galatians," in *Romans and Galatians* in Cornerstone Biblical Commentary, Vol. 14 (Wheaton, Ill.: Tyndale House, 2007); F. F. Bruce, *Commentary on Galatians* (Grand Rapids: Eerdmans, 1982); E. DeWitt Burton, *The Epistle to the Galatians* in *ICC* (Edinburgh: T.& T, Clark, 1921); James D. G. Dunn, *The Epistle to the Galatians* in *Black's New Testament Commentary* (Peabody, Mass.: Hendrickson, 1993); Ronald Y. K. Fung, *The Epistle to the Galatians* in *NICNT* (Grand Rapids: Eerdmans, 1988); Timothy George, *Galatians* in *NAC* (Nashville: Broadman & Holman, 1994); Richard N. Longenecker, *Galatians* in *WBC* (Dallas: Word Books, 1990); J. Louis Martyn, *Galatians* in *AB* ((New York: Doubleday, 1997); Heinrich Schlier, *Der Bief an der Galater* (Göttingen: Vandenhoeck und Ruprecht, 1949); Ben Witherington III, *Grace in Galatia: A Commentary on Paul's Letter to the Galatians* (Grand Rapids: Eerdmans, 1998).

EPHESIANS

For information on Ephesians, see: Marcus Barth, *Ephesians* in *AB*, 2 vols. (Garden City, N.Y.: Doubleday, 1974); F. W. Beare, "The Epistle to the Ephesians," in *IB*, Vol. 11 (Nashville: Abingdon, 1953); F. F. Bruce, *The Epistle to the Ephesians* (London: Pickering and Inglis, 1961); E. J. Goodspeed, *The Meaning of Ephesians* (Chicago: University Press, 1933); Ernst Kaesemann, "Ephesus and Acts," in *Studies in Luke-Acts*, ed. L. Keck and J. Martyn (Philadelphia: Fortress, 1980), 288–97; J. C. Kirby, *Ephesians: Baptism and Pentecost* (London: S.P.C.K., 1968); Andrew T. Lincoln, *Ephesians* in *WBC* (Dallas: Word Books, 1990); P. T. O'Brien, "Ephesians 1: An Unusual Introduction to a New Testament Letter," *New Testament Studies* 25 (1978–79): 504–16; A. Van Roon, *The Authenticity of Ephesians*, in *Novum Testamentum* Supp. 39 (Leiden: E. J. Brill, 1982); Pamela J. Scalise and Gerald L. Borchert, "The Bible and the Spiritual Pilgrimage," in *Becoming Christian: Spiritual Dimensions of Spiritual Formation*, ed. Bill J. Leonard (Louisville: Westminster/John Knox, 1990), 31–45; Heinrich Schlier, *Christus und die Kirche im Epheserbrief* (Tübingen: Mohr, 1930); id., *Der Brief an die Epheser* (Duesseldorf: Patmos, 1957); E. F. Scott, *The Epistles of Paul to the Colossians, to Philemon and to the Ephesians* (London: Hodder & Stoughton, 1930); Klyne Snodgrass, *Ephesians* in *NIVAC* (Grand Rapids: Zondervan, 1996).

PHILIPPIANS

For further information concerning Philippians, see: G. B Caird, *Paul's Letters from Prison* (Oxford: University Press, 1976); Fred B. Craddock, *Philippians* in *Int* (Atlanta: John Knox, 1985); Gordon Fee, *Paul's Letter to the Philipians* in *NICNT* (Grand Rapids: Eerdmans, 1995); J. A. Fitzmyer, "Philippians," in *Jerome Biblical Commentary*, ed. R. E. Brown (Engelwood Cliffs, N.J.: Prentice Hall, 1968); David Garland, "The Composition and Literary Unity of Philippians: Some Neglected Factors," *Novum Testamentum* 27 (1985): 141–73; Gerald F. Hawthorne, *Philippians* in *WBC* (Waco, Tex.: Word Books, 1983); J. B. Lightfoot, *St. Paul's Epistle to the Philippians* (Grand Rapids: Zondervan, 1953); Ralph P. Martin, *Philippians* in *New Century Bible* (London: Oliphants, 1976); id., *Carmen Christi: Philippians 2:5–11 in Recent Interpretation and in the Setting of Early Christian Worship* (Cambridge: University Press, 1967); Richard R. Melick, *Philippians, Colossians, Philemon* in *NAC* (Nashville: Broadman Press, 1991); H. C. G. Moule, *The*

Epistle to the Philippians (Cambridge: University Press, 1897); Peter T. O'Brien, *Commentary on Philippians* in *NIGNTC* (Grand Rapids: Eerdmans, 1991); Moises Silva, *Philippians* (Chicago: Moody Press, 1988); Frank Stagg, "Philippians" in *BBC,* ed. C. J. Allen, Vol. 11 (Nashville: Broadman Press, 1971); Frank Thielman, *Philippians* in *NIVAC* (Grand Rapids: Zondervan, 1995); see also the articles on "Philippians" in *R&E* 78 (1980): 309–92.

COLOSSIANS

For further information on Colossians, see the following works: Markus Barth and Helmut Blanke, *Colossians* in *AB* (New York: Doubleday, 1994); F. F. Bruce, "Colossians, Epistle to the," in *ISBE* (Grand Rapids: Eerdmans, 1979), I. 732–35; David E. Garland, *Colossians and Philemon* in *NIVAC* (Grand Rapids: Zondervan, 1998); Eduard Lohse, *Colossians and Philemon* in *Herm* (Philadelphia: Fortress Press, 1971); Ralph P. Martin, *Colossians: The Church's Lord and the Christian's Liberty* (Grand Rapids: Zondervan, 1972); C. F. D. Moule, *The Epistles of Paul the Apostle to the Colossians and Philemon* in *Cambridge Greek Testament Commentary* (Cambridge: University Press, 1957); Peter T. O'Brien, *Colossians, Philemon* in *WBC* (Waco, Tex.: Word Books, 1982); Eduard Schweizer, *The Letter to the Colossians* (Minneapolis: Augsburg, 1982).

1 & 2 THESSALONIANS

For comments on 1 and 2 Thessalonians, see, for example: Ernest Best, *The First and Second Epistles to the Thessalonians* (New York: Harper & Row, 1972); Gerald Borchert, *Discovering Thessalonians* in the *Guideposts Home Bible Study Program* (Carmel, N.Y.: Guideposts, 1986); F. F. Bruce, *1 & 2 Thessalonians* in *WBC* (Waco, Tex.: Word Books, 1982); James Frame, *A Critical and Exegetical Commentary on the Epistles of St. Paul to the Thessalonians* in *ICC* (Edinburgh: T. & T. Clark: 1912); Beverly Roberts Gaventa, *First and Second Thessalonians* in *Int* (Louisville: John Knox, 1998); Michael Holmes, *1 and 2 Thessalonians* in *NIVAC* (Grand Rapids: Zondervan, 1998); D. Michael Martin, *1, 2 Thessalonians* in *NAC* (Nashville: Broadman & Holman, 1995); Leon Morris, *The First and Second Epistles to the Thessalonians* in *NICNT,* rev. ed. (Grand Rapids: Eerdmans, 1991); Earl J. Richard, *First and Second Thessalonians* in *SPag* (Collegeville, Minn.: Liturgical Press, 1995); Charles A. Wanamaker, *The Epistles to the Thessalonians: A Commentary on the Greek Text* (Grand Rapids: Eerdmans, 1990); Ben Witherington III, *1 and 2 Thessalonians: A Socio-Rhetorical Commentary* (Grand Rapids: Eerdmans, 2006).

1 & 2 TIMOTHY, TITUS

For further information on the varied views of the Pastoral Epistles, see: C. K. Barrett, *The Pastoral Epistles in the New English Bible* (Oxford: Clarendon Press, 1963); J. M. Bassler, *1 Timothy. 2 Timothy. Titus* (Nashville Abingdon, 1996); Raymond F. Collins, *1 & 2 Timothy and Titus* in *NTL* (Louisville: Westminster/John Knox, 2002); Martin Dibelius and Hans Conzelmann, *The Pastoral Epistles* in *Hermeneia* (Philadelphia; Fortress, 1972); Gordon D. Fee, *1–2 Timothy, Titus* in *Good News Commentary* (San Francisco: Harper & Row, 1984); Donald Guthrie, *The Pastoral Epistles* (Grand Rapids: Eerdmans, 1990); A. T. Hanson, *The Pastoral Epistles* (Grand Rapids: Eerdmans, 1983); E. Glenn Hinson, "1–2 Timothy, Titus," in *BBC* (Nashville: Broadman Press, 1973), 299–376; Luke Timothy Johnson, *The First and Second Letters to Timothy* in *AB* (Garden City, N.Y.: Doubleday, 2001); J. N. D. Kelly, *A Commentary on the Pastoral Epistles* (New York: Harper & Row, 1963); Walter L. Liefeld, *1 and 2 Timothy, Titus* in *NIVAC* (Grand Rapids: Zondervan, 1999); William D. Mounce, *Pastoral Epistles* in *WBC* (Nashville: Thomas Nelson, 2000); Thomas C. Oden, *First and Second Timothy and Titus* in *Int* (Louisville: John Knox, 1989); E. F. Scott, *The Pastoral Epistles* (New York: Harper and Brothers, 1936); Philip H. Towner, *The Letters to Timothy and Titus* in *NICNT* (Grand Rapids: Eerdmans, 2006).

PHILEMON

The commentaries on Philemon are usually linked with longer works such as Colossians. For information on this letter, see: Joseph S Fitzmyer, *Philemon* in *AB* (Garden City, N.Y.: Doubleday, 2000); David E. Garland, *Colossians and Philemon* in *NIVAC* (Grand Rapids: Zondervan, 1998); Eduard Lohse, *Colossians and Philemon* in *Herm* (Philadelphia: Fortress, 1971); C. F. D. Moule, *The Epistles of Paul to the Colossians and to Philemon* (Cambridge: University Press, 1962); Peter T. O'Brien, *Colossians, Philemon* in *WBC* (Waco, Tex.: Word, 1982); N. R.

Petersen, *Rediscovering Paul: Philemon and the Sociology of Paul's Narrative World* (Philadelphia: Fortress, 1985). See also P. N. Harrison, "Onesimus and Philemon," *Anglican Theological Review* 32 (1950): 268–94.

HEBREWS

For further information on the Book of Hebrews, please consult, among other works: Gerald L. Borchert, *Assurance and Warning* (Nashville: Broadman, 1987), 153–202; id., "A Superior Book: Hebrews," *R&E* 82.3 (Summer 1985): 319–32; G. W. Buchanan, *To the Hebrews* in *AB* (Garden City, N.Y.: Doubleday, 1981); F. F. Bruce, *The Epistle to the Hebrews* in *NICNT* (Grand Rapids: Eerdmans, 1964); Fred B. Craddock, Luke Timothy Johnson, et al., "Hebrews," in *Hebrews–Jude* in *NIB* (Nashville: Abingdon, 1998); Donald Hagner, *Hebrews* in *A Good News Commentary* (San Francisco: Harper & Row, 1983); Luke Timothy Johnson, *Hebrews* in *NTL* (Louisville: Westminster/John Knox, 2006); William Johnsson, *Hebrews* in *Knox Preaching Guides* (Atlanta: John Knox Press, 1980); Craig Koester, *Hebrews* in *AB* (Garden City, N.Y.: Doubleday, 2001); William L. Lane, *Hebrews 1–8* and *Hebrews 9–13* in *WBC* (Dallas: Word Books, 1991); Thomas G. Long, *Hebrews* in *Int* (Louisville; John Knox, 1997); Edgar V. McKnight and Christopher Church, *Hebrews–James* in *SHBC* (Macon, Ga.: Smyth & Helwys, 2002) and the older work by B. F. Westcott, *The Epistle to the Hebrews* (Grand Rapids: Eerdmans, 1967 [reprint of 1909]).

JAMES

For further information concerning the Book of James, please consult, among other works: Peter H. Davids, *Commentary on James* in *NIGNTC* (Grand Rapids: Eerdmans, 1982); id., *James* in *New International Biblical Commentary* (Peabody, Mass.: Hendrickson, 1989); Martin Dibelius and H. Greeven, *A Commentary on James* in *Herm* ((Philadelphia: Fortress, 1976); David A. Hubbard, *The Book of James: Wisdom that Works* (Waco, Tex.: Word Books, 1980); Luke Timothy Johnson, *The Letter of James* in *AB* (Garden City, N.Y.: Doubleday, 1995); Sophia A. Laws, *A Commentary on the Epistle of James* (San Francisco: Harper & Row, 1980); Ralph Martin, *James* in *WBC* (Waco, Tex.: Word Books, 1988); Edgar V. McKnight and Christopher Church, *Hebrews–James* in *SHBC* (Macon, Ga.: Smyth & Helwys, 2002); David P. Nystrom, *James* in *NIVAC* (Grand Rapids: Zondervan, 1997); Kurt A. Richardson, *James* in *NAC* (Nashville: Broadman & Holman, 1997); James H. Ropes, *A Critical and Exegetical Commentary on the Epistle of St. James* in *ICC* (Edinburgh: T. & T. Clark, 1916); Harold S. Songer, "James," in *BBC*, ed. Clifton J. Allen, Vol. 12 (Nashville: Broadman Press, 1972), 100–140.

1 & 2 PETER, JUDE

For helpful works on the Petrine Epistles and Jude, see: Richard J. Bauckham, *Jude, 2 Peter* in *WBC* (Waco, Tex.: Word Books, 1983); Ernest Best, *1 Peter* in *New Century Bible* (Grand Rapids: Eerdmans, 1971); Gerald L. Borchert, "The Conduct of Christians in the Face of the 'Fiery Ordeal' ([1 Pet]4:12–5:11)," *R&E* 79 (1982): 451–62; Raymond E. Brown, et al., *Peter in the New Testament: A Collaborative Assessment by Protestant and Roman Catholic Scholars* (Minneapolis: Augsburg, 1973); Philip Carrington, *The Primitive Christian Catechism* (Cambridge: University Press, 1940); Fred B. Craddock, Luke Timothy Johnson, et al., "1 Peter" and "2 Peter and Jude," in *Hebrews–Jude* in *NIB* (Nashville: Abingdon, 1998); F. L. Cross, *1 Peter: A Paschal Liturgy* (London: A.R. Mowbray, 1971); F. W. Danker, "2 Peter 1: A Solemn Decree," *CBQ* 40 (1978): 64–82; Peter H. Davids, *The Letters of 2 Peter and Jude* (Grand Rapids: Eerdmans, 2006); John H. Elliott, *A Home for the Homeless: A Sociological Exegesis of 1 Peter, Its Situation and Strategy* (Philadelphia: Fortress Press, 1981); J. N. D. Kelly, *A Commentary on the Epistles of Peter and Jude* (London: Adam & Charles Black, 1969); Scott McKnight, *1 Peter* in *NIVAC* (Grand Rapids: Zondervan, 1996); J. Ramsey Michaels, *1 Peter* in *WBC* (Waco, Tex.: Word Books, 1988); Douglas J. Moo, *2 Peter and Jude* in *NIVAC* (Grand Rapids: Zondervan, 1996); J. H. Neyrey, "The Form and Background of the Polemic in 2 Peter," *Jounaal of Biblical Literature* 99 (1980): 403–31; Bo Reicke, *The Disobedient Spirits and Christian Baptism* (Copenhagen: Munksgaard, 1946); J. A. T. Robinson, "Jude," "2 Peter," in *Redating the New Testament* (Philadelphia: Westminster Press), 1976), 140–99; E. G. Selwyn, *The First Epistle of Saint Peter* (London; Macmillan, 1958); Donald Senior and Daniel J. Harrington, *1 Peter; Jude and 2 Peter* in *SPag* (Collegeville, Minn.: Liturgical Press, 2003).

1, 2, & 3 JOHN

For further information on the Johannine letters, see: Raymond E. Brown, *The Epistles of John* in *AB* (Garden City, N.Y.; Doubleday, 1982); Rudolf Bultmann, *A Commentary on the Johnnine Epistles* in *Herm* (Philadelphia: Fortress, 1973); Gary M. Burge, *Letters of John* in *NIVAC* (Grand Rapids: Zondervan, 1996); R. Alan Culpepper, *1 John, 2 John, 3 John* in *Knox Preaching Guides* (Atlanta: John Knox Press, 1985); Thomas F. Johnson, *1, 2, and 3 John* in *New International Biblical Commentary* (Peabody, Mass.: Hendrickson, 1993); John Painter, *1, 2, and 3 John* in *SPag* (Collegeville, Minn.: Liturgical Press, 2002); David Rensberger, *1 John, 2 John, 3 John* (Nashville: Abingdon, 1997); D. Moody Smith, *First, Second an Third John* in *Int* (Louisville: John Knox, 1991); and the old standard work of Bruce F. Westcott, *The Epistles of Saint John* (Grand Rapids: Eerdmans, 1996).

REVELATION

For further discussions on Revelation, see: David Aune, *Revelation 1–5*; *Revelation 6–16*; *Revelation 17–22* in *WBC* (Dallas: Word Books, 1997; Nashville: Thomas Nelson, 1998); Gerald Borchert, "Revelation," in the *New Living Translation Study Bible* (Wheaton, Ill.: Tyndale House, forthcoming c. 2008); M. Eugene Boring, *Revelation* in *Int* (Louisville; John Knox, 1989); John Wick Bowman, *The Drama of the Book of Revelation* (Philadelphia: Westminster Press, 1955); G. B. Caird, *A Commentary on the Revelation of St. John the Divine* (New York: Harper & Row, 1966); Adela Yarbro Collins, *Crisis and Catharsis: The Power of the Apocalypse* (Philadelphia: Westminster Press, 1984); Robert G. Clouse, ed. *The Meaning of the Millennium: Four Views* (Downers Grove, Ill.: InterVarsity Press, 1977); W. Hulitt Gloer, "Worship God! Liturgical Elements in the Apocalypse," *R&E* 98 (Winter 2001): 35–57; Paul D. Hanson, *The Dawn of Apocalyptic,* rev. ed. (Philadelphia: Fortress, 1979); Philip Edgcumben Hughes, *The Book of Revelation* (Grand Rapids: Eerdmans, 1990); Craig Keener, *Revelation* in *NIVAC* (Grand Rapids: Zondervan, 2000); George Eldon Ladd, *A Commentary on the Revelation of John* (Grand Rapids: Eerdmans, 1972); Bruce J. Malina, *On the Genre and Message of Revelation: Star Visions and Sky Journeys* (Peabody, Mass.: Hendrickson, 1995); Leon Morris, *Apocalyptic* (Grand Rapids: Eerdmans, 1972); John P. Newport, *The Lion and the Lamb* (Nashville: Broadman Press, 1986); Eugene Peterson, *Reversed Thunder: The Revelation of John and the Praying Imagination* (New York: Harper Collins, 1988); D. S. Russell, *The Method and Message of Jewish Apocalyptic* (Philadelphia: Westminster Press, 1964); Leonard Thompson, *The Book of Revelation: Apocalypse and Empire* (New York: Oxford, 1990); Arthur Wainwright, *Mysterious Apocalypse: Interpreting the Book of Revelation* (Nashville: Abingdon, 1993).

THE DIDACHE

Kurt Niederwimmer, *The Didache* in *Herm* (Minneapolis: Augsburg/Fortress, 1998).

Preface

The writing of this Worship Introduction to the New Testament has been for me a worship experience in which for the past two years I have intensely pondered many ideas and arisen in the wee hours of the morning to make sure I would not forget some fresh insight. This task has allowed me to revisit each of the New Testament books and to review countless notes that I have collected over many years of teaching the New Testament. Indeed, at times during the writing of this work I began to sing songs such as "How Great Thou Art!" as I reflected on the greatness of God and the gift of Jesus to humanity. I realize that for an academician to make such an admission in print may sound overly pious, but I do confess that however the reader might respond, this work coming toward the end of my life is a sincere reflection of my dependence on the mystery of God that has touched me in Jesus.

This work is my gift to my students and to the churches that have nourished me for decades. To them and to God I am humbly indebted because I have grown in the process of my encounters with people of faith. I am not the brash young lawyer that I was when I first prayed for God's forgiveness and offered my life in service to the Lord. I thank God in Christ for the pilgrimage that has brought me to this point, and I pray that my readers will find this work to be of some assistance to them as they journey through the pages of the New Testament. If by God's grace some may find this work helpful in opening their minds and spirits to sense something of God's presence in their lives, then I have received an added blessing.

But prefaces are places where we normally offer our thanks to those who have been of assistance to us as writers, and I am more than ready to do so. My first thanks belong to my dear wife who has read many of my manuscripts in the past and carefully suggested that I discard my first attempt at writing a work on worship. I did so with some pain, but I have been doubly blessed for following her wise advice. I have already dedicated other works to her.

Second, this work I thankfully dedicate to my close associate, the late Robert E. Webber, whom I helped bring to Northern Seminary from Wheaton in his closing years of teaching, and who later asked me to join him at the Institute for Worship Studies where he was the founding president. In that role he offered me the opportunity and pleasure to direct the thesis program for the doctoral students in worship. Now, after having read well over a hundred worship theses and proposals, I have learned a great deal about worship in a field in which I had earlier only scratched the surface.

Third, concerning this present work on worship, I also wish to express my sincere gratitude to my students, who come from an almost unbelievably wide range of denominations and who have taught me much about the broad parameters of worship and how worship impacts Christian communities. They are truly in the forefront of a wholesome ecumenical revival in worship.

Fourth, I am deeply indebted to my editor, Trent Butler, who has made many helpful suggestions and stimulated me throughout the work on this manuscript. He is a dear friend of many years standing.

Finally, to my readers, I offer my prayer that you might use this work to reflect on your patterns of worship and consider how you might become agents for bringing worship renewal to your communities of faith.

Cordially in Christ
Gerald L. Borchert, Thesis Director
The Robert E. Webber Institute for Worship Studies
Palm Sunday 2007

INTRODUCTION

Responding to Mystery

Worship in the New Testament

Encountering God in Jesus Christ is an experience with mystery. You may be able to analyze your reactions to the encounter, but the person of Jesus ultimately resists analysis, even though Albert Schweitzer, in an early-twentieth-century study, made an attempt to do so. Like John in writing his first letter, we may be able to speak about what we have sensed with our eyes, our ears, and even with our touch (1 John 1:2); but we cannot put ultimate reality into a test tube or computerize a person. There is a numinous quality about God and Jesus to which philosophers and theologians have given the designation the *mysterium tremendum,* which essentially means that such mystery is beyond our understanding or control.[1]

This concept reminded me of a rather homey but surprising experience when I was teaching in Cameroon. One of the nationals described the death of his wife as "wunde-ful." The fact that he used the term repeatedly in the conversation caught my attention. He did not mean that it was a happy experience, but that it was awesome and brought him to a sense of wonderment and fear. The Bible often refers to our relationship with God as the "fear of the Lord." Indeed, the psalmist declared that such fear is "the beginning of wisdom" (Ps 111:10). The "fear" of the Lord is the starting point for authentic worship.

Purpose of This Book

The purpose of this book is to detail the New Testament's responses to mystery in the coming of Jesus by reflecting on the lessons in the Gospels, the worship and life of the early church, and the expectations that have enlivened worship down through the ages from our inspired texts.

In this era of changing mind-sets worship is in the forefront of the church's concern. Worship is an issue that touches our lives at their very core and engages our minds in intense differences of opinion. We argue about worship patterns, feel strong emotions in varying worship settings, and often judge churches by the extent to which their worship services conform to our personal comfort zones. Indeed, this era has often been called the period of worship wars. Actually, history reveals that differences of opinion about worship are not new.

Now, in achieving my goal for this book, I am not simply writing a theology of worship based on New Testament texts. We already have several such helpful studies.[2] Instead, I turn in the direction of writing a different kind of introduction: an interpretation of each book of the New Testament with a distinct focus on the contribution that each makes to our understanding of worship. Instead of extracting ideas out of the texts and then formulating my theology of worship, my intention is to supply the raw materials to enable you as concerned Christians in various churches to confront the biblical texts yourselves in their varied styles, formats, and literary presentations. The anticipated result should be that you, my readers, with your New Testaments in hand, will be able to critique your present patterns of worship and develop new approaches of responding to divine mystery, which will reflect deeper understandings of worship.

Over the years of being a member of many international dialogues and having served as the chair of the Commission on Doctrine and Interchurch Cooperation for the Baptist World Alliance, I have become very conscious of the fact that when we begin any conversations by rehearsing our theological presuppositions about a subject, we generally end up where we began. But if we begin with an openness to the biblical texts themselves, several results can follow: we stand a better chance of allowing our views to be judged by a strategic outside authority (the New Testament), of having our views modified, and of developing new insights and patters for worship from our foundational texts. Of course, we all start with presuppositions, as Rudolf Bultmann stated many years ago. Those presuppositions are based either on naive imbedded theologies or have been formulated over years of being socialized to think in certain ways. My point in this work, therefore, is to afford my readers a resource for developing new deliberative theologies of worship based on the authority of the Bible. What you, the reader, add to that source is your decision, but hopefully you will recognize what is rooted in the New Testament and what is not.

In this era of changing ways of thinking and communication, it is imperative to be clear on the general sources of our faith, namely: Scripture, tradition, reason, and experience (the so-called quadrilateral). All of them play a part in who we are as worshiping people of God. I would, however, request of us as a pilgrim people who are continually learning more about relating to divine mystery that we be very sensitive to the foundational texts of our faith, namely the Holy Scriptures, which can through the Holy Spirit provide new insights concerning worship for every new generation. In this process I am fully aware of the "Marcionite" danger, of using only the New Testament as my source, but time and space prevent me from expanding this study into the Old Testament.

Besides, my colleague at the Institute for Worship Studies, Andrew Hill, has begun that process with his helpful work, *Enter His Courts with Praise*.[3]

The Bible's Image-rich Nature

To recognize the centrality of our foundational texts is especially important for the growing number of young people and others who represent the "postmodern" mindset with a thorough attachment to "image-rich" communication patterns. If you are among this group and have not already discovered the fact, I trust that you will be surprised to learn that our ancient book called the New Testament is image-rich in its presentations. Moreover, because of the immanent arrival on the generational horizon of people with a "digital" mindset and a familiarity with computer links to countless Web sites and more information than our minds can absorb, we need to be prepared to rethink the ways we do worship without losing the sense of divine mystery.[4]

In this work I am not attempting to provide full footnotes or references on almost every statement I make, as I did in some of my commentaries.[5] Instead I have included at the beginning of this book additional works that can be consulted by the reader. In the discussion that follows I will include a few footnotes as needed on some points. My hope is that in this work you, the readers, might focus on significant ideas as we move through the biblical stories and passages, not as prooftexts for worship, but as contextualized thought-provokers that can stimulate reflection on your own patterns of worship. In this manner, hopefully, you may discover afresh from the contexts of each book some of the overarching perspectives on worship that are often lost when we fail to grasp the contributions of the New Testament writings in their contexts.

Having just completed my work on the dramatic visions of Revelation,[6] I began to wonder what it must have been like for John to set down in writing his inspired visions that both touched his "then-contemporary world" and suggested directive perspectives about the future. His dynamic apocalypse straddles two worlds; and, if any work in the New Testament is rich in images, his treatise surely is a model. The book literally vibrates in a newfound symphonic beat with the postmodern and emerging mindsets that seem better able to synthesize sense perceptions than we who are "moderns" are usually able to do with our logical and scientific patterns of viewing reality. Although I certainly make no pretense here of writing a profound work, I thought that perhaps it might be intriguing to provide an overview on worship throughout the New Testament. I am the first to admit that these are *my* reflections, but they come after decades of teaching the New Testament in seminaries and colleges around the world.

Experiences behind This Work

Worship is often viewed as the way humans approach God. Indeed, one might even gain the impression from some folks that worship is not primarily about God at all but about human preferences or tastes in relation to the way they experience their faith or religion. So before I begin these reflections on the

New Testament and worship, which have been exciting to me and prayerfully will be for you as well, let me detail for you how this student of the New Testament became involved with teaching doctoral students in worship.

This book of reflections comes at the convergence of two significant events in my life. The first, as I have indicated above, comes at the completion of writing my work on Revelation. The second is my collegial relationship with Robert E. Webber. By now, it should be clear to you, dear readers, that I have written commentaries or major articles on most of the New Testament books, but I can say that I have been really stimulated in writing my work on Revelation and communicating something about the rich images of a work that may seem strange to many. So my dear wife (who has been a longtime professor of Christian education and a director of ministry supervision) asked me if I was going to write something else that might be fairly encompassing and appeal not merely to academics and students but also be significant for general church people as well.

Then, when Bob Webber spoke with me several years ago about his concern for the thesis segment of the doctoral program at the Institute for Worship Studies, I pondered only briefly before becoming involved in the school. The idea of working with worship students challenged both my wife and myself like an angelic chorus beckoning us to broaden our horizons and reflect more on God and the Christian's responsibility for worship. This teaching experience has blessed us both. But I became a little troubled by some of my students who seemed to lack a broad base for understanding the New Testament as the foundational source of their studies. I also have been concerned with my New Testament students reading introductions that focused primarily on authorship and dating questions, while failing to encounter the early worshiping communities themselves. So when I began to insist from my worship students on a broader base for their written work, it led me to read the New Testament afresh. The result is this present work.

My graduate students at the Institute are generally very bright and are from a vast array of backgrounds: all the way from Greek Orthodox on the one hand to Church of God and Assemblies of God ministers on the other. Moreover, many of them are professors in their own colleges and seminaries. My seminary and college students have been and are likewise from a broad set of backgrounds. In terms of my own background, it is appropriate that I should add a brief statement so that you might know who I am. Besides having graduated from the University of Alberta and law school in Canada, and attending Baptist seminaries, I have studied with the Presbyterians at Princeton; the Methodists at Duke; the Roman Catholics in Boston and Bethlehem; the Lutherans in Hamburg; the Anglicans and others at Cambridge; with professors from various denominations at the Graduate Theological Union, Berkeley; and with archaeologists in Jerusalem. Each has left an imprint upon my life. Although they are not responsible for any of my mistakes, they all have contributed significantly to my understanding of Christ's church and to my sense of divine mystery and our human attempts at responding to God's wonderful goal of bringing us into the kingdom as precious children of the Lord.

Reflections on Scripture and Worship

In this present work, all biblical citations are my own from the original Greek and Hebrew. I am not attempting here to provide a commentary on styles or patterns of worship, although some perspectives will obviously emerge for the reader. Neither am I suggesting some typical, new, quick-fix programs on worship for the future. What I am hoping to elicit from readers is a willingness to reflect on the formation of their faith and to re-envision the basic foundations of Christian worship for today. In this process we need to be open to bringing together in the matrix of our minds the feelings and other senses that God has given to us. We also need to recognize again that the Triune God who has acted in creation and redemption continues to act today and demands from us appropriate responses to the divine touch upon our lives. We are people who are called in this new millennium to follow in the footsteps of our self-giving Lord Jesus Christ (cf. 1 Pet 2:21).

The Nature of Worship

But the question can be raised: What is worship? As I was growing up as a young person in Alberta, Canada, I thought worship was done in my typical Baptist church on Sunday mornings and Sunday evenings, and that it involved singing, praying, and preaching about Jesus and the people of the Bible by the pastor or some visiting minister. Then, about once a month, a communion service was tacked onto the worship experience. Since that time, I have come to realize that such a definition is merely about a worship "service." The idea of "service" stuck in my mind so that when I was in seminary and read Karl Barth's Gifford lectures on *The Knowledge of God and the Service of God* I began to realize that response to God, "service of God," was really a much bigger concept than mere meetings about God or about my little promises of commitment during such "services."[7]

The service of God involves one's entire life of responding to God and divine mystery. Then, when I read Bob Webber's book on *Worship Is a Verb,* and when I reached his final chapter, "Worship as a Way of Life," my mind responded with an excited "Amen!"[8] For me, Bob's concluding thoughts summarized what "responding to mystery" involves—it is the way one lives the whole of one's life. True worship can never be pigeonholed as a segment of life. It is not merely liturgical activity in a building. Of course, our liturgies and congregational actions can reflect authentic worship, but worship demands one's life involvement. Otherwise, such actions are simply elements of busyness. Moreover, merely because some priest or minister follows a prescribed liturgical formula does not make that activity worship. God can still say to us, "I never knew you," or, "Leave me!" (Matt 7:23; 25:41). Those words haunted me in the past. Yet they have also brought me to realize a far more significant reality.

Our work and service for God is absolutely essential, but it must represent a genuine spirit of self-giving *for God* and not for our own advancement or benefit. The point is that it must be *a response to God!* During our lives on earth, we grow in the ways we respond to divine mystery. Here we have not yet reached the perfection of response, but growth is part of God's sanctifying process in us, of our becoming holy. It is a vital process in our pilgrimage to maturity with God.

Worship and Life

With this understanding in mind, I have linked worship and life constantly together in this study of responding to God. I have made this connection just as Paul and others have done in their epistles. As Jesus indicated in his severe criticism of the Pharisees, that connection must be made. I contend that worship is a response of our entire lives. The early church understood the unity of one's entire life and condemned Christians if they tried to bifurcate or segment their lives, as is evidenced in the repeated condemnation of those who called themselves followers of Jesus and practiced either or both the eating of meat offered to idols (idolatry) and immoral behavior (see my comments on Acts 15:20, 29; Rom 1:21–23; 1 Cor 6:18; 10:14; Rev 2:14, 20; 9:20–21). Both represent the failure of an authentic response to God. Unity of a person's words and actions is essential in the true worship of God (cf. 1 John 3:18; James 1:22; 2:14–17).

Encounter with God

Responding to the mystery of God is the way we express worship in our lives. It means that God is the divine subject of our relationship, and we respond to the action of God in Christ Jesus. Martin Buber, the brilliant Jewish philosopher, expressed the relationship of humans with God as "I and Thou" in his classic work. Although, for me, he reversed subject and object in his description of the divine "meeting" with the human, his general thinking was very significant. This concept was enhanced by Emil Brunner in the English translation of his work when the meeting was defined as the "divine-human encounter." In this encounter our role is to respond. We never become the directors of the meeting or become divine ourselves (not even our so-called "souls"). Therefore, neither humans, political powers, nor servants of God (including angels) deserve worship. As John in Revelation pointedly learned, worship belongs only to God (Rev 19:10; 22:8–9). May we thus live our lives so that they will respond authentically to the mystery of God in worship.

So now, my dear readers, I bid you to join me in this intriguing journey through the New Testament as we seek to decode anew the biblical stories and messages in this era of transition. May our commitment be to learning from the texts, and may we be prepared for insights that will enable us to develop new blended and convergent approaches to worship that will not alienate any of the generations in our congregations but will assist them in the very difficult task of synthesizing worship patterns for all of our people.

As we move to glimpse the images of worship in heaven or on earth, the realities of our sin-stricken cosmos and our frail attempts at responding as the people of God, let us remember that early Christian experiences of worship were often forged in the fires of rejection and outright hostility. Accordingly, in any re-envisioning that we may wish to entertain, we should always be aware of the fact that ancient perceptions are invaluable for guiding future directions. We should also realize that if we fail to understand the past, we are doomed to repeat its errors in future contexts.

In an effort to encourage your revisioning process, I have attached at the conclusion of each chapter or section a major question or questions that hopefully will stimulate further reflection and discussion on worship as it pertains to the context of that book of the New Testament. I trust that these questions will provoke the emergence of new ideas for your worship communities in the coming years.

Finally, whatever we may be able to accomplish for God in this world, let us continually remember: "To God alone belongs the glory!"

QUESTIONS

1. How would you define worship?
2. What is your evaluation of the author's close linking of worship and life?

PART I

Testifying about Jesus
Reflections on Worship in the Gospels

Interpreters have compared the New Testament Gospels to various forms of literature, but none of those forms is quite adequate to characterize them. They are not merely biographies, although they have biographical features. They are not just stories or chronicles about a hero, although Jesus is certainly very heroic. They are not simply histories or historical reports about a special time and person, although they certainly contain authentic historical details. They are not really memoirs, although they contain memories. They are not just announcements of victory or good news, although they obviously contain proclamations of great significance. They are not simply theological treatises, although they are packed with theological significance. They were in fact a new genre of literature developed by Mark and expanded by Matthew and Luke and then brought to full flowering by John.

To attempt a brief categorization of these documents, I would ask you the reader to visualize our Gospels as being like testimonies and, as the Greek heading for each book indicates, each is "according to" (*kata*) a genuine follower of Jesus. If one can think in picture forms, each Gospel can be compared to a portrait that bears the personal stamp or characteristic of each of the four writers or evangelists. They are not simply like photographs because each picture or testimony is a little different from the others, but the same Jesus is present in all of them. To illustrate, when I was in Thailand on one of my journeys, I asked an artist to paint a picture of my dear wife from a small photograph that I carried in my wallet. He produced a marvelous large portrait of her, but it is not like any portrait that an Anglo-American would have painted, because the eyes are just a little different. He painted what his mind visualized. Similarly, in terms of the Gospels it is not inappropriate to accept and regard each book as an authentically inspired picture of Jesus—the evangelist's true testimonial statement concerning the Lord. Moreover, each of the four Gospels was recognized very early as a standard or a canonically accurate representation of the awe-inspiring Son of God for Christians.

Of course, other so-called "gospels" attempted to mimic the canonical works. These included the Gospel of Thomas, the Gospel of Philip, the Gospel of Mary, the Gospel of Judas, and even a Gospel of Truth, the latter purportedly written by Valentinus, who sought to become the bishop of Rome but was rejected. We have known of the existence of these so-called "gospels" for centuries. Indeed, I did my dissertation on the Gospel of Philip years ago at Princeton. Even though their presence may periodically make the headlines in our newspapers and magazines, none of them will ever be categorized by the church as a "fifth gospel." Moreover, the early defenders of Christianity, such as Irenaeus in the second century, inveighed against them because their writers sought to lead Christians away from the truth and promote heretical tendencies such as Gnosticism, just as the First Epistle of John argues. These books were clearly never regarded as authentic representations of Jesus, the mysterious, incarnate Son of God, who lived and sacrificially died for the sins of humanity and was mysteriously raised by God as the vindicated Savior of the world.

For the purpose of this book, we must recognize that many of these other so-called "gospels" advocate a different view of God in a structured essential dualism, a different understanding of Jesus as an "alien messenger," a different concept of the world as negative, a different meaning of salvation as escape, and a different perspective on worship—even of the sacraments or rites. For example, in the Gospel of Philip the highest sacrament is the "bridal chamber" or "union"; and, until one experienced that rite, the person was not really considered a full-fledged devotee of the religion.[1]

Now, the reader should discover here that, while the approach to matters of worship in each of the canonical Gospels may be slightly different, all four of them witness to a genuine underlying commonality of commitment to the Triune God and to the theological substructure that demands integrity of life for believers, patterned on the model of the self-giving Jesus. These Gospels belong together as the church's inspired witnesses concerning Jesus in matters of faith and life, and particularly here—in our concerns for worship.

The early church forthrightly rejected any attempt to eliminate what some found were differences in the stories through harmonization efforts such as was attempted in the second century by Tatian in his *Diatessaron.* The early Christians knew of the slight variations in such matters as times, names, places, numbers, and the order of incidents reported. They accepted these variations in the Gospels as inconsequential to the testimonial presentations, an idea that usually frustrates readers today. Each evangelist's Gospel was regarded as nevertheless fully reliable and as truly representative of the Lord's life and work while on earth. Even more significant, each Gospel was seen as faithfully directing readers to a genuine response of worship before the Triune God.

Finally, the order of the Gospels in our New Testament is not the order in which they were written. Clearly Mark was written first. The order was selected because Matthew provides a recognition for the church that Jesus was the fulfillment of Old Testament messianic expectations, Mark emphasizes the awesome Jesus as God's Son, Luke presents the caring nature of God in Jesus, and John identifies Jesus as none other than God fully incarnate in human form. Each portrait of Jesus is crucial for developing an adequate response to God in Christian worship. To these priceless testimonies in the New Testament our attention is now directed.

QUESTIONS

1. Why do you think that people usually collapse the four Gospel witnesses into one conceptual account concerning Jesus' time on earth and fail to see the Gospels as various portraits of Jesus?
2. Have you done so? Why? Why not?
3. How can you help others in the church to be prepared for taking four different worship journeys with Jesus?

1

Matthew

Fulfilling Old Testament Expectations in Emmanuel[1]

In repeatedly fulfilling the Old Testament Scriptures, Jesus in Matthew is portrayed as condemning superficial worship practices and providing the means for everyone to respond appropriately to the presence of "God with us" as humans.

Introduction to Matthew

How intriguing is the story of Jesus in the Gospel of Matthew for Christian worshipers who may have heard repeatedly that the book was intended for the Jews. That view, however, is only partly correct, because it was actually intended to help Jews realize that God in Jesus had come for the Gentiles as well. To accomplish this task Matthew had to demonstrate for his Jewish readers not merely that Jesus had, in fact, fulfilled the prophecies of the Old Testament but also that he greatly expanded their old concepts of the Messiah's entry into the world. He was none other than the mysterious "God with us" (Matt 1:23). Moreover, because Matthew understood both Jewish thought and worship patterns well, he employed these prophecies to highlight the fact that the coming of Jesus initiated the beginning of a new era that encompassed both Jews and Gentiles.

As with all the Gospels, our knowledge concerning the authorship of this work is the result of reports about the book in a few early statements from the second and succeeding centuries. The Gospel itself does not contain much information about the author. The title *kata Maththaion* ("According to Matthew") was added by later scribes for identification. The Gospel, however, does indicate that a certain tax collector was Matthew (see 9:9), whereas in

Mark and Luke he is called Levi (Mark 2:14 and Luke 5:27). Yet note that he is also called Matthew in the list of the disciples not only in this Gospel but in the other Synoptic Gospels as well (Mark 3:18 and Luke 6:15; cf. Matt 10:3). The author/evangelist of this Gospel was undoubtedly a Jew who was very familiar with the Old Testament and the Jewish worship practices. Yet his citations of Old Testament do not appear to come from the Hebrew text. They were probably either from a Greek version of the Old Testament such as the Septuagint (LXX) or merely quotations from memory. One obvious reason for such speculation about Matthew's Hebrew knowledge is his discussion of the entry into Jerusalem (an important event in today's worship calendar).

He cites the poetical text of Zechariah 9:9 and then strangely indicates that there were two animals (an ass and its colt) waiting for Jesus and he rode on "them" (*epano auton* [pl.], see Matt 21:7). The point is that much of Hebrew poetry is written in couplets wherein both lines virtually mean the same thing. So did Jesus actually sit on two donkeys, or did Matthew not understand the Hebrew? This question (patently related to our important Christian celebration of Palm Sunday) is not easily resolved, and the translators today often fuzz the problem by failing to indicate the presence of this plural in Matthew.

Another matter is that some scholars have argued strongly that Matthew was the first Gospel to be written (the Griesbach theory of the eighteenth century), a view that in part goes back to an earlier theory of Irenaeus (late second century) and others who thought that this Gospel was first written in Hebrew and then was translated into Greek. Such a view is not very likely. It is far more likely that Matthew used an earlier form of Mark in Greek, together with some type of "sayings" source, which would account for the close connection of both Matthew and Luke to the accounts in Mark, but also provides a reason for the sayings statements which are common to Matthew and Luke yet are absent from Mark.

Yet one might ask: If Mark was probably written first, why was Matthew placed first in our New Testament? The answer is that the books of the New Testament are organized, not according to the date of their writing, but for other practical and theological reasons. Thus, Romans is placed first among the Pauline letters because it was regarded as Paul's fullest explication of salvation. Matthew was likely placed first among the Gospels because it is the only Gospel that specifically mentions the church and indicates not merely Peter's task in the work of the church (16:17–19) but a similar responsibility given to all Christians. It also includes the promise that Christ's presence would be "in the midst" of even two or three of Christ's followers (18:18–20). With these brief preliminary remarks related to introductory matters in mind, we turn to the text of Matthew and its importance for our understanding of worship concerns.

The Beginning and the Ending of Matthew

I have often suggested to my students that they should read the beginning and end of a Gospel. Then they might better understand what is in the middle. That process is hardly advisable in reading a mystery, because it will usually spoil the unfolding of the plot. Most readers, however, already know how this story ends, and our point in studying the Gospels is to gain insights from our reading to enhance our lives and our worship. The first of Matthew's prediction/ fulfillment statements appears in the first chapter after the genealogies and concerns the coming of "Emmanuel." The evangelist reminds us that Emmanuel means that the amazing "God" we worship is actually "with us" (Matt 1:23). Significantly, the Gospel also ends with the promise that the risen Jesus will be "with you always" to the end of time (28:20)! The point of the Gospel, therefore, must be to present the divine messenger of God as the one who had been with them and would be with his followers (note also 18:20) to the end of this earthly reality. To sense the mysterious presence of God and God's Son Jesus in their lives, according to Matthew, is essential for all Christian worshipers.

The question that immediately suggests itself then is: Where did Jewish readers of the Old Testament think that God was most clearly made evident? The immediate answer is, of course, in the context of mountain scenes such as at Mount Sinai, Mount Gerizim, Mount Carmel, and Mount Zion. The list could be extended from the episodes of Abraham through Moses to David and Elijah, etc. Because of the importance of mountains to Jewish worship, Matthew quite naturally highlighted mountains in his presentation of Jesus. Therefore, early in his Gospel Matthew initiated Jesus' teaching by giving a new set of instructions generally called the "Sermon on the *Mount*" (5:1–7:27).[2] Later Jesus is pictured as climbing the hills beside the Sea of Galilee and sitting down to dispense healing (15:29–31). Then, in Matthew's final teaching section, after Jesus left the Temple Mount and issued his indictments and his stunning announcement about the Temple's hopeless future (24:1–2), he looked over those buildings from the Mount of Olives, sat down, and began to deliver his stirring eschatological (futuristic) message concerning the ultimate expectations for his own followers and the rest of humanity (24:3–25:46).

Jesus in Matthew's Gospel

There is no doubt, therefore, that Matthew pictured Jesus as the divine successor to, and even "Lord" of, both Moses and Elijah, the two great figures of Israel who represented the law and the prophets. Matthew pointed to Jesus as the one who would lead the people of God into their new "eschaton" (their last days). Moreover, it is no accident that the careful reader can easily identify five specific teaching sections of Jesus in Matthew's Gospel. These instructional sections were no doubt purposely patterned on the fact that the core of Jewish thinking, worship, and obedience rested on the "five" books assigned to Moses (known as the Torah or the Law). Pointedly, each one of the five teaching sections in Matthew is punctuated by the evangelist with the concluding words indicating that the section is "finished" (cf. 7:28; 11:1; 13:53; 19:1; and 26:10) so that it should not be difficult for the astute reader to gain the implication that here is a new way of worship and life, a new Torah.[3] It is also no accident that all three of the Synoptic Gospels rehearse the fact that in the worship experience of the transfiguration on the mountain both Moses and Elijah are portrayed in submission to the Son of God. Matthew followed Mark in announcing that the new Elijah predicted in Malachi 4:5 (also 3:1) had already come, namely, John the Baptist (cf. Matt 17:9–12 and Mark 9:11–13).

Furthermore, in initiating this mountain thinking, Matthew indicated that the last temptation of Jesus occurred on a mountain (Matt 4:8), in contrast to Luke 4:9 where it takes place in the Temple area (a matter that will be discussed in the section on Luke). Finally, Matthew concluded his story of Jesus' resurrection on a mountain in Galilee (28:16), with Jesus issuing his lofty proclamation that all authority (*exousia*) in heaven and earth is vested in him and that he had the right to issue the divine threefold imperative (28:19–20) involving: mission (to go and disciple people everywhere), liturgical response (to baptize), and instruction (to teach). Picturing Jesus in relation to mountains was Matthew's way of indicating that the awesome Jesus is the one who calls forth his followers to the full implications of authentic worship. Moreover, in this conclusion Matthew emphasized the fact that the "good news" of "God with us" was not merely intended for the Jews.

"Chosen People" and Gentiles in Matthew (1:1–4:25)

Nevertheless, accepting the universality of that message was difficult for a people like the Jews, who had long believed that they were selected as a "chosen people," yet had forgotten that as heirs of Abraham they were called, not merely to bask in the self-oriented worship that belonged only to Israel, but to be a blessing to the nations (the Gentiles, see, among other texts, Gen 12:2; 22:18; 28:14 and the implications of the Book of Jonah). They had to learn anew that the God they worshiped was not confined to a particular piece of geography or to a particular group of people.

So Matthew began his work by reminding his Jewish readers that even the genealogy of David and Solomon was marked by the insertion of four women connected with those who might otherwise be despised, namely Tamar, Rahab, Ruth, and the wife of Uriah the Hittite (Matt 1:3, 5, and 6). Moreover, he chose to point out in the birth story that while the Jewish religious leaders were quite aware of the place where the Messiah was to be born (2:5), those who first actually honored and worshiped the baby Jesus in Bethlehem were Gentile (Mesopotamian) star gazers (2:1, 11). Apparently Matthew wanted his readers to realize that their Jewish religious leaders were too busy with their own concerns to search for and worship the messianic baby! The ruler Herod wanted the foreigners to do the careful work of finding the so-called king for him, not so that he could worship Jesus, as Herod claimed (2:8), but so he could kill him.

So, as was the case involving the earlier people of Israel, the Messiah had to return to Israel (the promised land) from Egypt (2:15). Matthew's goal in presenting the story of Jesus, however, was not to lower the standards of the Jews to that of the customs of the Gentiles (5:47) and their empty worship practices

(6:7) but to lead the Jews to understand that the Gentiles could also legitimately love and worship God and accept God's new way of life (2:11).

The Sermon on the Mount (5:1–7:27)

The Beatitudes

Matthew provided a new set of perspectives from Jesus, generally known as the "Beatitudes," in which the Lord promised the kingdom of heaven and its concomitant blessings to those who do not follow the ways of the world but instead model integrity in worship and life by accepting the legitimacy of humility, mercifulness, poverty, suffering, and other such patterns of life not merely as human misfortunes to be rejected but as qualities to be employed for God's glory (5:3–11).[4]

Such patterns were experienced by the prophets, who in life were generally rejected by Israel, but who in fact early demonstrated that they understood the true nature of worship and modeled integrity of life for God's people (5:12). In coming to the world, Jesus did not seek to abolish the messages of the Torah and the Prophets. His goal was to bring his people to a more perceptive understanding of God's eternal purposes. Such a view was very different from the wooden perspectives of many Jewish interpreters and their worship practices (5:17–20).

The Antitheses

In general Jesus focused on the Torah not as a set of rules but as the new inner way of life that exemplified a true relationship with God. Matthew chose to illustrate this style of thinking and action by several examples often called the "Antitheses." He began by referring to two segments of the Decalogue (Ten Commandments). First, Jesus is seen as redefining the prohibition against killing by placing it in the context of worship—namely, making an offering to God at the Temple while being at odds with another human (5:21–26). Just imagine if you were there and hearing Jesus' words in the *north* near the Sea of Galilee—about someone who had made the long trek *south* to the Jerusalem Temple and then remembered an unresolved dispute back in the *north* land. Jesus seemed to imply that the worshiper was supposed to go back to Galilee and clear up the dispute before proceeding with the worship. Would you not think that idea was a bit ridiculous? Why not just finish the worship experience and then go back and seek to mend the relationship? But such was not the advice of Jesus.

Next he redefined adultery by advising that one should gouge out a sinful eye (5:27–32). Is that the way you would think of handling lust? Does he not seem to suggest that worship-oriented confessions and change of heart necessitate more than mere words of contrition?

The third antithesis involves the Deuteronomic marriage code and the question of faithfulness to the marriage vows (Deut 24:1–4). Jesus took such vows very seriously as actual commitments before God (Matt 5:31–32; 19:3–9). He made no distinction between a husband and a wife in terms of adultery. In that day faithfulness was regarded as the responsibility of the wife, not the husband! (Note the story in John 7:53–8:11.) A man could put away his wife if he found in her anything displeasing to him. Because of masculine insensitivities to wives, however, Moses provided a divorce certificate to protect the rights of women by not letting them be put out of the house without any recourse or support.[5] Notice that even the disciples did not want to be treated on the same basis as the women and in protest cried that if as men they would be so treated then it was probably "best not to get married" (Matt 19:10)! Jesus hardly acceded to their childish hurt feelings, and instead informed them that it was just unfortunate if they did not understand their commitments to God and faithfulness to their wives (19:12).

In the fourth antithesis, Jesus confronted the familiar Levitical custom of oath-taking, in which the rabbinic scholars developed levels of seriousness. Some oaths were regarded as ultimate because the objects of support on which the oaths had been based were directly connected with the worship and reverence of God, whereas other oaths were merely of earthly import. Jesus refused to acknowledge such a difference between the sacred and secular because the source of all creation is God (5:33–36). Since God's original intention was integrity in all aspects of life, a person's word should be sufficient (5:37; cf. Lev 19:12; Num 30:2). While taking an oath might have seemed to imply seriousness before God as in worship, Jesus suggested that the practice actually proved that people intended to lie and cheat others and even God, so that they attempted by the use of oaths to signify their truthfulness.

In the fifth antithesis, the rules of retaliation (cf. Exod 21:23–25; Lev 24:19–20; Deut 19:29) came under Jesus' scrutiny (Matt 5:38–42). Instead of seeking justification for "getting even" or the satisfaction of revenge (cf. Cain and Lamech in Gen 4:23), Jesus' method—as Glenn Stassen correctly identified—is the overcoming of the negative initiatives in life by the positive.[6] For example, in the case of the Roman forced labor rights of "Angareia"—the soldier's right to demand carrying a burden for a specified distance (cf. Simon of Cyrene in Matt 27:32)—Jesus advised overcoming such an evil practice by accepting double duty (5:41). Our postmodern world, in which freedom and self-determination are regarded as supreme rights, often exhibits little understanding or acceptance of such servitude. On the other hand, our world shows little understanding of the absolute "lordship" of God or the mystery of Christ. Even Christians who use the term "Lord" frequently in worship too often live their lives without evidencing an actual understanding or commitment to that idea.

The sixth and final antithesis (5:45–48) in essence offers the foundation for the application of Christian worship to life. Loving those who love you proves to be exceedingly easy, but one who truly knows and worships the loving God realizes that God loves the unlovely (even us) and that God's grace extends to the unworthy just as the rain falls on all people without distinction (5:45). Similarly, true responsive love in Christ's followers should extend beyond the normal "quid pro quo" of reciprocal love, (here designated as the way of the "Gentiles") to a mature or perfected quality of love modeled by God (5:47–48).

Authentic Human Worship

Having illustrated the alternative way in the world for Jesus' followers, Matthew turned to a number of specific teachings on authentic human worship. In the sixth chapter he focused on the humble, nonpublic nature of genuine piety. He opened this section with Christ's stern warning against seeking public recognition for one's piety (6:1) and emphasized his advice by highlighting the human lust for praise following the parading of a significant donation either to the Lord's work or to another "good cause." While such gifts often benefit others and may be associated with God's mission, Jesus made it clear that the benefactors should not expect divine recognition for such gifts because they already had received their desired praise (6:2–4).

As we reflect on this matter, consider how much and how often we as humans, even as Christians, love to have our names attached to buildings, rooms, and a host of other worthy projects represented in named scholarships and publicly displayed art pieces such as statues. Meanwhile, it is often very difficult to obtain gifts for the general expenses of the church or other institutions. Following this line of argument, the evangelist next moved to Jesus' critique of the display of piety in public prayer. Instead of parading one's prayer piety either before fellow worshipers in community services or in front of the pubic in general, Jesus instructed people to pray in private and watch how God would respond to such devotion (6:5–6). Jesus' advice, however, is not a condemnation of public worship, but rather a direct hit on self-centered concerns that arise from a desire for public acclamation. Moreover, prayer is not to be judged as being appropriate because of its multiplicity of words or its cleverly crafted phraseology (6:7). In the Hellenistic/Gentile world, which revered classical patterns of argument and logic (rhetoric), Jesus' critique summoned his followers to address their prayers to God as a father in a humble, direct, and forthright manner. Brilliant, long-winded, repetitive petitions, or flowery ascriptions to God, do not influence God.

The Lord's Prayer

In place of playing word games with God, Jesus provided a model that has come to be known as the "Lord's Prayer." In this prayer God is simply addressed as our heavenly Father (6:9). Consider this in the context of a Jewish world and their response to mystery. They had ceased to use the name of God (*YHWH*)–even inserting the Hebrew vowels for *Adonai* in the written text–for fear of taking God's name in vain (Exod 20:7). They regarded the deity as *so* awesome, transcendent, and remote that communication with God was best done through mediating angels.

Jesus simply and intimately called God his Father. The Jews viewed such an act as blasphemous and deserving of death (Matt 26:65–66). Yet God is hardly unconcerned about his people like some remote dictator. Instead, God is similar to a loving human father, who would hardly give his child a serpent if she asks for a fish or a stone when he asks for bread (7:8–11). Still more remarkable in that context, Jesus taught his disciples to address God by the intimate family designation of "Father" as well.[7] Such a means of address did not seek to make God in the image of humans, as happens so often in our contemporary, narcissistic thinking. Such intimate address sought to raise human sights to the reality of the incarnate God in Jesus, who cares intimately for God's creation. The Lord's Prayer that follows is a model of simplicity, but equally is an example of dependence and humility as petitioners are led to recognize the mysterious role of the holy God in their provision, forgiveness, and protection (6:9–15). God and Jesus are the only ones worthy of a Christian's full honor and reverence (3:11; 8:8; cf. Rev 5:9–14).

Public Piety

In the next segment of chapter 6, Matthew reflects on Jesus' reaction to a public show of fasting. Once again, Jesus did not attack the liturgical practice. He criticized those who attempted to gain personal attention by appearing to be engaged in a self-denying, worship-oriented activity. Jesus countered by advising his followers to assume an appearance that did not reveal any indication of a self-effacing activity, leaving any affirmation of such devotion to God rather than drawing attention to themselves in fasting (Matt 6:16–18).

The Final Judgment

Matthew climaxed this magnificent set of instructions by reminding his readers that Jesus mapped out two ways of attachment to God by reference to the building of two houses: one destined to survive great traumas, such as a flood, while the other would clearly be destroyed (7:24–27). Many who read texts such as this one hardly consider that Jesus could be serious about such a fateful end, but Matthew had no difficulty believing that the disobedient would suffer a horrible end. Indeed, he emphasized this fact by noting that Jesus used the ancient expression of tragedy for the unfaithful by indicating that there would be punishment followed by a "weeping and gnashing of teeth" (24:51; cf. for example Job 16:9; Ps 35:16; Lam 2:16). Moreover, Jesus clearly is portrayed eschatologically as sitting on his magnificent throne and separating people into two groups based on their integrity: some would be welcomed into the eternal kingdom prepared by God (Matt 25:34) while the others would be delivered into eternal punishment (25:46). The point is that *not* everyone who enunciates a worshipful commitment to Jesus as "Lord" is in fact a true worshiper of God. Only the one "who does the will" of the heavenly Father (7:21) is a true worshiper. A life of obedience must accompany worship and words of commitment to God. The bifurcation of worship and practice is doomed to be rejected by God (7:22; 24:50–51; 25:44–45).

The Miraculous Jesus and the Disciples' Derivative Authority (8:1–11:1)

In this section Matthew combined the miracle stories of Jesus (chapters 8 and 9) from Mark chapters 1, 2, 4, and 5 with some teaching segments to provide a powerful testimony concerning the presence of the awesome God in their midst. As representative of God, Jesus expected integrity in worship and he pinpointed that requirement as Micah did, by demanding mercy and not sacrifice (Matt 9:13; cf. Mic 6:6–8). Then Matthew concluded with instructions concerning the call of the disciples to a servant nature, and also with their commissioning by Jesus both to heal and to have power over the hostile spiritual forces (Matt 10:1). For the early Christians who were living and worshiping in small house churches and who were persecuted by both religious and political authorities, the affect of this part of Matthew's Gospel must have been incredibly empowering. But it was not a "pie in the sky" presentation, because it contained a clear warning that in the world they should not expect to experience peace, but rather hostility (10:34–39). Yet their servant efforts would certainly be rewarded (10:40–42).

The Identity of Jesus, Hostility, and the Parables of Mystery (11:2–13:53)

The issue of Jesus' identity is next introduced by reference to John the Baptist's question. The answer actually led, not only to Jesus' identification as the Messiah, but also to John's as the expected Elijah and to the conclusion that they both were rejected by the people (11:1–19). What follows is a series of pericopes indicating the growing hostility epitomized in worship issues–namely Sabbath controversies (12:1–14) and charges of blasphemy (12:22–37). But besides healing many, Matthew made it clear that Jesus was the long-anticipated hope for the Gentiles (12:12:15–21; cf. Isa 42:1–4).

This section concludes (13:1–53) with a series of parables, with some drawn from Mark 4. The fact that Matthew collected both parables and miracles in groups is an indication of the way Matthew wrote–namely he thought by combining events or ideas into larger patterns for ease of treatment. Whereas the impact of miracles was empowerment, the impact of these parables is mystery. They seem clear and yet their meaning is not quite obvious. For that reason one needs ears to hear (13:43), an expression familiar in the Book of Revelation. The disciples said they understood (13:51) but their actions indicated otherwise.

Unveiling the Mystery in the Kingdom (13:54–19:2)

The mystery hidden in the miracles and the parables (13:54) is brought to focus by Matthew through the Jewish misunderstanding of Jesus' identity in no other place than his own synagogue–and it resulted in a failure to honor him

(13:55–58)! Then, like a predictive unveiling, John's death foreshadowed the death of Jesus (14:1–12). And in the midst of several more miracles, Matthew juxtaposed inauthentic Jewish worship lustration or washing rites (15:1–19) with the acceptance of a Gentile woman's pleas for healing (15:21–28). The stage is thus set for a series of the central unveiling events concerning Jesus by the Pharisees' demand for a sign and by the disciples' failure to perceive (16:1–12).

These crucial events began with Peter's climactic worship confession and his failure to achieve perceptive integration. The confession was under divine inspiration and upon it hung the future of the Church (16:17–19), but Peter's application was devilish and needed to be completely altered (16:22–23). As a result, in a "cross motif" Jesus summoned his disciples to a unified commitment of confession and life if they would expect to experience the Kingdom (16:24–28). Then, in the strategic unveiling at the transfiguration encounter on the mountain, Peter's perception was once again flawed. Jesus was not just another prophet like Moses and Elijah. He was God's Son! He was to be obeyed and worshiped (17:5–8)! Following this, as a contrast, in the valley the other disciples had another hard lesson to learn, namely that the power of healing is not vested in the human will but is based on one's reliance on God (17:14–21).

This section concludes with a powerful discourse by Jesus on what it means to be the church, the people of God. It is not pomp and ceremony in worship, nor power and authority in the community, but rather humility that is the key to becoming part of the kingdom of heaven. Humble children were Jesus' example of kingdom people (18:1–6) and searching for lost, helpless sheep was Jesus' goal (18:10–14). In this context Jesus repeated the well-known "binding and loosing" statement made at Caesarea to Peter (18:18; cf. 16:19). The rabbinic expression relates to the responsibility for communicating the expectations of the Torah for acceptability by God. In the church it refers to the task of communicating the gospel, which implies both grace and judgment. And rather than ten men necessary for the formation of a synagogue and corporate prayer, the church in worship can be composed of two or three people (not necessarily men; cf. Gal 3:28) and there would be the presence of Emmanuel (Matt 18:20)!

The Interchanges in Jerusalem (19:3–22:46)

This section of Matthew's Gospel uses most of chapters 10–12 of Mark, with a few editorial additions. These texts will be discussed later in Mark. The conflict between the Pharisees and Jesus in Mark 12:38–40, however, gives rise in Matthew to the important addition concerning the condemnations of the Pharisees by Jesus that follow hereafter and are significant for our discussion of worship.

The Woes on Hypocrites (23:1–39)

To warn readers about self-centered, narcissistic patterns of worship before God, Matthew, unlike the other evangelists, chose to detail for Christian disciples in chapter 23 a long series of "woes" against the Pharisees, whom he likened to hypocrites. These skillful teachers of the Law sat in the seat of Moses (the honored place in the synagogue), but they were repeatedly condemned in Matthew, *not* because of their zeal for learning (23:3), but because their finely crafted words and distinctions in defining models of piety actually missed God's intentions and led people astray. Moreover, their own acts of piety were merely empty shells that resembled a graveyard of whitewashed tombs that gave the appearance of beauty but were actually filled with ugly, dead skeletons (23:27–28). These leaders wore wonderfully woven robes and prayer shawls, bound their bodies with showy phylacteries, and loved to be identified with special honorific titles and with priority of place in worship celebrations.

They, however, completely missed God's intentions in worship (23:4, 5–7, 8–12). They were exceedingly precise in tithing regulations, even to the point of tithing tiny seeds. Yet like blind trackers in the wilderness, they missed the major points along the path of living in integrity and committing themselves to the caring service God expected of them (23:23–24; cf. the scathing comments of Ezekiel in his attack on the religious leaders of his time in Ezek 34:1–10, and God's intention of becoming the shepherd himself in 34:11–24). Jesus likened the Pharisees to slimy snakes who used the houses of worship (synagogues) for their own purposes—including condemning, persecuting, and even whipping those who disagreed with them. Jesus concluded that they were destined for nothing less than hell (Matt 23:31–35)!

The End of Jesus' Ministry (24:1–28:20)

As Jesus came to the end of his ministry in Jerusalem, Matthew portrayed him as knowing that most of Israel would not recognize the presence of "God with them." Jesus wept over Jerusalem for the people's lack of understanding and integrity. Moreover, Jesus indicated that the center of their Jewish faith would soon be destroyed and they would not see him again unless they could worship him and confess that he is the one "who comes in the name of the Lord" (23:37–39). So he died forsaken—even by the disciples (26:56)—and betrayed—even by Peter who had made a great confession (26:73–74; cf. 16:16–9; 26:33–35).

But that self-sacrificing death about which Jesus earlier spoke (26:26–29) was not the end of the story. When he died, the veil of the Temple was amazingly ripped from the top to the bottom as God judged worship to be false in the rejection of his Son (27:51). Yet a Gentile centurion was filled with awe and confessed that the dying one must have been a "Son of God" (27:54). Afterward, Jesus was buried in a rocky tomb. Matthew alone reports that these same so-called pious Pharisees set a guard to prevent Jesus' devotees from taking his body and claiming he had risen from the dead (27:62–66). A mere rock door and humans, however, could hardly hold the one in whom "all earthly and heavenly authority" was vested. So Jesus arose from the dead as he had predicted (16:21; 17:22–23; 20:17), to the surprise and awe of even his own followers (28:10). He is alive today, and Emmanuel is now "with" his people, directing them in mission, worship, and instruction as the representative of the Triune God (28:19) "until the end of time!" (28:20).

WORSHIP SUMMARY

From the beginning to the end of his Gospel, Matthew provides a portrait of Jesus as both the very presence of God on the one hand and the ultimate descendant of Abraham on the other. He pictures Jesus as far superior to Moses and Elijah and fully worthy of worship, even though the Jewish religious leaders, who paraded themselves as the authorities on God and worship and who relied on Moses, completely missed the coming of their Messiah. Instead, Matthew portrays the Gentiles as the first to worship Jesus. Moreover, they are given the promises made to Abraham, and the gospel of the kingdom of heaven is thus proclaimed to them. The life and teachings of Jesus throughout Matthew epitomize the integration between authentic worship and life, whereas the Pharisees and their patterns of religion receive harsh condemnation as merely false shams of worship. The stark differences in Matthew provide an ideal measuring tool for the examination of worship practices by contemporary Christians.

QUESTION

1. As you think about how most of the Jews in Matthew's day failed to acknowledge Jesus because of their traditions concerning worship and life, would you and your church be ready for a visit from Emmanuel, or would your worship traditions impede such a visit?

2

Mark

Encountering the Awesome Jesus[1]

The awesome Jesus in Mark silenced superficial witnesses concerning the Son of God and shocked the world into a new relationship with God by his words and actions.

The Strangeness of Mark

We turn now to a reflection on Mark and the impact of this Gospel on our understanding of worship. Before turning our attention to worship, however, it is crucial to review some matters of introduction, since Mark provides us with an important glimpse into the history of our early witnesses concerning Jesus and the nature of gospel writing. Not only is the presentation of Jesus in Mark awesome, but this Gospel itself is rather strange, awesome, and challenging. It resides in the history of Christianity, however, as a strategic document. Paul and others wrote letters before Mark wrote his Gospel, but Jesus' followers preferred to tell the stories of Jesus rather than put them to pen and ink. Witnessing was an oral experience authenticated by the personal presence of the witness. But as the personal witnesses of Jesus began to die, they were leaving no authoritative written record of their Lord's life, his teachings, and his perspectives on worship. In this vacuum Mark burst on the scene. Tradition as early as Papias (second century) seems to indicate that the writer of this Gospel could be the John (Mark) mentioned in the Acts (e.g., 13:5, 13 and 15:37–39), in Paul's letters (Col. 4:10; Phlm 24; and 2 Tim 4:11) and also was an assistant of Peter in Rome (e.g., 1 Pet 5:13), but the actual linkage through Eusebius (fourth century) is not quite as early as one might like for certainty.[2] Nevertheless, in Mark a new genre of literature was born. This book provided Christians with a new vehicle for expressing their faith. Indeed, Mark first suggested the connection between the nature of the good news ("gospel," Mark 1:15) about Jesus with a type of literature, a Gospel (1:1).

While the book did not gain many advocates as the primary standard for the written "good news" of Jesus in the early church (few commentaries on Mark were penned in the first Christian millennium), a close synoptic analysis makes it obvious that Mark served as the basis for Matthew's and Luke's more developed Gospels. Tatian, in his second century attempt to harmonize the Gospels (the *Diatessaron*), certainly knew it. But the abrupt beginning of Mark, with nothing about the birth of Jesus (see Matthew and Luke) or his origin (see John), and the absence of appearances of Jesus after the resurrection meant that the church often passed it over for the other Gospels. Yet the apparent absence of both a beginning and an ending has continually suggested to me that they were probably lost from the autograph itself since no record of their existence can be found. The two conclusions of Mark after 16:8 are clearly later additions, and the extant ending with only the fear of the women can hardly be the finish of the book.[3]

Mark is indeed a strange book! Perhaps the strangest aspects of Mark involve the elements that also characterize it as a most enticing work. The reader hardly has begun scanning the book before finding that events take place "immediately" (*euthys*, e.g., 1:12, 18, 20, 21, etc.). The reader becomes quickly aware that what Jesus taught and did shocked people (e.g., 1:22, 27; 2:12; 4:41). Moreover, this awesome Jesus seemed to be fully in control even of the spirit world (e.g., 1:25–26, 34; 3:11). As a result, some scholars in the nineteenth century gleefully argued that Mark was "the" primitive report about the miracle worker, Jesus, and included what he taught without much theological molding or addition to the stories.

The Messianic Secret

At the close of that century, Wilhelm Wrede issued a bombshell that shocked those scholars intent on isolating the historical Jesus from the Church's faith. Wrede discovered in Mark what he called the "Messianic Secret," a prevailing theme in which Jesus repeatedly forbad both spirits and humans to speak about him. The effect was that the so-called secret actually enhanced Jesus' stature in the Gospel.[4] This discovery doomed attempts to separate the historical person, Jesus, from the church's confession about him.

Since that time, however, scholars have periodically sought to define new means to do the same type of separation in the second and third quests for the historical Jesus with what I consider not much more success. The confessions about Jesus in the Gospels are tied so intimately with the presentations of the mysterious figure of Jesus in the stories of the Gospel that the quester's attempts to shed the so-called outer skins of the stories to get to the kernel of the presentations generally result in constructing subjective portraits that seem to reflect the preconceptions of the searchers. That Mark is a powerful witness to a mysterious Jesus goes without much contradiction. You cannot comfortably confine Jesus to mere human categories, and that fact makes this Gospel's presentation very appropriate for a reflection on worship. So to the text of Mark I now turn.

Call to Worship the Holy One (1:1–2:17)

The unclean spirit's designation of Jesus as "the Holy one of God" is an apt description of the awesome Jesus in Mark (1:24). The Gospel, however, does not seek to lead the opposing spirit world to acknowledge Jesus' nature. Mark wants believers to confess and worship the Son of God. Mark's unfolding stories are aimed in that direction, but they surprise the reader. The disciples do not actually enunciate Jesus' nature. Peter did summarize the idea at Caesarea Philippi; yet he became all confused about the actual task of Jesus and spoke thereafter like Satan rather than like an inspired disciple (8:27–33). The authentic confession had to wait until the cross, where *not a disciple but a Gentile Roman soldier* guarding the crucifixion site recognized Jesus as Son of God (15:39).

The interconnection between words and actions as the foundation for a true understanding of worship is illustrated as early as chapter 2 of Mark when, in healing the paralytic, Jesus also forgave his sins (2:5). The religious leaders were angered that Jesus "blasphemously" assumed the authority of God in such a move. But Jesus countered their criticism by asking whether it was easier to forgive or to heal (2:9–10). The answer, of course, is that only God can do both. Stunned, the people correctly glorified or worshiped God because mystery was in their midst and they had experienced the blessing of God on a human (2:12). God does not demand worship, but gives humans the free choice to decide concerning worship, while also giving them opportunities to witness the actions of the divine in the world. Yet that option, as the Book of Revelation indicates, will not always be available to people (cf. also Phil 2:11).

Worship Challenges (2:18–3:6)

The religious leaders soon threw down several worship challenges. Why, they asked, did not the disciples of Jesus act as "good worshipers" and fast (2:18)? Jesus answered simply. For his followers it was not fasting time; it was party time. Both are valid experiences of worship, depending on the appropriate occasion (2:19). His worship opponents were not satisfied. They followed Jesus and criticized his disciples for eating grain directly from the fields and thereby breaking several Sabbath rules. In countering them, Jesus not only quoted from the story of David about eating sanctified bread but also indicated they had in fact totally misunderstood Sabbath. The Sabbath was in reality a gift for worship and not an end in itself. Beyond that fact, as the Son of God, Jesus claimed to be Lord of the Sabbath (2:27)!

Then his critics watched him in the synagogue to see if he would beak the law himself and heal on the Sabbath. His question to them was: Is Sabbath a time for doing good or evil? The answer for them was obvious: Sabbath was a time to stop doing any work, and they had their prooftexts from the Torah (e.g., Exod 31:12–15). So the Pharisees joined with the Herodians, their regular opponents, and began to plot Jesus' death (Mark 3:6). It did not take long for the Jewish leadership to determine that they could not tolerate such a mysterious miracle worker upsetting their institutions and their nicely formulated rules of worship. He would have to be eliminated.

Opposition to Jesus' Continued Ministry (3:7–5:20)

Yet Jesus continued to preach, heal, and cast out evil spirits (Mark 3:7–12). He appointed twelve followers to do so as well (3:13–19; cf. 6:7–13). As he proceeded, the issues became more intense; and their implications for worship became more clearly defined. He was charged illogically with being possessed by a demon and casting out Satan as a follower of Satan (3:22–23). He responded with the stern warning that confusing the forces in the spirit world was an unforgivable sin (3:28–29).

Moreover, he made it clear that mere human family relationships were not determinative for membership in the family of God (3:31–34). Indeed, in the parable of the soils (also referred to as the parable of the sower) it becomes evident that the issue of fruitfulness and acceptability in God's realm is not dependent on the sower or the gospel (the seed) but on the readiness of persons (soils) to receive the unentangled gospel (4:1–20; cf. the thorns choking the new sprouts). It is a matter of readiness for response.

The Markan Sandwiches (5:21–6:56)

One of the strangest phenomena in Mark is what can best be described as the "Markan sandwiches." One story is inserted into the middle of another story, and the combination is vital to the meaning of both. Such is the case of the stories of faith and healing in respect to both the dying daughter of Jairus, the synagogue leader, and the poor woman with a bleeding disorder (5:21–43). Jairus was desperate to have Jesus come to his home and heal the girl, but while they are en route, another story arises, concerning a helpless, sick woman. Unbeknownst to the crowd, she believed that if she could merely touch Jesus' cloak, she would be healed. Confirming her belief, she was instantly made well in accordance with her faith.

Following this exchange, however, a messenger arrived to inform Jairus that his daughter had already died. Jesus instructed the leader to have faith. They arrived at Jairus' home amid loud wailing. Still, the people laughed at Jesus for coming to heal the girl. Nevertheless, Jesus astonished them all by calling the girl forth from the dead (5:42).

The point, is that a worship leader may not have the faith of a person who would normally be overlooked or rejected by the worshiping community. Indeed, Mark positioned the next pericope in Jesus' hometown, where unbelief made it difficult for Jesus to do many miracles in that setting (6:1–6).

Ceremonial Questions (7:1–9:1)

In chapter 7 Mark takes up ceremonial questions. The leaders began to criticize the disciples because they did not follow the custom of ritual washing of their hands. Jesus countered their criticisms by charging them with being hypocrites. He cited Isaiah's condemnation of the people for following human traditions and parroting the words of worship without exhibiting a worshipful heart (7:6–7; cf. Isa 29:13). Then he charged them with employing manipulative temporary dedications of their wealth ("Corban" in the text) to avoid the responsibilities of caring for their parents and thus violating the intention of the commandment to honor one's parents (Mark 7:9–13; cf. Exod 20:12; Deut 5:16). Moreover, he asserted that defilement is not measured in terms of external matters of worship procedure but results out of an internal fraudulent mindset from which emerges all forms of sin (Mark 7:18–23).

Mark then focused on Jesus' reactions to Peter's confessional confusion at Caesarea Philippi (noted above, especially in Matthew 16), and warned his listeners that, if they would be his disciples, worshipful words were not enough. They, too, would have to take up the way of the cross and follow him. The human tendency is for self-preservation and self-advancement, but the way of discipleship is self-denial and sacrifice. Attaining the acceptance and the glory (praise) of God means to accept the "shame" of Christ to avoid ultimately being shamed by Christ (8:34–38). In a society in which shame and honor were vivid realities of existence, Jesus' message must have hit his listeners with tornado force.

The Transfiguration (9:2–50)

The doublet of stories in chapter 9 offers some fascinating worship insights. When Jesus took three inner-core disciples up on the mountain (probably Mount Hermon, which is just above Caesarea Philippi) for a brief retreat, they were in for a huge surprise. While up there, Moses and Elijah appeared and conversed with Jesus, who was awesomely radiant. Peter's immediate reaction was to respond by suggesting the erection of three worship shrines (to Jesus and the two great figures from the Old Testament) and to continue their retreat in worshipful contemplation (9:5). To his shock a dark cloud fearfully enveloped them and a voice thundered, "This is my specially loved Son. You listen to Him!" (9:7). Then it all vanished and they were alone with Jesus.

The experience must have made an indelible impression on them. (See 2 Pet 1:17–18.) After instructing them further, Jesus led them down from the mountain (9:7–13). When they came down to the valley, another sight greeted them: the other disciples had been trying to heal a young lad with a debilitating spirit without success. After Jesus healed the boy, the disciples asked him why they were powerless to drive out the spirit. Jesus responded that it takes prayer to control such spirits (9:14–29).

The worship point of the two stories should be apparent to readers. Some disciples wanted to continue in their mountaintop spiritual experience without perceiving who Jesus is. When they learned the truth, Jesus returned them to the valley of life and ministry. Others, however, were trying to do ministry without their time of prayer and retreat. They, too, failed miserably. To be effective disciples, followers of Jesus need *both* perceptive prayer *and* divinely appointed task. The chapter then proceeds with a discourse on humility and integrity, as Jesus took a child and illustrated for them the meaning of a trusting spirit (9:33–37). Moreover, he took salt and illustrated for them its uselessness if it fails to fulfill its intended purpose (9:50).

Final Instructions (10:1–52)

With chapter 10 the Gospel turn towards Judea and Jesus' final instructions before the inevitable conclusion. Less than a year had elapsed in Mark's accounting (see my comments on John), and the end was near. In this setting Mark continued his focus on children with another of his "sandwiches" as the disciples tried to prevent children from coming to Jesus (10:13–16) and as Jesus referred to his followers as "children" and reminded them how hard it is to enter God's realm (10:24–31). Between these two segments lies the story of a rich man who was seeking to complete his preparation for God's acceptance by keeping rules of life and worship while maintaining his wealthy status. He had to learn like a child that God's concern is not with human status (10:17–23).

Then Mark added the pericope of the quest for status in Jesus' realm by his own disciples, James and John. They, too, had to learn that the way of discipleship was not through gaining "chief-seats" but through servanthood. Furthermore, to follow Jesus meant to be "baptized" into his suffering and death (10:35–45).

Entering Jerusalem (11:1–13:37)

The stage was set for the entry into Jerusalem (11:1–10). Unlike the presentation in John, Mark emphasizes the victory nature of the entry because the Lord was about to act next in an awesome manner. Once again the evangelist employed a sandwich presentation to accomplish his task. Using the two segments of the cursing of a fig tree, Mark placed the cleansing of the Temple between them. Mark was implying that because the Jewish leaders had used the Temple for their own economic gain and not for prayer and worship (11:15–17; cf. Ezek 34:2–3), the Temple worship services had become as dead as a cursed fig tree (11:12–14, 20–22). Jesus added that prayer is not merely some liturgical manipulation of words. It is an active engagement with divine power (11:23–25).

The leaders, who controlled the institutions of Judaism, did not take the challenge to their authority lying down. Instead, they began in earnest to plot Jesus' death (11:18) and to challenge his authority openly (11:27–33). Their attempts to catch him incriminating himself on the matters of taxes, the resurrection, and the priority of the commandments, however, failed miserably. Jesus countered their questions by affirming the legitimacy of earthly realities, but, more significantly, by stressing the ultimate reality of the divine realm and God's requirements for worship and life (12:1–34). In concluding this segment, Mark selected a widow's tiny donation to the Temple as Jesus' example of authentic worship. The Lord proclaimed that the widow had superseded all the large donors in generosity because she had given her all (12: 41–44).

Jesus shocked his disciples as they extolled the magnificence of the Temple buildings. He announced that the beautiful stone edifices used in worship would soon be destroyed (13:1–2). Moreover, he alerted them to the coming of apocalyptic traumas (13:14–23), but he forewarned them not to be led astray by prophets who calendared the end of time, since *even he* was not privy to such information (13:32)!

False prophets who claim to know the when and where of the end in hopes of attracting devotees to their systems of worship and ways of thinking are not a new phenomenon. They will constantly appear to confuse people and to gain a following. Our task is to take seriously our worship of God and the fact of Christ's victory over evil, but not to presume to know what even Jesus did not know concerning the future while he was on earth.

Death of the Son of God (14:1–16:8)

The death story of Jesus is then initiated by another sandwich in which the two segments of the traitorous plot by Judas (14:1–2, 10–11) highlight the central pericope of the anointing of Jesus for his burial (14:3–9). Moreover, as a contrast with John, Jesus' final meal with his disciples in Mark is regarded as a Passover meal (14:12). At this supper Jesus identified his betrayer as one who dipped in the same bowl with him, indicating that perhaps as a last act of grace Judas was allowed to recline in a place of "honor" next to Jesus (14:20; see also my comments on this matter in John). At that meal Jesus distributed to the disciples both the blessed, broken pieces of bread representing his torn body, *and* the cup symbolizing the covenant of his poured blood for many. Then he promised he would not again drink of the contents of that cup until the inauguration of the kingdom of God (14:22–25). These acts of Jesus represent for Christians a lasting covenant of Christ's freely given sacrificial life for his people's salvation or redemption (cf. 10:45). The church's worship celebration of the Lord's Supper is both a covenant reminder of his death and a proclamation of his victory (cf. 1 Cor 11:24–26). It is not merely a worship service of "remembrance." It is also a worship service that proclaims victory and the expectation of Christ's return.

Gethsemane then provides a series of lessons for worshipers. First, the failure of the disciples to watch and pray with their Lord (Mark 14:37–38) is only a symbol of the human difficulty to enter into long periods of silent retreat with God. Second, Gethsemane and the disciple's [Peter's] futile attempt at responding to force is only an example of how easily Christians under pressure choose the ways of the world rather than those of God (14:46). Third, Gethsemane and Peter's later denials also reflect the vulnerability of humans to run and forsake Christ when force and pressure are exerted against their faith (14:50, 66–72).

Jesus was destined to die–as he predicted. Also, as he predicted, he would mysteriously conquer that death in his resurrection (cf. Mark 8:31; 9:9, 31; 10:33–34), even though the appearance stories themselves are missing and have been lost from the Gospel. What remains in the text is sufficient because it contains the story of the empty tomb and the stunning appearance of the angel, who announced to the women not to be shocked by what they saw (16:1–6). Instead, they were instructed by the angel to tell the disciples and especially the mourning Peter (cf. 14:72) that Jesus would meet them shortly in Galilee (16:7).

As the gospel began, Jesus was introduced as the "Son of God" (1:1). Such was confirmed in the death story when Caiaphas, the high priest, asked his conclusive question and Jesus asserted "I am" (14:61–62). At the cross when his blood was shed for humanity (14:24), the Roman centurion confessed that Jesus was "in truth, the Son of God!" (15:39).

He is, however, not now dead. He is alive. The awesome Jesus, the Son of man, will return on the clouds with amazing power and glory (13:26). The question for us is: Does our worship and life reflect such a wonder-inspiring Jesus as our Lord?

WORSHIP SUMMARY

Indeed, is our worship merely reduced to a series of rote practices and words, or does it actually represent, in the spirit of Mark's portrait of Jesus, the conviction of the victory of Christ over death and the anticipation of his return? Moreover, do our lives and worship evidence both periods of retreat with Christ on the mountain and service in the valley with humanity? The awesome Jesus of Mark expects both from true Christian worshipers.

QUESTION

1. Would the awesome Jesus of Mark surprise you in your worship and life? Why? Why not?

3

Luke

Journeying with the Caring Jesus from His Glory to His Power[1]

In the mystery of the caring Jesus the marginalized of society are able to experience the peace and glory of the Lord and find acceptance as true worshiping people of God.

Luke is unquestionably the best storyteller in the New Testament. Just mention such stories as the good Samaritan, the rich man and Lazarus, the lost coin and the prodigal son, the little Zacchaeus, the shepherds and baby Jesus, the boy Jesus in the Temple, the widow and the judge, the Pharisee and the publican, and the magnificent Emmaus journey. These stories are found only in Luke. More importantly for this study, you will quickly discover that they are not only marvelous stories; they also have significant implications for worship.

Connections to Acts and to the Old Testament

Luke's stunning portrait of the caring Jesus epitomizes the unity between worship and life. But it can hardly be understood adequately without holding in mind that Luke's Gospel was followed by a second volume known as the Acts of the Apostles. While no manuscript evidence suggests that the two were ever joined in circulation, it will be imperative when interpreting both books to remember that the evangelist purposely formulated his account of the beginnings of the church to mirror the life of Jesus in his Gospel.

This Gospel portrays Jesus in several modes—such as, as a new Moses and as a new prophet like Elijah. In him the Old Testament finds its fulfillment, and in him is epitomized the loving God, full of loving kindness or tender mercy (*hesed*), who earlier through his messengers and prophets cared for the poor and the despised of humanity. To reflect on Luke's picturesque testimony of Jesus, "the Son of the Most High" (Luke 1:32), should enable the reader to recognize why authentic Christian worship is clearly experienced with a sense of thanksgiving in spite of many human hardships in life.

Introducing the Gospel

This two-volume work was traditionally assigned to Luke, the beloved physician and coworker of Paul (cf. Col 4:14; 2 Tim 4:11; Phlm 24). The followers of F. C. Baur called that attribution into question. They considered a book such as Acts to be dialectically unreliable and politically oriented. W. K. Hobart soon countered with a traditional approach by arguing that Luke's language indicated he was a physician. Henry Cadbury then responded that linguistic studies could merely confirm that Luke was an educated person. Sir William Ramsay, beginning as a devotee of Baur, retraced much of the Acts' travel material and concluded that Luke was a reliable historian. Then more recently Hans Conzelmann categorized Luke as primarily a theologian and not as an historian. Today it is probably best to understand that Luke was in fact quite a reliable historian but also was a very capable theologian.[2] Moreover, I see no reason now to refer to him other than as Luke, a Gentile companion of Paul.

Luke may well have written this Gospel after Jerusalem fell to the Roman special legate Titus in 70 C.E., since Luke has interpreted the "sacrilegious desolation" of Mark 13:14 as "Jerusalem surrounded by armies" (Luke 21:20). Such a dating would also mean that Luke wrote Acts after Paul was dead and that he left the book as we have it open-ended to imply that although Paul was in chains, the gospel cannot be chained or confined (Acts 28:31). It is impossible to tell whether he intended to write more.

Another matter concerns the recipient, Theophilus (Luke 1:3; Acts 1:1). He is otherwise unknown but appears from the Gospel introduction to be someone of importance to Luke, such as a wealthy sponsor (*kratiste*, "very noble"). He was apparently a Christian worshiper who was interested in receiving a clear account of matters related to Jesus and the early church (Luke 1:4). Alternatively, the name "Theophilus" could possibly be a surrogate for some unknown Christian(s) since it means "lover of God." As will become evident almost immediately when turning to the text of Luke, issues of worship must have been very important to both Luke and his reader(s).

As I indicated in connection with Matthew, reading the beginning and the end of a Gospel should provide some insight into the work in question. In this case one quickly notices that this Gospel begins with a mysterious encounter in the Temple of Jerusalem and ends in the Temple with the disciples joyfully worshiping God as they awaited with anticipation the promise of an endowment by God following Jesus' resurrection (24:49–53). One, for example, should also notice clues such as the details that both the baby Jesus and the boy Jesus are brought to the Temple (2:22–24, 41–51), and that the temptations in Luke end in (or "on") the Temple (4:9). One also quickly learns that cities are important to Luke, especially Jerusalem. Accordingly, Acts picks up the story from the Gospel in Jerusalem (for Luke the religious center of the world) and ends in Rome (the political center) as the good news is carried from city to city throughout the Mediterranean world (Acts 1:3–8; 28:17–30). But now our attention is turned to the unfolding of this captivating Gospel text.

Opening in the Temple (1:1–80)

Typical of Luke's historical concerns, the Gospel opens by setting the first story about a priest, Zechariah, in Jerusalem in the time of King Herod. Typical also of Luke is the focus on worship. Immediately the reader is placed in a numinous worship context in the Temple, with an angelic visitation and a surprising announcement to the priest: he and his wife—elderly, childless, and righteous—would have a baby. The scene is reminiscent of the miraculous birth stories of Isaac and Samuel (Gen 17:1–7, 15–27; 21:1–3; and 1 Sam 1:1–19). The disbelief of the priest at the angel's stunning promise of God's answer to the couple's prayers, however, resulted in the priest's temporary dumbness and the people's perception that some type of divine visitation had occurred in their worship sanctuary (Luke 1:18–22).

This first visitation story is followed by an even more astounding angelic visitation and an even more astonishing announcement to the virgin Mary that she, too, would have a child. While she also asked "how" such a birth was possible, the response of the divinely appointed visitor was that it would be miraculously accomplished by God's self. The reply resulted not in her doubt or disbelief, as with Zechariah but in her humble acceptance of the miracle (1:26–38). The reader should be aware of this model of a spiritually formed contrast at the very beginning of Luke, who often uses complementary stories containing both a man and a woman as a mark of his inclusiveness.

These amazing birth stories involving the coming of the "Son of God," Jesus (1:35), and of his preparatory prophet, John (1:76), led Luke to provide two marvelous canticles or poetical ascriptions of praise to God, both of which the church has used repeatedly in worship. The first is now known as the "Magnificat," the song of Mary (1:46–55); and the second as the "Benedictus," the song of Zechariah (1:68–79). The themes in these hymns of praise and joy (1:46–47, 79) are an acknowledgment of God's holiness and righteousness (1:49, 75), of God's purpose to save and deliver the chosen people (1:47, 68–69, 71, 73, 77), of God's mercy to those who honor God (1:50, 54, 72, 78), of God's loving care for the unfortunate (1:52–53), of God's righteous indignation at the haughty and unconcerned rich and powerful (1:51, 53) and of God's goal in providing hope and peace for the chosen people (1:78–79). These themes are repeatedly explicated in the Gospel as the reader is led to worship by experiencing the glory of God in Jesus.

Jesus' Birth and Childhood (2:1–52)

The birth story of Jesus is again contextualized by Luke in history and worship as the glory of God was revealed in an angelic visitation to lowly, fearful shepherds (people of the land, *am ha'aretz*). They were given the joyful announcement that a Savior, Christ the Lord, had been born in a borrowed stable in David's city (2:1–12). This visitation was highlighted by a divine choir worshiping and giving glory to God while promising peace to those who please God.[3] The shepherds responded immediately, and their report engendered widespread wonderment, the accompanying response to the presence of divine mystery in the world.

The presentation of the baby Jesus in the Temple is a reminder that family worship begins early in a child's life. It is here framed by the presence of Simeon and Anna, two saintly senior citizens, who recognize who Jesus is and thank God for the coming of God's salvation/redemption (2:22–40). Simeon's brief worship response now encapsulated in the canticle *Nunc Dimittis* proclaimed Luke's themes of peace, salvation, acceptance of the Gentiles, and of the coming anguish (2:30–32, 34–35).

The next appearance of Jesus in the Temple on Passover (probably about the time of his *bar mitzvah*) seems to celebrate his maturing stage in life: namely, of coming into acceptance before God and the people of God (2:52), as evidenced in believer's baptism in some Christian circles and in confirmation in others. It, likewise, elicited amazement (2:47). Luke patently intended it to clarify Jesus' divine Sonship and responsiveness primarily to God (2:49). It functions as a defining moment with his mother in this Gospel, much as the Cana wedding celebration serves in John (John 2:4–5; cf. the kinship question in Mark 3:31–35 as well as in Matt 12:46–50 and Luke 8:19–21).

The Beginning of Jesus' Ministry (3:1–7:17)

Luke again contextualized the beginning of Jesus' ministry in Roman history before he introduced Jesus in an outdoor worship setting of John the Baptist and his ministry (Luke 3:1–3). The point of the Baptizer's preaching and the ritual of baptizing is noted as preparing for God's salvation by condemning inauthentic worship such as mere outward practices of repentance that did not issue in changed lives. To be ready for the Messiah who would baptize with the Holy Spirit necessitated observing the close interrelationship between worship and life. Genuine children of Abraham bring forth the "good fruit" of ethical life. Lack of such integrity would lead to judgment (3:7–17). Jesus confirmed his commitment to the need for such integrity of worship and life by submitting himself to baptism. Luke then adds that, as Jesus was "praying," God confirmed his "delight" in his Son (3:21–22; cf. the servant song at Isa 42:1). Luke ties this section together by inserting the genealogy from Jesus back to Adam and making it clear that Jesus' ministry was not merely directed to care for Israel but was intended to deal with the sin of the entire world (3:38).

Before engaging in his ministry, however, Jesus faced his own life temptations: of using his authority to care for his own needs (making bread), of compromising with evil to achieve his goals (gaining the world inappropriately), and finally of using show and miraculous power to gain adherents (Temple miracle). While none of Jesus' temptations would be temptations for us who are merely human (since temptations are the measure of the one being tempted), these general areas of Jesus' temptation are not irrelevant to us in our worship and life. Moreover, these temptations of the devil are merely examples of that which Jesus faced throughout his life (4:13) and were present up to the very end, as is evident in his prayer on the Mount of Olives (22:42–44), symbolic of the integration of his life and worship.

Luke chose to begin Jesus' ministry in a synagogue service in his hometown (Nazareth), where he read from Isaiah concerning the coming year of Jubilee with its reversal state for the poor and oppressed. When Jesus announced in a worship setting that the great Jubilee had arrived with him, the people first reacted with amazement, which soon turned to outright hostility when Jesus likened his ministry to those of Elijah and Elisha in their care of Gentiles (4:16–30). Although Luke did not here add the arrival of God's judgment from Isaiah 64:2, the rejection of Jesus implied judgment would certainly come.

Luke next adopted the familiar healing and call stories of Mark (Luke 4:31–6:16) and used a "Sayings Source" containing teachings such as the Beatitudes from Sermon on the Mount in Matthew (6:20–49). Then, in the story of the healing of the centurion's son and the accompanying discussion on "worthiness," he spotlighted for his Gentile reader(s) the fact that Jesus had not found in all Israel such faith (response to divine action) as the Gentile centurion had exhibited (7:9). Luke joined that story to the one in which Jesus raised a widow's son to show us how an unimportant, poor woman provided a model for worship not only in glorifying God but also in confessing that God had "visited" God's people in Jesus (7:16; cf. the canticle at 1:68).

Acceptance and Rejection (7:18–9:50)

Luke added two pericopes—the alternatives represented by John the Baptizer, who had truly fulfilled his prophetic task (7:18–28), and the Pharisees, who had rejected God's plan (7:29). Next Luke powerfully illustrated acceptance and rejection. In one of Luke's great stories, a sinful woman slipped in and disturbed a Pharisee's diner party by humbly weeping and worshipfully anointing Jesus' feet in the presence of all. When the Pharisee scoffed at the discredited woman and Jesus' acceptance of her action, Jesus proclaimed that her sins were forgiven. Those at the table became incensed at Jesus' assumption of such authority, but Jesus responded by pronouncing "peace" on her as the result of her faith in Jesus (7:36–50). The bestowing of peace on people who acknowledge the power and presence of God is a crucial aspect of Christian worship.

When turning next to the three Marcan linked stories of Peter's confession, the transfiguration, and the healing of the boy with an epileptic spirit, one notices some special phenomena in Luke's use of the stories, which are of particular importance for our study. Both the confession and the transfiguration are introduced with Jesus (and the disciples) praying, signaling that these significant stories should not be divorced from a worship context in Luke. The first story includes the confession and the speech about taking up the cross from Mark and ends with a unique eschatological announcement by Jesus that some present would not die until they experienced the kingdom (9:27). An eschatological expectation of the return of Jesus is essential for adequate Christian worship. That statement has given rise to speculation about whether Luke had a mistaken view of the *parousia* (the coming of Christ, cf. 9:26). Would it not be better to view Jesus' remark as Luke's understanding that Jesus was speaking here of the post-resurrection coming of the Spirit and being "clad' with divine "power" (*endusesthe...dunamin*, cf. 24:49) as the Gospel ends? Recognizing the double perspective of "the already and the not yet" in Jesus' predictive statements is very important, and its relevance for our participation in worship today is crucial. Jesus' presence in the Spirit can be with us now, but we still await his final presence.

The second and third stories also contain special points. In the transfiguration account his "departure" is mentioned in the conversation with the Moses and Elijah (9:30–31). The word used here is his "exodus" (*exodon*), which immediately suggests linking God's earlier freeing of Israel with Jesus' action in the cross and resurrection. The "exodus" was the foundation of Jewish worship (e.g., the Passover haggadah). For Luke, Jesus' exodus is the foundation of Christian worship. As such, it highlights part of the "already" nature of our faith. The third story of healing the epileptic ends with the recognition of the "majesty of God" (9:43) in Jesus, a concept that is crucial for authentic worship and is related to both aspects of our eschatology (our perspectives on the end of time and our expectations of the future).

Facing Jerusalem (9:51–18:43)

The end of chapter 9 signals a dramatic shift for Luke as Jesus set his face like a poised arrow to go to Jerusalem and his "lifting up" (*analempseos*, 9:51; cf. Paul's setting of his face to go to Jerusalem in Acts 20:22–25, 36–38; 21:13–14). The stories from this point in the Gospel until his entry into Jerusalem (19:28) encompass segments of a long travel story (or reflections on the way). The destiny of Jesus was firmly set. The pericopes in Luke are organized to clarify his road to death, but also to instruct his readers on proper perspectives for worship and life. A disciple's task is not to call judgment on others (9:54–55), nor is following Jesus to be a whimsical adventure from which one can temporarily be excused. It is a life commitment (9:57–62). Servants of Jesus are arrayed against Satan (10:18) under the guidance of the Holy Spirit (10:21–24).

Luke's linking of the good Samaritan (10:25–37) with the contrast between Mary and Martha (10:38–42) and the discourse on prayer (11:1–13) focuses on integrity in worship and life. The representative Jewish worship leaders (a priest and a Levite) are both portrayed as inauthentic in comparison to the despised Samaritan who modeled care for an unfortunate victim of violence (10:37). In contrast, the busy, caring Martha was just too busy to care for her own spiritual development (10:41). Therefore, Luke directs us to Jesus' model prayer of dependency on God (11:2–4) and calls us to appropriate responses of asking, seeking, and knocking on God's door because God earnestly desires to give the Holy Spirit to those who pray (11:9–13).

Next, the Pharisees' lack of integrity is the subject of a lengthy analysis (11:14–12:3). Luke perceptively illustrates this through Jesus' fascinating story of the rich fool. This man thought primarily of himself, his endowments, and his readiness to rest on his laurels. In fact, he was even praying to himself (12:19)! That proved to be a fundamental mistake. He failed to understand that almighty God had the last word and demanded the man's life (12:20–21). In contrast, Jesus called his followers not to trust in things of this world (12:22–34) but charged them to be vigilant, faithful (12:35–48), and to count the cost of discipleship (14:25–15:2).

Next comes a story pf Jesus healing a badly crippled woman on the Sabbath. The leader of the local synagogue severely criticized Jesus because in caring for the woman he broke their rules of Sabbath. Jesus thundered back that he, and those like him, were blatant "hypocrites!" They separated worship from life! He countered with a rare assertion by referring to the healed woman as a "daughter of Abraham." It was an incredible statement for a Jewish man to make, since in the synagogues men thanked God that they had not been made women. Jesus thus shamed his learned critics but elicited joy from the people because of his care (13:10–17). Yet the final picture was already in focus for Jesus, so Luke added the touching story of Jesus weeping over Jerusalem like a mother hen who is unable to collect her little chicks (13:31–35).

The parables of the lost sheep, the lost coin, and the lost son enhance our understanding of the caring God who actively seeks the company of God's lost children and rejoices in their presence (15:3–32). These parables provide an important perspective for our worship by depicting the hand of God outstretched toward mere mortals. The parable of the fraudulent steward, however, reminds us that false and manipulative people actually attempt the impossible: namely, trying to serve two masters (16:1–13). The classic story of the rich man and Lazarus (16:19–31) testifies that how we act has eternal consequences and that even if someone would miraculously return from the dead, unconcerned people would still refuse to listen to the message. Then, the moving story of the tax collector and the Pharisee teaches that displays of public show and self-interest in worship are patently empty rituals, while God rewards unshowy, genuine humility in worship, even if so-called religious people regard such humble worshipers as rejects (18:9–14). The priceless story of Zacchaeus then sums up this section by assuring readers that the radical transformation that the church proclaims affecting all of life actually can occur, as it did with the despised chief of tax collectors (19:1–10), who returned the gain he received from his earlier manipulative practices—a true test of authentic worship.

Entering Jerusalem (19:1–22:53)

The arrival of chapter 19 signals the end of Jesus' journey to Jerusalem. Luke introduces the entry with Jesus' parable concerning servants of a king. Some were rebellious while others were very productive. Still others acted slovenly. The king knew how to treat them all (19:11–27), just as Jesus knew how to discern people and their actions. The entry that followed illustrates the differences in observers. While the Pharisees complained, Jesus' disciples exemplified an acceptable attitude of worship as they praised God and blessed their "King" as they proclaimed "peace in heaven and glory in the highest" (19:38). The parallel with the birth of Jesus and the angelic choir's divinely oriented response of "peace on earth" and "glory to God" is ironic (2:14) since it was now evident that God's gift of Jesus was hardly received by the world graciously. Therefore, Luke reminds us by the next brief but touching story that Jesus again wept over Jerusalem because its people did not recognize and respond appropriately to Jesus—the one who could bring them peace (19:41–42).

As the hostility continued to intensify, Jesus employed a statement from the Psalms to announce his verdict: the construction stone rejected by builders (the people who were supposed to worship and serve God) is in actuality the key or marker stone (Jesus) for the building (20:17; cf. Ps 118:22; 1 Pet 2:6). Instead of genuine dialogue on what counted in life and worship, trickery became the tool of his critics. But they did not succeed (Luke 20:7–8, 26, 40), for Jesus turned the tables on them and judged their lack of integrity by reference to their worship and life practices. While Jesus' critics dressed in ritualistic gowns, loved special religious titles, and demanded the chief places in worship, their ruthlessness in the seizure of widows' property was worthy of damnation (20:45–47). Their end was in sight. The Temple, the earthly worship center, was doomed (21:5–6), and Jerusalem would be destroyed (21:20). Jesus also indicated that true worshipers would certainly suffer from such ruthless people (21:12, 16–17), yet his followers were forewarned that they should not become troubled or alarmed by predictions of the ultimate end (21:8–9). Instead, they should recognize the signs of times (21:25–31) and not be led astray by false rumors. Their duty and our continuing worship imperative is to watch and pray for endurance and fortitude (21:36).

Judas, Satan's instrument, then hatched the plot to kill Jesus (22:1–6). This traitorous act set the stage for the "Last Supper" of Jesus with his disciples, an event that epitomizes a worship response for Christians. In Luke, as in the rest of the Synoptics, it is a Passover meal (22:15; Mark 14:16; Matt 26:17). But in Luke the distribution of the cup and the eschatological promise that Jesus would not drink of it again until the kingdom of God (Luke 22:17–18) precedes (yet also follows) the breaking and distribution of the bread (22:19). Such an order of the elements is not usually observed in churches today, but it is a reminder that according to the various Jewish Seder services the cup is taken more than once in the Passover meal. The important point for Luke, however, is that with both elements Jesus offered his prayer of "thanksgiving" (*eucharistesas*), the source of why, in some traditions, the Lord's Supper is called the Eucharist (22:17, 19). Then into this eucharistic context Luke sets Mark's dispute about the priority and greatness among the disciples (cf. Mark 10:42–45). Jesus' response is expanded here. It is applied not merely to chief seats in the kingdom but also in this table context it is used to highlight humility of both the server and the served (Luke 22:24–27). This two-fold humility should have great import for our theological interpretations and worship practices that have constructed an elevated "office" at the Lord's Table! Our divisions of clergy and laity at the Table hardly represent Luke's understanding of relationships among Christians. We are all merely humble servants of Christ in all of life—in worship and outside of worship.

The Gethsemane story in Luke is pointedly focused on prayer and temptation (22:39–46). The eight verses of this pericope mention prayer five times, indicating how significant Luke regarded prayer as the means of maintaining spiritual strength and of resisting the "power of darkness" in the face of temptation (22:53). Prayer involves the genuine struggle of humanity with the powers of evil. Jesus gave us a model for responding to God in the face of trauma.

Jesus' Trial and Death (22:54–23:56)

In the trial story before Pilate, Jesus' innocence was proclaimed three times (23:4, 14, 22). Even so, Pilate finally gave in to pressure from the Jews and delivered Jesus to be crucified (23:25). In spite of the injustice thrust upon him, the Savior issued words from the cross as he died that revealed his caring nature. He prayed for the forgiveness of his killers who had no overall conception of what they were doing (23:34).

Jesus had been prepared for this moment. He, likewise, graciously promised the hope of paradise to the repentant criminal (23:43). Then in prayer he entrusted his spirit to the Father (23:46). As they died, even the perceptive criminal recognized Jesus' innocence (23:41), as did the Roman centurion who was on duty at the cross (23:47). Luke will later employ this theme of innocence repeatedly in the Book of Acts with reference to the followers of Jesus, as in the cases of the falsely accused Stephen and Paul (e.g., Acts 7:51–53; 26:32).

The Resurrection (24:1–53)

So Jesus died and was buried by Joseph from Arimathea, an authentic member of the Sanhedrin (Luke 23:50–51). The followers of Jesus expected nothing more, except for the appropriate final burial preparations by the women (23:55). Little did the women realize, however, the surprise that would await them after the Sabbath, because the tomb was amazingly empty. Instead of finding a body, they encountered two awesome angelic visitors who questioned them about their search for the "living" Jesus among the tombs (24:1–5). When the women reported their encounter with the mysterious figures and indicated the reminder of Jesus' earlier instructions, the whole story was sloughed off by the men (with the exception of Peter) as an unbelievable fairy tale (24:10–11). The disciples were not prepared for mystery. But it confronted them in spite of their doubts and unbelief.

That report was only the beginning of Luke's resurrection account. He next introduces the magnificent story of the journey to Emmaus (24:13–33). While readers quickly guess that the mysterious stranger who met the two weary disciples on the road was Jesus, they are nevertheless drawn into the gripping account by the intriguing question-and-answer exchange, including the references to Scripture. In the next table scene the reader may become as surprised as the disciples by the discovery that Jesus was recognized in the breaking of bread! Then mysteriously he vanished.

The significance of this numinous experience of mystery for worship can hardly be over emphasized. It initiated a startling change. Although the weary disciples had lacked energy to continue their journey, the revelation of the presence of Jesus at the table transformed them into inspired witnesses. They immediately returned to the rest of the followers of Jesus in Jerusalem to report on their remarkable experience. That encounter with the risen Lord was enhanced by learning of an appearance to Simon (24:34). It was soon confirmed by the appearance of Jesus to the community of disciples, with his eating of food proof that he was not some ghostly apparition (24:36–42). Jesus was not dead. He was alive and was with them!

The Gospel then moves to its conclusion, as Jesus issued his standing commission for them to be his witnesses to the world, beginning in Jerusalem (24:44–48). Jesus demanded a response from his worshipers, but he also issued a clear instruction for them to wait for the coming promise of divine power to fulfill his commission (24:49). For Christians today both the commission and instruction are still pertinent. The clear summons is for Christians to respond and be witnesses of the living Lord. To fulfill that call, they need to encounter divine mystery in the power and direction of the Holy Spirit.

The Gospel then ends where it began—in the Temple. In this case, however, it involved the disciples who at Bethany had received the Lord's blessing as he was drawn up and away from them (24:51). In joyful anticipation, the disciples returned to Jerusalem to await their future and to bless God in worship for the divine conclusion to the earthly life of the caring Jesus.

WORSHIP SUMMARY _____

Waiting in worship for the power of God was not an end in itself for the early Christians any more that it is for Christians today.

Effective worship goes beyond merely sitting on comfortable pews in "services" at church. Instead, it will lead to the empowerment of God for witness and service in life. From the beginning to the end of this Gospel, Luke presents Jesus, like God, as Savior (cf. 1:47) who modeled for humanity the integrated life of worship and service. He clearly condemned pseudo-practitioners of worship—such as priests, Levites, and Pharisees—while elevating the lowly and despised—such as the shepherds, the good Samaritan, caring women, and a hated tax collector—because of their newfound trust and integrity. Luke expected his readers to respond similarly in worship and life to the mystery of God.

May the joy that the early disciples experienced in seeing the risen Lord be present in Christians today, and may the blessing that the early Christians offered to God be repeated continually by contemporary believers as they accept their commissions of witnessing to the world (cf. 24:52–53).

QUESTIONS

1. Do your personal and corporate worship practices lead you to care for those who are poor, minorities, inflicted with horrible diseases, and/or are rejects of humanity?
2. If they do, why? If not, why not? Can you illustrate your answers?

4

John

Worshiping the King: The Word Who Became Flesh[1]

The mysterious "Word of God" became human and embodied in himself all the aspects of Jewish worship including both the role of the Lamb of God in taking away the sin of the world and the dying and victorious King of Israel.

My pilgrimage with the Gospel of John has lasted almost my entire lifetime, beginning when I was confined to an isolation hospital while I was in grade school and took the opportunity to put most of the gospel to memory. My academic journey with this precious book since that time spans decades, in which I have penned scores of articles and commentaries (both a shorter one and a much longer two-volume commentary). The Gospel is an amazing resource for spiritual development. Early on, Clement of Alexandria designated it as the "Spiritual Gospel." Moreover, it is a model for characterization, since each person described in the Gospel is pictured as not only a historical personage but also as representing a specific type of person engaged either positively or negatively in life and worship.[2] In addition, this Gospel is a phenomenal resource for theology,[3] My task in this present work, however, is to detail briefly how it is also a magnificent resource for reflections on worship.

Introducing John's Gospel

In the early twentieth century, some scholars, such as Rudolf Bultmann, posited that some unknown second-century elder in Asia penned the Gospel.[4] The discovery of the Roberts Fragment in Egypt (now housed in the John

Rylands Library), which can be dated to the early second century, has made such a view quite speculative. Moreover, a number of scholars believe the author cannot be John, the son of Zebedee, because they consider the thought process to be too developed to be the work of an early writer from Palestine.[5] I have sought to deal with these matters at length in my commentary and will only add here that early tradition seems to support the view that John lived into the nineties of the first century and that he wrote the Gospel.[6]

The Gospel's Structure

The gospel is a finely organized work that is also strategic for worship. It begins with a profound eighteen-verse prologue that was probably written after the main part of the book was finished. The prologue highlights who Jesus is and was while on earth, a basic starting point for Christian worship. Thereafter, what follows in the rest of the chapter are several stories of "witness": first involving John, the ideal witness, who elsewhere is called "the Baptist" (but not here); and concluding with three other cameos of witness. Then follows in chapters 2–4 the "Cana Cycle," a series of "witness" pericopes concerning Jesus beginning in Cana and ending in Cana. After this first cycle comes a group of seven chapters (chs. 5–11), which I call the "Festival Cycle." In these chapters Jesus replaces the Jewish worship calendar. Chapter 12 is like a new beginning to the second half of the book and concerns the movement of Jesus to his appointed "hour," the hour of his glorification as the dying King of Israel. The next five chapters (chs. 13–17) I designate as the third or "Farewell Cycle." This cycle is not merely a series of discourses. It begins with a crucial worship act of foot washing, prepares the disciples for Jesus' departure, and then ends with an encompassing prayer. The book concludes with two sections, each two chapters long, involving first the death story of the King (chs. 18–19) and then the marvelous resurrection stories (chs. 20–21). Chapter 21 appears in the form of an appendix, but the Gospel did not circulate without this appendix, so it must have been added almost immediately as an afterthought.

With this organization in mind, I have space only to note some representative features of the worship content, including the well-known text in John 4:24, one of the important thematic keys to the Gospel. Clearly God is spirit, and so naturally one must worship in spirit and truth (both of which are great themes in the Gospel). To worship as God has directed, one must understand who Jesus is!

Who Is Jesus? (1:1–18)

That message forms the introduction to the Gospel. Jesus is the mysterious one who was from the absolute beginning and has been active in all creation (1:1–3). Indeed, life itself vests in him, and enlightenment results from his visitation to earth (1:4–5). The reference to John warns the reader not to confuse a witness *to him* with *him*, a not too infrequent human tendency (1:6–8). Moreover, one must be aware that those who should have most likely recognized his presence (the Jews) in fact failed to perceive and honor him (1:9–11), because such recognition does not come from human effort, parental relationship, or any human desire (1:13)! Becoming a transformed child of God is the result of God's gift to us and based on human receptivity (1:12).

This incarnate Word "tabernacled" or tented (*eskenosen*) in the world (1:14) just like the worship tent of Israel had provided a sense of God's numinous presence in the desert. Like the tabernacle, Jesus represented the earthly appearance of God's glory (1:14–15). Since no human could actually look upon the direct appearance of the Almighty (Exod 33:20), God provided various alternative means for recognizing his presence. That presence was most completely exegeted (*exegesato*) or represented in Jesus (1:18).

Witnesses to Jesus (1:19–51)

Sadly, those who should have been ready for his appearance were more interested in protecting their institutional worship structures, and so they even misunderstood the coming of his prophetic forerunner (1:19–22; cf. Mal 4:5). That prophetic witness, John, recognized his own humble servant nature in the presence of such a "worthy" one (John 1:27). Indeed, as a model witness he introduced his followers to Jesus and was not concerned about losing them (the so-called "sheep-stealing" syndrome) or retaining them for his own benefit. Instead, John knew his role with God and acknowledged Jesus as the one "from above" (cf. 3:27–33). He also recognized Jesus' role as the Son of God and the "Lamb of God who takes away the sin of the world" (1:29, 34, 36). When John introduced his followers to Jesus, however, they seemed to be more concerned about the accoutrements of their new leader's position (his dwelling place) than about his role with God (1:38). When John introduced his followers to Jesus, he began to lead them to a new understanding of both his role and theirs (1:39–42). Indeed, to the guileless newcomer, Nathanael, Jesus announced that he would be like the place of Jacob's dream-filled worship encounter–Bethel ("the house of God," 1:51; cf. Gen 28:12).

Worship in the Cana Cycle (2:1–4:54)

The Cana Cycle provides some interesting insights into worship. While some ministers in their marriage ceremonies employ the Cana marriage story as a basis for Jesus' sanctification of marriage, that notion is hardly the point of the pericope. Instead, the story reveals that even his mother attempted to use Jesus for her own purposes. She quickly learned a fundamental principle in all worship–namely, obeying Jesus was the proper basis for a relationship with him. His disciples began to learn how to recognize the "glory" (*doxan*) of Jesus in human affairs (John 2:1–11). Such recognition is fundamental to worship.

The second story takes place in Jerusalem at Passover time and involves the cleansing of the Temple. The point of this story is that it is illegitimate to use worship places as settings for one's personal gain. Another perspective becomes increasingly clear–Jesus embodies in himself (and replaces) all the key aspects of Israel's life and worship. Accordingly, the worship center of Israel's faith was no longer to be the sanctuary of the Temple (*hieron*; 2:15); instead, mysteriously, it was to be the sanctuary (*naos*) of Jesus' own person ("body," *somatos*), which would be destroyed and raised on the third day (2:13–22). Therefore, the key to true worship is authentic believing *in him*, not merely liturgical involvement in an earthly structure or mere words of confession (2:23–25).

The third story involves Nicodemus, a man in transition. His coming to Jesus at night (*nyktos*) reflected the state of his life (3:2) and his need to learn the meaning of being born from above (*anothen*; 3:7). With such learning he could differentiate between what is merely of earthly import and what is of heaven (3:12). He was just like the Israelites in the desert who needed a miracle to heal them of their disobedience and snakebites. While Moses made a bronze serpent for them to look upon and be healed (Num 21:4–9), Jesus is the one who, for Nicodemus and us, is similar to the lifted-up serpent, yet who not only supplies merely physical healing but also is the *source* of eternal life (John 3:14–15). Pathetically, however, while that bronze snake of Moses was not the divine source of healing and life, the Israelites later worshiped it. As a result it had to be destroyed (2 Kgs 18:4). The story is a vivid reminder that religious symbols can become substitutes (idols) for God.

Attached to this story is the best-known verse in the New Testament (3:16). To understand its significance we must recognize the interconnectedness of John 3:16–18.[7] God certainly loves us and sent Jesus (3:16). God's purpose was undoubtedly not condemnation but the salvation of the world (3:17); yet if one does not believe, the reality is that such a one is already condemned (3:18)! To believe in Jesus means to have begun a new journey with God in our lives and worship, all of which will then reflect that we belong to the light (3:21).

With this meaning in mind, the evangelist added the next pericope, which sets Jesus in the territory of the rejected Samaritans, speaking with a woman of poor morals. The discussion of who can supply good drinking water quickly turns into a review of the woman's life. The woman counters Jesus' comments with the question of the correct venue for worship (4:20)–similar to, "What is the best church or denomination?" When Jesus shifted the question instead to the correct "spirit" for worship, the woman tried to move the question to the best teacher for worship. She quickly discovered that she was conversing with him. In his response Jesus employed the now famous *ego eimi*–"I am!" of God to Moses (4:26; cf. Exod 3:14). To believe and honor Jesus, God on earth (God's "only son," *monogenes*, John 1:18) is the route of worship (cf. 14:6)!

Such a pattern brings the Cana Cycle to a conclusion in the fifth story. Here an official begged Jesus to come and heal his dying son (4:47). When Jesus told him to go home because his son was now well, the man believed Jesus' word and departed, learning on the way home that the healing was a reality (4:50–51). This realization led to further believing, and this witness affected his entire household (4:53).

The Festival Cycle (5:1–11:57)

The next cycle involves seven chapters (5–11). Since the heart of Jewish worship was expressed in its festivals, the evangelist of the Fourth Gospel pictured Jesus as the replacement to the Festival Cycle (cf. Lev 23).

The Sabbath

John began his festival accounts with an unidentified feast, which has caused confusion among scholars. For example, Rudolf Bultmann moved chapter 5 to a point after chapter 6 because he thought it fit the movement of Jesus better. Then he reasoned the feast should be Pentecost.[8] If he would have understood the Jewish mind-set and the content of chapter 5, he would have recognized that the subject was Sabbath and that for the Jews every feast is in fact a *shabbot* to the Lord.[9]

In this pericope Jesus healed a man on the Sabbath. The man had suffered his illness for thirty-eight years (the length of Israel's time in the wilderness from Kadesh to Zared; cf. Deut 2:14). The healing led to a confrontation with the Jews (John 5:9–16). The Jews considered such healing as work on the Sabbath and thus worthy of death (cf. Exod 31:12–15). Jesus countered by claiming to have divine authority even over the Sabbath. Therefore, he was in charge of both ultimate life and judgment (John 5:19–30). The gauntlet was thus thrown down. Observance of Sabbath for Jesus was not ultimate, although the Jews had argued that even God was subject to Sabbath (their understanding of Gen 2:2–3). Instead, celebration rites such as festivals (and even Sundays!) are subject to God and God's work in the world. They are gifts of God for our benefit in worship and are not ends in themselves.

Excursus on the Life of Jesus and Passovers in John

Many think that Jesus' ministry lasted three years. I would argue that such thinking is a misunderstanding based on a poor interpretation of John. Every cycle and surrounding section of the story of Jesus in John contains a notation related to Passover except the last: Passover allusions begin with "the Lamb of God who takes away the sin of the world" (1:29) and end with the notation that it was the Day of Preparation (the day when the lambs were killed for Passover) when Jesus died (19:14, 31; cf. Passover in 2:13, 23; 6:4; 11:55; 12:1; 13:1; 18:39). For John, Jesus was the ultimate sacrificial lamb, fulfilling Scripture (19:36–37). After he died once for us all, there was no more need for Passover—in the resurrection era! If one reads Matthew, Mark, and Luke, however, one will soon learn that Jesus' ministry lasted at the most for one year. That amount of time for the presence of God's Son on earth was about all the Jewish world with its worship and rituals could take. The question is: Could we have taken more?

We can celebrate Christ's presence on earth in our liturgies today, but do we really think we could take his presence in our churches? Worth pondering, isn't it?

Passover

The second pericope in the Festival Cycle begins the movement from Passover (John 6) to Passover (ch. 11). This pericope contains the only two signs (in John)/ miracles (in the Synoptics) that are present in all the gospels. The text concerns the meaning of the exodus in light of the coming of Jesus. The story involves two related episodes loaded with worship significance: the feeding of the five thousand (6:5–13) and the walking on the water (6:15–21). Like most of John's stories, these are rich in symbolism.[10]

Jesus' feeding of the people is a reminder of God's feeding of Israel in the desert. The five loaves and two fish make seven, the perfect number, and the twelve remaining baskets are a reminder of the number assigned to God's care for his people. This story in John symbolically replaces the liturgical initiation of the Lord's Supper that appears later in the Synoptic Gospels. In John 13, a point parallel to the other Gospels' Lord's Supper narrative, a new dominical ordinance (command) of foot washing and love is inaugurated.

The walking on the water is a reminder of God's control of the sea in the exodus, and the use of *ego eimi* ("I am") is a reminder of Moses' historic worship encounter with God in the desert at Horeb (John 6:20; cf. Exod 3:14). The discussion of eating the true bread and the contrast with the bread given by God during the time of Moses confirms that a comparison with the exodus was in mind (John 6:25–34; cf. Exod 16:15).

The murmuring reaction of the Jews (6:41) is also a reminder of the many times that the Israelites grumbled in the wilderness (e.g., Exod 16:2–3). To their credit, in later ritual celebrations of the Passover Haggadah the Jews acknowledge their earlier grumbling.[11] Such patterns of murmuring have been and no doubt are also present in churches today–perhaps even in worship matters?

Tabernacles

The third set of stories, encompassing chapters 7–9, deals with the Festival of Tabernacles, celebrating God's leading by smoke and fire/light in the wilderness. This set of stories is later linked to a Jewish liturgical water ceremony and to messianic expectations. The evangelist brings all these segments together in a phenomenal collage of reflections.

The messianic expectation (somewhat like our celebration of expectation at Advent) was introduced by Jesus' brothers (John 7:3–6) and expanded by the crowd (7:25–31). Then John brought the expectation to a head on the last day of Tabernacles ("the great day," 7:37) and added a brief notation concerning "living water." To the Jews it was a reminder of the hostile Tabernacles' experience in the century before Jesus, which revolved around the frustrated prayers of the Pharisees for water because of their empty cisterns in the cities and villages after a hot summer. A great worship conflict ensued (not unlike some of our worship wars). The face-off between the Pharisees and Sadducees involved the dumping of the sacrificial water by the Sadducean high priest/king, Alexander Jannaeus, at Tabernacles. Then when the Pharisees threw citrons at the high priest, they were slaughtered in the Temple precincts.[12]

In the present story, on the last day of Tabernacles Jesus proclaimed to the people that he was the source of "living water" (7:37–38) and the means for the coming of the Spirit (7:39). This segment of John provides a forceful example of just how contextually relevant were the messages of Jesus. The Tabernacles episode here ends with an argument about whether Jesus could in fact be the Messiah, including whether he was actually born in Bethlehem (7:42; cf. Matt 2:1; Luke 2:4–7). John must have smiled at this point, knowing the answer to such speculation concerning the promise of Advent.

The conflict then intensified in chapter 8. The focus shifts slightly in terms of Tabernacle worship as Jesus declared himself to be (*ego eimi*) the "light of the world," namely, the epitome of the pillar of light that led Israel in the night (John 8:12; cf. Exod 13:21–22). The lighting of lamps was a significant liturgical practice in Israel's history and symbolized the sense of the divine *hesed* ("mercy") in their midst.[13] But the conflict became even more hostile as Jesus insisted that he embodied the ultimate truth and was the way to freedom (John 8:31–32). His opponents asserted that they were free and claimed a reliance on Father Abraham. Jesus responded that he was superior to Abraham (8:58) and that they did not follow the ways of Abraham or God. Indeed, they were children of the lying devil (8:30–44). The result was hardly unexpected. The Jews were prepared to stone Jesus (8:59).

The evangelist then illustrated the point of the conflict through the story of the blind man (ch. 9). Refusing to debate the issue of theodicy (the problem of evil) with his disciples, "the light of the world" healed a blind man with spit and dirt (9:6–7), reminiscent of the way God mysteriously formed Adam from the dust of the earth and brought him to life with breath (cf. Gen 2:7). As might be expected, the healing occurred on the Sabbath (John 9:14). The question then was: Would the authorities accept the healing as an act of divine grace or focus on their ritualistic rules? The answer was predictable. Tragically, their rules made it impossible for them to recognize the agent of God's grace (9:16, 24). Earlier, the religious authorities would have shunned the man from acceptability in worship because of his handicap. Now they listened as he forcefully explained the legitimacy of God's agent based on the healing (9:31–33), but they soon shut their ears to his argument and excommunicated him from the synagogue (9:34). As Jesus sadly noted in closing this discussion, religious rules of worship and life can actually prevent us from recognizing God's awesome presence and work in our midst (9:39–41).

Dedication (Hanukkah)

The fourth section involved the festival of Dedication (Hanukkah), one of the two major post-Mosaic feasts, along with Purim. This feast of the rekindling of the lights, coming just prior to the winter solstice, reminded the Jews of the liberating of Jerusalem by Judas Maccabeus. It raised in their minds all sorts of messianic expectations. In this Gospel, however, the feast provides for a reflection on Ezekiel 34 and Jeremiah 23, with their messages concerning the false leaders of Israel who fleeced the people. These texts also pointed to the promise of the coming of God's special agent. In this first mashal (extended parable) John identified Jesus as the door or means of access to God (John 10:1–9) and the good shepherd who would care for the flock (cf. John 10:11–18 and Ezek 34:11–15, 23–24).

In his account of the incident John, demonstrated that this festival, coming in winter or the stormy (*cheimon*) season, also represented the spiritual quality of Israel (John 10:23) because the die had been cast. Israel would rather kill their shepherd (10:31–33) than listen to his voice (10:25–29).

Passover Again

The fifth and final section of the Festival Cycle returns to Passover with the story of Lazarus. The resuscitation here forms a kind of window or a foreshadowing of the death and resurrection stories of Jesus. It also supplies for the church one of the most-used texts (along with John 14) for funeral services because of its promise that whoever believes in Jesus can expect never to experience lasting death. A hope in a resurrection was in fact an important element of Pharisaic theology. The mourning Martha asserted it very well (11:24). Jesus however, wanted to lead Martha, Mary, and the accompanying mourners to a perspective beyond mere mourning and a distant hope in resurrection. His goal was to direct their understanding to the power mysteriously inherent in the "I am" and actually present with them! Jesus encompassed within himself the power of "resurrection and life" (11:25). Did Martha or the others recognize this power? The answer is a resounding "No!" In spite of her confession–"I believe" (11:27)–she also told Jesus not to open the grave because "He stinks!" (11:39). She is like many Christians today who can confess their faith in church, but their lives actually reveal doubt and lack of belief. Their worship can be quite powerless and unrelated to life!

The Jewish high priest, the supposed symbol of worship leadership, revealed a very different mindset. He was willing to play the manipulative "means-ends" game, using unjust means (killing Jesus) to achieve what he considered was an appropriate goal–the saving of Israel (11:49–50). John recognized the irony in the statement because the death of Jesus was to be the genuine means for saving not only the Jews but the whole world (11:51–52). It was finally the time for Passover, the great festival of hope in the midst of death (11:55)! But the Jews hardly acted like the children of God. They were more like the ancient Pharaoh instead.

The Coming Hour (12:1–50)

Chapter 12 initiates the second half of the book, the beginning of the end.[14] While many Christians refer to the Jerusalem entry with palm branches and shouts of "Hosanna" to the "King of Israel" as the "Triumphal Entry," both Jesus and the Johannine evangelist thought differently. John's understanding of the event led him to place the anointing scene before the entry (12:1–8; contrast that it comes after the entry in the Synoptics; e.g., Mark 11:1–10 and 14:3–9). In this entry various perspectives were present: the people shouted their worship praises (John 12:13); the disciples were confused (12:16); the Pharisees were angry and bemoaned Jesus' popularity (12:19); while the Greeks wanted to get into the action (12:20).

Jesus understood that the event marked his entry into death (12:23–24). It is important for worshipers on Palm Sunday not to miss this point in John. The King was going to die, and his followers were invited to follow him in this journey (12:25). Darkness was coming, but so was a new hope through death (12:35–36, 45). Yet it was going to be traumatic even for Jesus (12:27). Many might consider believing in Jesus, although their understanding would be darkened and they would probably seek human affirmation rather than the acceptance of God (12:42–43). Jesus knew that worship that costs nothing is worth just about that much!

The Farewell Cycle (13:1–17:26)

Having thus introduced Jesus' journey to death, John initiates the third major segment (chs. 13–17)—the Farewell Cycle—with another reference to Passover (13:1) and a symbolic act of washing the disciples' feet (13:4–12). That ritual act was to epitomize the role of Jesus' followers. While the church's two major ordinances or sacraments of baptism and the Lord's Supper are not specifically explicated in John (though they are symbolically represented in John 3 and 6 as well as at the cross in 19:34), this act of foot washing is treated as the primary order or command (ordinance) for believers (13:14). Moreover, the pattern of such servant humility is further highlighted by Jesus' "new commandment": to love one another (13:34). Furthermore, recognition by the world of those who were in fact Jesus' disciples (followers) would come not so much because of their words or even in worship services, but as the result of their lives of love (13:35).

Jesus' Departure

The second pericope in this Farewell Cycle was initiated by Jesus' announcement that he was going away (13:33, 36). What follows is the disciples' expressed sense of lostness and aloneness. In response, Jesus issued words of comfort that are often used by Christians in funeral services concerning Jesus' preparation of "a place" for them to be with the Father (14:1–3).

In their confused state of mind, they wanted to know where he would be and wanted him to give them a "trip-tik" (a map) to that "place." When he told them that "he" (note the ego eimi saying at 14:6) was the route to the Father, they, in their naiveté, wanted him to show them the Father, little realizing that such a request would mean their deaths (cf. Exod 33:20). Then, trying desperately to remove the veil from their minds, Jesus sought to help them understand that in him they were facing nothing less than the mysterious divine reality itself–the subject of their worship! He was in fact to be identified with the Father. If that thought was too much for them, then he suggested that they reflect on his incredible works (John 14:11). Who was capable of such acts? No mere human!

Excursus on the Trinity

These verses have led historically to some very strong arguments concerning the relationship between the persons of the Trinity, particularly in reference to the *filioque* clause in the creeds. Was the Spirit sent from the Father only (Eastern Church; see John 15:26) or from the Father "and the Son" (Western Church; see 16:7)? So committed were proponents to their views that they actually excommunicated opponents for expressing the other view. From my viewpoint, it is important to realize that precision in such matters may not be so important, since in the New Testament itself even the Trinitarian descriptions vary so that in contrast to the familiar order of Matt 28:19, the order in Rev 1:4–5 and 1 Pet 1:2 is Father, Spirit, and the Son, which I believe to be the order the divine persona were experienced.

The Role of the Holy Spirit

Tucked into chapters 14–16 are five strategic *parakletos* (counselor, comforter) sayings that define the role of the Holy Spirit for Christians.[15] These verses are crucial for a sense of both the role of the Spirit in our relationship to the triune God and for an understanding of the functions of the Spirit in the lives of believers.

In the first saying the "Paraklete" was to be a substitute "*in* them" for Jesus who had been "*with* them." The Spirit would not leave them alone or orphaned (14:16–18). Next, the Spirit would become their new teacher and would bring them a sense of "peace" (14:26–27). Then the Counselor would keep them from becoming scandalized and losing their faith in God during times of difficulty and persecution (15:25–16:4). The Adviser would also use the believers to convict their opponents concerning their sinfulness, the righteous standards of God, and the judgment that awaited them (16:7–11). Finally, the Supporter would become their companion guide in their pilgrimage to true life and would in turn bring glory to Jesus (16:12–5). The pertinence of these verses for spiritual formation and for worship in spirit and truth (cf. 4:23) should be obvious.

Parable of the Vine

In moving to the beginning of chapter 15 and the heart[16] of the Farewell Cycle, one is confronted with the second of the Johannine mashals or extended parables (the first being the mashal of the good shepherd and the door in ch. 10). Here Jesus is likened to a vine, and believers are represented as branches that need to be sustained by the relationship to the vine. The worship point is very clear: we must get our relationship straight. Believers are not the vine. Unless the branches abide or remain in the vine, they will have no life or energy. They will become useless and will be fit for removal and destruction (15:4–6).

When they do maintain the proper relationship with the vine (Jesus), several results will follow: they will produce fruit (15:5); their petitions will be heard (15:7); they will glorify God (15:8); they will obey Jesus and continue in his captivating love (15:9–10); and they will experience an abundance of joy in their lives (15:11). The picture is a wonderful representation of a believer properly aligned in worship and life with God through Christ. Such a believer is called a "friend" of Jesus (15:14), a designation given earlier to God's "friend" Abraham (e.g., 2 Chr 20:7; Isa 41:8).

Abandonment

The text that encircles both the core pericope of the vine mashal and the Paraclete passages concerns abandonment. Whereas in 14:1–11 John dealt with the disciples' feeling of being left alone or abandoned, in 16:16-33 Jesus reminds them that even though he would not leave them alone but would come to them, they would abandon him! Yet the Father would never abandon him in his trauma (16:32). This discussion in chapters 14 and 16, which deals with the genuine nature of loss and aloneness that comes to all humans and must be treated realistically in our worship, prepares the reader for the magisterial prayer of Jesus in chapter 17. It also provides a helpful Johannine response to the often difficult and debated abandonment text that appears only in Mark 15:34 (cf. Ps 21:1) and has lead to some horrible theological constructions by separating God from the sacrifice of Jesus on the cross.

Jesus' Prayer

Jesus' prayer in chapter 17 is a model for all worshipers. It contains a series of phenomenal petitions. Jesus begins by setting the correct focus for prayer—bringing glory to the Son so that he can bring glory to the Father. Such glory is not new. It is the glory that Jesus always had from the beginning of time. Jesus the Son has glorified the Father by finishing the work assigned him—dying as a sacrifice to bring believers eternal life (17:1–5).

Then Jesus prayed for his disciples. He asked that they might be kept safe and preserved from loss in a hostile world and that they might experience a deep and abiding joy in the midst of life's traumas (17:11–13). In praying for their safety, Jesus did not request their removal from the world because that would mean that their witness in the world would be lost. Instead, he prayed for their protection from the onslaughts of the evil one (14:14–15). Then he prayed that they might become holy and true just as he had been a model for them in his life of holiness (17:17–19).

His next petition has become one of the great unmet hopes of the church–Jesus' prayer for his people's oneness. That prayer is not focused on unity for its own sake. As I often reflected when I was the chair of the Commission on Doctrine and Interchurch Cooperation for the Baptist World Alliance, that petition was focused on mission to the world–namely, that the divided and hostile world might come to believe in Jesus when they saw the unity of the believers (17:20–21). For some unholy reason Christians would rather fight with each other than pray with each other. As a result, much of the world continues to slough off the Christian witness as merely nice words with no meaning.

Jesus concluded his prayer with petitions that believers might ultimately realize their great hope to be with him in his glory (17:24), and that, in the meantime, they might live in the spirit of love with each other (17:26).

When one studies this prayer, one is impressed with one overarching theme. The prayer of Jesus is not like many of our prayers that often focus on ourselves, our families and friends, and our petitions of "give me." Instead, Jesus concentrated *not* on praying for himself and his welfare but on praying for the believers and their integrity as Christian disciples. We certainly do have Christians who exemplify such qualities. Would for God's sake that many more of us could learn how to pray like Jesus prayed. Maybe Christians would then become greater examples of love and hope in this fractured world.

The Death Story of Jesus (18:1–19:42)

Having concluded the Farewell Cycle, John presented his moving version of the Death Story of Jesus.[17] He opened the story with the betrayal and arrest of Jesus presented in a quite different manner than in the other Gospels. We see no kiss of Judas, but rather a picture of Jesus in full control of the situation. Jesus identified himself with the now classic words of the divine, *ego eimi*. When he repeated them, his captors fell on the ground, obviously because no one can stand before the mysterious presence of revealed deity (18:5–6). Yet having submitted to his captors, Jesus still instructed them to let his disciples go because his goal was to protect them (18:8–9; cf. 17:12). Peter, however, attempted to intervene in the situation with force (18:10–11), little realizing his puny sword had little effect in the divine drama. Peter's time of testing would come as Jesus had predicted (cf. 13:38). When it did, Peter proved to be a threefold failure at the charcoal fire (18:15–17, 25–26) before the cock awakened him to the reality of what he had done (18:27).

The subplots of the manipulative high priests and of the frustrated Pilate only heighten the drama as the steady drumbeat of the death story moves to its conclusion when the Lamb of God was crucified on the same day that the

Passover lambs were slaughtered (19:14, 31). The spineless Pilate is not given the benefit of washing his hands in John. He is just as guilty as Judas and the Jewish leaders for his part in "delivering" (*paradidomi*, 18:2, 30, 35; 19:16) Jesus to be crucified. None of them are excused! Yet when the Jewish leaders tried to change the charge on the cross from "the King of the Jews," it appears that Pilate finally found a backbone and refused to accede to their manipulative wishes (19:22).

For those who often wonder about whether God cares for them when they hurt, they might ask the question about where was God when Jesus was going through this traumatic experience. The answer John would undoubtedly give is that God was right there with God's Son (for example, cf. 5:20; 11:41–42; 16:32). Maybe the fact that Pilate refused the last request of the high priests to reduce the confessional nature of the words on the cross is a hint in that direction. Throughout the Gospel and particularly at the cross, Jesus is described as fulfilling Scripture. Such fulfillment is a testimony of God's supervening will in the ministry of Jesus (for example, cf. 19:24, 28, 36).

Jesus died the spotless Lamb of God before the *crucifragium* (the breaking of the legs) could be administered, and, like a slaughtered lamb at Passover, he was pierced (19:32–34). Readers who wonder at the strange outflow of "blood and water" from Jesus (19:34) should not seek for a mere physical explanation of that phenomenon in this highly symbolic, worship-oriented book. We should recognize that at the cross John was also pointing to the fact that Christ's overflowing care for Christians in both the water (baptism) and blood (the Supper) was being proclaimed. The liturgical significance here should not be missed. For that reason John added the special note of the Johannine witness to this event for succeeding Christians, just as he did later in the resurrection stories (19:35; cf. 20:29; 21:22–23).

For John, symbolism is a very powerful conveyor of meaning, and for him the cross was the strategic "hour" (*hora*) when, in history, God brought God's purposes to fulfillment in Jesus (see 2:4; 4:21, 23; 5:25; 7:30; 8:20; 12:23, 27; 13:1; 16:32; 17:1). Likewise, for John symbolism in worship is a significant way that a rational human can express the depth of the experience of responding to the mystery of the divine reality.

So even at the end, Jesus, the Son of God, was in charge and determined the time he "delivered" his spirit and actually died (19:30, 33). For John, the King was dead. Really dead! No matter what any later folk traditions might say or theological constructs might suggest, Jesus really died. He was symbolically buried with a hundred pounds of spices, enough for any king (19:39)! This would end the average story of a hero. Any focus on worship would then be a mere sham. But not this story!

The Resurrection (20:1–21:25)

This story had an unexpected ending for all the followers of Jesus. Mary Magdalene reported to the disciples that the tomb was empty and that the women did not know the reason why (20:1–2). Peter and the Beloved Disciple hastily ran to the tomb to check out the report. John makes a point of telling the reader that the latter outran the former and "believed" when he saw the tomb (20:8). Mary, however, is the first to encounter the risen Jesus, and initially thought—mistakenly—that the story of Jesus would then just continue as it had before (20:11–17). But everything was now different! Jesus, the Lord, had to make that point clear to her and the disciples.

It was the first day of the week (our Sunday), and the frightened community had gathered to consider the events. John emphasized this fact by the next meeting of the community one week later when they again gathered (20:19, 26–the eight days in our Western reckoning was the next Sunday'). In their first "worship meeting" with the risen Jesus, John summarized the relationship that would eventuate for the church with their Lord. In that summation, the risen Lord: (1) blessed them with his peace, (2) commissioned (sent) them into a ministry of forgiveness, and (3) bestowed on them the Holy Spirit, their other Paraklete (20:19–23; cf. the earlier Paraklete texts in 14:15 ff.). One of their members, Thomas, however, had missed this first gathered experience with their Lord and needed to be reconfirmed into the ministry for Jesus. Thomas doubted the legitimacy of the others' encounter and firmly set his parameters for believing and worship (20:24–25). On the next worship day he joined the believers in their gathering. Jesus again honored them with his presence and "peace." Moreover, he took seriously Thomas' conditions for proof of the resurrection (20:27). As a result of that encounter, Thomas, the former doubter, issued the most significant confession concerning Jesus found anywhere in the New Testament: "My Lord and my God!"

As the Lord instructed in the story, that confession would become the basis for all legitimate Christian confessions concerning Jesus and of "blessing" in worship for the entire church (20:28–29). The beginning and the end of this Gospel are thus coordinated. The Word which is God in the beginning (1:1) and which became incarnate ("human," 1:14) in Jesus is here confessed as Lord and God!

With the above confession the evangelist originally drew the Gospel to a magnificent conclusion (20:30–31). But something had not been said which needed to be treated. That concern involved Peter and the Beloved Disciple. So the evangelist added an unforgettable postscript. The context was another resurrection encounter, this time apparently mirroring an earlier calling of the disciples from their fishing business (cf. Luke 5:1–10).

This time Peter needed to be reinstated, but the other disciple first recognized Jesus (John 21: 7; cf. 20:8 for another contrast between the two). When they came to land, a strange site met them; a *charcoal fire cooking fish accompanied by bread* (21:9). The symbolism is unmistakable. Fish is the symbol of the Christian mission/task and bread the symbol of Christ's continuing presence. But there is here much more. Only in two places in the entire New Testament does a "charcoal fire" (*anthrakian*) appear (cf. 18:18). It is as though a very pertinent message was intended in the story: namely, that to be restored by Jesus, one must deal with one's past performance. Peter had to return to a charcoal fire! To confirm this view, Jesus asked Peter three times (note the specific reference in 21:17) if the disciple "loved" him, mirroring his three denials of chapter 18.[18] Forgiveness and restoration to service is possible, but not without facing the awesome God with the reality of one's sin!

After the restoration one, final question remained concerning the other disciple. That question is also very pertinent to worship and life for all Christians: What about comparisons with others in one's life, service, and death? The answer for Peter and for every Christian is a resounding: That concern is none of your business (21:23)! The calling is to follow Christ no matter what the cost! So concludes the "spiritual gospel" with a colophon testifying that this witness concerning Jesus is absolutely authentic (21:24). May we as later readers and worshipers be faithful to the purposes for that witness!

WORSHIP SUMMARY

From beginning to end this Gospel is laced with important worship implications. The divine Word of God became incarnate in Jesus (1:14), and was proclaimed to be God's unique Lamb, the Savior able to take away the sin, not merely of the Jews, but of the whole world (1:29–36; 4:42; 19:14, 31). For John, Jesus replaced, in his own being, the sanctuary of the Jewish Temple (2:19) and the Jewish worship festivals (chs. 5–11); offered a superb model of prayer (ch. 17); defined new life in terms of being born of water and the Spirit (3:5); and explained the worship relationship with God in terms of the Spirit and truth (4:24). In his death, the King of Israel powerfully symbolized both baptism and the Lord's Supper (19:34–35). In his resurrection he bestowed on his followers the gift of the Spirit (20:22), the promised Paraklete (chs. 14–16). To believe in Jesus, the loving gift of God, will lead to eternal life and escape from judgment (3:16–18). To confess and worship him as Lord and God (20:28) and to serve him by caring for his sheep (21:15–18) is a strategic goal for this Gospel. Nothing less than the integration of words and actions, of worship and life (cf. also 1 John) is a sufficient response for the Johannine evangelist.

QUESTIONS

1. What does it mean in your worship understanding to follow the ordinance (command) of Jesus to wash one another's feet? What would go through your mind, if you were in the same situation as the disciples?

PART II

Devoted to the Forming of New Christian Worshiping Communities

Reflections on the Book of Acts

Studying the Book of Acts is for most Christians a refreshing pursuit of reflecting on how God can touch mere humans as they experience through the presence of the Holy Spirit the continuing work of the risen Jesus. In perusing this captivating document, the reader encounters not merely power and acceptance but also hostility and rejection. The stories in Acts, like the stories in the Gospels, provide contemporary Christian communities of faith with vivid guidelines for dynamic patterns of life and worship. To ponder these stories can be immensely rewarding.

5

Acts[1]

This magnificent book provides a stirring selection of vignettes about how Jesus mysteriously continued to touch the lives of the early Christians so that they were able to respond confidently in the face of charges, threats, violence, and even death itself without turning away from the true worship of God.

Introducing Acts

The Book of Acts is a unique work in the Christian canon. It not only provides a singular set of insights into the exciting beginnings of early Christianity and its expansion from Jerusalem into the larger Hellenistic world, but it is also a fascinating resource for the study of early Christian life and worship. To reflect on the stories of this book is to be gripped anew by a sense of power that was present in the early communities of faith and to be reminded that such dynamism *could still* also be experienced in contemporary churches, even if they have, at the moment, sunk into the lethargy of mediocre familiarity in the worship of God.

The title "The Acts of the Apostles" that was later attached to the book is a little misleading. Acts is not a complete record of the early church's activities; nor does it contain accounts concerning the ministries of all of the early disciples. Luke selected what he wanted to emphasize for readers. Indeed, the Greek word for "Acts" (*praxeis*) is used only once in the book (Acts 19:18) and at that place means "magical practices." That meaning would probably seem very foreign to Luke as a title for his book. Moreover, Acts is not, as some have suggested, a book primarily about the acts of the Holy Spirit. The last third of the book hardly mentions the Spirit at all. Luke's second book could possibly be described as the continuing "work" (*ergon*) of Jesus[2] through his disciples, but Jesus should not be viewed as unable to work without the disciples. Furthermore, Acts should not be viewed as being about how the gospel reached Rome, because believers were in Rome before Paul reached the capital city (cf. 28:15). What can be said is that Acts presents the reader with a marvelous selection of stories, speeches, memories, and insights from early Christianity that challenge believers even in our era with our possibilities in Jesus for dynamic life and worship.

As indicated in the earlier discussion on the Gospel of Luke and the caring Jesus, Acts is the second part of a dual work by Luke. It is imperative, therefore, to remember the interrelationship of these two books in this study. We will not attempt to repeat what was said concerning a number of introductory matters related to Luke-Acts except to remind the reader that Sir William Ramsay at the beginning of the twentieth century argued quite convincingly that wherever he was able to check concerning the travel information in Acts, Luke was not only a fine historian but also a reliable geographer. Some of the stories in Acts were purposely included to mirror stories from the life of Jesus in Luke's Gospel. The book is loaded with theological implications for life and worship.

Luke is a superb writer and organizer of his materials. Luke's plot development in Acts is nothing short of remarkable! Each section of Acts ends with a skillfully designed summation so that the reader should have no difficulty in following the development of his work. Moreover, each major section contains at least one sermon or speech that provide(s) insight into the meaning of the story(ies) in that segment. I will attempt here to concentrate briefly on matters pertaining to church life and worship.

Luke's Introduction (1:1–11)

Acts opens, as does Luke's Gospel, by addressing Theophilus (Acts 1:1; Luke 1:3) and picks up where the earlier treatise ended: with the concluding appearance of Jesus prior to his ascension and with the promise of the coming power through the Spirit (Acts 1:2–11; Luke 24:50–52). When Jesus spoke to the disciples about the kingdom of God (Acts 1:3), they interpreted Jesus to be speaking of the kingdom being restored to Israel (1:6), a common problem in misunderstanding even today among Christians who often think that their church institutions and their worship patterns are equivalent to God's reign.

Jesus' commission (1:8) outlines the expanding work of the church. But it is not merely to be pictured as a series of expanding concentric circles as some of my students have often thought. The text does not say Jerusalem, Judea, and the world. Samaria is inserted in the program, implying that Christians must be willing to glance sideways and not forget the rejects of society. Indeed, one of my doctoral students wrote a magnificent musical honoring the worship of God concerning Trinidad, the West Indies, and the world. But he missed this important side road that we must be willing to take as Christ followers to fulfill our destinies as Christians. I had to help him understand his important omission. This introduction then concludes with a directed question concerning the disciples' hesitation (1:10) and identifies their failure to recognize that the new era was beginning without the physical presence of Jesus.

Establishing the Early Church (1:12–2:47)

The next section, the first major one, involves the formation or establishment of the early church (1:12–2:47). Of course, business matters had to be handled. Since one of the disciples had been a traitor, he needed to be replaced at the first meeting of the new Christian community. Such a "successional" or replacement pattern for one of the twelve was not to be a continuing policy when one of them died, because, when James was killed, he was not replaced or "succeeded" (12:2). Sometimes Christians erroneously think that church order is unrelated to church life and worship.

The insertion, or side comment, made concerning the 120 persons at the meeting is also important at this point (1:15). Readers often overlook this aside, but for Luke it seemingly represents the fact that an independent Jewish community had been established with its own *Sanhedrin* (council) able to make its own decisions and appointments.[3] The selection of Matthias as a replacement for Judas at this council meeting was handled as one might expect in the pre-Pentecost period–by lot according to Jewish patterns of selection (1:26). Thereafter, however, it appears that such selections by the community were made more directly through the Spirit rather than by lot (6:3; 13:2; etc). Thus, our own patterns of selection by vote–either secret or otherwise–are neither a part of traditional Jewish worship or community procedures, but are rather a reflection of the influence of Greek principles of selection.

In this section the early church was officially birthed in a miraculous manner at Pentecost. The disciples were "filled with" the Spirit (2:1–4). Luke no doubt intended this incident to reflect the miraculous birth stories in his Gospel. Note another comparison with the Gospel: Zechariah was "filled with" the Holy Spirit before he delivered his beautiful hymnic blessing to God (cf. the Benedictus in Luke 1:67–79). Prior to that event the promise was made to Zechariah that his son John would be "filled with" the Holy Spirit in the womb (1:15).[4] The tongues event was also a marvelous "means of identifying God's power in communicating so that everyone heard in his or her own tongue or language (2:6). Luke obviously intended this event to represent a divine reversal of the confusing breakdown of communications at Babel in the beginning of the Bible (Gen 11:7–9) when people sought, not to worship God, but to prove that God was insignificant and not worthy of worship. In both instances God's mysterious power proved to be overwhelming for human reason.

Peter's long four-point sermon in this context then elucidates these events as a fulfillment of God's intentions predicted in Joel 2:28–32. The sermon is well organized and (1) relies on the Old Testament, (2) instructs concerning the historical Jesus, (3) proclaims the resurrection, and (4) challenges hearers in the name of Jesus Christ to a worship response by repenting, being baptized, and by receiving the Spirit (Acts 2:14–39). The result was the formation of a huge new community that received the message and turned to God (2:41). But it must be remembered that such revivals are the work of God and not merely the result of human effort.

Luke closes this section with two very significant summary conclusions (2:42 and 2:43–47). The first is a fourfold identification of characteristics in an authentic worshiping community: namely, one that is (1) oriented to correct teaching and preaching; (2) evidences *koinonia* or fellowship; (3) experiences the presence of the Lord in the common meal; and (4) is marked by prayer (2:42). Unfortunately, churches too often choose to emphasize one aspect of a worship response to God over the others and thereby lose the divinely intended synthesis for church life and worship. If you would reflect a little, you can probably determine what kind of a church you attend.

The second summary statement illustrates another of the early church's attempted efforts at building community–by holding things in common or sharing their possessions, much like some earlier Jewish Essenes may have done.[5] Ultimately, most in the church failed to adopt holding possessions in common as an ongoing practice. Such failure is understandable because of many factors, not the least of which were lying and cheating (e.g., Ananias and Sapphira, 5:1–11) as well as inconvenience and failure of fair distribution (e.g., 6:1). At least the early church tried to evidence a genuine sense of unity in the worshiping community under the Lordship of Christ and the Spirit (cf. 4:32–37). Nevertheless, the question for us is: How do we treat our brothers and sisters in Christ, especially the poor?

Challenges Facing the Jewish Church (3:1–5:42)

The second major section of Acts (3:1–5:42) involves the challenges facing the early Hebraic church. The Jewish authorities reacted to the early Christians much as they had to Jesus, especially since the Christians copied the pattern of Jesus in doing miracles. In fact, they did them in the name of Jesus (e.g., 3:6). They also preached in his name (3:16; 4:12), proclaimed his resurrection (4:2), and, when threatened, even refused to cease using his name (4:17–22). Instead, they prayed for boldness to follow their Lord's example (4:29–31). Indeed, when they were thrown into prison and were mysteriously released by an angel, they responded to the heavenly command and returned to preach about Jesus in the Temple, the Jewish worship center (5:19). On the other hand, when human authorities commanded them to cease and desist their activities in the name of Jesus, the believers sternly refused and issued a countercharge against the authorities for hanging Jesus on the cross. They also proclaimed that God was to be praised by clearly reversing those evil actions in the resurrection and by exalting Jesus as the divine Savior able to forgive sins. God had made them witnesses of the resurrection and given them the power of the Holy Spirit in their lives (5:29–32).

Gamaliel's speech highlights this major section. In his address to the Supreme Council or Great Sanhedrin, Gamaliel, one of the foremost rabbis in Jewish history, warned the authorities to be careful because their activities could be opposing the God they sought to worship (5:39). The Jewish high council's refusal to take his advice offers a commentary on their view of God and their emptiness as leaders of worship. In the conclusion to this section, Luke emphasized that although the disciples were beaten and warned again not to mention the name of Jesus, they rejoiced that they had joined their Lord in suffering. In addition, they continued to preach about Jesus not only in their homes but even in the Temple precincts (5:40–42)! Such strength of Christian conviction is an inspiring example of believers who have truly met Christ, know how to worship, and have received the power of the Spirit in their lives.

The Growth of the Greek-speaking Church (6:1–9:31)

Helping the Greek-speaking Widows

The third major section of Acts (6:1–9:31) concerns the development of the early Greek-speaking Church. A concern over assistance to the Greek-speaking widows reflects such growth. The early solution to the problem provides a model of a life response even for churches today. Rather than the twelve trying to micro-manage the church by tackling the problem themselves and deviating from their special assignments of witnessing, the church appointed seven persons to care for the financial concerns of the widows (to wait "tables," *trapeza*, the Greek term is used for banking even today).

Instead of selecting members from a "good old boys network," the church appointed representatives who themselves had Greek names. The result was not only confidence on the part of those who were concerned, but all others also had confidence because those selected were known to be responsible members of the worshiping community and were "filled with" the Spirit (6:3). The response was rooted in a genuine relationship with God and with the rest of the community. What a contrast to many contemporary church committees and to their selection processes. Could it be a reflection on the basic composition of our churches?

Stephen's Example

What becomes more intriguing is that those selected for the financial administrative duties actually proved through their Christian integrity to be models of integrity in both worship and witnessing. Stephen, according to Luke, actually became a mirror image of Jesus and, like Jesus, he was charged in his witnessing with breaking the "law" (the Jews' inspired book) and opposing the "Temple" (their institutional structure; see 6:13–14). By condemning Stephen, the Jewish authorities once again set institutionalism (book and structure) over against God and authentic worship response. In his magnificent defensive speech Stephen, traced Israel's history, including her failure to understand God's intentions for God's people and true worship. He reminded them that in their past their forefathers had turned to a golden calf in the wilderness and had persecuted God's prophets (7: 2–3, 7–8, 16, 19–20, 25, 30–34, 35–42, 44–48). Then he charged that they were no different than in that day.

His condemnation of the authorities ensured that he would follow Jesus to death. Just like Jesus, Stephen modeled a true dependence on the God he worshiped as he prayed for his killers' forgiveness (7:60; cf. Luke 23:34). Luke adds two brief notes of Stephen's affirmation by God (Acts 6:15; 7:56), which are much like Jesus' acceptance by God (cf. Luke 9:35; 22:43). The summary statement at the end of the Stephen story concerning Saul (otherwise called Paul) and the persecution that followed (Acts 8:1–3) serves Luke as a literary window to introduce the coming of a transformed Paul.

Philip's Example

Luke chose next to introduce a second administrator, Philip. His integrity and openness to others is highlighted (8:4–40) in the expansion of early Christianity beyond the boarders of the Hebrew-speaking Jews in Judea. The first of the three new stages in his mission is to the rejects of Samaria (8:4–5). Philip preached and cast out evil spirits (8:5, 7) much like Jesus and the early disciples did in the Gospel (cf. Luke 4:36; 9:1–2).

During this mission Simon, the magician (linked by the church fathers to Simon Magus, a wily heretic), who had gained many followers through the exercise of the magical arts, became enticed by the movement and was himself baptized. Later when Peter and John arrived from Jerusalem and prayed for the believers to be empowered by the Spirit of God, Simon sought to buy the miraculous gift. He was summarily condemned for his wicked and manipulative spirit and forthrightly confronted with the need to respond in repentance (8:22–24). Seeking to profit or gain manipulative power by using God and the resources of the church is clearly not merely a modern phenomenon in Christianity. It has been around for ages. God, however, is to be worshiped, and the church is not to be used for personal benefit or for personal ambition.

The second story of Philip involves the Ethiopian eunuch (8:26–39). This fascinating pericope is a reminder that according to the law in Deuteronomy 23:1 a eunuch was forbidden ever to enter "the [worship] assembly of the Lord." The eunuch was regarded as an outcast from God. Isaiah 56:3–5 promised, however, that the day was coming when the eunuch would be restored, his worship on the Sabbath would be accepted, and he would be given an "everlasting name" or an inheritance. Philip explained to the African reject that what he was reading from Isaiah 53 concerned the coming of the Messiah. Indeed, the coming had already taken place in Jesus. The eunuch accepted the testimony, responded with the liturgical act of being baptized, and in joy was added fully to the genuine people of God (Acts 8:35–39).

Many Christians tend to miss the point of the brief third story of Philip at Azotus (8:40). Azotus is the new name for the ancient city of Ashdod. Philip had entered traditionally Philistine territory (indeed, the area near Gaza that has contained the traditional enemy of Israel)! Moreover, the good news was being carried along the coast and even as far north as Caesarea, where the Roman legions were stationed. The expansion to Caesarea and the Gentiles will be treated shortly in Acts 10 and 11.

Saul of Tarsus

Luke was stressing that the true worship of God in Christ Jesus has no borders and should not be restricted nationally, culturally, politically, economically, or sexually (cf. Gal 3:28). Someone stood in the way of the gospel's advance–the fire-breathing Saul of Tarsus. He was devastating the church ("the Way"). While doing so, he thought he was being a faithful worshiper of God. Accordingly, God had to do something, and Jesus acted! The blinding encounter of Saul with Jesus reminds readers that the Book of Acts is about the continuing "work" of Jesus. As Moses asked God, "What is your name?" so Saul asked and was shocked to learn that he was mysteriously confronting Jesus. He was actually persecuting Jesus and not merely the believers (Acts 9:5–8). To complete the transformation process, Jesus turned the tables on Saul and intriguingly used one of the persons Saul had intended to persecute to heal the then praying Saul. One should never think of Saul as an unfaithful person, but clearly as a misguided devotee of Jewish religion. Similarly, many (Christians and non-Christians) today mistreat and persecute others in the name of God. The story is indeed a touching one as the fearful Ananias trusted his heavenly vision, responded obediently by going to the persecutor who was by then praying, and addressed him as "Brother Saul" (9:10–17). The zealous persecutor became a transformed worshiper, was baptized, and began to proclaim Jesus (9:20). Soon the zealous champion of Jewish power himself became one of the persecuted believers. Like a helpless victim, he had to escape by being lowered over the wall in a basket, an incident he never forgot (9:23–25; cf. 2 Cor 10:33).

When Saul returned to Jerusalem, the church did not receive him like a hero since the Christians were afraid of him. Barnabas did accept him and ran interference for him among the believers. During this time Saul responded by preaching about Jesus and, in fact, raised the hostility level among the Jews (9:26–29). So the believers sent him home to Tarsus to relieve the tensions. Luke then sums up the result of this miraculous transformation with a brief encompassing analysis to the effect that the churches of Roman "*Palestina*" experienced a time of peace and comfort in the Spirit (Acts 9:31). The gospel was able for a time to advance "unhindered" (cf. 28:31) as it moved into uncharted waters.

Peter and Gentile Christianity (9:32–12:25)

The fourth major section of Acts concerns the ministry of Peter and the previously unexplored path of legitimate Gentile Christianity (9:32–12:25). The section opens with a familiar Lucan literary pattern of employing a pair of stories involving a man (Aeneas) and a woman (Tabitha, or Dorcas) who are recipients of Jesus' awesome healing power through Peter (Acts 9:32–41; cf. the pairs of Zechariah/Mary and Simeon/Anna in Luke 1 and 2). With such a beginning in identifying the significance of Peter for early Christianity, the stage was set for one of Luke's great transitional worship stories. This one involved

Peter and Cornelius (Acts 10:1–11:18)–a meeting between an Eastern Jewish Christian and a Western Gentile-Roman.

Peter and Cornelius

The Roman centurion in Caesarea *Maratima* (by the sea) is described as a faithful follower of God in terms of holistic worship (active prayer life and financial support of the poor, 10:2). Unexpectedly, Cornelius received a divine visitation indicating that God would fulfill his prayers for divine guidance; but, first, Cornelius had to contact Peter in Joppa (modern Tel Aviv/Jaffa, 10:5, 8). In the meantime Peter was resting from his ministry when he also received a mysterious visitation–a sheet coming down from heaven filled with a zoo of animals. Peter received a command to kill and eat. Faithful to the worship and dietary rules of Kosher, Peter refused but was immediately censured for contradicting God's direct command. After this vision was repeated "three" times (a clear message from God), Peter awoke and tried to determine the meaning of the strange numinous experience.

Suddenly, the Spirit announced to Peter that "three" Gentiles were at the door seeking an audience (10:9–19). Obviously, Peter perceived the significance of the human visitors, because contrary to Jewish customs, which forbade sharing meals with Gentiles (cf. 10:28), he invited them in as his guests and then went with them to Caesarea (10:21–24). When Peter arrived in the provincial capitol, Cornelius fell down in worship before Peter. Peter quickly informed the Gentile not to confuse him, as a human messenger, with God (10:25–26; cf. a similar instruction by an angel in Rev 19:10; 22:8–9). Then as a window into the immanent change, Peter rejected the senselessness of "the seven last words of a dying church: 'It's never been done like that before!'" as he moved into the new era (10:28–29). In listening to Cornelius' report, Peter recognized that the wall of separation between Jew and Gentile was breaking down (cf. Eph 2:14–16). He responded with his enunciation of the gospel concerning Jesus (Acts 10:34–43).

In Peter's sermon, scholars have found a major key to identify one aspect of early Christian worship: namely, the elements in the early church's preaching or *kerygma*. They are: (1) Jesus was specially appointed by God to bring the good news (10:38); (2) he fulfilled the prophetic expectations of the Old Testament (10:43); (3) in both his words and deeds Jesus represented the new era of God's blessings and opposed evil and the devil (10:38); (4) he was rejected by the Jews and was put to death on the cross (10:39); (5) but God raised him from the dead and made the victory evident (10:40); (6) his followers are commanded to bear witness to these facts and call people to repentance (10:39, 41–42); and (7) everyone who responds and believes will receive the forgiveness of their sins and begin a new life with Jesus Christ as their Lord (10:43).

To the shock of Peter and the Jews who were present, the Holy Spirit came to the Gentiles (10:44–46) just as the divine power had been evidenced among the Jews at Pentecost (2:3–12) and among the Samaritans later (8:17). God was doing something new in expanding the community of his people, and he made these new beginnings evident through the presence of the Spirit in their worship. Could Peter then refuse to admit the Gentiles into the community of believers or refuse them the entrance rite of baptism? The answer seemed obvious. He baptized them in the name of Jesus Christ (10:47–48).

Peter and the Jerusalem Church

The church in Jerusalem heard about the strange happenings in Caesarea and summoned Peter to headquarters (11:1–3). They forced Peter to answer the question: Why did he not maintain the Jewish-Christian tradition, but instead did something new by accepting the Gentiles without them becoming Jews first? When Peter recapped for them the various aspects of his mysterious numinous vision and the incidents that followed, they remembered John the Baptist's prediction that the one coming would baptize with the Holy Spirit (cf. Luke 3:16). The church then overrode the complaints of the circumcision party and praised God that a new era in worship and the life of the church had dawned. (Can God do new things in the church today? Can we recognize such actions?)

Then Luke provides another window with the reminder that persecution was still present, but that preaching was continuing. He prepared the reader for the next major stage by having Barnabas retrieve Saul from his home in Tarsus. Together they did follow-up work in Antioch, where the believers became nicknamed for the first time as "Christians" (10:19–26).

Peter and Herod Agrippa I

Back in Jerusalem, persecution became intense. Luke illustrates the situation with another of his fascinating stories. Herod Agrippa I –a favorite of the Jewish establishment because, although a Herodian, he was at least of Maccabean descent–moved to quash Christianity by starting to round up the disciples. He had James (son of Zebedee) killed. Praised by the Jews for that act, he imprisoned Peter just before Passover time and had him closely guarded (12:1–3). The memory of the earlier murderous Passover of Jesus must have raised a terrifying specter for the early church which, responded with fervent prayer–sometimes the only avenue that is open to Christian worshipers (12:5). But prayer must never be viewed as a powerless act of worship.

What follows is a lesson in worship. God answered the prayers of the Christians by amazingly sending an angel to release Peter in middle of the night. After Peter realized what had happened to him, he headed straight for the house of Mary, the mother of Mark, where the Christians were praying for him. On coming to the door, he knocked. One can imagine the fear in that house. Was the knock from Herod's secret police? When the maid, Rhoda (Rose), came to the door, she could hardly believe it was Peter outside. Without opening the door, she rushed to tell the others. Those who were praying told her that she was out of her mind or that she had just seen an apparition (12:15; cf. Luke

24:11). When she insisted, they finally opened the door. To the astonishment of all the Christians, Peter was actually there (12:6–16). The story needs little comment except to remember that God gave the Christians exactly what they had requested in prayer. Yet they were hardly ready to believe that their prayers were actually answered. One must not forget in this context that God had released Peter and John from prison once before (5:19). God is not powerless, even though Christians often fail to believe their own prayers.

The section ends with the wheels of God's justice turning to deal with the Herodian murderer who, like the Roman emperors, assumed a divine posture and failed to honor and worship God (12:21–23). The crowd acclaimed Herod Agrippa I as a god. As a result, the true God's angel struck him dead. The section concludes with a very brief summarizing announcement of the increasing power of God's word and a signal that a new section was about to start (12:24–25).

Barnabas and Paul Travel to the Gentiles (13:1–25:35)

The fifth major section of Acts (13:1–15:35) begins to work out the wider implications of the Caesarea story with the mission to the Gentile world by Barnabas and Saul (whose Greek name was Paul). While this section is often called the first missionary journey, it would be a mistake to understand the missionary travels like a preplanned vacation journey in which one was following a "trip-tik" with reservations along the way prepared by a travel agent. Sometimes the missionaries were thrust on their way and barely escaped from hostile places with their lives. Moreover, Luke did not even view the mission as initiated by the church or the missionaries. Instead, it began during a period of worshiping the Lord including fasting (a practice not observed by many Christians today). God, through the Holy Spirit, led them to appoint Barnabas and Saul as missionaries. The church in response prayed and laid hands on them as a sign of their commissioning (13:1–3), a worship pattern that many succeeding churches have adopted.

In Cyprus and Antioch

The missionaries began their work (*ergon*) in Cyprus, the home province of Barnabas. In Paphos, the capital, the gospel was shared for the first time with a Roman senior senator (the proconsul, Sergius Paulus). Then, just as Moses had confronted the magicians of Pharaoh, Paul judged the fraudulent trickery of the proconsul's magician, Elymas, and punished him with blindness (13:4–12). While John (whose Hellenistic name was Mark) had started with the missionaries as their assistant (*hypereten*, 13:5), he abandoned the mission almost immediately (13:13).

They next traveled to Perga and then to Antioch in Pisidia. There, as Stephen did in his earlier speech/sermon, Paul recited Israel's repeated failures (13:16–22) leading up to the gospel of Jesus (13:23–38). Paul focused on the fact that "everyone who believes" can be freed from his or her sins. In addition, he warned the Jews not to become scoffers as the prophets had predicted

(13:39–41). When the Jews became jealous over the crowds attracted by the missionary preaching concerning freedom, Paul and Barnabas turned away from the Jews to concentrate their mission on the Gentiles (13:46–47).

Then Luke repeated his predictive statement concerning a "light to the Gentiles" which he first used in Luke 2:32. Indeed, Luke even added a preliminary summary statement concerning the gladness and thankful worship expressed by the Gentiles because of their realization of eternal life (13:48). As the hostility of the Jews grew, however, the missionaries, in the traditional sign/rite of judgment, shook the dust from their feet and departed for Iconium, realizing the joy that had come to the Gentiles (13:51–52).

In Iconium, Lystra, and Derbe

The situation was hardly different in Iconium, where the missionaries scarcely escaped without being stoned (14:1–15). So they fled to Lystra, where they encountered a man crippled from birth. When he displayed faith, Paul told him to stand up; and he was healed. The people supposed that Barnabas and Paul were the gods, Zeus and Hermes, come down to earth in human form. So they made preparations to offer sacrifices to them (14:8–13). Rather than accepting the liturgical accolades of the people and their priests, however, the disciples, in a traditional evidence of humility and rejection of such a worship abomination, tore their clothes seeking to make clear that they were merely men serving the living God (14:14–18).

In a strange twist of events, such as during a sports event when a hero can quickly become the audiences' goat, the people turned on the missionaries and stoned Paul after hostile Jews came from the two previous cities and cast aspersions on him (14:19). Fortunately, he recovered and the missionaries left for Derbe, where they encountered less hostility. When they had finished their mission in Derbe, they returned through the previously visited cities and established leadership groups in each church. After worship involving prayer and fasting, they committed the Christians in that region to the Lord and headed back to Antioch in Syria, where they reported that God had opened the way for the Gentiles (14:23–27).

Judaizing Opposition and the Council's Resolution

On their return to Antioch, however, they encountered Christians from Jerusalem who were insisting that Gentiles had to become liturgically circumcised Jews to become Christians (15:1). A great controversy followed. As a result a council meeting was held in Jerusalem. In this meeting Peter argued that not even the Jewish Christians could achieve acceptance with God through circumcision and the law. His argument reflects the logic Paul developed in the Epistle to the Galatians. (See my comments on chapter 2 of that letter.)

The decision of the council (Acts 15:19–20, 28) is a vivid instructional model for handling a very difficult concern. On the one hand, the Jewish Christians agreed not to add the Jewish worship rite of circumcision for the Gentiles to become Christians (contrast 15:5 with 15:19, 28). On the other hand, the Gentiles were charged to observe four restraints (15:20, 29) that, on analysis, seem to fall into two categories. The first category concerns fundamental ethical norms that actually go back to what the Jews called the Noachim rules/ethics. Since everyone was regarded as a descendant of Noah, it was agreed that God patently forbade immorality and idolatry for all people. (Note the condemnations of Paul at 1 Cor 6:18; 10:14; and of John at Rev 2:14, 20.) The second category, however, is a little different and involves Jewish understandings of ritual and community or table rules concerning blood. If Jewish and Gentile Christians were going to be part of the same worshiping community, then the Gentiles would have to give up the practices of drinking blood and eating meat with the blood still in it (things strangled). Honoring the blood rules was crucial to Jewish sensitivity and their understanding of worshiping the God of creation.

While the brief statements in Acts do not make this distinction fully evident, a realization of the differences within Judaism helps to clarify the decision and provides a basis for the resolution of difficulties. Being able to separate fundamental moral issues within the community from perceptions of worship practice and cultural sensitivities is absolutely crucial when seeking to resolve crises in the church. Some things are morally not even open to question or negotiation, while others are matters of community harmony. Both must be honored for spiritual growth to take place in the church; however, to achieve a resolution in difficult situations, it is imperative to understand which category is being discussed.

Luke concluded this section on this first mission to the Gentiles with a summarizing report to the mixed congregation of Jewish and Gentile Christians at Antioch. When they heard the report from Jerusalem, they were filled with joy and were strengthened in their faith (15:31–32). Today with so many disputes in churches, there is a desperate need for Christians to learn how to reach peace-enhancing decisions that will maintain moral integrity but will also contribute both to worship and to the communication of the gospel.

Paul's Second and Third Travels (15:36–21:14)

The sixth major section of Acts involves Paul's second and third missionary enterprises (15:36–21:14). The account opens with a vigorous dispute between Paul and Barnabas over including on the mission Barnabas' cousin, John Mark, who had abandoned them on the first mission trip. The result of the dispute was that the partners separated and went in two different directions, with Paul choosing a new partner, Silas (probably the Silvanus mentioned in an early letter at 1 Thess 1:1 and later in 2 Cor 1:19, cf. also 1 Pet 5:12), who was one of the reporters from the Jerusalem decision (Acts 15:22). The gentle spirit of Barnabas apparently was effective in the restoration of Mark to the good graces of Paul, which is an untold story (note Col 4:10; Phlm 24; cf. 1 Pet 5:13). In every worshiping community the people should pray for a few members like Barnabas who earlier had even been a rescuer of Paul (cf. Acts 9:26–27).

The Call to Macedonia

Passing again through the cities of Galatia that were on his first mission, Paul recruited Timothy to join them on this mission and had him circumcised (16:3). This ritual act by Paul often troubles readers who find that Titus was not required to do so (cf. Gal 2:3). As pertaining to worship rites, Paul was not inconsistent here. Titus was obviously a Gentile, whereas Timothy (having a Jewish mother) was to be regarded as a Jew. Paul himself did not renounce his Jewishness, but he understood that his salvation did not come from the Jewish worship rites or obedience to the law. His rationale is very clear. He was neither anti-Jewish nor anti-Gentile. He was pro-Christ and wanted people to be who they were "in Christ."

After traveling through Galatia and Phrygia, Paul had planned to take his mission north to Bithynia and stay in what is today Asia Minor. But God through the Holy Spirit/the Spirit of Jesus (16:6–9) had other plans for him. In a new visionary experience of the numinous, God directed Paul to go to Macedonia and Europe.[6]

The story of Paul at Philippi is one of Luke's great accounts (16:11–40). Philippi was a Roman "colony" receiving that revered status in 42 B.C.E. after the battle in which Antony and Octavian (Augustus) defeated Brutus and Cassius. The defeated soldiers were settled there and not permitted to return to Rome.[7] Apparently no synagogue was there (not the required ten Jewish men present?). So the Jews, primarily women, were meeting for worship and prayer by the riverside, where they had the necessary running water for ablutions. Paul stayed in Philippi with a woman from Thyatira in Lydia (no doubt why we call her Lydia) in Asia Minor. A possessed slave woman accosted Paul on the street. A soothsayer, she served the business interests of her masters. When she followed the missionaries repeatedly and shouted that they were servants of God, Paul (as did Jesus before him) charged the devilish spirit in the name of Jesus to leave her (16:18; cf. Luke 8:28). The woman was healed, resulting in lost income to the owners. They hauled the missionaries before the authorities for unlicensed religious practices in a Roman colony (Acts 16:19–21). Paul and Silas were then summarily beaten and thrown into prison. Instead of bemoaning their state, however, the missionaries worshiped God in song. Miraculously, in a strange earthquake the prison chains and gates were unlocked (16:25–26). But Paul and Silas did not try to escape. Instead, the jailor who thought he would be executed for losing his prisoners was so moved by the spirit of the missionaries that he and his household became believers and were baptized (16:29–33). The question has often been asked: Why did Paul insist that the magistrates come to the prison and apologize for beating them after the authorities learned that the missionaries were Roman citizens and freed them (16:37)? Was Paul being proud and unforgiving? The answer lies in Paul's understanding of Roman law and the political situation. For the authorities to apologize meant that Christianity at that juncture would not be treated as an unlicensed religion and, therefore, would be permitted freedom of worship! His action was essential for recognizing the legitimacy of Christian proclamation and worship in a Roman colony.

The missionaries then moved along the Egnatian Way to Thessalonica, the capital of Macedonia (17:1–9). Following his customary pattern, Paul began proclaiming Jesus in the Jewish synagogue. After three weeks, the Jews became incensed at the large group of Gentiles that were attracted to Paul and his message. The Jewish leaders caused an uproar in the city, in violation of Roman laws of "peace" (*pax*). In support of their position, the Jews charged the missionaries with "turning the world upside down" and serving another "king" contrary to the laws of Caesar (17:6). Instead of trying to ferret out the issues or holding the missionaries as prisoners, the authorities took a security bond from the Christians against further unrest. The Thessalonican believers then sent the missionaries on their way. At Beroea the situation was not much different, except that the Jews were less hostile until some came from Thessalonica and inflamed them (17:13). This time Paul was immediately shipped off to Athens with the promise that Timothy and Silas would follow (17:14–15).

In Athens

The account at Athens is another of the marvelous Lucan stories (17:16–34). The undaunted Paul was aroused when he beheld all the statues and temples to the gods in that ancient city known for its multitude of "worship" centers and cult images. He began immediately to preach about Jesus and the resurrection in the synagogue and in the market ("forum" or *agora*, 17:17). The Greek and foreign rhetoricians who enjoyed debate were ready to investigate this new "philosophy," and so Paul was summoned to speak in defense of his views on the Areopagus (Mars Hill, the court and defense center of Athens). It was located just below the famed Acropolis on which stands the Parthenon and the holy shrine of the Erecthion (the only double-faced temple and worship center dedicated to both Athena and Neptune).

Five centuries before Paul, Socrates had stood before the same tribunal and was charged with "atheism" because the great philosopher had deprecated the Greek gods. In his defense Paul cleverly avoided that charge by confirming that the Athenians were both very religious and clearly worship-oriented because they even possessed an altar to "an unknown god." That unknown God, the Creator of all things, was the one that Paul was proclaiming. In support of his view he even quoted from their own philosopher-poets (Aratus and Cleanthes). Then he moved beyond their views to indicate that God should not be thought of in terms of representative statuary or friezes. God made himself known in the person of Jesus, whom God raised from the dead. Given their orientation to immortality only of the soul, the idea of resurrection sounded crazy to the Greek philosophers, and they broke up the meeting.

Some contemporary scholars have argued that Paul's message here hardly represents Pauline thought, but is Lucan in orientation. That Luke reported the speech and did so in Lucan style is undisputed, but to argue that the speech could not represent the brilliant Paul who was knowledgeable in both Greek and Hebraic thought patterns is, I would suggest, without merit. Paul's ability in rhetoric is evident in Romans and elsewhere, as even Bultmann acknowledged years ago in one of his dissertations.[8] Moreover, to argue as others have done that Paul was a failure in Athens because he used philosophy instead of the Bible in his presentation of the gospel is also lacking in adequate perception. Paul's context was very different at Athens. He wisely employed in his communication the framework not of the Bible but the thought patterns of his philosophical listeners. This story, accordingly, provides a very important lesson for all those who would seek to communicate worship pattern and theology to varying audiences. Those of us who were brought up with a modern framework of thought and are trying to communicate with postmodern people must be aware of their orientations. Both generations have different ways of thinking. Moreover, Luke provides his own evaluation of the event by indicating that some Athenians weighed his words seriously and that some became believers, including one of the council members (Dionysius). In Luke's literary pattern he also mentioned a woman (Damaris) here (17:33).

In Corinth

From Athens Paul headed for Corinth, the capital of Achaia. Luke reported another interesting encounter (18:1–16). Here Paul met Aquila and Priscilla, fellow Jewish tentmakers who had been expelled along with other Jews from Rome by Claudius in the early fifties. (See Suetonius, *Divus Claudius* 24.4.) Silas and Timothy also again joined him. His experience in the synagogue here was a familiar one. Paul responded to the Jews by shaking out his clothes as a Jewish sign of condemnation and began preaching next door (18:6–7). Intriguingly, Crispus, the leader of the synagogue, and his family as well as many Corinthians became Christians and were ritually initiated into the new covenant people through baptism (18:8).

The Jews, however, decided to make a full-scale legal attack on the missionaries and took the case to Gallio, the senator/proconsul. He presided over the case at the *bema* in the market (*agora*). When Gallio heard that the Jewish complaint was a matter of Jewish worship practice, he dismissed the case. The new ruler of the synagogue, Sosthenes, ended up getting beaten for disturbing the peace (18:12–17). One cannot help but wonder if this Sosthenes later became a Christian and was the same one who assisted Paul in writing to the Corinthians (see 1 Cor 1:1). Did the worship of Jesus finally make an impact on him?

Luke concluded this part of the segment of Acts with a brief description of Paul traveling across the Aegean Sea for a short stop at Ephesus before returning to the imperial province of Syria. Before departing from Cenchreae, the seaport of Corinth (home of the deacon Phoebe, see Rom 16:1), Paul had his hair cut because of a traditional Jewish liturgical vow he had taken (Acts 18:18) as he readied himself for worship in Jerusalem. (For the Jews the expression to "go up" at Acts 18:22 always implied going to Jerusalem.)

The Return to Syria and the Third Journey

The second half of this section begins without much fan fare. Paul began his third mission trip by retracing his steps through the provinces of Galatia and Phrygia on the overland trans-Asian Roman highway system that linked Tarsus to Ephesus. What parts of the highway he used at this point and whether or how close he came to the tri-cities of Colossae, Hierapolis, and Laodicea is not entirely certain. What is clear is that he came to Ephesus. where the eloquent speaker Apollos also came to Ephesus and was instructed in the way of God by Priscilla and Aquila since he had not received Christian baptism. (Acts 18:24–28). Soon thereafter, Apollos became one of Paul's close associates in mission (cf. 1 Cor 16:12).

IN EPHESUS

In Ephesus, once again Paul began his mission in the synagogue, but after three months was forced to change his mission center to the hall of Tyrannus. There he continued to minister to both Jews and Greeks for an additional two years (19:8–10). Luke's account of the Ephesus mission makes for captivating reading, beginning with the miraculous healings in which mysteriously even cloths that had touched Paul's body carried healing power for the sick (19:11–12). Such patterns of genuine healing seem to be rather rare in the Western rationalistic world and are often viewed with great skepticism, but they should not be dismissed as mere ancient quackery because the power of the Holy Spirit is still evident in the church today. The issue is that humans cannot force the Spirit to act in such miraculous ways. God through the Spirit, not humans, is in control. What happened next in the story is a confirmation of this fact. The priest's sons attempted to copy the miracles using the names of Jesus and Paul, but in a comedy of errors evil spirits attacked the sons; and they fled naked and wounded. The message was clear—do not mess in the spirit world without the power of God's Spirit (19:13–16). As might be expected, the impact of these mysterious events on the city was astounding, and people began responding in large numbers by to turning to God and abandoning their pagan ways, even burning their costly books of magic (19:17–20).

Such responses, however, were only the beginning. Worship ceremonies honoring Artemis attracted thousands of pilgrims each year to Ephesus. The silversmiths became wealthy selling statues of Artemis. These smiths, seeing how effective Paul was in gaining converts to Christianity, became concerned for their "idol" souvenir business and created such a stir in the city that it nearly caused a riot in the gigantic theater. The quick thinking of city administrators (*asiarchon*) averted the riot. They pleaded with the crowd that the worship at the Temple of Artemis was hardly in danger from a few visiting miracle workers proclaiming another god. More persuasively, they informed the proud citizens that their independence as a city was in great jeopardy if the Romans should come from their provincial headquarters at Pergamum due to the potential for immanent rioting (breaking the "peace") (19:23-40). ' One thing should be apparent from this event: namely, when the gospel and authentic worship practices confront the combination of people's pocketbooks and pseudo-worship practices, the result is inevitable hostility. Failure to understand such a reaction is absolute folly. Even Paul thought he could deal with the issue by logic, but was fortunately restrained by his friends from entering the riot scene (19:30).

IN TROAS

Once again Paul was on the road. This time he planned to return to Syria and Jerusalem. Before doing so, he had to make a concluding visit to Macedonia and Achaia, the two provinces of Greece (20:1-4; cf. 19:21-22). After completing those visits, he returned to Asia and Troas (near the site of ancient Troy).

Here Luke added another of his fascinating episodes of spiritual power, this one involving Paul's intensity in preaching (20:7-12). A young man, Eutychus, was sitting on the windowsill listening to Paul. He went to sleep, fell out of the upper story window, and died. Thankfully, Paul was able to restore the young man, and apparently continued in worship and instruction until dawn.

WITH THE EPHESIAN ELDERS

Determined to reach Jerusalem for Pentecost, Paul bypassed Ephesus and landed at Miletus. Then he called the Ephesian elders to come to him and delivered one of the most touching messages Luke records. Luke pictured Paul, much like Jesus before him, undeterred on a fateful journey to Jerusalem, despite knowing that imprisonment and suffering awaited him (20:22-23, 25; cf. Luke 9:52-53). In this speech Paul forewarned the leaders of the church ("shepherds of the flock") that unscrupulous people "(wolves," cf. the imagery in John 10:11-12) would soon come with malicious and divisive intentions that would fracture the worshiping community. Therefore, the leaders of the church needed to be on their guard (Acts 20:28-30). Paul concluded his address by reminding them about how self-giving he had been with them, even working to support himself. In so doing he modeled an otherwise unknown saying of Jesus about it being more blessed when one gives than when one expects to receive (20:35).[9]

Paul's departure was painful for the Ephesian elders because they realized that they would not see him again. In prayer and with weeping as though experiencing a preliminary funeral rite similar to that of the woman anointing Jesus for burial (cf. Mark 14:8), they sent him on his way (Acts 20:37-38).

The scene was replayed at Tyre (21:4, 5) and again at Caesarea (21:10-12) as Paul maintained his commitment to go to Jerusalem in spite of the suffering that awaited him. For those who are closely aligned to God in worship and life, such spiritual insight is not novel. This section is then concluded when the people realized that Paul could not be deterred from his goal of Jerusalem even if it meant to die for the name of Jesus. So they acceded to the "will of God" (21:14), as Jesus did in the garden (cf. Luke 22:42).

Paul the Prisoner Goes to Rome (21:15–28:31)

The seventh and final major section in Acts involves Paul's arrest, imprisonment, and journey to Rome (Acts 21:15–28:31). It opens with Paul's arrival in Jerusalem and his report concerning his mission.

Paul's Arrest in Jerusalem

He willingly acquiesced in the elders' plan for him to join in a vow of recommitment to God at the Temple. This vow represented a final effort to convince the Jews that as a Christian he was still a loyal Jew (21:17–24). Engaging in such a Nazarite vow was indeed a sizable commitment of time and expense.[10] His agreement to do so should not be viewed as an expedient compromise of Paul's theology because he had already done so earlier (18:18). Even in the Corinthian correspondence he outlined such a perspective to win people for Christ (cf. 1 Cor 9:20–23). Here Paul demonstrated one of his fundamental perspectives in matters such as worship: he was neither anti-Jew nor anti-Gentile; he was pro-Jesus. Moreover, he was not a manipulator of worship or life. His goal was the service of Christ. The Jerusalem plan backfired when Jews from Asia spotted Paul in the Temple and falsely charged him with bringing a Gentile (Trophimus) into the inner court of the Jews and beyond the warning wall (the *Soreg*), which terminated the Court of the Gentiles (Acts 21:27–29).[11]

The tribune and his soldiers quickly emerged from the nearby Tower of Antonio which Herod the Great had built adjacent to the Temple to control the worship proceedings in the Temple. They promptly stopped the minor riot that ensued. The hostile crowd continued their demands for Paul's death, as they did for Jesus earlier (21:36; cf. Luke 23:21). In typical fashion, Luke included Paul's defensive speech in the Temple—another historical rehearsal of Paul's conversion and call. The hostile Jews listened to his testimonial speech in Hebrew, including his admission of participating in the death of Stephen (22:20), but when he reached his call to preach to the Gentiles, they once again shouted for his death (22:22).

Seeking to determine Paul's apparent guilt and to gain a confession, the Roman tribune condemned him to the cruel Roman practice of "examination" by scourging. In defense of his innocence and demanding appropriate justice, however, Paul called on his Roman citizenship (22:25), leaving the tribune uncertain of the reason for the riot. To clarify the situation, the tribune summoned the Sanhedrin into session. In his defense Paul split the council by claiming to be a loyal Pharisee and emphasized his spiritual experiences with God and his belief in the resurrection. The Pharisees exonerated him and defended him over against the Sadducees, who in their skepticism denied spiritual encounters with mystery such as Paul described (23:9). Fearing violence between the parties, the tribune returned Paul to the Antonio fortress (23:10).

Learning of an assassination plot against Paul, the tribune decided to rid himself of his prisoner and the accompanying turmoil. Accordingly, he sent Paul to Caesarea and the governor of the imperial province, Felix, but without an adequate charge (23:26–30). Felix's attempt to solve the problem quickly with a hearing at Caesarea hardly succeeded. Then Felix and his new Jewish wife, Drusilla (who were not known for their morality), summoned Paul to learn more about Jesus. Felix was shocked to find that Paul had the courage to confront them on the moral issues of their lives and the eternal consequences. The governor could hardly accept such bold implied accusations and dismissed Paul, hoping of course that Paul would arrange for a bribe and that he could conveniently release him (24:24–26). Such, however, was not forthcoming, and Paul languished in prison for an additional two years (24:27).

Following the removal of Felix by the emperor, Festus took his place. Immediately, he sought to deal with leftover matters from the previous governor. One of those issues concerned Paul. Festus, after a brief, frustrating hearing at Caesarea, tried to please the Jews (25:7–9) by suggesting that a follow-up session be held at Jerusalem. Paul, knowing that he would be waylaid and killed en route and that he was innocent of all charges, immediately appealed to Caesar for recourse. Festus was forced to respond by granting his appeal (25:10–12).

A state visit to Festus by Herod Agrippa II and his wife, Bernice, both of whom may have been siblings of Drusilla (the new wife of Felix), followed. Since Festus did not have an adequate charge to send to the emperor, he asked the king of the northern province to assist him in formulating the charge. Accordingly, once again Paul set out his testimony (26:19–23), indicating that he had been obedient to the vision for God (26:19) and that Christ, in his death and resurrection, fulfilled the Old Testament prophecies concerning the coming Messiah (26:22–23). Festus' reaction was that he thought Paul was crazy, but Agrippa understood Paul's intentions and asked Paul if he thought that he could get Agrippa to become a Christian so quickly. Not one to back down, Paul pressed forward with the hope of such a commitment (26:28–29). In the end, Paul might not have converted Agrippa, but the King did reiterate one of the themes of Luke: namely, that Paul (like other Christians) was not guilty. For Luke, believing in and worshiping Jesus was hardly a treasonable offense (26:32; cf. Pilate's judgment in Luke 23:4). Yet having appealed to Caesar, Paul could not be set free by subordinate authorities, a fact Agrippa conceded. So to Rome, Paul was sent.

On the Sea to Rome

During the sea voyage (27:1–28:13) it became increasingly clear that neither the ship's captain nor the sailors nor even the centurion were in charge. Rather, the prisoner, Paul, who embodied an awesome sense of confidence as a result of his relationship with Jesus, took control. It was late in the season–when the Mediterranean became very rough for ancient ships. Against the firm advice of Paul, the sailors attempted to get as far as the port of Phoenix on Crete rather than wintering at Fair Havens (27:8–12). As soon as they set sail, the tempestuous wind known as *"Eurakulo"* arose (27:14, like us, they named their storms!).The only option open to the sailors was to let the ship run before the wind, but they knew they could have been heading for the isolated shores of North Africa and the ancient graveyard of shipping. Having tossed cargo and everything they could sacrifice overboard, as the sailors in the story of Jonah did, they lost hope of being saved (27:18–20; cf. Jonah 1:4–10).

In the pit of the sailor's despair, Paul counseled everyone not to fear because the God he worshiped (*latreuo*) had promised him that everyone would survive the wreck on an island (27:23–25). When the boat came near land, the sailors feared the boat would break up on the rocks, so they planned to escape in a lifeboat during the night. Perceiving their intentions, Paul informed the centurion that unless they stayed together, they would not survive. Accordingly, the soldiers cut away the lifeboat, and the company aboard ship was left to wait anxiously for the morning to arrive. At that point, Paul demonstrated his worshipful reliance on God by following Jesus' earlier model at the Last Supper by taking bread, giving thanks to God, breaking it, and eating it in their presence. With Paul's confident worship example in mind, the entire crew relaxed and also took nourishment (27:34–35; cf. Luke 22:19).

The next day, the ship ran aground on a reef and began to be broken apart by the waves. As the ship broke up, the soldiers were prepared to follow Roman custom and kill all the prisoners to prevent their escape. The centurion prevented the slaughter, and all the company came safely to land on broken pieces of the ship (Acts 27:44). On the island of Malta the survivors built a fire after gathering wood. A poisonous snake emerged from the hot fire and grabbed Paul's hand. The island natives were convinced that he would die, believing that the god "Justice" (*Dike*) was executing judgment. When Paul threw the snake into the fire and survived the bite, they quickly changed their minds and were ready to treat Paul as a god (28:3–6). Then, when the father of the island chief became ill, Paul prayed for him and touched him with healing. The other people on the island recognized the spiritual strength that Paul had gained from relationship with God, and they came for healing as well. When the company was able to board another ship, the people supplied them with gifts to cover all their needs (28:10). The remainder of the trip to Rome was uneventful except to note that when the believers from Rome came to greet Paul on the Appian Way about thirty-three miles from Rome, they expressed their gratitude to God in prayer and were strengthened by his safe arrival (28:15).

Paul in Rome

Although Luke included only a few notes on Paul in Rome, those he did include are very significant for our understanding of spiritual power and a worship-filled life. Upon his arrival in Rome, Paul contacted the Jews located in Rome and explained his reason for being a prisoner was his worship of God and the hope of Israel in Jesus. Later he preached at length to them about Jesus and the kingdom of God. When, as usual, some of them began to dispute his preaching, he repeated to them the words of Isaiah 6:9–10 about the people closing their ears and eyes so as to be unable to accept God's word to them. Then Paul announced that God's salvation would instead be accepted by the Gentiles (Acts 28:28). The book closes with Paul under armed guard but able to witness freely while he awaited the disposal of his case (28:30–31).

Whether Luke had intended to write more concerning the fascinating story of Paul or other early Christians is unknown. That Paul was dead by the time Luke penned these words is quite probable. Why Luke did not write more is open to speculation. Reports concerning the first Christian century are at best very sketchy. But the concluding words of the book are very suggestive when they indicate that although Paul was in chains, his preaching about Jesus Christ and the kingdom of God was being done both "boldly" (*parresias*) and "unchained" (*akolytos*). Perhaps what we should take from this book is that the church in every era is called upon to write the worship conclusion to this two-volume work.

WORSHIP SUMMARY

These amazing vignettes in Acts about the continuing work of Jesus within the early worshiping community should stir every reader to a new sense of vitality and power that comes with responding to the awesome God in Jesus. He is the one who empowered his frail worshipers to proclaim his resurrection (4:13–22) in spite of being jailed and who sent them back to speak again in the worship center of their persecutors (5:17–26); who inspired them to reorganize their worshiping community (1:15–26) for correct teaching, fellowship, liturgy, and prayer (2:42); who challenged them to share their goods with the poor in the face of human greed and possessiveness (4:32– 5:11; 6:1–7); who gave them courage to forgive in the presence of persecution and death (7:54–60); who bestowed on them a gracious spirit to accept a persecutor into their midst and call him a brother (9:1–31); who helped them break down barriers and welcome people who were different (8:4–40; 10:1–11:18; 15:1–34); who called them forth by the Holy Spirit to mission beyond their comfort zones (13:1–3); who pushed them to share the gospel after they had been continually rejected and stoned (14:1–27; etc.); who assisted them in singing praises to God in prison rather than seeking to escape when they were freed (16:25–34); who filled them with boldness in the presence of political authorities (13:6–12; 24:1–26:32); who gave them peace and the ability to calm frightened people by demonstrating God's superintending presence through worship in the midst of calamity (27:33–38); and who granted them guidance and insight even while they were in chains (27:9–32 and 28:28–30).

May we also sense a freedom to communicate the gospel boldly. Moreover, whether we are young or old, experiencing persecution or living in a context of liberty, may we focus our lives on truly worshiping God and realize that the gospel of Jesus cannot ultimately be shackled by the enemies of Christ. The Book of Acts is a continuing testimony that the God of mystery who calls us to himself in Christ Jesus can help us respond with courage, just as the Lord did for the early Christians. And may God receive all the glory.

QUESTIONS

1. How exciting is your worship of God?
2. What could contribute more to your sense of God's presence in worship?
3. What might be hindering your worship and life from becoming as dynamic as the experiences of the early church in Acts?
4. How realistic to you are these stories? Why?

PART III

Caring for and Counseling the New Christian Worshiping Communities

Reflections on the Pauline Epistles and Hebrews

The twenty-one books known as the New Testament epistles give us firsthand evidence of the early church struggling with practical and theological issues, many involving the meaning, practice, and implications of worship. Thirteen of the letters are traditionally attributed to Paul, the featured missionary in the final chapters of Acts.

Before any of the Gospels were written, the leaders of the early church began to pen epistles containing advice for the early Christians on varying matters such as: correct theological reflections about God, Jesus, and the Holy Spirit; implications of Christ's coming for salvation both at present and in the future; the nature of the new communities of faith that had been birthed; legitimate perspectives on worship and mission to the world; and proper patterns of living for believers in a hostile world. These early Christian letters to the young or recently formed churches are comparable in form, but witness a wide variety in their contents and in the issues they address.

The first and major segment contained fourteen books composed of thirteen works assigned to Paul plus Hebrews.

The early scribes placed Paul's soteriological or salvation letters (Romans, the two Corinthian letters, and Galatians) at the beginning of the collection. The second group in the Pauline corpus comprised the christological letters or epistles defining Jesus Christ. They include Ephesians, Philippians and Colossians. The third segment involving the two Thessalonian letters deals with eschatology, or documents about expectations of the future or last times. The fourth section can generally be identified as the personal letters. They include what is generally termed the three "Pastoral" letters (the two to Timothy and the one to Titus). The short book of Philemon was also added.

Because Hebrews was joined to the Pauline corpus, it has frequently been suggested that Paul wrote Hebrews, but such is virtually impossible since the Greek is of the neo-classical/Alexandrian type and is not the *Koine* or popular, everyday Greek of the Pauline works.

This study on worship naturally pays particular attention to Romans, the Corinthian correspondence, and Ephesians among the Pauline corpus. In Romans Paul lays out his mature thinking on the nature of the gospel and its implications for life and worship, and in the two Corinthian epistles he deals specifically with many issues related to church life and worship. Ephesians can serve Christians as a significant resource or handbook for spiritual formation and worship. In the other epistles, including those that are not Pauline, I have concentrated on their focused concerns, which are also exceedingly pertinent for Christian worshipers today.

Study of this section should provide vital insights into the life and worship practices in the early church and thus should offer some helpful perspectives for contemporary churches as they struggle with conflicts and difficult problems, including the reevaluation of their worship programs, patterns, and formation as Christians.

QUESTIONS

1. Have you ever thought that the early church was ideal? When and Why?
2. Did it truly have problems like ours in worship and life?
3. Why do many people today idealize the early church?
4. What does such a view do to our perspectives on the letters of Paul?

6

Romans

Accepting the Power of God for Salvation and Worship[1]

In this strategic Epistle to the Romans, Paul provided an interpretation of the threefold nature of Christian salvation as a basis for authentic worship and he rejected the patterns and implications of pseudo-worship among both Gentiles and Jews.

The Book of Romans is an indication of Paul's magisterial ability as: a Christian teacher of the doctrine of salvation or wholeness in Christ; a superb rhetorician in matters of critique and defense; an insightful promoter of Christian mission; a sensitive evangelist to the Hellenistic world; a transformed Jewish rabbi; an able analyst of God's purposes in history; and a perceptive advocate of appropriate relationships to God in worship and life. This book has become a cornerstone in the structural development of Protestantism, with its themes of "Scripture alone," "faith alone," "grace alone," "Christ alone!" It is also being restudied anew by Roman Catholics who have found it to be a great resource for worship and spiritual formation.[2]

Weaknesses in Interpreting Romans

I remain firmly convinced that major weaknesses exist in interpretations of Romans within the Western Protestant church since Luther. The weaknesses result from an overemphasis on justification and a failure to consider seriously the other aspects of the salvation process. This failure has resulted within evangelicalism in an over-stressing on gaining an initial commitment to Christ,

85

with a failure to give sufficient attention to matters of growth in worship and the Christian life. It is not an either/or but a both/and. The worship rite of baptism has often become something like fire insurance throughout Christianity (both East and West), which cares for one's eternal destiny. But more astonishing, about which I have frequently critiqued my own Baptist brothers and sisters, is the fact that I have found the not-too-infrequent phenomenon that some Baptists have been baptized two or more times in Baptist churches (reminiscent of Jewish water rites of lustration or purification)! When the primary emphasis in the church is placed on the initial commitment to Christ and baptism, the question becomes, What means does one have for publicly expressing growth in the relationship with God and the desire to respond in a commitment of oneself more fully to Christ, other than being invited to repent and become baptized as a "real" Christian? Naturally, one can always indicate a personal desire for a fuller commitment to Christ by going to seminary and becoming a pastor or other minister. That pattern can take place in any denomination, whether it means becoming a priest or a minister.

When a pattern of rebaptism in evangelical churches is linked to the desire for counting baptisms as a sign of church growth, then the church or minister can easily succumb to Madison Avenue's perspectives of success in the church. Please do not think here that I am opposed to evangelism, because for years I taught evangelism in seminary at the doctoral level. Moreover, I would not for a moment intend by my critique to provide fodder for those who are either afraid to do evangelism or who criticize the importance of evangelism. Rather, I firmly believe with Paul that one of our tasks as Christians is making the gospel known to the world. Yet, I am seriously concerned that we also advocate a holistic view of salvation and growth in Christian life and worship, which I clearly find in Paul.

Introducing Romans

No reputable scholar today would join the nineteenth-century radical critic Bruno Bauer and suggest that Paul did not write Romans. The book stands as the capstone of Paul's writings. The scribe for this letter was a man named Tertius (Rom 16:22), and the book was probably written from Corinth some time between 56–58 C.E., during Paul's three-month stay in that city (Acts 20:3). Clearly, one purpose of the letter was to anticipate Paul's moving his mission emphasis west toward Spain. First, he had to visit the Jerusalem Christians and deliver the financial aid collected from the churches in the Greek provinces (Rom 15:25–26). He obviously had not yet visited the Christians in Rome (1:13) but looked forward to coming there with the hope of establishing the church in Rome as a base of support for his intended mission work in Spain (1:12; 15:24). Paul's earlier bases had been Antioch in Syria for his first set of missionary visits (cf. Acts 13:1–3) and then Philippi (cf. Phil 4:15; 2 Cor 11:9) for his mission to both northern and southern Greece (Macedonia and Achaia). Now it was time for him to move on (Rom 15:23). In preparation for his visit to

Rome, he apparently chose the deacon Phoebe from the church in the seaport of Corinth (Cenchreae) to carry this letter and develop the connections for him. Accordingly, he requested that they treat her appropriately (16:1–2).

Unlike the other Pauline letters, Romans does not treat specific problems in the church. Instead, Romans is a kind of letter of introduction in which Paul sets out for them his understanding of the gospel. By doing so, Paul provided not only for the Roman church of his time but also for Christian readers throughout the centuries a marvelous resource in developing their understandings of Christian thought, life and worship. To this crucial text, therefore, attention is now directed with the realization that this analysis must necessarily be very brief and concerned primarily with matters related to worship in the context of an intense theological presentation.

Romans: The Introduction (1:1–4)

The introduction to Romans is like a beautifully complex Chinese box, as new statements emerge out of previous ones and form a magnificent presentation of Jesus Christ and Paul's relationship to him. Paul made it absolutely clear with four descriptions (a slave, a summoned one, an apostle, and a separated or marked-out one) that he was not self-directed, but rather was answerable directly to Jesus. Jesus is identified as the one who fulfilled the prophetic anticipation of the authentic descendent of David, as well as being the genuine Son of God and Lord as evidenced by the Spirit in the resurrection (Rom 1:1–4).

If one needed a rationale for worshiping Jesus, it is plainly here. Moreover, Paul realized that he was appointed by God as a special agent to pass on the gospel. Fascinatingly, he defined the gospel as "obedience of faith," an expression that unites two concepts which Christians since Luther have frequently separated (1:5). They are our obedient effort or working for Christ and our believing or trusting in Christ, both of which are quite Pauline, but church polemics have bifurcated them (cf. Eph 2:8–10; Phil 2:12–13; cf. also James 2:14, 17).

Romans: The Thesis (1:16–17)

After this introduction, Paul moved immediately to spell out the major thesis for his letter (1:16–17). In the ancient world, which emphasized shame and honor, Paul proclaimed that the gospel is hardly a message of shame, even though many might think so because Jesus died on the cross. Instead, it is a message of power (*dynamis*) for everyone (historically to the Jew, and then to the Gentile). The reason is that God acted to reveal in the gospel God's fundamental perspective for dealing with the people of the world (namely, divine righteousness). The entire process of salvation from beginning to end involves faith.[3] Then Paul supported this thesis with a quotation from Habakkuk 2:4, and emphasized "living" by faith. It is not a static concept in which salvation is completed when one believes, but a dynamic concept that involves all of life (Rom 1:17)! Such a complete perspective is crucial as a basis for worship.

Total Failure to Understand God's Way in the World (1:18–2:29)

Paul turned to show that both the Gentiles and the Jews failed to understand God's way in the world. The first argument (1:18–32) is a direct critique of Hellenistic worship and life. Paul begins this section with a thunderous condemnation by God of evil activity and idolatry among the Gentiles. He charged them with knowing about God's existence through creation but deliberately suppressing the truth (1:18–20). Furthermore, not only did they fail to worship God appropriately with honor and thanksgiving, but they stupidly fashioned their own idolatrous gods modeled on created beings. One cannot help but hear Luther's sharp words in the background to the effect that humans will choose *entweder Gott oder Abgott* (either God or an idol).

The results of the choice by humans for idolatry rather than God have been devastating in the world. Paul defined the consequences by means of three parallel statements of "God delivered [*paredoken*] them…" (1:24, 26, 28) which reflect a three-part Hellenistic view of the human personality (heart, passions, and mind).[4] The fateful degeneration of humans is here clearly articulated as beginning with the choice of the *will* (heart) in favor of the created order over the Creator of the cosmic order. That choice has led to various personal sins (1:24–25). These sins are followed by sexually explicit sins of the *passions,* which reject foundational standards on which society is built (here Paul refers to homosexuality, 1:26–27). These sins, he argued, in turn lead to all sorts of sins against society as the *mind* and human thought processes become corrupted (1:18–31). The conclusion, of course, is God's judgment leading to the sinner's death. Then, in a strong conclusion, he declared that by extension the sins no longer remain personal sins of an individual, but instead they end in conspiracies to sin and in community sinning (1:32). Paul's summation is clear: improper worship results in the disintegration of society.

He then turned from the Gentiles to their critics–the smug Jews. He reminded the Jews that God would also judge them when they failed the repentance test (2:1–4). Clearly their lives did not indicate that God's perspectives were written on their hearts (wills, 2:6–15). Then referring to the Jewish concept of the human personality and the "two inclinations" (the *yetzer hatov* [the good] and the *yetzer harah* [the evil]), Paul judged the Jews harshly for inconsistency between their words and actions. While they boasted about their relationship to God, their lives revealed a very different inclination. He judged them as blind guides, ignorant teachers, fraudulent proclaimers of the Ten Commandments and the Torah, and people who disconnected life from worship (2:17–24).

To make his point very clear, Paul focused on the Jewish worship rite of circumcision, which for them had become a status symbol. He insisted that rites without inner commitment of the worshipers were meaningless. Worship rites are a matter of the "heart," not merely external actions (2:25–28)! The implications for Christian rites should also be obvious. Moreover, Paul concluded that such rites should lead to genuine praise of God and not be used as human status symbols (2:29).

Paul employed a style of argument similar to the "Cynic and Stoic Diatribe." This fact led Bultmann to assume that Paul's philosophical foundation was basically Greek in orientation. Like some other Germans of his time, Bultmann rejected any attachment to Jewish theology and the Old Testament.[5] But while Paul was astute enough to use the style of the Greek philosophical teachers, his theology is rooted in his Jewish heritage transformed by his encounter with Christ.

The Value of Jewish Heritage (3:1–20)

Paul next turned, in fact, to the value of the Jewish heritage. Paul repeatedly affirmed the strategic value of that heritage. Still, he insisted that more is needed for a relationship with God than the mere adoption of one's heritage, since heritage does not save one from sin (3:1–8).

In support of the fact that even the Jews are sinners, Paul formulated a "florilegium" type prooftext or midrashic chain of verses constructed from the Psalms and Isaiah to prove that even the Jews were sinners. He summarized his argument by announcing that the purpose of the Torah or law was not to save but to make clear both the nature of sin and the need for justification—becoming right with God (3:19–20).

All Are Sinners (3:21–31)

Paul thus clarified his position that neither human achievement nor keeping worship and other rules could serve as a basis for becoming acceptable to God. Having cleared away these potential roadblocks, Paul enunciated his next major thesis—that everyone is a sinner, has fallen below God's expected standards; and is desperately in need of God's assistance for divine acceptance. That acceptance has been made available through faith in/of Jesus Christ, whose death was God's means of providing humans with forgiveness (3:21–26).[6]

The impact of this section is that our acceptance by the holy God is both because of Christ's faithfulness and because of our acceptance by faith of Christ's dealing with our "guilt" (3:25).[7] Accordingly, the law or Torah is not discarded. Rather Paul acknowledged it as an important means for identifying our failures with God and helping us to turn to God's way of acceptance (3:28–31). Worship then is *not the means* for salvation *but the response* to God's action in providing salvation!

The Example of Abraham (4:1–25)

With his thesis concerning sin and God's way of acceptance in focus, Paul turned, like a good logician, to the story of Abraham (4:1–25) for support. Being an astute rabbi, he knew how to use his sources. He compared Genesis 15:6 with 17:9–11 and insisted that Abraham's faith and his acceptance by God preceded the inauguration of the rite of circumcision. A worship rite or sacred symbol such as circumcision is therefore a sign, Paul contended, of *the already existing reality of acceptance with God* ("reckoned") and *not the means* to that reality (4:11)! Relationship with God precedes worship rites in obedient acknowledgment of God. This distinction was crucial for Paul and should be important for Christians (when they reflect on their rites such as the Lord's Supper and baptism).

Paul added that the promise of inheritance did not come through law or its obedience since that would be a misunderstanding of the role of law (4:13–15). Finally, he argued that, since Abraham's faith rested on God's grace like that of later Christians, Abraham was not merely the father of Israel but the father of all who have faith. Moreover, since Abraham had faith that God could enliven Sarah's womb, his acceptance by God was like that of Christians who believe that God raised Jesus from the dead (4:16–25). Worship thus centers in the acknowledgment and celebration of the resurrection of Jesus Christ, not in the performance of rituals to gain God's attention and blessing.

Faith and Reconciliation with the New Adam (5:1–21)

Paul drew this segment of his argument to a conclusion by introducing the implications of faith for the reconciliation of humanity. Paul outlined his threefold view of salvation: justification, sanctification in holy living, and glorification as the ultimate hope. The result of *justification* by *faith* should be peace with God, which provides the foundation for a deep sense of joy because of the *ultimate hope* for sharing in the *glory* of God. This, in turn, should be evidenced presently in a growing sense of the *love* of God in Christians who are empowered by the Holy Spirit for consistent, holy *living* (Rom 5:1–5; similar triadic thinking appears in 1 Cor 13:13; 1 Thess 1:3, 9; etc). Paul uses the term "salvation" here because, for him, to "be saved" includes all three aspects of the process: justification, sanctification, and glorification, not just the initial step of justification. (See his fuller perspective at Rom 5:9, 10).[8]

Now, the realization that God had worked out the reconciliation of humanity to himself through sending his Son Jesus so gripped Paul that he could not help but launch into praising God (5:11). Unfortunately, for many Christians today the idea of being reconciled to God often becomes a mere theological statement so that the thought of bursting into praise over such an idea can seem to be unusually emotional. But to grasp this reality is nothing short of awesome. Until we grasp the joyous mystery of being reconciled to God, we can never truly worship.

To support his conclusion that God mysteriously had worked out the means for the reconciliation of all humanity through Jesus (5:10–11), Paul included a vivid comparison between Christ and Adam (5:12–21). While Paul affirmed that death had accompanied sin in all people (5:12), he carefully identified the fact that grace "might" reign in righteousness to life for humans through Jesus Christ (5:20–21). Paul did indicate that the implications of Christ's work were universal in significance, but Paul was not a universalist (5:18). Nor did he argue that everyone would ultimately be saved. By repeating the phrase "much more" in his comparisons (5:15, 17, 20), Paul argued from Christ back to Adam rather than the reverse, because for him it was Christ who made clear the very sad nature of the human plight. Still, in Christ new hope was given so that, while law provided the realization of judgment, Christ could provide the gracious hope for life (5:21).

Baptism and Life with Christ (6:1–7:6)

For those who are joined to the New Adam (Christ), certain implications follow. Altering the question of 3:8 slightly, Paul asked another "Diatribe-type" question about the possibility of continuing to sin so that grace could be made more evident (6:1). The answer, as one might expect, was again a resounding negative (*me genoito*)! This opening question is then followed by other questions about living in sin, and pointedly about the significance of baptism and such a pattern of life (6:2–3). Paul was certainly ready to answer his own questions. The initiatory rite of the Christian church implies a conscious identification with Christ–namely, a willful death to the old way of life and an acceptance of resurrection to the new life with Christ.

Paul even used the Hebrew concept of *halak* ("to walk") to insure that his readers would take seriously their new life (6:4). For Paul *halakah* implied recognizing the authoritative way. Union with Christ was not a trifling matter. Having died to sin meant living in the way of Christ (6:5–11; cf. Phil 2:5). Allowing the sinful nature to control one's life was a rejection of the baptismal commitment, a misunderstanding of the implications of worship, and a return to the old life, not of grace, but of law (6:12–14).

The mention of law raised for Paul the old specter of slavery. Such a thought brought another of his harsh negative responses (6:15). The realization that he had been freed from such slavery brought his worshipful prayer of thanksgiving (6:17) and a challenge to his readers to pursue the route of sanctification (6:19), the end of which would be the gift by God of eternal life or glorification, the last stage in the salvation process (6:22–23). So, like a woman who had been bound to her husband during his lifetime but had been freed from her marriage at his death, Christians are likewise freed from bondage to the law and now belong to Christ and his way, which is the life of the Spirit (7:1–6). The life of the Spirit or walking in the way of Christ reveals that our baptism represents a valid confession enabling us to give thanks to God (6:17) who saves us by providing for our justification, sanctification, and glorification.

The Struggles of the Christian Life (7:7–8:17)

The next section is a critical part of Paul's argument, but readers often fail to understand it because they assume that the struggles Paul was referring to must have been during his life before he became a Christian. Instead, this text very much represents one's life as a Christian and the struggles that a believer faces on the difficult journey to sanctification (7:7–8:17). It is an important corrective to much of the pie-in-the-sky Christianity that is passed off as an authentic message of the New Testament, but is actually merely a hollow shell of true life. To think that Christians are not tempted by the ways of the world or by disillusionment is unreal and does not even represent Paul's *own* life and despair at times (e.g., 2 Cor 1:8). No one who seeks spiritual growth in worship and life should be unaware of this text. It should be prayerfully pondered like the Lamentations and even the Imprecatory (cursing) Psalms of the Old Testament. Struggle and despair are part of the human psyche. To deny their existence for Christians means failing to recognize the realities of life. God understands our hurts and mercifully comes to us in our woes, as God did for Paul here.

This section again is very dialogical and contains another group of Diatribe-type questions concerned with law, sin, goodness, and death (7:7, 13, 24). As far as law is concerned, Krister Stendahl, Christiaan Beker, and E. P. Sanders are correct in their arguments that "law" here applies to the law of Moses, but this thesis is only the beginning of the issue. Torah or law concerns a whole way of thinking and living, and Paul would hardy equate law with sin.[9] I do not here propose, a la Stendahl, to modernize Paul. To assist in the interpretation, I do suggest that Paul was a superb psychologist. If one substitutes the psychological designations of *ego*, *superego*, and *id* for the "I," the "law" and "sin" in Romans 7, the meaning should become fairly evident. For Paul, one more crucial element belonged in the equation—an element missing in much of modern psychology and pointing to the superiority of Pauline thinking. That element is the presence of the Holy Spirit. Paul clearly understood that human beings and particularly Christians were enmeshed in a life struggle. Christians (ego) are quite aware of God's demands (the superego); however, they are not completely freed from temptation by the evil one (sin), and they struggle to overcome temptation. They are in fact locked in a great war with evil (7:14–15). Indeed, they do not always succeed in overcoming temptations. At times they succumb to a deep sense of failure and are tempted to give up (7:24). But Christians are not like others, for they have another resource (the Holy Spirit) in their struggle. That resource enables them in the depth of their traumas to pray worshipfully: "Thank you, gracious God, that we can rely on you through Jesus Christ, our Lord!" (7:25). The worship life is not limited, then, to times of peace, quiet, wholeness, and joy. In life's deepest struggles, believers can cry out through the Holy Spirit to God, asking for forgiveness, for strength to overcome temptation, for guidance through the darkest night. Eventually such prayer turns to thanksgiving for Jesus and our ability to rely on him. Worship is part of all of life, not just one segment of it.

What then is Paul's evaluation of life and temptation? Christians should willingly accept the fact that at present they are *split persons* wanting to do God's will but not always doing it (7:25). Happily, that conclusion is not the end of the matter. Unfortunately, the ancient editors of Romans started a new chapter at this very strategic point in Paul's argument. Readers should not pause here, because the answer is given in the beginning of chapter 8. Despite our split personal responses, those who belong to Christ Jesus are not condemned! Besides, Christians have been introduced to a new way of life. Not only can they thank God (7:25) for their Lord, but they can face life in the Spirit, which frees them from the condemning power of the law (8:1-2).

When God sent Jesus, the law was not set aside. Rather, the law became fully incorporated into Jesus so that the Christian's "walk" (*halak*) is not now done to conform to rules but to the Spirit of God (8:3-4). Moreover, to allow the things of this world (flesh) or the requirements of the law to dominate one's thinking and life is to return to the old way of death. To focus one's life on the ways of the Spirit in response to God brings God's promised life of *shalom* (peace, 8:6). Yet having set out the way of the Spirit, Paul did not retreat to enunciate a new superficial way of life by issuing a new set of rules. Instead, he reminded his readers of their split nature—that, although they often conformed to the ways of death, their spirits were very much alive. In the resurrection of Christ Jesus the promise is that their lives would be transformed (8:10).

Their task, however, was to accept the mysterious leading of the Spirit and not return to their earlier slavery, for they were now children of God (8:14-15). Indeed, as God's children they had direct access to God through prayer. As precious children of God, the Spirit would even assist them in the articulation of their prayers when they were at a loss as to how to pray effectively. Paul's double use here of "Father" (*abba, ho pater*, 8:15; cf. Gal 4:6) in both Aramaic and Greek probably reflects his knowledge of Jesus' prayer instructions to his disciples (cf. Matt 6:9; Luke 11:2) and indicates just how important prayer was for Paul.

Paul did not want Christians to live with rose-tinted glasses as though their lives would not have problems, or prayer and the worship of God would keep them from suffering and persecution. It did not do so for Jesus! So Paul closed this section with both a promise and a warning—Christians are truly God's children and can expect their appropriate inheritance of life with Christ, but they must be willing to suffer with him (cf. Phil 1:29) to experience their ultimate goal of salvation or glorification (Rom 8:17). Worship, then, is offered through persecution and suffering as well as through good times and health. Worship glorifies God and Son Jesus in all situations of life, knowing God is present in the Spirit through those situations. The worshiper turns an eye to the future glory, not to the present gore.

Present Life Versus Future Glory (8:18-39)

To emphasize his previous point, Paul turned to compare the present life, where one's sanctification is being enacted, with the future glory that is to be expected. The present time is one of suffering, and one in which the entire created order is experiencing a state of meaninglessness, decay, and death. But the creation and the believers will not remain in that state, because a glorious future awaits not only the children of God but also all of creation.

Paul indicated that, in the meantime, not only believers but even the creation seems to be in a mode of prayerful "groaning," awaiting the expected hope (8:18–25). While in this state of frailty and confusion, Christians may not fully know how to pray. Paul again assured his readers that the Spirit understands the inner motivations of humans and knows how to make the pleas according to God's will even below the level of conscious articulation (8:26–27). Moreover, God is fully able to work out God's purposes in every situation because God knows who are the chosen and acknowledged people of faith and those who will ultimately gain the state of glory (8:28–30).

So, with a conviction of the superintending power of God in mind, Paul continued his argument against any possible opponents with a series of conclusive questions that can be summarized as: Who is able to stand against God and God's people in the light of God's ultimate gift of God's own Son? The answer of course is, "No one!" The follow-up question is: What can separate Christians from God's love? Again, the answer of course is, "Nothing" (8:31–39)! To which one is powerfully inclined to add "To God be the glory!" Worship is the only response when we recognize the power of God and the pervasiveness of God's love.

Israel's Future (9:1–11:36)

Romans 9–11 are not merely an excursus in Paul's argument. They are very integral to his thinking.[10] A major question must have bothered Paul in the light of his answer concerning God's superintendence of God's people. That issue was the question of Israel. After all, God had blessed Israel as God's children with special covenants and the inspired law, with divinely oriented worship and with promises concerning the future, to say nothing of Israel's history and the fact that Jesus came from them. The list was so overwhelming for Paul that he had to pause and praise God for this reality (9:1–5). For us, as with Paul, many experiences and thoughts in daily life give rise to opportunities for worship, not merely those in the planned routines of institutional worship. The worshiper has been given a twofold perspective: understanding both the present traumas and the future glory.

"Why? Why?" Paul must have asked himself repeatedly. Why did Israel not receive Christ? His only answer was that God was not the reason for their failure. The answer had to be in Israel itself. Not all descendants of Israel, he reasoned, could have been the chosen people, just like Esau who was a son of Isaac was not included (9:6–7). Then Paul launched into a long defense of his thesis by citing ideas from Isaiah 64:8 and Jeremiah 18:1–6 concerning the potter's role over the clay (Rom 9:20–21), as well as from Hosea concerning God's right to name whom he wished as his accepted children (Rom 9:25–26;

cf. Hos 1:9–10; 2:23) and from Isaiah concerning only a remnant being left and the coming of a rejected cornerstone (Rom 9:27–33; cf. Isa 10:20–23; 8:14; 28:16; cf. also Ps 118:22–23; Matt 21:42; Acts 4:11; 1 Pet 2:6–8). Paul reasoned with his head, but he could not give up the idea with his heart, and so he prayed for Israel's ultimate acceptance in spite of their misdirected zeal, lack of understanding, and failure to submit to God's way of gaining acceptance (10:1–3). In doing so, he modeled for us that prayer should be offered to God when we do not understand, when we think something should be in God's will but does not occur, or when people do not seem to accept the gospel. We should certainly pray for people and people groups who, as far as we can see, do not know or have not accepted the gospel.

This concern for his people turned Paul's attention to mission and the need for both confession with the mouth concerning Jesus' lordship *and* belief in the heart concerning Jesus' resurrection. That confession that "Jesus is Lord" (10:9) became the symbolic identifying mark of early Christianity during the period of persecution when Christians refused to confess "Caesar as Lord" and also declined to put a pinch of salt on Caesar's altar in worshipful homage. In the face of the current hostility from the enemies of Christians, and in anticipation of any coming persecution, Paul once again addressed the question of shame and honor. He indicated that believing in Jesus was not a mark of shame. Anyone relying on Jesus would be saved whether they were Jew or Gentile (10:11–13; cf. 1:16). So, in another Hellenistic-type set of "florilegium" prooftexts, or Jewish midrashic chain of verses, Paul asserted the God-given necessity of proclaiming the gospel to a disobedient world (10:14–21).

He could not give up on his concern for Israel, however. Had God rejected them? His response again was a firm negative (11:1). Even though the people were disobedient, Paul needed to provide a rationale for his life and the given situation. Just as with the people of Israel who in prior times had killed the prophets, Israel had continued to follow the this same pattern and had again become hardened, but as Elijah learned, God still had faithful ones (11:3–10). Yet was their stumbling the ultimate rejection of God? Paul could not agree with that scenario and issued another firm negative. Then what was his resolution to the issue? The stumbling permitted the salvation of the Gentiles (11:11). Like a wild olive branch the Gentiles replaced the natural olive branches (11:17). Paul viewed himself as an agent in accomplishing that grafting. His hope was that the coming of the Gentiles would spur the Jews to follow suit (11:13–14).

That Paul was increasingly disappointed in Israel's rejection goes without saying. But he warned the Gentiles not to follow the haughty pattern of the Jews in negating the proper responses to God and boasting about their status with God. God was fully capable of removing wild olive branches if God had done so with natural branches. Furthermore, God was quite capable of regrafting the natural branches into his tree of salvation (11:18–24). Since he believed firmly in God's ability to fulfill God's promises, Paul dreamed of and expected God's reinserting of Israel into the trunk of the olive tree (God's people) when the fullness of the Gentiles had been accomplished.

The questions remain: When could such a phenomenon occur? How does Paul's hope conform to the conditional nature of prophecy outlined in Jeremiah 18:7–10? The answers to those questions were not available either to Paul or to us today. What Paul did provide in his conclusion to this discussion on Israel was a little insight into his magnificent sense of God's mystery and a lofty doxological response (11:33–36). As mere human beings who worship the Creator and Redeemer, we must readily admit that we do not understand beforehand how God works; however, we can observe how the holy God is engaged in bringing together everything to fulfill the divine purposes in the world. With Paul we can confess, "To God be glory for ever. Amen" (11:36).

The Call to Transformation (12:1–15:13)

The last major section of Romans (12:1–15:21) may give the appearance of being a unrelated attachment until one reaches chapters 14 and 15. At that point it becomes clear that Paul has not deviated from his plan to set out for the Romans his perspectives on the gospel and their application to life. He began with a foundational appeal that would have sounded a little strange to his Hellenistic readers. Life surely was answerable to God, and perhaps it could be regarded as an element of worship or sacrifice (12:1); but Paul called for that worship to be opposed to conformity with the current *aion* or "age" (12:2). Paul's theology was based on his commitment to the concept of two ages or two domains. While he lived in the current domain, he did not advocate allegiance to it.

He called for transformation to another domain. Indeed, he even called for a transformation of the "mind" (*nous*, 12:3), an idea that would have sounded quite foreign to those with ancient philosophical leanings. Most parts of the person, they would have argued, could be sloughed off at death as the *nous* (mind/soul) ascended to the divine realm to be incorporated into the divine soul, but surely they would have thought that only those who were very base persons would really have distorted minds. Yet that was not Paul's view. He knew that all had sinned (cf. 3:23) and that such sinning had penetrated even to the way people thought (1:28). So for a person to be properly related to God in life and worship demanded total transformation—including the mind!

Transformed thinking, Paul counseled, would then lead to having a clear perception of who one is and what one's gifts are (12:4–8). As he indicated to the Corinthians, not everyone is blessed by God in the same way. Christians with varying gifts form one body of different members (cf. 1 Cor 12:12–26). Love is the basis for exercising all the gifts, and members should make love the foundation for the treatment of others (Rom 12:9; 13:8; cf. 1 Cor 13:1–13). Paul's contemporaries would have regarded the Christian way, as he outlined it, as a high moral standard since it involved not only the pursuit of harmony and the rejection of evil but also, surprisingly, the refusal to take vengeance, an uncommon perspective in that world. To know and worship God meant that one could trust God to carry out judgment (12:10–21).

Paul's discussion on the state and the honoring of officials has led to many inadequate interpretations, including the theory of the "divine right of kings" and the insistence by tyrants and dictators on total obedience (13:1–7). One needs to view this text in the context of the whole New Testament, beginning with Jesus' answer to the trick question posed to him concerning whether it was appropriate to pay taxes to Caesar. Jesus' answer was to give Caesar what belonged to him, but to give to God what belongs to God (Matt 22:21; Luke 20:25). Jesus quickly silenced the tricksters. Yet one must not suppose that Jesus' focus was on Caesar.

God demands ultimate loyalty in worship and life, while the state deserves what belongs to the state. Patently the state does not deserve the loyalty that belongs to God. In 1 Peter 2:17, we will find a clear distinction between honor, love, and fear. The first belongs to the political authorities, but not the other two. As he wrote Romans, Paul was convinced that the political authorities were just and he addressed the entire issue from such a perspective. Even so, he would never give the emperor the reverence due to God. The situation was very different by the time John wrote the Book of Revelation. Nevertheless, while he viewed Rome like a terrible beast, even John warned his readers of the consequences that would follow if they would take the sword against the Roman beast (Rev 13:9–10).

By citing some of the Decalogue laws pertaining to society, Paul reiterated his position that love was to be the driving principle of community life (13:8–10). In addition, he supported his view by placing the society issue in the context of an eschatological perspective. He challenged the Romans to live, not for worldly gratifications (*epithymias*), but with a sense of their final salvation in mind. He did so intriguingly, however, by using the liturgical language of their baptism and calling for them to "put on [*endysasthe*] the Lord Jesus Christ" (13:11–14). Thus, worship experiences provided language and experience to interpret daily life situations.

Somewhat reminiscent of the problems with the Corinthians in their lack of concern for other believers with weaker sensitivities in matters of worship and eating idol meats (1 Cor 8:1–22; 10:14–30), Paul turned to food issues and calendar matters related to worship. He called for the Roman Christians to be conscious of those who might be weak in their faith and to accept responsibility for their colleagues. Food for Paul was to be eaten with a sense of thanksgiving (*eucharistei*) to God. Passing judgment on others was not to be in our hands (Rom 14:1–12). The Christian's responsibility was to "walk in love." Modeling living in peace and building up one's neighbor was Paul's goal. Since God's kingdom was not constructed on the basis of earthly food laws and the like, the Christian ought to be very careful not to place a stumbling block in the way of another child of God or cause such a one to fall away from the faith (14:10–23). Instead, those with strong consciences should be considerate of those who have worship worries about what is unacceptable in the sight of God.

The goal of the Christian is to have one's mind conformed (*phronein*) to that of Christ Jesus (15:5; cf. Phil 2:5) so that the entire church might praise or glorify (*doxazete*) God (Rom 15:6). In concluding this section, Paul returned to his initial thesis of "to the Jew first and also to the Gentile" (1:16), and was himself lifted to a state of worshipful praise as he reflected on Christ's own model of becoming a servant to the circumcised (the Jews) and thereby validating God's promises to their ancestors while also opening the way for the Gentiles to praise God (15:7–9). In his wonderful praise of God, Paul constructed another of his fascinating set of Hellenistic "florilegium" prooftexts, or rabbinic chain of verses, drawn from the Psalms, Deuteronomy, and Isaiah about singing and praising God for the acceptance of the Gentiles (15:9–12). He closed this very practical section with a prayer of hope for their joy and peace in the power of the Holy Spirit (15:13). Devoting our minds to God's marvelous ways of working out salvation for us and for all who will believe leads to worship and prayer. Such worship often includes reciting familiar Bible passages that express our feelings much better than we can express them.

Paul's Summary, Plans, and Greetings (15:14–16:27)

The final chapter and a half (15:14–16:27) involve Paul's summarizing advice to the Romans, an outline of his plans to visit them, an expectation that they will support him in his forthcoming mission (*synanapausomai*, 15:32), and a long series of greetings establishing his relation to them through many other believers. He concluded this magnificent work with one of the great worship prayers in the Bible. In this doxology he prayed for their strength in the gospel that he had outlined and their understanding of the phenomenal fulfillment of God's mysterious promise concerning their acceptance as believing Gentiles.

WORSHIP SUMMARY

This letter to the Romans, with its encompassing view of salvation, challenges the Christian community to take seriously a holistic view of worship by rejecting both Gentile idolatry with its implications for unholy living (1:18–32) and common Jewish bifurcated worship and life practices involving verbal confessions without life commitments (2:1–3:8). Instead, it calls for a turning away from all sin (3:9–28) toward the way of faith (1:16–17; 3:27–31), exemplified by Abraham who walked with God (4:1–24). The life of faith is a continued worship response that is represented in our baptism and will be culminated in our glorification (5:1–6:23). God does not expect that Christians will achieve perfection on earth, but God does call us to recognize what God has done and to rely on the power of the Spirit in the process of transformation (7:4–8:39). Mere human views of believing in God and paltry mortal worship practices are no guarantee of authentic responses to God, or faithful worship. Jewish failures to recognize the coming of Christ serve as a forceful warning for Christians to evaluate their own lives (9:1–11:32). True worship of God implies the transformation of the worshiper's "mind," or foundational sense of meaning and purpose in life (12:1–2). This change would be evident in believers' worship practices and in the ways they treat others both in their personal relationships and in their public lives (13:3–15:6).

Paul closed with the lofty ascription: "To God alone who is wise may there be glory forever through Jesus Christ!" So with Paul and all of God's people, may we join them in our "Amen!"

QUESTIONS

1. Have you ever been ashamed of the gospel?
2. How does such a condition affect the way we worship?
3. Does our view of Paul's three stages of salvation in Romans have anything to do with the way we worship?
4. Or, with an understanding our own psyches in relation to God?
5. Or, with the way we live in our communities? Explain.

7

First Corinthians

Dealing with Frustrations while Building New Worshiping Communities[1]

Paul cared greatly for his children in the faith. Through his corres-
pondence with the Corinthians, he sought to lead them to appropriate
worship responses to the mysterious work of Christ on the cross so
that their pride and their perspectives on sex, food, marriage, legal
concerns, possessions, support of the poor, relationships with others,
activities in church, views of spiritual gifts, and future hopes would all
be modeled on the love of the Lord Jesus.

If you would ask average ministers of today if they would have welcomed
receiving an invitation to become the pastor or priest of the First Church of
Corinth, most would probably express great hesitancy at the very idea of being
a party to such a possibility. Who in their right mind would want to take on such
a parish? It was indeed loaded with problems that did not vanish, even after
good advice. Such a conclusion probably haunted even the apostle Paul.

Reflect for a moment on Paul's words in 1 Cor 16:5–12: "I will come to
you *after* I have gone through Macedonia. *I am* [indeed] *going through Macedonia*
[!] and *perchance* I will spend some time with you..." Then he added that he
hoped "to remain with [them] for a time...*if the Lord allows it.*" He continued,
"*If* [or when] Timothy comes, *see to it* that he is treated *tranquilly,*" reminding
them that Timothy "*is serving the Lord just as I am...Don't let anyone treat him*
with contempt." Moreover, Paul commented concerning Apollos, "*I strongly*
encouraged him to come to you...But it is not his desire now." Yet he also added that
Apollos indicated he would come "*when* he has *the opportunity.*" Why did Paul

100

write these words that I have placed in italics? What is your reaction to these summary statements of Paul? Do you have the strange feeling that none of the missionaries really wanted to visit the Corinthians? Bear in mind that later Paul indicated he did visit them, and it turned out to be a particularly "painful visit" for him (2 Cor 2:1). As we see here and many other places in Paul's letters, the early church was not born a perfect entity! It had all the warts and problems of any congregation—indeed, even more! It is hard to find the model of the New Testament church. As you will quickly discern, if you did not know already, those problems intensely affected the Corinthians in their worship.

Introducing the Corinthian Letters

Corinth was an unusual city in the Roman Empire. In the Greek period it had been the headquarters of the Achaean League in 196 B.C.E. It stood firmly against the advance of Rome.[2] As a result, when Rome finally captured Corinth in 146 B.C.E., the Romans, under Lucius Mummius, devastated and burned it. It stood in ruins for a hundred years until Julius Caesar recognized its strategic value, lying on the narrow isthmus between the Adriatic and Aegean Seas. Accordingly, in 44 B.C.E. he ordered it to be rebuilt. It became a fascinating new colonial city that attracted hoards of people from the empire, becoming the crossroads seaport between east and west.

While stevedores loaded and unloaded ships or hauled them over the narrow isthmus between the two ports of Lechaion and Cenchreae, the sailors fully enjoyed their shore leave. As a result, the city became notorious as a place of loose morals. Indeed, even Strabo, the Roman geographer and historian, after detailing some interesting notes on Corinth, stated sarcastically, "Not for every man is the voyage to Corinth!"[3]

Interestingly, the English word for dried grapes or raisins is *currants,* which is related to the name Corinth and testifies to the widespread presence of grapes and thus to wine in that region. Dionysus, the god of wine and partying, was well-known in Corinth. The religious orgies of women connected with this cult will be discussed further in 1 Corinthians 12–14.

Interpreting the Corinthian letters has become a vehicle for engendering various views and countless arguments concerning the roles of women in the church. But it is important to remember that the female "deacon," (*diakonon*) Phoebe (Rom 16:1),[4] was from none other than Cenchreae—the eastern port for Corinth.

Virtually all major scholars agree that Paul was the author of these letters. Some, however, might argue that 2 Corinthians is composed of more than one letter. For example, 6:14–7:1 is viewed as an inserted leaf from another letter, clearly breaking the flow of the surrounding thought patterns, and chapters 10–13 are said by some to be a different missive, since they are seen as harsher than the rest of the epistle.

Besides these minor issues, we must look at the nature and the amount of contact and correspondence that passed between Paul and the Corinthians. Paul's first visit there was probably between 51–53 C.E., since the inscription found at Delphi indicates that Gallio, the proconsul before whom Paul appeared (Acts 18:12–17), was appointed to that position by Claudius during his twenty-sixth acclamation (52–53 C.E.).[5] Senators were normally appointed to such posts for one year at a time, with a possible one-year renewal.

Our 1 Corinthians was obviously not the first letter that Paul wrote to these people, since he indicated that he wrote an earlier lost letter to them (see 1 Cor 5:9) which may have read much like the strange leaf in 2 Cor 6:14–7:1. In 1 Corinthians he indicated that people from Chloe's household had given him information about the church (1 Cor 1:11). Further, he noted (1 Cor 7:1) that he had received correspondence from the Corinthians themselves. That correspondence has not survived. He had also received a delegation from them (1 Cor 16:17).

Paul's Introduction (1:1–9)

This letter opens with some very important notations. Paul, who was called by the will of God to be an apostle or chosen missionary[6] (along with Sosthenes[7]) addressed the Corinthians not only as the "church" (*ekklesia*) of God but as a result of Christ's work in them he also designated them "sanctified" (*hegiasmenois*) and "saints" (*hagiois*)–basically, holy people (1 Cor 1:1–2).

Then Paul listed a series of outstanding qualities or characteristics about them, such as eloquent and knowledgeable, spiritually gifted, eschatologically (futuristically) oriented, and blameless (1:4–8). I suspect the average reader might wonder what an amazing group of Christians these Corinthians must have been. Are they the same Christians that he very soon took to task?

Why did Paul start in this way and almost immediately thereafter launch into a series of critiques concerning their actions? Was he being insincere and merely flowery in the typical way Hellenistic letters usually seem to open? Yet all one has to do is read the beginning of the Galatian letter to know that Paul can open a letter with absolute disgust. What then was his purpose when we know that 1 Corinthians is filled with criticisms? The reason seems to be that Paul was confident that God would see to it that the Corinthians would succeed in following Christ because "God is faithful" (1:9). But when one reads 2 Corinthians 13:2–4, it seems as if he had become a little exasperated with his converts! The indications that his task of spiritual formation with them would not be an easy one are already present in this first letter.

A Call to Unity (1:10–25)

In beginning the body of his letter, Paul emphasized that unity in Jesus was an essential element of an effective church (1 Cor 1:10). He knew that the closer the people moved in their reverence for Christ and his divine leadership, the closer they would be drawn to one another. Instead of a close-knit community of faith, however, he had learned that the Corinthians were involved in internal strife by choosing up sides as to whom they wanted to follow. Some could be referred to as the "founders" group, because they tried (poorly) to imitate Paul (their founding missionary). Others were the "logicians," apparently inspired by Apollos (a captivating speaker; see Acts 18:24); still others were "traditionalists" after Cephas/Peter (the outspoken leader of the original Twelve). Then there were the "super spiritualists" who probably prided themselves on their one-upmanship by choosing only the name of "Christ" (1 Cor 1:12).

While these designations probably did not represent actual schisms, the implications for tensions in patterns of worship would be apparent because, not only did Paul ask if Christ could be divided, he also placed before them a fundamental question concerning worship and their relationship to God: were they "baptized in the name of Paul?" (1:13). He reminded them that the focus of the gospel was not to be on superficial differences that elevate human separations. Instead, it should be on the mysterious power derived from the saving act of Christ on the cross (1:17), which enhances unity. The distinction is crucial because the driving force of one is *centrifugal* while the other is *centripetal.* Then, to highlight his point that neither the patterns of the Greeks nor of the Jews provide the answer, Paul dismissed the styles of the philosopher-sophists, the rabbinic-scribes and the logical-rhetoricians and indicated that the awesome foolishness of God is wiser than human thought, and the weakness of God is more powerful than human strength and action (1:20–25).

Human Weakness and Divine Power (1:26–3:3)

To respond properly to God in worship one must begin with an overwhelming sense that God is not merely human! Human achievement is not what counts. We as creatures are in reality merely nobodies in comparison to God (1:26–28). Boasting before God is impossible (1:29). The world does not understand this fact, because, if people would have understood, they would not have crucified Christ the Lord (2:8)! Humans and the evil powers may possess some knowledge; however, like the white witch in C. S. Lewis's *The Lion, the Witch, and the Wardrobe,* they do not understand the deeper "mysteries" of God, as Paul points out (2:6–7). Therefore, people did not comprehend the reality of the Lord, nor of authentic glory, and they crucified Christ (2:8).

So in addressing the Corinthians Paul countered that, although they had become Christians and in their commitment had left the ranks of the "unspiritual" (*psychichoi*), because their worship of God was actually immature (3:2) and had not translated into changed lives, they were basically still oriented to the ways of the world (or the "flesh"–*sarkinoi*). Paul's challenge to them, therefore, was to become people who would accept and follow the new orientation (*pnuematikoi*) to the ways of the Spirit of God (2:14–3:3).[8]

Call to Holiness (3:4–4:21)

Using illustrations from farming and the building trade, Paul sought to help the Corinthians understand that they were now to be a holy people–like a temple in which God's Spirit resided (3:16)–and that God was very serious about them evidencing the reality of holiness in their lives (3:6–23). Unfortunately, they had become big "wind-bags" (*physiousthe,* 4:6), judging others (4:2–5) and boasting about themselves and their possessions (4:7–8). Paul refuted their high-mindedness by indicating that he was a servant (3:5; 4:1), while also reminding them that he still had the important task of communicating God's hidden mysteries to them (4:1). Yet instead of regarding him as a crucial part of their worship and life–like a father whom they should imitate (4:14–16)–they and others treated him as if he were the final act in the arena, when the condemned people were thrown to the lions as the climactic event to show that they were the refuse of humanity (4:9–13).

Problems in the Church (5:1–6:20)

Having thus laid the foundation for a correct understanding that God should be the center of their lives and worship, Paul turned to deal with their problems. First, they had a highly embarrassing morality issue that resulted from a completely inappropriate sense of God's presence and leading in their church. Their arrogance as a community must have nauseated Paul, since he stressed that even the pagans would have been repulsed by the sexual activity of one of their men (5:1–2).[9] People frequently desire to separate the worship of God and practical life, but for Paul such a division was impossible. Not only did he command them to excommunicate the man (5:2–3), but he charged the Corinthians to assemble in a church worship meeting with his (Paul's) "spirit" present and in the name of Lord Jesus to hand over ("deliver," *paradounai*) the man "to Satan." From his background in the synagogue, he understood the nature of various patterns of discipline.[10] His intent, however, was not to use the church meetings and worship to condemn the pagan world. The outsiders were already being judged by God (5:12)! Instead, his interest was to establish the authenticity of worship and life in the church because he knew such was the basis for genuine spiritual power (5:9–13).

The early church clearly had a strong sense of the mysterious presence of God within the community of faith. This presence served as a powerful force against the devil. To be excluded from community worship and life would therefore open a person to the strangling powers of Satan. Such a person who had earlier experienced the protecting power of the Lord would be rendered spiritually helpless and would long for a return to the support of God and God's people (5:4–5). The goal was not punishment but restoration (cf. 2 Cor 2:5–11). Unfortunately, in the contemporary demythologizing world many churches witness an appalling lack of the unfathomable sense of God's supervising presence. Moreover, while severe and often unfair methods of punishment have been eliminated from much of church life, most discipline has likewise also disappeared. Any remaining discipline is vigorously threatened by contemporary litigation.

In summarizing this situation, Paul used a picture from Jewish worship practices associated with Passover. Before the celebration of the Seder, a house was to be cleansed of all the *hametz* (fermented grain or leaven) as a reminder of that special night when the people of Israel ate the pascal lamb and the unleavened bread of haste before being freed from Egyptian slavery. On that historic night the angel of the Lord "passed over" their homes and spared their "firstborn" (Exod. 13:3–10). The Corinthians, however, failed to recognize that they were living like unredeemed people and that their marvelous redeeming Passover Lamb (Jesus) had already been sacrificed for them. It was, therefore, long past the time when the leaven of their immorality should have been cleansed from their lives. They should have been living in the worship state of those who had thankfully been freed from the clutches of such sins (1 Cor 5:5–8).

Next Paul introduced the subject of lawsuits and called on the church to be responsible in helping members settle disputes among themselves. In a passing note that probably shocked these rich[11] Corinthians, he set the entire subject of being cheated and defrauded into an eschatological context by announcing that as God's holy and worshiping people (*hagioi*) they would be a crucial part of the eternal judgment process (6:2). Accordingly, they should become ready for their roles in the eternal court by dealing fairly with such minor earthly situations (6:4–8). Paul himself did not collect earthly possessions, but rather focused on worshiping or revering God, who in the self-giving Jesus had given him both the gifts of new life and ministry. On the other hand, the Corinthian desire for possessing and collecting "stuff" seemed to be highly inappropriate. The Corinthians' possessions had become a stumbling block. Perhaps the church today, and Christians especially in the Western world who are interested in developing a proper perspective on worship, could learn a valuable lesson from the apostle.

Paul returned at the end of chapter 6 to the morality and sin issues of the Corinthians. Not only did he condemn activities identified in the Decalogue, such as idolatry, adultery, and stealing (cf. Exod 20:3–4, 13–15), but he also included homosexuality, greediness, and drunkenness as sins, indicating that none of these activities would be acceptable in the kingdom of God (1 Cor 6:9–10). Frankly, the Corinthians needed to be made aware of what "transformation" implied (6:11). In a dialogical *coupe de grace* (which in newer translations is indicated by the Corinthians' views being placed in quotations marks), Paul achieved his goal by employing a method of argument similar to the Cynics and Stoics, and literally smashed the Corinthians' simplistic arguments.[12] When they tried to justify their loose living by reference to eating food, Paul declared that food and body alike would one day be destroyed (6:12–13)! In the process he also reminded them that the human body was the "sanctuary" (*naos*) of the Holy Spirit. They *did not own their bodies* because they belonged to the Lord! Therefore, worshiping and glorifying God was the task assigned to the body, not immoral behavior (6:18–20). He insisted that honoring God with proper responses should be the purpose of every Christian![13]

Answering the Church's Questions (7:1-40)

As Paul moved into chapter 7, he began to answer some questions the
Corinthians raised. Unfortunately, their letter (7:1) to him has not survived, so
we must glean what we can from Paul's answers in this epistle. This chapter
involves a collage of various matters pertaining to marriage and sexual concerns.
From his first set of answers, one would surmise that he was tackling an ascetic
issue in marriage. It is almost as though a married man came home from a
religious/worship meeting at which he had promised the Lord that to be holy
he would refrain from having sex with his wife. That announcement to his
wife probably created a major stir in the church, so Paul had to remind both
parties that sex is a legitimate part of marriage. Such a decision of abstaining
from sex should be a joint decision and should not be of indeterminate length.
Otherwise, Satan could tempt the parties (7:2-5). Then he quickly added that
his counsel on these matters was not legislative but appropriate advice since
he himself was not in need of such activity and he could wish more people
were like him (7:6).

Paul set the entire concern for sex and marriage in the context of one's
relationship to God and identified both the desire for marriage and for singleness
to be a "gift" (*charisma*, 7:7) from God! This text reminds me of two incidents.
When I was attending and speaking at a conference in a Roman Catholic
monastery, a priest of a rural parish pulled me aside and expressed his loneliness
at being without a wife; he glamorized what it would be like to be married. He
obviously did not have the gift of singleness, even though his church insisted on
it! The other event occurred when a senior, unmarried Protestant seminarian
came to me after interviewing with some executives of his denomination and
informed me that he was told: "Unless he would be married, they could not
place him in a parish." The ostensible view was that those churches would
not recognize the gift of singleness! Is it not fascinating how we determine the
ways of God for others?

Paul continued his exposition by indicating that whether one is circumcised
or uncircumcised, whether a slave or a free person, one should not bemoan
the fact of one's status because God understands and cares for the state of all
who are Christians (7:17-24). Of course, if the opportunity arose for a slave to
become free, it should be taken (7:21). But this recognition of understanding
one's state before God was then employed by Paul as a basis for indicating
the importance of having an eschatological (futuristic) perspective in life and
worship. Paul believed that the time was "very short" when the Lord would
return. Accordingly, for him whether one was unmarried or married was
not the primary issue. It was living and worshiping in the expectation of the
Lord's coming and the dissolution of the present world (7:25-31). One might
naturally ask: If Paul had known that two millennia would pass, would he have
given the same advice? One can merely respond that between the writing of 1
Thessalonians 4:15 and Philippians 1:21 Paul had already guessed that Christ

was not going to return before he died. Nevertheless, his belief in the importance of the Lord's coming did not change. He firmly lived and was ready to die with the conviction that Christ's *parousia* (coming presence) should be the basis for all of one's worship and life.

In the matter of entering into marriage, Paul's view was that a Christian should only marry another Christian (1 Cor 7:39). Clearly that view has caused great discontent in places such as Japan, where young Christian women have told me that there are just not enough Christian men available. But Paul believed intensely that marriage was a worshipful agreement between both the parties and God. What then of existing marriages between a Christian and a non-Christian? Paul's advice was not to break the marriage (7:12–13) because God could still be in it (7:14) and the Christian could be the agent for the non-Christian coming to Christ (7:16). But what if the non-Christian refused to continue in the marriage? Then the Christian is "not bound" since Christians are summoned to live in peace (7:15). This text provides an important clue to the way that Paul, a former rabbi, thought about issues of marriage, divorce, and remarriage.[14]

Christian Liberty (8:1–11:1)

In the next three chapters (8:1–11:1) Paul turned to the subject of Christian liberty in the overall context of pagan and Christian worship practices. Paul would have agreed whole-heartedly with the Corinthian Christians that an idol has no existence (8:4). But that agreement was about as far as he would go with them. They had been flaunting their knowledge (8:1) and had misused that knowledge to the detriment of others (8:9). Because they realized that idols were actually nothing, they had participated in pagan worship and ritual ceremonies at pagan temples (8:10). Their involvement had led others (who did not have their understanding) to participate willingly in the pagan worship ceremonies as well. As a result, these Corinthian Christians were, in essence, encouraging the others to sin ("a stumbling block" (*proskommma*) for others (8:9). Their freedom in matters of worship, therefore, caused grief to Paul and was to be regarded as a sin against Christ (8:12). Such a use of freedom was intolerable for Paul (8:13).

Having thus stated that he would not knowingly cause anyone to fall, he approached the subject of his own rights as an apostle (9:1–2). He was not afraid to defend his financial rights in ministry alongside those of others (such as Cephas) and to state his claim for support from the churches where he ministered (9:3–12). As a basis for his defense, he readily cited the pattern for the generous support of the worship leaders in the Old Testament—namely, the priesthood in the Temple (9:13). Having done so, he stoutly refused to exercise his rights because of his responsive indebtedness to Christ and his concern for the free acceptance of the gospel by non-Christians (9:12, 15–7). In this approach he set the financial example of how the missionary enterprise of the church should be conducted to those who had not heard or believed the gospel. Support should not be expected from those who had not yet encountered the mystery of Christ nor had developed a loyalty to the Lord. Support should come from those who had clearly experienced the forgiving grace of Christ and could express their gratitude by giving to God's work. Paul's primary obligation was his response to Christ for sharing the gospel with others (9:17–23). Their support of him was at that point *not his concern.* Indeed, it was just the opposite (9:15). He wanted them to discover the awesome Christ. Moreover, in that communication he was clearly aware that, he was responsible to heed his own message (9:24–27).

In something like stream-of-consciousness thinking, Paul turned to the issue of the sinful failures of the Israelites and their tragic worship in the desert. Using typological thinking patterns familiar to the rabbis (but strange to most of us), he described the exodus events in christological terms that could be translatable for his Greek Christian worshipers. The passing through the Red Sea becomes a baptism into Moses (10:2). The manna and water in the desert become "supernatural food and drink" that are not unlike the Lord's Supper (10:3–4). Indeed, the "Rock" from which the water emerged is identified as "Christ," which actually is said to follow them, not unlike the presence of the *shikinah* in the Tabernacle and the continuing presence of Christ among Christians (10:4).

The positive aspects of Paul's typology then give way to the negative, as the sins of Israel in the desert become the vehicle for him to deliver a set of shrill warnings to the Corinthians (10:5–6, 11–12). The Israelites' wilderness idolatry (e.g., the worship of the golden calf) and their immorality–note the direct linkage between the two[15]–led to the death of thousands (10:7–9; cf., for example, Exod 32:1–35 and Num 21:4–9; 25:1–18). Moreover, the grumbling of the Israelites must have seemed to Paul a vivid representation of the incessant complaints and troubles of the Corinthians. His warning to them was that they should not put Christ/the Lord to the test because they could be destroyed as the Israelites were in the desert (1 Cor 10:9–10). On the other hand, he counseled them that their reliable God was able to provide a means for overcoming any temptations or enticements to evil (10:13).

Participating in pagan rituals in their temples (cf. 8:10) was clearly outside permissible activity–forbidden for Christians. How could they in integrity participate in the Lord's Supper and also be partners to pagan worship or sacrificial meals? Of course, idols were nothing, but the demonic realm was real! The zealous God would not tolerate such syncretistic activity, especially in the case of mixing true worship and pseudo-worship (10:16–22). Well, then, what about eating in the home of a pagan friend who set food before them? Most of such food obviously came from pagan meat markets, associated with pagan temples or worship activity. Was eating in such a friendly setting also forbidden? The answer of Paul was clearly, "No!" If, however, the pagan emphasized the fact that the food was involved in a pagan worship ritual and therefore the meal was being treated as an offering to an idol, then it was patently inappropriate for the Christian to eat the food (10:23–28). The issue was not the Christian's conscience but the pagan's approach to the meal as an aspect of false worship. The way the Corinthians needed to approach any meal was to give thanks and glory to God for the food wherever they were. Thus, even eating was to be regarded by Christians as a worship experience before God and was not to be compromised (10:31)!

Church Worship Practices (11:2–14:39)

The next four chapters (11:2–14:39) are concerned directly with church worship practices. Paul began this section with instructions concerning the wearing of veils (namely adhering to a proper dress code for worship). The topic is definitely contextually driven both in time and dress patterns. In Jewish circles even today religious men wear head coverings in worship and elsewhere (*yarmulkes*), whereas the Greeks of Paul's day did not. The Romans, however, were hardly committed to follow Greek propriety customs. For example, while we do not have stone or pottery archaeological indications of men wearing veils in Corinth, we do have iconographic finds from elsewhere showing even a Roman emperor wearing a veil while worshiping.[16] Such a confusing style of worship would have struck the general Greek person as maddening.

In this section Paul does not discount a woman's right to "pray or prophesy [proclaim or preach]" publicly, but if a woman did so, she was duty bound to be properly attired. Likewise, Paul instructed men to be properly attired in worship—without a veil! The rationale that Paul gave—"the angels" (11:10)—may strike one as strange today. But as a former rabbi he regarded confusing patterns in society as arising from unnatural phenomena. There are two dimensions to approaching this statement. On the one hand, we recognize that the rabbis understood the good angels to be the guardians of order and integrity in matters pertaining to God. Veils on women were regarded as an acknowledgment that women were committed to the orders of creation and protection. Later, however, in the Book of Hebrews angels were described as having been demoted from authority (Heb 1:5–8), but they were still supposed to support Christians (1:14). On the other hand, the rabbis also reasoned that unruly angels who disobeyed the orders of creation, similar to the figures in Genesis 6:1–4, could pounce on unsuspecting women if they were not wearing the veil (the sign that they were under the authority of a protector). In the ancient story the unholy result of mixing "angelic" sperm with human genes was said to have resulted in the birth of strange creatures known as the *nephilim*, often translated as "giants" (Gen 6:4; cf. Num 13:33). Today we are hardly attracted to such views and are more concerned in protecting women and children from maniacs.

This text is both an affirmation of the equality of women before God and a recognition of the transition taking place within the perspectives of the church concerning service and the marriage relationship. Paul clearly articulated the idea of interdependence (1 Cor 11:11–12) already previewed in the beginning of the Bible: namely, not only that "woman was made for man" (cf. the Genesis 2 story), but that "man is born from woman" (the Genesis 3 story), even though she was subject to him as the result of the fall. The point is that the early stories themselves hinted that a movement toward equality would come, even though submission in marriage was practiced. What is fascinating to note is that the ultimate norms suggested by Paul (Gal 3:28) concerning the end of distinctions between race (Jew and Greek), economics (slave and free), and sex (male and female) are beginning to be realized in society but are often, ironically, more slowly recognized in many churches.

Many years ago when I was in law school, we had our first woman law student. Today there are women governors in politics, women executives in business, and women medical specialists; but in many churches we are still very hesitant about having women deacons and pastors or priests. Can only men lead us in worship? Can only men direct our response to God in prayer, preaching, and at the Lord's Table? I will certainly deal with the "silence" texts (1 Cor 14:34; cf. also 1 Tim 2:12) later in their contexts, but for the present this passage (11:2–14:39) should lead us to reflect on the nature of the eschatological movement inherent in the New Testament. Paul's overall purpose in these four chapters of 1 Corinthians is to recognize custom, good taste, and order, while at the same time affirming that equality in Christ is confirmed. He did not want the name of Christ to be desecrated by the inappropriate activity of Christians (1 Cor 11:16, 33; 14:33, 40). Such is clearly the purpose for his discussion on human hair and apparel.

His approach to the subject of the Lord's Supper in the next section is similar in its focus (11:17–34). The Corinthians had been using the Supper in a divisive manner. They were forming cliques for eating and not waiting for the others—probably the poor.[17] They were even getting drunk in their worship and fellowship meals. Was Paul ready to accept such activity as appropriate? Absolutely not! As far as he was concerned, they were a disgrace. He refused to grant that they had even celebrated the Lord's Supper (11:20–22).

As a result, they needed instruction concerning the true meaning of the Supper. Using a Greek rendering of the rabbinic terms for "receiving" and "delivering," or the authentic passing on of tradition (11:23; cf. 15:3),[18] Paul cited the establishment of the Lord's Supper by Jesus on the night he was betrayed as a triadic worship ceremony: Continue (1) to "do this" (*touto poieite*) (2) in "remembrance" (*anamnesin*), but only (3) "until he comes" (*achri hou elthe*). The Supper thus has three temporal dimensions: a present conduct, a looking back, and an expectation of termination in the future (11:24–26). All three elements should be evident in the celebration! Merely to look back (remember) truncates the Supper and turns the table into something akin to a gravestone in a cemetery. Moreover, Paul emphasized to his frivolous converts that the celebration of the Supper must not be entered lightheartedly because the Lord, who is the judge, understands human intentions or motivations (11:27–32; cf. Heb 4:12).

Paul clearly envisioned the Lord's Supper to be part of a community meal, not merely a segment in the middle or tacked on to the end of an otherwise jammed worship and preaching experience. The churches at that time were primarily small house churches. For the Supper, Paul had in mind a close community of brothers and sisters in Christ participating in a meal together. Community of authentic fellowship (*koinonia*) is the reason he instructed the Corinthians to wait for one another in the meal (1 Cor 11:33). If they could not do so, he counseled them to eat in their own homes (11:34). Today our churches are often much bigger. Although we have "pitch-in" or served suppers, they are seldom associated with the Lord's Supper (which has become very formalized in our settings). While we are not likely to return to the style of the early church, perhaps a concerted reflection on what the Supper was in Paul's time might engender some creativity into our later formalities and encourage us to recover some of the lost meaning in our worship celebration of the Supper. It also might help us to imagine what John had in mind when he thought about the marriage supper of the Lamb (cf. Rev 19:9)!

The next section involving speaking in tongues and the gifts of the Spirit has been the subject of both widespread controversy and comment. It is not the intent of this writer to discuss the legitimacy or illegitimacy of the phenomenon in contemporary churches, but rather to explicate the issues pertaining to worship as they are outlined in chapters 12–14 of this epistle and to attempt to set the discussion of Paul in its historical context. Doubtless, the early church experienced strange "spiritual" phenomena as the power of God confronted them (e.g., Acts 16:16–18; cf. 19:11–17; 20:9–12). Paul opened 1 Corinthians 12 with a recognition of this fact, telling them that formerly they had been seduced (*apagomenoi*) by inarticulate or senseless (*aphona*) idols who led or "moved" them (12:2). Whatever he meant by this statement, it reflects a different sense of the spirit realm than is usually recognized in the Western world today.

In that time and setting people acknowledged spiritual realities and were "moved" by spiritually demonic forces that the early church confronted openly. It is akin to some of my experiences in Africa when I encountered the power of God defeating the powers of the juju leaders and making them helpless even to use a plot of land where they previously practiced their magical rituals. The ghastly dances of the Baal worshipers in the biblical story of Elijah (1 Kgs 18:28–29) are a striking reminder to readers of the differences in such world perspectives. One only needs to read reports such as those of Strabo and others[19] concerning Bacchic and Dionysiac frenzied, orgiastic dances of women to thank God that we do not live in a context like that today.

Yet the former American Ku Klux Klan rituals were not far removed from the beastly actions of the Pythian priestesses of Dionysius. We must be constantly aware that in the contexts of the Bible the transforming powers of Christ were in an open battle with evil forces, and Christ's Spirit had not taken hold of human sensitivities. Moreover, humans can easily revert to the ways of the devil and respond as agents and instruments of those demonic forces so that the world periodically learns of human pogroms (annihilation efforts), such as those of the Nazis and Jews or the Tutsis and Hutus. The question remains: Do you realize that demonic forces can infect the church today?

Simply because many in the present-day Western world may not experience firsthand such spiritual phenomena does not mean that the demonic is nonexistent nor powerless. We can easily dismiss or demythologize the spiritual realm. With such thinking we truncate the powerful presence of the Holy Spirit. Indeed, many Christians today are afraid of any mention of the Holy Spirit unless "it" is institutionalized, strictly controlled, and relegated to the role of mere confessional words in worship. God, however, cannot be poured into the teacups of human thinking or controlled by mortal ingenuity. Paul knew that fact very well. The Spirit can easily render our verbal arguments or ritual formulas meaningless. Accordingly Paul challenged the Corinthians to realize that the foolishness of God is still wiser than human understanding (cf. 1 Cor 1:25). Moreover, he was very conscious of opposing spiritual forces when he wrote that no one by the Spirit could both assert, "Jesus be damned!' and also confess, "Jesus is Lord." He meant that the power of God was present in authentic worship and confession to exclude from effectiveness the power of inconsistent confessions of the opposing spiritual realm (12:3).

Clearly for Paul the various gifts that the Spirit freely bestows on humans were not designed and implemented by the human will but by God's grace (12:4–11). They are also not meant for our own personal satisfaction, but for the benefit of the entire Christian community (12:7). Since Christians are recipients and not determiners of the gifts, all differences of station in life are reduced to commonality, because there is only one Spirit and one baptism that unites us all in one body (12:12–3; cf. Eph 4:4–7). Notice the close connection between true worship and genuine community! But Paul was also quick to add that the unity of the body did not mean uniformity in the body. All Christians are not endowed with the same gifts any more than all parts of the human body are identical. His point was that all Christians–whatever their calling–contribute to the common purposes of God for the church and therefore there should be no sense of personal superiority among the members (1 Cor 12:14–26).

In listing the various gifts (12:8–10) and callings (12:28–30), however, Paul clearly recognized that some gifts were more strategic in fulfilling God's purposes in the world and therefore advised the Corinthians to desire from God the more useful gifts (12:31) for evangelism and edification without dismissing the legitimacy of the other gifts (14:2–25). In employing this tack on the subject Paul actually modeled for them how they should evidence the proper attitude toward the gifts and a Christlike perspective in all worship and life–namely, *the way of love* (12:31b–13:13)! In this sense love is not a gift but the God-given approach or spirit that should be inherent in the use of all the gifts. The Corinthians might be able to speak in tongues in the church (13:1), or have incredible powers of discernment and confidence in God (13:2), or even be willing to suffer martyrdom for Christ (13:3). Yet if they lacked genuine love (*agapē*), both their worship and contribution to the work of God would be meaningless (*outheis/ouden,* "nothing")! While motivation based on true love is effective and enduring, motivation based on all forms of seeking to fulfill one's desires or to gain personal recognition will fade into dimness and nonexistence when the permanence of eternity arrives (13:4–12).

Then Paul closed his great chapter on love with a triad that has become famous throughout the world of the church–"faith, hope, and love." One should understand that Paul used many triads to make his points in the epistles. He even used this same famous triad in a different order elsewhere (e.g., 1 Thess 1:3)[20] because in his expositions the last element of his triad often served for him as the focus of that discussion. In the first Thessalonian letter the focus is upon the need for hope! In this letter the focus is upon love. The Corinthians' self-interest in the matters of worship and "spirituality" prevented them from achieving maturity and truncated their church life.

The purpose of chapter 14 for Paul, therefore, was that of seeking to guide the Corinthians into maturity (1 Cor 14:20) concerning their speech patterns. Because they emphasized in their worship that speaking in tongues was a sign of their superior spiritual status as Christians, Paul took pains in demonstrating to them via a number of illustrations that their assumptions were completely erroneous. Clarity in communication (14:7–11) was crucial for edification (14:12).[21] Putting one's self into neutral during a worship service so that the tongue was left to jabber did not communicate intelligibly. While such a practice might benefit a person's self, it is hardly to be judged as edifying for the community since others are not able to join in the prayer or praise (14:13–17). Paul clearly did not denigrate the personal experience of speaking in tongues (14:18), but without further clarification he reduced its value in public worship to one-twentieth of 1 percent as compared to intelligible speaking (14:19).

The goal for Paul was once again order and appropriateness. Speaking in tongues in a worship meeting might well be recognized by other Christians as an indication of the presence of the Divine in the speaker's life, but for a visiting non-Christian it would be regarded as an indication of craziness in the church similar to some pagan forms of worship (14:23).[22] If, however, the exercise of speaking in tongues was accompanied by a clear communication of its meaning, it could be acceptable in worship. Even then only a minimum of such activity should be included and only if it were carefully regulated, because all communication is subject to the will of the communicator (14:26–32). God is not honored by confusion (14:33).

The second part of verse 33 brings us to a section that has been greatly debated. Complementarians (in contrast to egalitarians) have employed this so-called "silence" text (along with 1 Tim 2:9–14) to argue that the authoritarian view of the family should be applied to the church and to the exclusion of women from many ministerial roles in the church.[23] The problem, of course, is that verses 33–34 seem to fly in the face of the earlier direct statement of Paul that women can pray and prophesy in the worship service when properly attired

(1 Cor 11:5). Moreover, it relies on the law for its support, a strange pattern of argument for Paul who generally relies on Christ for his model. The text itself is enmeshed in a series of textual problems related to the displacement of these verses to a later point in some manuscripts. The result is that even a careful conservative scholar like Gordon Fee is unable to defend its authenticity here.[24] In addition, it is impossible to find any law in either early Jewish or Greek documents that would deny women the right to speak in public. There are, of course, rules and customs for women to be responsible to their husbands, but that is an entirely different matter and can be treated more at length in the sections on *Haustafeln* (early Hellenistic household codes) and in their Christian applications. As will be discussed later in texts such as Ephesians 5:21–6:9, it is extremely interesting to note that the entire pattern of Hellenistic family codes is strikingly modified as a result of the coming of Christ. The issue here then is not a matter of church order but of order in the family! If, therefore, family order impinges on the church, it is to be settled at home and not in the church! Whatever is done in the church and in its worship should be done decently and orderly (1 Cor 14:37–40).

The Resurrection (15:1–58)

The climax of 1 Corinthians comes in chapter 15, in which the issue of the resurrection is explicated. The resurrection is "the hinge point of Christianity," and this chapter is "one of the most strategic chapters in the New Testament."[25] Here again Paul employed the rabbinic terms for the authentic passing on of tradition ("receiving" and "delivering," cf. 11:23) to establish the centrality of Christ's resurrection and its historical reality as the basis for all of Christian worship and life (15:1–11). It would have been totally pointless (*kenon*, "empty") for Paul to preach or teach about Christ's power and for them to believe and so live if, as the Greeks generally thought, the soul was eternal and resurrection was impossible (15:12–14). Paul would then be an empty worshiper, a fraudulent proclaimer of the gospel, and Christian faith would be an incredibly tragic misunderstanding of reality (15:15–19). The resurrection of Christ, however, is the absolute assurance that God can deal with the results of all human sin (even from the very beginning; note the reference to Adam in 1 Cor 15:21–22), as well as the results of the starkness of mortality and death (15:21, 26) and the oppressive power structures of evil (15:24). The eschatological wheel of ultimate victory for God began to turn radically with the resurrection and the worship of the victorious Christ. It will not stop until everything is subjected to God (15:28).

How then, Paul asked, can the Corinthians participate in the strange pagan-like ritual of being baptized on behalf of the dead and still not believe in the resurrection? Likewise, he queried, how could he suffer so much for his proclamation of the resurrection, if it were impossible? Their strange worship rituals and his genuine suffering did not make any sense if there were no resurrection (15:29–32). Their Greek bifurcation of the real and phenomenal realms (separation of body and soul) needed to be radically reconstructed. As seeds die when sown so that a new plant emerges, the future immortal body, which will gain its new life because of the resurrection, will be directly connected to its former human/mortal nature. But it will have been mysteriously changed by God (15:42–50) in a split second, an *atomo* (the smallest segment of time, 15:52).[26] These former mortals will then not only praise and worship God because "Death is devoured in victory" but will also express their thanksgiving to God for that victory achieved through "our Lord Jesus Christ" (15:54–57). Anything one does in the name of the Lord, therefore, is never meaningless (*kenos*) and should result in confidence and a sense of assurance in life's work (15:58).

Concluding Notes (16:1–24)

Paul ended his letter with some intriguing brief notes involving a reminder that the Corinthians' worship meetings (on the first day of the week) needed to contain the elements of sacrificial *giving* for the poor (in this case the needy of Jerusalem, 16:1–4), and an encouragement to faithful and courageous *living* in love (16:13–14). As a sign of response to God and the authentic nature of the Christian community as a closely knit family of God, they should in their worship meetings greet each other with a holy kiss (*philemati hagio*, 16:20; cf. also Rom 16:16; 2 Cor 13:12; 1 Thess 5:26; 1 Pet 5:14), a practice that by the time of Justin Martyr (second century) apparently was associated closely with the Lord's Supper, or Eucharist, much like the "giving of peace" in some of our churches today.[27] The concept of the holy kiss in worship was later abandoned by the church, probably because of its sexual implications and possible misunderstandings as cultural perspectives changed.

Finally, in summarizing his letter he employed an interesting play on word sounds as he reemphasized two very different aspects of worship—namely, those who failed to love the Lord would be cursed (*anathema*), but faithful Christians instead would pray for the Lord's coming (*marana tha*). Paul's closing words here were a reiteration that he really did love them in Christ Jesus (16:22–24)!

WORSHIP SUMMARY

This letter to the Corinthians is one of Paul's most practical missives. At the heart of almost every issue—from dealing with conflict, to the spiritual nature of life, to confronting immorality and financial cheating, to marriage and divorce, to eating idol meats, to ministerial support, to the role of women in the church, to community meals and the Lord's Supper, to gifts of the Spirit and speaking in tongues, to the crucial subject of the resurrection—Paul is keenly aware that authentic worship is basic to a correct understanding of the church and the place of Christ in the life of Christians. Worship is not a mere tangential concern for Christianity. It is foundational to the lives of the believers and their responses to the living God!

QUESTIONS

1. Can you list six or seven problems that Paul encountered in Corinth?
2. Beside each one, can you indicate the worship dimensions involved?
3. How would you rate the Corinthians as worshipers?
4. Now, in your own mind, how do you and your church compare to the Corinthians?

8

Second Corinthians

Practicing Reconciliation among Worshipers

After writing 1 Corinthians (c. 54–55 C.E.), Paul made a painful visit (2 Cor 2:1) and wrote a letter of tears (2 Cor 2:4), which is now lost. Then, later, he seems to have gotten a good report concerning them from Titus (2 Cor 2:12–17; 7:5–6). This information apparently sparked Paul's desire to write 2 Corinthians. One question that remains concerns the seeming change of attitude in the final four chapters of 2 Corinthians. Did Paul receive another disturbing report concerning them? This question has raised a black hole of speculation into which we will not here plunge.

Emerging from the Spiritual Wilderness through Prayer (1:1–14)

The letter we know as Second Corinthians begins very differently than does First Corinthians. Instead of leveling incriminations at the Corinthian church, Paul was very conciliatory here. The word comfort (*paraklesis*) is constantly repeated in verses 3 through 7 of the first chapter. In verses 8 through 10, Paul indicated that he himself had been overwhelmed with despair from pressures in Asia and had almost lost hope. Yet he had come through the experience with a new confidence that the awesome God of the resurrection had been able to rescue him and give him a new sense of vitality.

It is important, however, to notice how crucial Paul regarded prayer (a central element of true worship) in the overcoming of his own sense of being undone. He mentioned not merely his own prayer life but the concerted prayers of the Corinthian church that were strategic in his battle with the problems in Asia (2 Cor 1:8, 11). For him God was obviously not some *deus absconditus* (a remote or absentee god), nor was prayer a mere formality in worship. God for Paul was the very personal director of his life. Prayer was the serious act of addressing a holy and caring Savior. This chapter, therefore, should serve as an encouragement to all Christians who go through periods when trials seem to be overwhelming, when God seems to be remote, and when worship seems to be meaningless. Even the great apostle to the Gentiles experienced wilderness periods in his life, but he learned again that it was not his wisdom but the powerful grace of God that would sustain him. He wanted the Corinthians to realize the strategic role of worship in life so that they would be prepared for the coming Day of the Lord and they would be able to thank God that they were able to support Paul during his period of being in the pit of desperation (1:12–14).

Paul's Difficult Commission (1:15–3:18)

After reviewing his plans, correspondence, painful visit with them (1:15–2:4; see the discussion above in the introduction to these letters), and their disciplining of the perverse man in his earlier letter (cf. 1 Cor 5:1–5),[1] Paul told them that he had accepted his difficult commission from Christ with total sincerity (2 Cor 2:17). He compared himself to a captive being led in a Roman triumphal march. Imagining the procession moving forward and sweet smelling flowers being thrown out to cover the stench of the streets, he viewed himself like the sweet smell of Christ for those "who are being saved." But for those in the world without Christ he knew the stench of death was intensified by his mission (2:14–16).

Continuing to articulate his mission and the Corinthians' role as his "personal letters of reference" concerning his effectiveness in that mission (3:2), Paul remembered the historic encounter of Moses with God on Mount Sinai. Following that unique worship experience, Moses descended from Sinai and delivered to Israel God's foundational recommendations for their society (the Decalogue) written on stone tablets. At that time the reflected glory of God even encompassed the face of Moses so that he was forced to cover his countenance to protect the Israelites from the derivative presence of God (3:7; cf. Exod 34:29–35).

Then Paul's mind focused on the reading of the Old Testament, which was at the core of synagogue worship. He concluded that the Jews did not understand the intentions of God in sending Jesus, so Paul likened their misunderstanding in reading the old texts to the veil put on Moses' face to hide God's reflected glory (2 Cor 3:7–14). When people's hearts are changed (3:3)[2] and they turn to the Lord, Paul understood the picture as completely altered. The veil is accordingly withdrawn and the believers begin through the Spirit to see God's glory more clearly and to evidence changing aspects of reflected glory in their own lives (3:16–18).

The Calling to Ministry (4:1–7:16)

The purpose of all persons called into ministry, such as preaching and leading in worship, therefore, is to function as servants (*douloi*) of the Lord because God again mysteriously calls forth, as in the first act of creation, the "light to shine out of the darkness" in humanity (4:1–6 cf. Gen 1:3). Basic to Christian worship, proclamation, and life is the church's confession of "Jesus as Lord" (2 Cor 4:5).[3] This confession brought Christians into direct conflict with Roman worship because of their stout refusal to acknowledge the claim, "Caesar is Lord." In contrast, Paul viewed the task of Christians to be one of *spreading* "the knowledge of the glory of God in the face of Jesus Christ" while the Lord enlightens the hearts of people who have been blinded by "the god of this present age" (*ho theos tou aionos toutou*, 2 Cor. 4:4–6). Paul was convinced that church leaders must never lead from a sense of superiority because, as he stressed, all Christians including himself were merely instruments like clay pots, holding a transcendent treasure that belongs only to God (4:7)! Thus the focus of the Christian life must be on the awesome power of God that raised Jesus from the dead. Only God can and will raise us. Only God offers divine grace to the world. Our appropriate response is worship, namely "thanksgiving" (*eucharistian*, 4:14–15), the name that some churches give to the Lord's Supper.

Paul acknowledged that Christian life and ministry are difficult. Nevertheless, because our strength does not vest in ourselves but in God, we must never give up. Christians should be a people who have gained an eschatological vision of a future glory and respond accordingly as they are motivated by a perspective of how the unfathomable, unseen, eternal realm impinges on our transient earthly world (4:16–18). To make his point absolutely transparent, Paul employed three salient illustrations. First, our human bodies are currently like fragile tents that can be devastated by a strong wind, but in the end we can expect to have an eternal building prepared by God (5:1). Second, when we die, we will not become some bodiless souls or spirits, as the Greek philosophers argued.[4] Instead, we will be "super-clothed" (*ependusasthai*) in better bodies with which to communicate and to express ourselves (5:2–5). Third, we should not be afraid that we will become homeless when we die because when we leave this earthly realm, we will be at home with the Lord.

Paul knew the Corinthians' past lives and their continuing attraction to views similar to those of other Greeks like the pre-Gnostics and Epicureans, who considered that the actions of the body did not affect their ultimate status. Paul understood that the Corinthians' lives and actions on earth were fully known to God. Therefore, he added a sobering word of warning for his children in the faith: that they would be rewarded according to their actions (5:6–10). Like many narcissistic people today, they were focused on self-interest and thought that Paul was a little crazy in his concern over integrity rather than positions in life (5:12–13).

For Paul, however, the love of Christ in his death and resurrection was the new motivating factor of his life, and the worship of God in Christ governed all of his actions (5:14–15). Indeed, he was absolutely convinced that people could be transformed by Christ and their responses and motivations in life could be thoroughly altered (5:17). Accordingly, he believed himself to be an ambassador of a new life through which Christ would reconcile the world to himself (5:19–20) and sinners would be made right with God (5:21). He was absolutely clear that all transformation results from God's work (5:18) and is the basis for true worship. In spite of any problems, conflicts, or difficulties in his life (6:4–5, 8–10), therefore, his divinely appointed task was to call people to the gracious God (6:1, 6–7), who would transform their lives (5:17), cancel their guilt (5:19), and remove any defilements in them (7:1).

Christian Finances (8:1–9:15)

Having reviewed his experiences with them in chapter 7, Paul turned in 8:1 to a crucial evidence of authentic worship—namely, their pattern of financial support for the needy. Although he had broached the matter briefly at the end of 1 Corinthians, he confronted the issue vigorously at this point, since he obviously did not believe that they took their responsibility for others seriously. He employed several arguments to convince them of their failure. First, he challenged them by the example of the Macedonians. Even though they were obviously under great stress from outside pressures (namely, "tribulations," *thlipseos*) and were themselves in deep poverty, nevertheless the Macedonians were extremely generous, even beyond what was reasonable (8:2–3). Second, to emphasize their responsibility, Paul cited the example of Jesus—who though he had at his disposal the riches of God, adopted the state of poverty for their benefit (8:9; cf. Phil 2:6–8). While he refused to issue a command to them concerning their financial responsibilities (2 Cor 8:8), his intent to use all his powers of persuasion is quite apparent. He called them to give not according to their lack but according to their bounty and in concern for equality (8:12–4). In a spirit of conciliation, he indicated that while such a reminder was probably unnecessary, he nevertheless included it so that neither he nor they would be embarrassed in the future (9:1–5). He recalled for them the maxim, "What one sows is what one can expect to reap," and added that giving should not be a matter of grief (*lupes*) or obligation (*anagkes*), because the acceptable giver is "cheerful," or one who has no regrets (*hilaron*, 9:7). Indicating that he considered the entire subject to be within the context of authentic worship, Paul closed his discussion on giving with an overpowering statement of thanksgiving—"Thanks be to God for his superlatively unutterable [*anekdiegeto*] gift!" (9:15).

Paul's Self-defense (10:1–12:13)

As indicated in the introduction, at chapter 10 a significant change in attitude seems to appear. It is as though Paul had received another report concerning the Corinthian church and returned to the task of defending himself. Apparently, some self-styled "super-false apostles" (11:5, 13; 12:11) had confused the Corinthians about Paul's "weaknesses" (10:1) and paraded their own proud authority (10:12). In response, Paul reminded the Corinthians that boasting should focus on the Lord (10:17); nevertheless, he agreed to enter into their foolish debate (11:1, 16). Scarcely into his boasting, however, Paul suddenly realized the absolute stupidity of such a style of argument (11:23), promptly reversed his strategy, and began to list his weaknesses and troubles (11:23–33). Even in speaking about his spiritual experiences, he merely selected an encounter of being lifted in the spirit to the "third heaven," an event that he described in such general terms that it would hardly have engendered the awe of his critics (12:2–5). Moreover, he quickly added the strange notation concerning his "thorn in the flesh," which reemphasized his weakness.

Paul even admitted that he prayed three times (the number representing encountering God), but he was not given the relief he desired. Rather, he was instructed that God's "grace was adequate [*arkei*]" for his needs (12:9). The point is that even Paul had to learn a practical worship lesson that Christ modeled for his followers in the garden when he prayed for the cup of suffering to be removed from him (cf. Matt 26:39). Prayer is not a means for manipulating God! Prayer is a means of conversing with the Lord, sharing our concerns, and of learning God's will for our lives as well as those about whom we are concerned. This understanding is critical for true worship!

Paul's Plans (12:14–13:13)

Paul ended this epistle with a series of warnings that he was about to return to them a third time (2 Cor 12:14; 13:1, 10) and hoped that they and their fraudulent teachers (12:13) would examine themselves and correct their actions (12:20–21; 13:5, 11). Otherwise, next time when he came, he would not spare them the proof (whatever it might have been) of his apostolic authority (13:2–4)!

WORSHIP SUMMARY

Second Corinthians is a very revealing epistle, since it provides insight into Paul's own struggles in life and his ability to worship God in Christ before, during, and following his despair and his painful encounters with his Corinthian children. His constant goal in ministry was to be a caring ambassador for Christ. He did not focus his letter on judgment but on reconciliation and restoration of deviant believers. He viewed his work as the removal of the concealing veil from the hearts and lives of deficient worshipers so that they might understand the transitional nature of human life and worship on earth. While the Corinthians forcefully challenged him to boast about his relationship with God and his spiritual experiences in worship, he turned their foolish challenge on its head and proclaimed instead his weaknesses and sufferings. Like a caring parent, he called them to compare their lives to that of Jesus and summoned them to caring for others.

In a concluding summation, he instructed the church once again (see 2 Cor 16:29) to demonstrate a community spirit of love and peace by greeting one another with a "holy kiss" (2 Cor 13:12; cf. 1 Cor 16:20) and receive the greetings of "the saints"–other Christians–everywhere. He closed his letter with the "triadic Trinitarian benediction" that even today is used repeatedly in Christian worship services throughout the world: the grace (*charis*) of the Lord Jesus, the love (*agape*) of God, and the companionship (*koinonia*) of the Holy Spirit (2 Cor 13:14).[5] May these quality gifts of the triune God continue to mark the worship of our churches everywhere today!

QUESTION

1. If you were given the opportunity of teaching two lessons on transforming worship for the Corinthians, what would be the focus of each of those lessons? Explain.
2. What is the relationship between worship and reconciliation?

9

Galatians

Freeing the Community for Worship and Life[1]

In this electrifying letter to the Galatians, Paul cursed anyone who tried to establish the legitimacy of acceptance by God through human effort, worship rites such as circumcision, or works of the law. He forcefully declared faith as the only basis for worship and the authentic route of responding to the awesome death and resurrection of Jesus and the leading of the Holy Spirit in the lives of Christians.

The Book of Galatians serves as the royal ruby in the diamond crown of the Pauline letters. I believe it to be a foundational work in building a Christian understanding of salvation and worship. It stands like the believer's *Magna Carta* on Christian freedom.[2] Martin Luther called it his "Katerina," comparing it to his beloved wife Katerina von Bora.[3] No other book in the New Testament has had a more profound effect on me, with the exception of the Gospel of John, than this little jewel of Paul. My "history" with this letter goes back to a time before I was born when my great grandparents were persecuted as Baptists by the Lutherans in Germany and moved to Russia, and then to Canada after their encounters with the Orthodox. Freedom to worship was their goal, and they found it in the western prairies of Alberta.

I was born into a commitment to liberty and a sense of freedom for all people before God. This sense was enhanced greatly when I taught in Israel and found a Jewish prayer book in one my jaunts to the bookstores. As I perused its pages, I was stunned to discover that the old Jewish prayer was still being published: "Blessed art thou, Lord our God, King of the Universe who hast not made me a heathen...who hast not made me a slave...who hast not made me a woman." A footnote was added that the women should pray "...who hast made me according to thy will."[4]

What is exceedingly significant for our notice here is that the order is the same as Paul's great affirmation in Galatians concerning the end of such distinctions (Gal 3:28). That discovery in the prayer book hit me like a powerful bomb as I returned to my study after revisiting the famous Western Wall (formerly called the "Wailing Wall"), where the women are still separated from the men. That reality seared my consciousness concerning the crucial nature of this book for all Christians. It provides a key to the correct understanding of Christianity. How we pray provides a microscopic glimpse into our views of God and worship. Failure to perceive this fact can mean that the worshiper may have a truncated view of God, as well as of both Christian faith and worship.

Introduction to Galatians

For the Book of Galatians, the authorship question raises no concern. If Paul wrote anything, scholarship is unanimous that he definitely wrote Galatians! Moreover, while he did not actually pen all the words (since he used an *amanuensis,* or scribe), he obviously did pick up the pen to write the authentication for the letter (6:11). The matter of dating, however, has been debated. Some scholars would place it in the middle 50s of the first Christian century, at about the same time as the writing of Romans. My opinion is that it was the first of the Pauline letters, written in the late 40s, in which Paul worked out the argument against the necessity of the Gentiles being circumcised to be recognized as Christians–an argument later used at the Jerusalem Conference. (See Acts 15.) As far as the recipients are concerned, I am not persuaded by the arguments of advocates for a north Galatian theory. I consider myself an American even though I was born a Canadian. I find no reason why Phrygians and others who lived in the Roman province of Galatia could not be called Galatians (Gal 1:2; 3:1). Modern attempts at reconstructing Paul's travels are basically arguments from silence.

Opening Charges against the Galatians (1:1–2:20)

Galatians is one of the most intense documents in the New Testament. It immediately gives the reader the impression that the very existence of the gospel was at stake, and Paul was ready to defend it with his life. If the Christian worshiper needs a lesson in what is really "worth dying for," then this letter is the exemplar *par excellence!* There is little doubt in this epistle about what Paul believed. He was ready to take on the entire church authority base (James, Cephas, and John, cf. 2:9) to rescue the gospel from misconception. The study of this book should be exceedingly high on the list of every Christian worshiper.

After a fairly normal Christian epistolary address, which hardly hinted at what was coming, Paul immediately launched into a lofty worshipful ascription to God and Jesus (1:3–5). Without even the slightest clue of a customary note of gratitude for his recipients, Paul then turned both barrels of an attacking rebuke on the Galatians, beginning with what in English would be something like, "I am stunned" (1:6). The charge that followed was brutal, as Paul condemned them for becoming turncoats, or deserters (*metatithesthe*), from Christ's amazing way of grace (*chariti*). Indeed, he was dumbfounded that it was happening so quickly (*tacheos*). He was so completely distressed that they had followed the direction of pseudo-preachers in adopting a false gospel that he issued the strongest curse of damnation (*anathema*) on *anyone*–even a heavenly angel, or himself–who would dare to preach such a false message. Protecting the authentic (received) tradition concerning Christ was so crucial for him that he actually reissued the *anathema* curse a second time (1:8–9).

We would misunderstand Galatians if we assumed that Paul's goal in advocating such a strong position was self-serving. As he clearly articulated in 1:10, he was not seeking to please either God or any human. His goal was faithful service to Christ. In pursuing that goal, he briefly reviewed his own previous life as a superior Jewish worshiper, scholar, and leader (1:13–14). Yet, despite that, he then became a transformed proclaimer of the gospel–one whom God personally called and instructed through an awesome direct revelation from Jesus Christ (1:11–12, 15–17). On the basis of that divine appointment, Paul was completely unwilling to settle for any compromise in the grace of the gospel and its far-reaching implications for all people, including the Gentiles, even if that meant confronting and condemning the so-called pillars of the church (1:18–2:14). He had learned that external matters in religious practice, such as circumcision and what he called "works of the law" (*ergon nomou*), could hardly justify (*ou dikaiothesetai*) anyone with God (2:16). The only adequate response to the work of Christ for any human being–including Jews (2:14–15)–had to be "living by faith" in/of "the Son of God" (*tou huiou tou theou*), who not only "loved" (*agapesantos*) us but died or "delivered" (*paradontos*) himself for us that we might be accepted by God (2:20). This atoning or substitute work of Christ for humanity is foundational for Paul's worship and life, which he would not nullify or dismiss for anything!

Self-evident Questions Calling to Faith (3:1–22)

It was obvious to Paul, however, that the Galatians had acted stupidly by casting off the basis of their faith (3:1). So using the style of the Cynic and Stoic Diatribe, he launched into a stern series of self-evident questions that proved that someone had hooked the Galatians (*ebaskanen*) in a crazy spell (3:14). The result was that they were constructing a worship pattern in a dream world and had lost all sense: (1) of the role of the Spirit; (2) of the mysterious or miraculous nature of divine action; (3) of their hopeless, attempts at gaining acceptance; and (4) of the significance of genuine faith (3:5).

They needed immediate serious instruction in matters of worship and life. The brilliant rabbi, Paul, had no difficulty meeting the challenge. If they wanted to be Jews, they had some lessons to learn. First, the genuine children of Abraham needed to be children of faith like Abraham (3:6–9). Second, if they thought that obedience to the law would make them acceptable to God, they should have understood that *total* obedience was required, or else they would be cursed. Christ actually nullified the curse by accepting the curse himself in the crucifixion. So, faith was now the only way to acceptance by God (3:10–14).

Third, if they had understood the nature of law (including Jewish ritual) and its relationship to the covenant with Abraham, they would have realized that law was instituted long after the covenant was installed.[5] Further, the covenant could not be changed after the death of one of the parties. Moreover, the relationship to Abraham, with its blessings in the covenant, was built on a promise and not on keeping a series of laws (3:15–18).

Fourth, according to rabbinic understanding, angels[6] delivered the law to humans, and its role was to serve as a means to judge people as sinners. Conversely, God's ultimate message of new life came directly from God's Son, who made it possible to be accepted by God through faith (3:19–22). All of these arguments should have convinced the Galatians to understand that they, like the rabbis, had raised the law virtually to the level of being *sui generis* with (or "a replacement for") God. But law is not God any more than the Christian's Bible is God. Both are a means to lead us as humans to God. Here confusion often arises. Neither the law nor the Bible is worthy of *worship*! That honor belongs *only* to God!

Christ and History (3:23–4:7)

What comes next in the text is the key to Galatians and to Pauline thinking.[7] In this section Paul divided history into two segments. The first was "before" (*pro*) the coming of the new faith (*pistin*), when humans were subject to the protective custody of the guardian (*paidagogos*), which was the law (3:23–24). The second period began when God acted to bring together in time a confluence of countless realities (*pleroma tou chronou*) in preparation for the coming of Christ (4:4). In the context of this unique event in history (the coming of Jesus), a new community of faith in Christ (*pisteos en christo*) was born, the members of which are called children of God (*huioi theou*, 3:26).

The identifying worship symbol of the members in this new community is their "baptism into Christ" (*eis christon ebaptisthete*, 3:27). Using a clothing image related to early Christian baptism, Paul indicated that those who have thus "put on" (*enedysasthe*) Christ are clearly united with one another in this new community. In it, distinctions of race (Jew-Greek), economic status (slave-free), and sex (male-female, 3:27–28) have ceased. Such is the basic thesis of the new community, the church. Unfortunately, important questions still remain today. Have we as Christians actually recognized the *full* implications of our identifying symbol in Christ? Do we understand that *we are all* adopted children (*huiothesian*) into this new community (4:5)? Or do we practice our identifying religious worship rite and then refuse to accept the significance of that rite?

Those questions do not end the inquiry. In this key passage Paul also pointed to a very important issue for worship itself when he recalled a word that probably goes back to Jesus! That very precious Aramaic word that he repeated was "*Abba*" ("Father," 4:6; see also Rom 8:15). As a Jewish rabbi, his former view of God had undoubtedly been that God was ultimately transcendent. Like his contemporaries, he probably had ceased even to use the *tetragrammaton* (the four letter Hebrew word *YHWH*, "LORD") for God, fearing the taking of it in vain. After becoming a Christian, his understanding changed. Paul had learned, as others before him had, to call God by the intimate designation of "Father."[8] Do we as Christians now realize that, in calling God "Father" in worship, we are *all* brothers and sisters of the same Father God (Gal 4:6)? So the questions must continue to be asked of us: How does our worship affect our lives? Are we still in bondage to the old ways of the world and making distinctions—or are we living, relating, and acting as authentic children of God, God's family (4:7)?

Inconsistent Living (4:8–5:21)

Paul challenged the Galatians' inconsistency in their lives. Specifically, they remained in bondage to the old ways because they continued honoring gods and demonic spirits that were not God, and persisted in celebrating pagan worship days. As with many today, their lives revealed a syncretism that mixed their worship of God in Christ and their commitments derived from their national and cultural heritages. Such a pattern of life distressed Paul (4:8–11). He could hardly understand their copying false teachers and their criticism of him and his work (4:12–20). So he used a rabbinic style of contrast to compare the silly Galatians to children of the slave woman, Hagar, rather than to the promised descendants of Sarah, the free wife of Abraham. Even though this type of argument may seem very strange to us today, it would have been quite logical for the rabbis and their successors in the schools of the Jewish Tannaim (4:21–31).

Freedom was the clarion call of Paul against his Judaizing opponents, but freedom did not mean license or libertinism (5:1; cf. 1 Cor 6:12–20). He was dead set against making any religious symbol, such as circumcision, a means to acceptance by God (Gal 5:2–12). In other words, Paul was not oriented to worship rites for their own sake. Indeed, he suggested that the false teachers who proclaimed the absolute necessity of circumcision should go further and castrate (*apokopsontai*) themselves. For Paul, worship rites were pointers to the inner life of the worshiper. The real test was to "walk" (*paripateite*)[9] "by the Spirit" (*pneumati*), which *excluded* submitting to the ways "of the world" (*sarkos*, 5:16).

The Authentic Walk with God (5:22–6:18)

In studying the closing *paraenetic* (ethical) sections of Paul's letters, it is imperative for the reader to be very cautious and *not interpret* the apostle as handing out a new set of legal prescriptions similar to the Jewish laws. Instead, in his ethical sections he identified the marks of authentic "walking" with God by the Spirit (5:22–24). When the Torah is correctly interpreted, then the same hermeneutical principle applies to the Old Testament laws. So, even though he had bitterly condemned the Judaizers, Paul was still able to conclude his ethical instructions with the amazing statement: "To all who follow this religious pattern, may peace and mercy be upon them; namely, upon the Israel of God" (6:16). His instructions are not a new set of rules! Instead, they were an indication of an authentic relationship to God through Christ. But human beings seem to prefer "rules" rather than a relationship to God–the Ruler!

Paul closed this emotionally charged letter without any of his typical greetings. Rather, he pointedly reminded the Galatians not to boast about their earthly rites–such as circumcision. The rites (even baptism) are not some "fire insurance" instruments for avoiding hell and its conflagration. They are important indicators of a new life. Therefore, they are not means of boasting, since glory belongs to the crucified Lord Jesus Christ, and what counts now is newness in Christ (6:13–15). Moreover, he warned them and their "stupid" colleagues (3:1)–in a final assault on their views (6:17)–that they should cease troubling him. Since they were so concerned about bodily symbols, they should take note that his body, like that of Jesus, bore the marks of suffering for God.

WORSHIP SUMMARY

To recognized the importance of this strategic letter of Paul is absolutely crucial for Christians. In it Paul minced no words as he issued several terrifying anathemas against all Christian interpreters who would install human activity and worship rites such as circumcision as the means to salvation. The gospel is not about what the church or Christian worshipers do. It is about what God in Christ has done (and continues to do) in the course of world history. According to Paul, all who put their focus for Christian salvation on human effort, such as laws and worship rituals, belong to the old covenant and are to be condemned! Yet his attack is not leveled at authentic, concerned human effort for others or at the importance of worship. Both are affirmed and encouraged as responses to what God has done in Christ for us. They are, however, not means to status with God! They are the results of relationship, not the means to relationship.

Well, in all honesty, where are you, dear reader? Is your commitment to rules and worship rites? Or is it to the Ruler? Is your commitment actually to the God in Christ whom we worship? If you have understood Paul in Galatians, you will know whether you should receive his blessing or his condemnation.

QUESTIONS

1. What do you consider to be the greatest danger to freedom in your contemporary worship and life?
2. What do you consider to be the greatest need today for achieving responsible worship? How do your concerns differ from Paul's concerns with the Galatians? Why or how?

10

Ephesians

A Handbook for Worshiping and Living as a Unified Community of the Spirit[1]

The letter to the Ephesians stands as a remarkable handbook of spiritual formation and worship in which Paul described an authentic relationship with God in Christ while rejecting all evil patterns of life. He defined the nature of genuine community spirituality, authentic new Christian morality, and appropriate family relationships as aspects of mature responses to God, all bathed in the context of prayer and worship.

The letter to the Ephesians gives the impression of being like a great poetical work written in free verse. Despite its rather elongated Greek sentence structure, in which the reader is at times led through a maze of unending connectives, the work can draw one to the very boundaries at which the Divine meets the human in a magnificent challenge concerning spiritual formation. To traverse its paragraphs of picturesque reflection with care can be a spiritual journey of significant personal growth and insight for the Christian worshiper.

Introduction to Ephesians

Ephesians has been a battleground for scholars. If one bases one's view of Pauline authorship on the style of Galatians, as do F. C. Baur and his Tübingen associates,[2] one would tentatively conclude that Paul could not have written this letter. If one does not confine Paul and his various secretaries (for example, see Rom 16:22) to a singular pattern of writing, then one should be willing to conclude otherwise.[3] My suggestion concerning the secretary (*amanuensis*) for Ephesians is that this person could have been someone who thought like Luke, because the imagery used of breaking down the barrier (*mesotoichon tou phragmou*, "middle wall," Eph 2:14) is not unlike the "warning wall" separating Gentiles from Jews in the Jerusalem Temple. Temple imagery is very strategic to Luke's thinking in both his Gospel and Acts. Moreover, the only place that the concept of "filled with the Spirit" (*plerousthe en pneumati*) occurs outside of Luke's writings in the New Testament appears in Ephesians 5:18 (see my discussions concerning these issues in both Luke and Acts).

The epistle is obviously a circular letter, since the words *en Ephesso* ("in Ephesus") are missing from our most reliable Greek manuscripts (1:1). The absence of a series of personal greetings at the end also testifies to its circular nature, since if the letter had been particularly addressed to the Christians in Ephesus,[4] it would be strange that such greetings would be missing at the end of a letter sent to a church where Paul had spent so much time.

Some scholars have argued that the entire cosmological framework of this epistle is non-Pauline. Indeed, Schlier, Schmithals, and others argued that the cosmological framework is Gnostic. The basis for that argument is that in Ephesians the devil is viewed as "the prince of the power of the air" (*ton archonta tes exousias tou aeros*). In Gnostic thinking, the evil powers resided in the lower heavens. To enter the ultimate spiritual realm, the *pleroma* (the "fullness" or heaven), an elect one had to pass through the realm of the planets and strip off the elements of the created order in a kind of purging not unlike the concept of Purgatory advocated by some churches even today.[5]

The letter to the Ephesians has sometimes been regarded as a baptismal sermon or liturgical rationale for that rite. Although some hints point in that direction, it seems clearer to use that line of argument with respect to Colossians. Ephesians, instead, appears to be not unlike a catechetical manual in which believers are instructed in their development as Christians.[6] But the letter is more than a manual. It is a work that challenges even the mature worshiper to grow in the divine-human mystery of Christ (1:9) and in the believer's relationship to Christ's "body," the church.

Opening Theological Argument (1:1–14)

After employing a brief form of the standard Christian address and greeting to a letter, Paul[7] plunged into the main part of the epistle, beginning with what is generally regarded as one of the most compact and intense theological arguments in the New Testament. He initiated this section with a liturgical formula "Blessed be God" (1:3), which he undoubtedly learned in his Jewish faith, probably even from his youth. He altered the formula radically by adding the "Lord Jesus Christ" and by his redefined eschatological perspective. That perspective concerned the realized nature of the Christian's current state and the future "blessings" being intimately attached to the experience of one's relationship to God and the divine realm through Christ (1:3).

Moreover, Paul emphasized the centrality of God's abundant graciousness in introducing Christians to the salvation process and the fact that praise (*epainon,* a significant aspect of worship) must not be directed to human achievement or ingenuity but only to God and God's glory (1:6). Accordingly, Paul highlighted the crucial premise that it was God who in love "chose" (*exelexato*) his followers (1:4), in a manner not unlike the way God chose Abraham, and Jesus chose his disciples. The purpose of that choice was not determined by humans but by God's will (*thelematos,* 1:5) to fulfill the divine goal God established from the beginning (1:4). That purpose was the freeing (*apolytrosin,* "redemption") of humans from the bondage of their own sins (*parapatomaton,* "wrongdoings," 1:7). This divine purpose was integral to what Paul identified as the great "mystery" of our faith—namely, God's desire to bring a sense of unity to all creation "in Christ" (1:9–10).

The mention of "in Christ" should alert the reader to one of the most significant concepts in Paul, namely his "Christ mysticism." As Sydney Cave reflected many years ago, it is not a mysticism built on a desire to escape the world and be alone, like Simeon Stylites, who lived for years away from people on the top of a pole, or like hermits who removed themselves to desert settings to be away from human influences and temptations. Paul's mysticism was community-oriented. For him, being "in Christ" meant being in the body of Christ, experiencing Christ together in worship and life.[8] Notice what follows: in Christ, God's purposes are accomplished (1:11); in him, Christians have hope and live to his praise and glory (1:12); in him, we have heard the true word; in him, we believed; and in him, we are sealed with the Holy Spirit (1:13). All aspects of the mystical relationship in Christ provide Christians with their knowledge of salvation, the assurance of their destinies with God, and their rationale for worship. Accordingly, all are directed as a community (the church) to praise him in his glory (1:14)!

Paul's Worshipful Prayer (1:15–23)

Paul was literally overwhelmed by this vision of Christ and about all he could do was to fall before God in worshipful prayer (1:16) and express both his thanksgivings and his petitions. His petitions provide a precious glimpse into the tender, Christ-filled heart of this famous apostle. He prayed that God would give God's children in the faith a wise (*sophias*) and revelatory (*apokalypseos*) spirit to know (*epignosei/eidenai*) the reality of Christ and their glorious (*doxes*) hope (*elpis*) as a holy people (*haiois,* 1:17–18). He asked that they might experience the amazing power (*dynameos*) of the divine in them that had been evident in the resurrection and enthronement of Christ, who now possesses with God all authority and power for all time (1:19–21). This amazing Christ is the undisputed leader (*kephalen,* "head") of the church! He gives the "fullness" (*pleroma*) of meaning to "his body" (1:22–23). The words are so inspiring that one is moved to join Paul in worshipful adoration of God in Christ.

Comparing Life in Christ with Life outside Christ (2:1–10)

Having thus reflected on the glory of Christ and having prayed for his children's growth in the Lord, Paul briefly glanced in the other direction. This comparative picture significantly enhances our wonder in worship at the marvelous work of Christ. Paul openly confessed that his Christian children had previously been under a devilish spell in which they were copying or imitating the ways of the evil one ("the powerful Prince of the air," *ton archonta tes exousias tou aeros*). In that former state they had been engaged in all sorts of evil practices and, as rebellious children, had sunk to the pit of being merely spiritless corpses (*nekrous*).

Fortunately, however, God–who epitomizes "mercy" and "love"–stepped into the tragic situation and enlivened (*synezoopoiesen*) these shadow people (*nekrous*, "corpses") "in Christ" by uniting them with the risen-enthroned Jesus (2:1–6)! Purely by the graciousness (*chariti*) of God can Christians experience a transforming way of life.[9] Nothing they can do on their own can accomplish it!

Once this transforming way of life goes into effect in them as humans, God continually expects that Christians will exemplify the model of Christ's work in them through their own positive actions (*ergois agathois,* "good works") for God (2:8–9). The close interconnection between Christ's work in us and our responsive work in the world for Christ is once again articulated. Our work can thus be understood as a responsive act of worship to Christ.

Dividing Wall Is Destroyed (2:11–22)

In further pondering the results of Christ's work, Paul concluded that old distinctions advocated by the Jews, such as bodily circumcision for identification purposes, were now meaningless. The symbolic "dividing wall" of Jewish worship–the warning wall in the Temple that separated the Jews and Gentiles–had been rendered insignificant (*lysas,* "destroyed") by Christ's death (2:13–14). In this process, Christ instituted a new understanding of "joint citizenship" (*sympolitai*) as a community of "saints" in God's "household" (*oikeioi*).[10]

This new household citizenship in Christianity was not based on keeping a set of rules, but on a relationship to God through the Spirit! Even those who had been estranged (*xenoi*) and formerly could only be mere associates (*paroikoi*) in the Jewish faith through Jewish ritual procedures were now brought together (*apokatallaxe,* "reconciled") before God and reconciled to one another in a "new humanity" (*kainon anthropon,* 2:15–19). Therefore, all are united by the indwelling Christ and are linked together with all God's messengers (including the apostles and prophets). Accordingly, worship is no longer confined to an old stone temple, but is evidenced in a new context–God's new sanctuary (*naon*)– epitomized in God's people, the place where God now "dwells" (*katoiketerion*) by the Spirit. Moreover, Christ Jesus is to be regarded as the "cornerstone" (*akrogoniaiou*) of the new pattern of worship (2:20–22).

The Mystery Revealed (3:1-21)

In proclaiming this revealed mystery (*mysterion*) of God's "good news" particularly to the Gentiles, Paul was fully conscious that, in spite of his own unworthiness, God had graciously given to him a strategic stewardship (*oikonomia*) in the divine household of being a minister (*diakonos,* "servant," 3:1-8). This new Christian household, the church (*ekklesia*), was God's chosen means through the Lord Christ of confronting the forces of evil in the world that were opposed to God (3:9-10).

In view of this conviction, Paul was again drawn to his knees in worshipful prayer (3:14) because he recognized both the strength of the enemy in the battle but also the positive, powerful, spiritual forces that were at work in the church. He longed for his children to recognize and receive the incredible resources (far beyond our comprehension) available both to him and to them in Christ (3:14-19). Then, having his thoughts ascend to the heavenly realm, Paul closed this section of the letter with one of the loftiest worship-oriented ascriptions to God and Christ found anywhere in the New Testament (3:20-21). May God give us as contemporary worshipers such a sense of divine power working through the glorious presence of Christ in our churches today! And Christians are encouraged to add their "Amen" (so may it be)!

The Lord's Prisoners (4:1-16)

With chapter 4 Paul initiated a series of important practical statements of advice. He reminded his children not only that he was a prisoner in the physical sense but that, in a much more significant relationship, he and they were also prisoners of the Lord (4:1). In that role he instructed them firmly to be sure that their lives represented integrity in their calling as Christians and that they exemplified unity in their worship and relationships with each other. He based his concern on the following realities: the oneness of God, the oneness of their faith, and the oneness of their baptism (4:2-6). For Paul, worship patterns, life conduct, and relationship to the Lord were inseparable because all of life is a gift of God. Moreover, all persons called to service within the community of faith are gifted by God for the edification (*oikodomen*) or enhancing of the entire body of Christ, so that all persons might grow into maturity and unity (4:11-13).

As indicated in 1 Corinthians 12, Christians need not be identical copies of each other; however, all do participate in the formation of the body. Here Paul emphasized the fact that a properly formed body with Christ at the head would be a defense against confusion from the clever (*kubeia*) manipulations and lying (*planes*) attacks of evil (Eph 4:14). When each part of the church evidences a working together (*energeian*) effectively, then the whole body develops in love (4:15-16). It is obvious in his letters that the evidence of love in the church is, for Paul, the true test of an authentic worshiping community and a mature body in Christ. In the midst of all of our disputes today, would that more churches actually displayed genuine Christlike love and not merely talked about it!

Ethical Instructions (4:17–5:20)

Having thus set the parameters very wide for his advice, Paul next listed a series of ethical instructions (4:17–5:20) that do not need to be repeated here, but that should be regarded as a paradigmatic outline of a "new morality." In the post–World War II era, the Western democracies were inundated with ethical theories that sought to overcome rigid legalisms and to proclaim instead "new" or different types of morality. Unfortunately, most of these theories were built upon subjective views of situational ethics in which a person's individual situation and/or sense of what was right and wrong (or, more precisely, what was thought to be " appropriate" and "inappropriate") became the rationale for acceptable/unacceptable conduct. Such ethical norms, however, were *not* actually a "new" morality, but in reality a very "old" morality emerging out of confusion inspired by the tempter and representative of the unproductive (*akarpois*) activity of darkness *(skotous,* 5:11). The so-called new morality was an important element in the development of much narcissistic thinking that is current in the world and has infected the church.

Human opinion, however, can never be an adequate Christian standard for moral behavior. Humans may try to play God in setting their own perceptions as the basis for ethics, but such hubris is merely a re-presentation or illustration of the sin of Adam and Eve in the garden, when mortals thought that they could become "like God" (Gen 3:5), or of the stories in the time of the judges, when "everyone did what was right in his own eyes" (e.g., Judg 17:6; 21:25). Only God who was revealed in the Lord Jesus is ultimately capable of determining such standards.

For Paul the ethical instructions in Ephesians 4:17–5:20 are rooted in Christ and are picturesquely portrayed in the worship rite of baptism through the "putting off" (*apotheisai*) of the old humanity (*palaion anthropon,* 4:22), as if stripping off an old garment, and the "putting on" or becoming endued with (*endusasthai*) a new nature (*kainon anthropon*), identified by the apostle with righteousness and holiness (4:24). These qualities are characteristic of a new transformed morality that is part of a new nature (4:24), and are genuinely representative of Christian ethics–the ethics of the "kingdom of Christ and God" (5:5). It is God who expects obedient living and who through the Holy Spirit provides for such direction in life.

The startling idea bringing up worship in this context of morality instruction can be easily overlooked. Rather than becoming drunk and carousing, the new Christian morality suggests an alternative–the hearty (*te kardia*) singing of "psalms, hymns, and spiritual odes to the Lord" (5:19).[11] Indeed, *all of life,* according to the apostle, is to be lived in "thankfulness" (*eucharistountes*) to God in the name of Jesus (5:4, 20). For some readers such instructions may seem to be pedantic and boring. Such a reaction may be because the devil (4:26; 5:6) has created confusion in the minds of even Christians so that dirty stories and silly talk (4:29; 5:4), anger, and immorality (4:26; 5:3) do not seem to be so bad after all. The way of the Lord is very different. Indeed, living in "imitation" of the loving Christ is for Paul a significant worship experience–namely, a pleasant-smelling "offering" and a "sacrifice" to God (5: 1–2).

The Household Code (5:21–6:9)

In the next section (5:21–6:9) Paul addressed the significant issue of household relationships under what is today known in academia as the rubric of Hellenistic Household Codes (*Haustafeln*). As I indicated earlier in connection with the interpretation of chapter 14 of 1 Corinthians, and chapter 2 of Ephesians, what becomes absolutely crucial in our explication of these texts is to pay particular note to how the Christian codes of Ephesians, Colossians, 1 Timothy, and 1 Peter differ from the normal codes of that earlier society. Since Ephesians is the fullest articulation of the Christian codes, I will give special attention to them here. It is imperative to understand that those codes were fundamentally prepared according to custom by the masters of the household for their underlings–such as wives, children, and servants/slaves. It is virtually impossible in Hellenistic literature to find household rules for husbands, fathers, and masters. They give rules, not receive them.

The Ephesian Code begins at 5:21 with a mutuality statement in which Christians are instructed to be submissive (*hypotassomenoi*) to one another because Christians are part of the household of Christ (just as all Romans belonged to the household of Caesar)! The master or Lord of the Christian household is Christ–not a senior male (a human patriarch) of a family. This perspective also applies to a correct understanding of the church and explains why Paul called himself a servant at the same time as he could refer to himself as an apostle (cf. Rom 1:1). He did not get confused about who was in charge of the church. Nor did Paul view himself as a CEO of the church! Unfortunately, often church pastors and bishops hardly even recognize that their actual models for leadership are frequently drawn from corporate institutions and military contexts rather than from the New Testament.

The first segment of this code refers to wives and husbands (Eph 5:22). This part of the statement concerning the submission of wives to husbands is not unlike familiar Hellenistic expectations in which males were in control of the household, but there is a significant change. Christ is designated as the Lord–not the husband. The rationale given is that Christ is the Savior of the church. Moreover, a new section has been added to the relationship that would not be found in Hellenistic codes. It concerns husbands who are instructed to love their wives so much that, like Christ, they, too, would be willing to die for them (5:25). The model then is not that of a controlling boss in a husband-wife relationship, but of Christ's self-sacrifice, which effected the purifying of the church (5:26–27). Moreover, as a little twist to the male ego, Paul reminds his readers that according to the biblical story of creation, it was the man who "leaves" and is joined to his wife, not the reverse (5:31). So the question that can be posed is: What happens when both husbands and wives acknowledge the "Lordship" of Christ in their relationship? The answer is the creation of a very different type of marriage. A new style of cooperative marriage is born in which selfishness gives way to the mutual serving of each other's needs!

A similar pattern applies to children and fathers. In the Hellenistic world, children had to obey their fathers, but in this Christian code it is not simply because fathers can demand it. Rather it is because children are subject to the Lord. Such a perspective was already presupposed in the Decalogue (Eph 6:1–3; cf. Exod 20:12; and Deut 5:16). What is new in this Christian code concerns the warning addressed to fathers. They were instructed to avoid provocative actions and punishment. Instead, instruction and discipline must conform to the recognition of who is the Lord of the family (Eph 6:4). So again a question is raised: What happens when parents and children conform to the recognition of Christ as the Lord of the family? The answer is, a new type of family life is initiated!

The code's third section applies a similar patten to slaves/servants and masters. According to both logic and custom, masters were generally viewed as being in charge of slaves; slaves had to obey masters, or they would be punished. In this Christian code, however, slaves are instructed to obey their masters out of reverence or respect for Christ (6:5, 7). In addition, their service was to be authentic and not a mere pandering, rendered to secure advancement or to avoid punishment (6:6). What is radically new in this part of the code, however, concerns the masters. Masters are pointedly informed to abandon the cruel threatening of their slaves. The reason given is the big stick of divine retribution! Not only the slaves, but, more relevantly, also the masters are subject to the Lord as the "Master." This Divine Master does not make distinctions in his judgments based on human status or position in society (6:9)! As I have suggested in my comments concerning the Letter to Philemon, the question can certainly be raised: What happens to slavery when slaves and masters are placed on a par before the Judge of the universe? The answer should be obvious—the ultimate demise of slavery was on the horizon!

The transformation of the household codes in Christianity was based on the sense of the presence of Christ in all relationships of life. Christ is to be acknowledged as "Lord" of all relationships! All of life is to be a worship response to the Lord. Such a premise for Christians is foundational to all relationships. For example, therefore, the pattern for the transformation of the primary relationship between husbands and wives is built upon the sanctifying power of Christ in the church, epitomized in the "washing" or baptism of Christians through the effectiveness of the Word (5:26). When worship or human response is appropriately directed to God, the result is the holiness of Christians in all aspects of life (5:27)!

Paul's Summary (6:10-20)

Paul announced his summarizing section with the words "*tou loipou*" ("finally," 6:10). In this section he portrayed the Christian as an ancient warrior dressed and armed for battle. The enemy is pictured, not as a mere human foe, but as the powerful forces of darkness under the command of the devil. Moreover, the soldier's armor is not merely forged by human industry but consists of the full resources (*panoplian*) of God (6:11–12). Paul brilliantly sketched the artistic presentation that follows. It involves truth, righteousness, the gospel of peace, faith, salvation, and the Spirit (6:14–17). As John Bunyan discovered when he wrote about Christian's battle with Apollyon (cf. Rev 9:11) in his classic work, *The Pilgrim's Progress,* no armor protects Christian's back. The warrior was helpless if he turned and ran from the battle. Therefore, he could only "stand" (*stenai/stete,* cf. Eph 6:11, 13, 14) and encounter the enemy head on. He did have one resource that would enable him to use all of the rest of the armor. That resource was prayer (*proseuches*), the secret of inner strength and the key to authentic worship (6:18). For God's warrior to resist the enemy and remain vigilant (*agrypnountes*), he had not only to pray for himself but also for others, including Paul (!), all of whom were in the same war of communicating the powerful mystery (*mysterion*) of the life saving gospel to world (6:19–20).

Closing Encouragement (6:21–24)

Paul closed this magnificent poetical work with a word of encouragement for his children in the gospel, and with his continued prayerful wish for their peace, love, and faith from God (6:21–24). The letter to the Ephesians is a marvelous resource for Christian instruction. It should be employed by every Christian congregation as a handbook for spiritual worship and formation so that the peace, love, and faith that Paul longed to see evidenced in all his churches might clearly be the mark of our communities of faith today.

WORSHIP SUMMARY

From beginning to end, this handbook for growing in maturity with Christ is oriented to worship. It starts in chapter 1 with a vision of Christ's work on earth and led Paul into the sanctuary of personal worship. Then it opens the way in chapters 2 and 3 for him to reflect on the power of the enemy, but also to praise God for the creation of a new unified community of faith that is the result of Christ having broken down the barrier that separated people. To this new community Paul had been called to be a minister concerning the mystery of Christ, a task that caused him to fall in humble worship at the very thought of the amazing power and love of the Lord. Then in chapters 4 and 5 he employed the concepts of the new unified community to outline the new Christian morality as a worshipful response to what Christ has done for humanity. The handbook concludes with an awe-inspiring portrait of the Christian warrior, who enters the spiritual battle of life fully aware of the need for a prayerful dependence upon God.

QUESTIONS _____

1. What do you think are the most important elements that need to be empha-sized in helping new Christians to develop mature patterns of worship in Christ?
2. What kind of a strategy would you employ in building mature Christians?
3. How do your thoughts compare with Paul's perspectives in Ephesians?

11

Philippians[1]

Modeling the Worshiping Community on the Mind and Pattern of Christ

In this amazingly joyful letter to the Philippians, Paul, while a prisoner, outlined at least six basic characteristics for having a vital Christian mindset for all of life and worship.

The letter to the Philippians is like a sweet-smelling rose that brings a smile to one's countenance in times of pain and difficulty. It was clearly written at a time when Paul was in prison (Phil 1:17); yet in this brief work he speaks more about joy and encouragement for Christians than in any of his other epistles (e.g., 1:4, 15, 19, 25; 2:2, 17–18, 19, 28; 3:1; 4:4, 10). If the Christian worshiper is not encouraged to have a glad spirit by this work, it is possible that he or she needs a new transfusion from the mind of Christ Jesus (2:5).

Introduction to Philippians

Few scholars would argue against Pauline authorship. Perhaps the one issue that remains involves the question of *where* Paul was in prison. The immediate surmise might be Rome, since he mentions the Praetorian guard (1:13) and Caesar's household (*Kaisaros oikias,* 4:22). But the guard was not merely stationed in Rome, and *Kaisaros oikias* could mean imperial servants throughout the empire. We know of Paul being imprisoned in Rome (Acts 28:16–30) and in Caesarea (Acts 23:33–26:32), but apparently he was also imprisoned more times (cf. 2 Cor 11:23). The tradition among the post–New Testament apostolic fathers indicates that Paul "bore chains seven times."[2] Some scholars think that these references could reflect an imprisonment in Ephesus. The sense among some was that Rome was too far away for Epaphroditus to bring support to Paul and for Paul to send him back to Philippi after his illness (Phil 2:25–30).[3] Where he was imprisoned will have to remain an unanswered question for the present, but the fact of his imprisonment in connection with this letter is not in dispute.

This letter of Paul literally pulsates with a sense of confidence in the Lord. Moreover, it is a model of encouragement for the church from the founding apostle/missionary to his Philippian children in the faith. Indeed, he called them to imitate him as they chose leaders based on their ability to follow his example (3:17). But he made this astonishing statement of modeling, not because of his own innate abilities or self-infused personal qualities, but because he himself had found his model in Christ Jesus (2:3–5). In fact, he took pains to clarify for the Philippians that he could have had great confidence in his own résumé as a Jew (from the tribe of Benjamin, properly circumcised, correctly educated as a Pharisee, zealous to the point of being a persecutor because of his views, and absolutely faithful to the legal prescriptions of Judaism–see 3:4–6). Yet that status list was for him actually worthless ("a lost cause," *zemia*) when it was compared to the incredible realization (*hyperechon tes gnoseos*) of the awesome Christ Jesus whom he worshiped as his Lord! Moreover, he came to understand that he could not earn acceptance by God through his own effort, but only through faith in Christ (3:7–9).

That realization led him to a life of worship in which his overwhelming life-desire was to know Christ, understand the power of the resurrection, and identify with his sufferings even to the point of accepting Christ's death as the model for his own life. His goal, however, was not martyrdom but like-mindedness with Christ, that he might experience Christ's promised resurrection (3:10). This worship-oriented motivation for Paul was the foundation for his amazingly positive outlook on life in the midst of traumas such as confinement in prison. To miss this crucial factor in reading Philippians is to misunderstand the dynamics of this priceless testimonial letter.

Perspectives for the Church and Its Worship (1:1–11)

After addressing the Philippians as saints (*hagious*) and their leaders as elders or overseers (*episkopois*) and deacons (*diakanois*), and following the typical Christian communication of grace and peace (1:1–2), Paul (with Timothy) began to enunciate a series of vital perspectives for the church and its worship. These perspectives are rooted in an explicit eschatological commitment to the significance of the coming of Jesus Christ (1:6, 10) and its implications for Christian worship–namely, giving glory and praise to God (1:11)!

In opening the body of this letter, Paul first highlighted prayer. In this emphasis on prayer he effectively balanced thanksgiving for the Philippians' genuine sense of community (*koinonia*) in the gospel (1:3–5) with his own heartfelt petition concerning their need for growth in Christian love and maturity (1:9–10). Such a focus on prayer may seem to some contemporary readers about as exciting as watching grass grow. Indeed, many surveys have made it quite clear that the average amount of time most Christians spend in prayer is pathetically low. To find Western Christians who spend at least ten minutes a day in prayer is actually surprising.

Such reports show that many Christians perceive God as quite remote and uninvolved in their daily lives. For Paul, however, prayer in worship was a foundational element of his Christian life. In this commitment to prayer he himself imitated (cf. 2:5; 3:17) the mindset or model of Jesus (e.g., Luke 3:21; 5:16; 6:12, 22; 9:18, 28; 11:1; etc.).

An Evangelical Perspective (1:12–18)

A second perspective evident in this letter is, for lack of a better name, what I call an "evangelical perspective." It grows out of an incredible sense of God's supervening presence in one's life and epitomizes one who knows how to worship and rely completely on God. Being in prison, Paul wanted the Philippians to understand that what happened to him in effect was advancing the gospel and that other Christians had been strengthened by his approach to imprisonment (Phil 1:12–14). But that is not the rest of the story!

Others were preaching about Christ out of a divisive spirit (*eritheias*) and were seeking to pile troubling pressure (*thipsin*) on Paul to make him collapse (1:15–17). His response was not what we might expect. Instead of condemning them, he rejoiced that even in their insincerity Christ was being proclaimed (1:18). As I read these words today, my only conclusion can be that for such a person the "mind of Christ" (see the worship hymn at 2:5–11) had been so infused into a human mind that the person reacted as Jesus did on the cross (Luke 23:34; cf. Acts 7:60). That quality of life must be what "transformation" really implies and what a life built on authentic worship of the self-giving God is meant to be.

To Live Is Christ (1:19–2:11)

The third perspective grows out of the second and can be summarized by Paul's assertion, "For me to live is Christ and to die is gain [*kerdos*]" (Phil 1:21). It is a perspective of "reversal"—death gives way to life (cf. 1 Cor 15:42). The ancients, who can be epitomized in the Egyptian pharaohs, were buried with their "stuff" so that they could be translated to a new realm fully equipped for the next life. Of course, their "stuff" did not make it to the next realm. The grave robbers and those of us who have done archaeology have been delighted that none of their "stuff" transferred. Such a concept of transference is not what Paul meant by his concept of what I have termed "reversal." His concern was not with "stuff," nor indeed with the accoutrements of humanity such as prestige and power. He lived life as fully as he could. Yet he was not concerned with "collecting" material goods or with building a résumé. He really affirmed the reversal model when he informed the Philippians that they had been given the privilege not only to believe in Christ but also to suffer for him (Phil 1:29).

The question for the world then is: How do you control someone who has this kind of a mindset? He lived life with a purpose and was self-giving. He did not take advantage of others but wanted to help them discover a new reason for living. In his zeal for what he believed, he did not accept revenge nor wish to kill others for which the world could punish him. He did not desire "stuff" that the world could seize to make him conform. And he accepted suffering as a divine calling.

He did not fit into the world's patterns. He marched to a different drumbeat. He honored and worshiped a different God! Ah! There is the clue. If you want to know why early Christianity had a sense of power, when to the world it seemed to be powerless, just reflect on the life of Paul and what motivated him. You actually can discover the secret to his mindset. It was in the One whom he worshiped!

Paul's worship response is encapsulated in his magnificent christological hymn at Philippians 2:5–11. This text has been thoroughly exegeted by Ralph Martin in his work on *Carmen Christi*[1] (see footnote 1 of this chapter), so I will not here retrace his excellent historical review. Instead, I am focusing on the hymn's importance for Paul's perspectives on worship and life. To ensure that his Philippian children understood the significance of their situation in Christ clearly, Paul introduced this hymn (2:1–4) by reminding them as Christians that they should not make themselves the center of their existence. The way they treated others was an indication of whether or not they were actually embodying the *missio dei* (the mission of Christ).

To worship God in Christ authentically meant that they needed to have the mind of Christ. He gave us the effective model by emptying (*ekenosen*) himself of the accoutrements (*morphe*, "form") of divine glory and entering the ranks (*morphen*) of humanity. He even stooped lower and humbled (*etapeinosen*) himself by allowing humanity to kill him, as if he were a horrible criminal. Yet human action is not the end of the hymn's story, because God exalted Jesus above the entire created order so that ultimately everyone, both living and dead, will worship him (bend the knee) and, in fact, acknowledge him as "Lord" to the glory of God! To worship Christ with the "mind of Christ" implies having a true humility like Jesus, but it also is rooted in a confidence of Christ as victor. This *Christus victor* theme is basic to all of Paul's thinking and leads naturally to the next perspective in Philippians.

The Work Perspective (2:12–3:21)

The fourth insight is what I have termed the "work perspective." Not only was Paul ready to die for Christ, but he gave himself to work in life for Christ and instructed his Philippian children to do so as well. Furthermore, he set his advice in the context of salvation (2:12). This verse has sometimes created a concern for Protestant readers, who wonder how work relates to salvation, especially for those who have been taught the force of Ephesians 2:8–9, that people are saved by faith and not by works, and who have forgotten that verse 10 in that context reminds readers that Christians have become Christ's work in order to produce good works. The same perspective is advocated here—namely, that our work for Christ is a reflection of or results from our relationship to Christ. While we do our work for Christ with a sense of our own frailty, we need to realize that it is actually God who is working through us to achieve his intentions in our world (Phil 2:12–13). Accordingly, even our work is a worshipful response to God. As such, Paul compares his life to a sacrifice (*thysia*)—namely, a liquid offering or libation—which is "poured out" (*spendomai*) along with the faithful lives of the Philippians as a representation (*leitourgia,* a term from which we get our word *liturgy*) of Christian faith (2:17). Moreover, Paul added that our work is done in a world filled with crooked (*skolias*) and corrupt (*diestrammenes*) persons (2:15) who do not know God and to whom Christians are like lights in the darkness (2:17; cf. Matt 5:14).

Since the world is filled with evildoers (Phil 3:2), Christians represent the authentic people of circumcision because they "worship (*latreuontes*) God in (by) the Spirit and glory (*kauchomenoi*) in Christ Jesus." In so doing, Christians do not put their trust in the ways of the world ("the flesh," 3:4), but rather in the power of Christ's resurrection (3:10). Their minds are therefore worshipfully directed to their destinies and the realm of heaven. They await their Savior's presence (3:20) and the ultimate transformation of their lives (3:21).

The Partnership Perspective (4:1–3)

As Paul moved to chapter 4, a fifth perspective emerges, which I designate as the "partnership perspective." Paul was not a "lone ranger" in his mind. He was not the center of his mission and, therefore, recognized the need for the community to work together in fulfilling the purposes of Christ. Accordingly, he encouraged (*parakalo*) those who seemed to be at odds with one another to work together, and for others to assist in bringing a collegial spirit among the workers (4:2–3). In this era when disputes are wide-ranging in churches and among denominations, it is imperative to recognize that the mind of Christ is not the source of our divisiveness. Simply to think we are right on issues does not mean that we represent the Spirit of God.

The devil can easily represent himself as an angel of light and confuse the church into adopting the ways of the world (2 Cor 11:14). In so doing, the devil achieves his goal of truncating our worship and stifling our mission. Paul instead attempted to pull the parties together by reminding them that all of their names are written in the "Book of Life" (Phil 4:3). To think that we alone represent the mind of Christ in any situation makes God in *our* image, and repeats the terrible sin committed in the garden of Eden story, in which humans turned the focus of their lives away from God and onto their own desires (Gen 3:5).

The Eschatological Perspective (4:4-23)

Paul closed his precious letter with a sixth perspective and a firm reminder for Christians to rejoice and live in the expectation of the return of the Lord (Phil 4:4-5). Throughout this epistle the astute reader will discover that the eschatological vision of Paul undergirds all of his perspectives on life and worship in this present world (cf. also 1:10, 28; 2:9-11, 16; 3:11, 20). Without this vision, Paul's perspectives would have faded into a cloud of good advice.

On the basis of this vision, however, he could call the Philippians to release their fears and anxieties (4:6; cf. 1 Pet 5:7) and rely on the God whom they worship by addressing their prayers, petitions, and thanksgivings, not to human powers, but to God who would give them peace and mold their minds to be like Christ Jesus (Phil 4:6-7). Their minds could then flower into the fullness intended by God so that everything they thought about would be channeled correctly in the model of Paul (4:8-9), and according to the mind of Christ (2:5).

WORSHIP SUMMARY _____

The letter to the Philippians provides the reader with a unique six-point conceptual model of what it means to have the mind of Christ and to live an exemplary worship-filled life. After initiating his model with an emphasis on prayer, Paul formulated the rest of his composite statement in terms of what I have categorized as the evangelical, reversal, work, partnership, and eschatological perspectives. Together these perspectives constitute a wholesome authentic life lived in a worshipful response to our Lord. In this brief epistle Paul revealed his mature inner motivations in life and provided a delightful insight into how God can encompass the mind of a Christian through the satisfying glory that is in Christ Jesus (4:19). Christian readers should readily embrace this outlook on life and joyfully join Paul in his lofty, prayerful ascription: "To our God...be glory for all eternity! Amen" (4:20).

QUESTIONS _____

1. Why was Paul such a positive Christian in the context of the difficulties associated with this letter to the Philippians? What was his secret?
2. What would it take for your worship and life to achieve a similar pattern?
3. How does the Christ hymn in chapter 2 guide your personal and corporate worship?

12

Colossians

A Baptismal Instruction Book for Life in the Christian Community[1]

This brief epistle to the Colossians is like a baptismal catechetical document in which new believers are instructed in the amazing nature of Christ Jesus and the significance of what putting on the new nature means for worship and life—namely, eschewing the old ways of the world and taking on the new ways of Christ.

Colossians is a fascinating book that seeks to correct false views and establish correct perspectives on what it means to be a baptized believer in Christ. It is like a catechetical document for new believers in Christ. While its content is directed to a rather specific situation at Colossae, it has great implications for all Christians even today. The city of Colossae had earlier experienced significance, having been on the main highway between the east (Mesopotamia) and Ephesus. Later, it was dwarfed in importance within the tri-city region of Phrygia that involved the so-called holy city, Hierapolis (cf. Col 4:13), and the more prosperous Laodicea (cf. 4:13, 15, 16). Well-known for its attraction to the magical arts, Phrygia boasted that the cult of Cybele, the great mother goddess, had arisen there because of a meteorite shower. The people were receptive to enchantment and also to Montanism, an early type of Christian Pentecostal enthusiasm, which developed there.

Introduction to Colossians

Paul, a prisoner in Rome along with Aristarchus at the time of writing Colossians (4:10), had apparently not been active in the founding of this church (cf. Col 2:1). That honor seemingly belonged to Epaphras (1:7), who was at that time also with Paul in Rome (4:12). Nevertheless, Paul was particularly concerned that these enthusiastic people were correctly guided in their development as new Christians so that they might not succumb to mythical theories and preachers of various religious mysteries. This book (like the more complete formation book of Ephesians) is a model for those who would develop instructional texts for believers.

Based on such verses as 1:13 and a style that varied from Romans, some scholars in past decades claimed that, Paul did not write this book. Such scholars insist that Colossians contains a post-Pauline realized eschatology. Those arguments are hardly as attractive to scholars today, since the book really makes no claim that the end time had arrived. Instead, it claims that a new type of life has begun for believers in taking on Christ Jesus as their Savior (1:14). Moreover, a change of an amanuensis (secretary) or the assistance of someone like Timothy (1:1) could easily account for any stylistic differences from Paul's other works. In addition, one certainly cannot make a case for a developed ecclesiology (church structure) in Colossians, since it makes little mention of any leadership positions. Finally, the mention of Onesimus (4:9) along with Tychicus accompanying this letter correlates well with the brief epistle to Philemon (Phlm 9).

Opening Prayer of Thanksgiving (1:1–14)

After a very brief introduction, this book also begins with a standard liturgical prayer of thanksgiving. Readers need to sense just how important the word-family of thanksgiving (*eucharistein*) is to this short letter by Paul. It is as though he wanted these novice believers literally to breathe the spirit of thanksgiving, since it appears in every chapter of the book (Col 1:3, 12; 2:7; 3:15, 17; 4:2) Further, one will observe that here Paul employs his famous triad, but in a different order than in 1 Corinthians 13:13. As I note in connection with some of Paul's earlier letters, such as 1 Thessalonians, the order often follows (unlike in 1 Cor 13:13) the order of salvation or transformation (as it does here): namely, faith, love, and hope—or the coming to faith, the growing in love (becoming holy), and the anticipation of the heavenly hope (Col 1:4–5; cf. especially 1 Thess 1:3, 9).

Indeed, in contrast to those who argue that salvation is primarily a total and instantaneous transformation, Paul would argue otherwise. It is imperative not to misunderstand or minimize the Pauline uses of the Greek present tense and its significance for the growth process in salvation (cf. for example 1 Cor 1:18). Paul illustrates the process nature of the Christian life by reference to terminology involving growth and fruit production (Col 1:6, 10; cf. 2:6–7). This idea is important for new believers to realize. Salvation is not all completed when one is baptized as a believer, or confirmed. Instruction continues to be a necessary element in Christian life and worship. The importance of growth in the "knowledge" of God's will and "spiritual wisdom" (or Christian integrity, 1:9) is clearly the reason why Paul wrote his epistles to the churches and particularly penned this one.

Paul prayed that they would experience the strengthening power of God, which was essential for their endurance and their sense of joy in the face of difficulty and hostility in life. Rather than bemoaning their situations on earth, they were counseled to remember that their amazing inheritance was to participate in the heavenly glory (*doxes*) with the saints (1:11–12). They were indeed part of Christ's realm (*basileian*) now and had been forgiven and redeemed from the dark (*skotous*) power of evil (1:13–14). Their calling was to grow and live in accordance with their ultimate hope.

Confessing Jesus the Christ (1:15–20)

Paul supported his prayerful counsel by detailing one of the most elevated confessions about Christ in the New Testament (1:15–20; cf. also John 1:1–18; Heb 1:1–14; and the various statements in Revelation). His goal was obviously to make sure that these novice believers did not think that Christ could be compared with Caesar or any of the pagan gods. Christianity was not just some fabricated philosophy or mystery religion concocted by human ingenuity (cf. Col 2:8). Christ was from the absolute beginning of time–a faithful replication of the mysterious, ultimate power in the universe and fully involved in all of creation (1:15–16).

What is more significant for them (and for us as well) is that through his death and resurrection Christ was established as the indisputable leader of the church (1:18). This crucial idea of the death and resurrection of Christ will be used later to tie the believers' baptism directly to their Lord. Here, however, the confession emphasizes that the office of "Lord" belonged to Christ and *not* to some *mere human being!* Only in Christ did ultimate deity reside in earthly form, and only through Christ's astounding sacrificial death on the cross (*staurou*) has reconciliation (*apokatalaxai*) and peace (*eirenopoesas*) with God been decisively offered to humans (1:19–20).

Call to Authentic Worship (1:21–2:3)

The point of this magnificent christological confession for Paul was not to initiate a theological discussion. His goal was to call these novice believers to authentic worship. They at one time had been alienated (*apellotriomenous*) from God and had engaged in all sorts of strange worship rites and evil practices. They needed to realize the significance of their reconciliation in Christ and to maintain a consistent Christian life response to their new Christian hope (1:21–23).

Helping to develop transformed lives in Christ–lives that responded to worship Christ–was Paul's goal in ministry, especially among the Gentiles (1:27). To that end he accepted suffering (see his personal testimony, 1:24) and took upon himself the seemingly endless responsibility of providing correct responsive advice and counsel to believers (1:28–29). That task included writing instructional letters to both them (the Colossians) and their Laodicean neighbors (2:1). Unfortunately, the other letter to Laodicea (4:16) has not survived.

Confronting Negative Matters (2:4–23)

Before turning to the positive matters of catechesis, however, Paul took the time to confront the negative matters in their contextual settings. He challenged them not to be deceived by fanciful words ("persuading speech," *pithanologia*, 2:4) or clever philosophical discussions related to the so-called elementary spirits or forces in the universe, which Paul viewed as mere human musings (2:8). That position did not mean that he refused to take the powers of evil seriously. On the contrary, he proclaimed that Christ had in fact stripped (*apekdysamenos*) the evil forces of their controlling power over believers (2:15).

Moreover, he regarded as now passé such liturgical requirements as circumcision (2:11) or the necessity of following earlier worship practices involving food and drink laws, or even observing special religious ceremonies/ celebrations to gain acceptance by God (2:16). This new perspective of Paul must be regarded as nothing less than revolutionary for a former strict Jew. It indicates just how transforming was the apostle's encounter and experience with Christ. These old worship practices had become for him a mere shadow reality in comparison to his worship of Christ (2:17).

On the other hand, the rite of baptism was not just a "mere" symbol for Paul. Baptism was for him a very important sign of the transformational process. In discussing this matter he employed the image of the exchanging of clothes, which for the early believers became a powerful portrayal of the exchange of their old life pattern for a new way of life in Christ. Indeed, the *Didache* informs us that running water was normally used for early baptisms. This pattern followed the model of Jewish ritual bathing that would wash *away* the "uncleanness."[2] The unique point of Christian baptism, in contrast to the various Jewish washings, however, is that baptism is modeled on the unrepeatable event of Jesus' death and resurrection. So, just as Christ died and was buried, Christians are buried with him in baptism. And just as he was raised by the Father, so Christians are raised to a new life in Christ (2:12; cf. Rom 6:1–11).

Instructions for New Christians (3:1–17)

These pictorial representations of death and resurrection and of the exchange of clothing then served Paul as the basis for instruction to new Christians. These novices in Christ were counseled to have a new mindset (Col 3:2) that would indicate their kinship with the resurrected Christ (3:1). They are to put to death all the ways of their former sinful lives, such as immorality, idolatry, greediness, anger, foul language, lying, and evil practices, just as though they were shedding their old clothing (3:5–9).

Instead, they are to "put on" a new mindset or a new nature, which is continually being transformed to become more and more like their Lord (3:10). In this new life pattern, old racial, ethnic, and economic distinctions between people are no longer to be of significance (3:11). The characteristics that mark God's people are to be qualities such as kindness, humility, patience, and forgiveness. Above all, believers are instructed to "put on" love and a desire for peace and harmony (3:12–15).

For such growth to continue, Paul wisely advised believers to let the message (*logos*) of Christ become resident in them so that their lives would be liturgies or worship responses of praise in song and hymn and spiritual song (3:16). As I indicated in connection with Ephesians 5:19, this group of song types is not meant to be an exhaustive list, but merely a representation of some possible types for expressing one's joy in the Lord. The important focus is in Paul's next verse: whatever the believer does should be a worship response of thanksgiving (*eucharistountes*) in the name (nature/spirit) of the Lord Jesus (3:17).

The Household Code (3:18–4:1)

As Paul moved to the conclusion of the book, he briefly added a few comments at 3:18–4:1 concerning the Christian version of the household codes (*Haustaflen*), a fuller example of which is contained in Ephesians 5:21–6:9 (see also 1 Pet 2:11–3:7). As noted in connection with the Ephesian codes, it is important to understand that the Hellenistic codes had no such sections for husbands, fathers, and slave owners. *They* did not receive such rules; they legislated the codes of conduct for their underlings.

Unlike the Hellenistic codes, Paul wanted to make sure that Christian households work well together under Christ. For households to represent the way of Christ, husbands must not be harsh to their wives (Col 3:19), fathers must not be provocative to their children (3:21), and masters need to be reminded that they are themselves subject to the great master of all (4:1).

Concluding Prayer (4:2–18)

Paul wrapped up his letter as one should come to expect—with a prayer for them (4:2–4). Even though he was in prison (4:3, 18), Paul was not self-centered or bemoaning his state of affairs. His personal concern was expansive, namely for opportunities to share the gospel (4:3) and for believers like the Colossians to be models of Christian integrity in life and worship (4:2). Then he added some brief notes on those who would carry this letter and some greetings from his companions in prison.

WORSHIP SUMMARY

This brief letter to the Colossians is a forceful example of how Paul exegeted in depth a major aspect of worship–baptism. He used various elements of Christian teaching to provide perspective on the subject. He made it eminently clear that baptism is not just a philosophical addendum to a religious idea. It is intimately related to the worship of Christ. This sacrament or ordinance is not meant to be a rite initiated to gain God's approval. It is a powerful response to the change that Christ has effected in the believer's life. Just like putting off an old garment and putting on a new one, it should signal a major change or transformation in the lives of new Christians concerning their relationship with God. It should also denote that a significant alteration has occurred in all their relationships with other people, especially in their own families.

Paul concluded this instructional manual for baptized believers with his own certification and his prayer for God's grace to be with them. May his wish for God's grace to them also be realized in us today (4:18)!

QUESTIONS

1. To what extent does your baptism actually impact the rest of your life?
2. How could a better understanding of baptism give more focus to your life as a Christian?

13

Thessalonian Letters

Living and Worshiping as an Eschatological Community[1]

In the Thessalonian letters Paul focuses on vital prayer and the power of Christian hope for impacting the life and worship of believers in the face of suffering and persecution.

The Thessalonian letters represent Paul's early attempt to deal with an issue that for Greek Christians became an assumed false supposition—namely, that when one died, the soul of the person sloughed off the bodily tomb and the freed soul ascended to be with the great eternal soul. Any idea of a bodily resurrection would have been viewed by their Greek neighbors with disdain.[2] See for example the story of Paul's encounter with the Athenian leaders on the Areopagus in Acts 17:16–33. For Paul, however, an idea of immortality of the soul was the equivalent of making at least part of a human being immortal like God. To fuzz the distinction between mortal humans and the immortal God was for him intolerable (cf. 1 Cor 15:12–19, 42–50). It completely negated any perspective on the worship of God who sanctified the unity of a person's spirit, soul, and body (1 Thess 5:23). By contrast, the Greeks and Romans actually had regarded their pantheon of gods in very human terms, possessing many of the frailties and committing many of the foibles of mere humans.

In addition to wrestling with the basic concept of immortality, the Greek Christians also struggled with trying to understand time sequences associated with death. Since I have dealt with some of these issues elsewhere,[3] I will not extend that discussion here except to deal with the texts themselves. My concern at this point is with particular concerns of worship and how our perception of the awesomeness of God impacts our sense of hope and eschatology.

Introduction to the Thessalonian Letters

In the late nineteenth century, some scholars regarded a concern for eschatology as a later development in Christianity, and therefore the Thessalonian letters were regarded by some to be pseudo-Pauline. Then Albert Schweitzer penned his famous *The Quest for the Historical Jesus,* in which he developed his analysis of Jesus as an eschatological misfit who died as a disappointed prophet.[4] While few accepted Schweitzer's conclusions, scholars immediately shifted their perspectives. Today most think that the Thessalonian letters are the first that Paul sent to his churches.

Although I took this position in writing my commentary on the Thessalonian epistles, I have since made a slight shift in my views.[5] I believe that the fiery letter to the Galatians was Paul's initial work, written in the late 40s of the first Christian century. I would argue that the Thessalonian letters were written after Paul fled from Thessalonica (Saloniki today) in the beginning of the 50s (cf. Acts 17:10ff). Most scholars would agree that the Thessalonian letters are genuine, though a few would try to argue that 2 Thessalonians is an attempt to copy Paul's style. Their rationale for the presence of different eschatologies in both letters has hardly been acceptable.[6]

First Thessalonians

Faith, Love, and Hope (1:1–10)

Following a brief salutation and greeting, Paul opened the body of his letter with a prayer. This prayer provides insight into the way Paul's mind worked. For those who have begun to recognize Paul's triadic thinking, they will probably immediately recall the most famous of Paul's triads (faith, hope, and love) in 1 Corinthians 13:13, which emphasized his concern for the Corinthians' apparent lack of loving service to others (cf. also the similar order of the triad in Rom. 5:1, 2, 5). First Thessalonians, however, uses the same triad in a *different order* (faith, love, and hope) because Paul's concern was not so much with the Thessalonians' love as it was with their hope (1 Thess 1:3), the last element of the triad being the focus of concern. In writing to the Corinthians' Paul focused on the "power" (*dynamis*) of the cross (1 Cor 1:17) in his effort to have them follow Christ's self-giving nature in developing relationships (1:11–13) and adopting humility as the basis of their wisdom (1:19–3:5).

Here, he challenged the Thessalonians to find confidence (*plerophosia*) based on the mysterious convincing "power" (*dynamei*) and presence of the Holy Spirit in their lives (1 Thess 1:5). Even more intriguing here is how Paul in 1:9–10 employed the order of the triad as a link to the three stages of the salvation process: (1) they "turned" (*epestrepsate*) from idols to God, (2) then they began to serve (*douleuein*) God, and (3) prepared to await (*anamenein*) the Son of God from heaven. Adequate worship of God begins with a clear turning to and living in dependence on God (faith), which leads to a self-giving commitment of service (love), which in turn issues in a genuine confidence that God is in charge of the future (hope).

Suffering and Persecution (2:1–16)

Having laid the foundation for his concern with their suffering, Paul offered them a personal testimony of his own life of suffering (*propathontes*) as well as his courageous response (*eparesia*) in the midst of great agony (*agoni*) and negative reaction to his proclamation of the gospel (2:2).

He boldly asserted that his real motivation was not rooted in a desire to deceive (*planes*), nor in any other base human tendencies (2:3) that arise out of a longing (*zetountes*) for the praise (*doxan*) of others or for personal gain (*pleonexias*). Instead, he assured them that his goal was integrity in worship and life—namely, to please (*areskontes*) God (2:3–6), who alone is the one who can evaluate (*dokimazonti*) the inner wills (or "hearts") of humans.[7]

When one understands how central and controlling the awe-inspiring vision of God was for all of Paul's life and thought, one gains a better perception of the nature of worship itself. Moreover, when the worship of God becomes the authentic core of one's life, then life opens in service to others. Accordingly, what follows in Paul's testimony is his description of himself both as a ministering "nurse" (*thalpe,* 2:7) and as a concerned "father" (*pater,* 2:11) in relation to his children. Contrary to those who would argue that Paul was a male chauvinist, his use here of such egalitarian illustrations concerning himself reflects the same mindset that is evident in Galatians 3:28. He wanted all Christians to be "servants" who would imitate him (1 Thess 2:14) in becoming "holy," authentically "righteous," and without blame (*amemptos,* 2:10)—characteristics of a true worshiper of Christ.

Indeed, Paul not only exhorted/counseled (*parakaloutes*) them to pursue their destinies as members of God's eternal kingdom (2:12), but he also prayerfully thanked God because he was convinced that God was in fact accomplishing his work in them through their suffering (2:13–14). In this process they, like Paul and others, were copying both the pristine model of the suffering Lord Jesus and that of the prophets before them. So, in their own suffering, they were providing additional proof of their persecutors' ultimate condemnation (2:15–16).

The Visitation Question (2:17–3:13)

While Paul longed to confirm his belief concerning their stability as Christians by a personal visit, he was at the time—because of Satan's harassment of him (2:18)—only able to learn of their faithfulness through surrogate visitors such as Timothy (3:2). His own experiences had taught him that the devil was no mere concoction of the mind. That was reason enough for his genuine concern about their potential temptation to turn away from authentic Christ-oriented worship and life when they learned of his troubles (3:4–5). Fortunately, Timothy's report comforted him (3:7).

He could not help but burst into a thanksgiving prayer for the joy that overwhelmed him (3:9). Moreover, he entered into a fervent or unceasing (*hyperekperessou deomenoi,* "night and day") prayer vigil that he might soon see them (3:10) and that God would keep them holy until the coming (*parousia*) of Jesus and all the saints (3:13).

Eschatology and Authentic Living (4:1–5:28)

Paul was convinced that a wholesome eschatology would provide his children with the basis for authentic living–namely, their sanctification (4:3)! Assured that they practiced love for each other (4:9) in their response to Christ's saving power, he nevertheless instructed them to evidence that pattern in an ever-increasing manner and avoid the temptation to become busybodies (4:11–12).

Paul turned briefly to their behavior and a concern that really seemed to trouble them. Obviously, some of their Christian colleagues had recently died. The believers in Thessalonica had begun to wonder whether Paul's view of the Christian hope was in reality true. Were Christians who died any different from their pagan neighbors (4:13)? Paul's answer was a resounding assertion of the Christian hope based on the death and resurrection of Jesus and the promise that, not only had their dead associates not died in vain, but also that Christ would bring their dead associates with him when he comes to receive his living followers into his new era (4:14–17).

Having stated in unequivocal terms his confidence in God's purposes, he returned to their situation and called them to keep alert and both comfort and encourage each other in their Christian lives (4:18; 5:11). In doing so, he re-employed his triad of faith, love, and hope and linked it to the elements of the Christian warrior's armament, which he would later expand in his magnificent warrior illustration at Ephesians 6:10–18 (cf. 1 Thess 5:8). Then he continued in his "parenesis" (moral exhortations) and advised them to continue in authentic Christian patterns of life (5:12–15).

He ended his instructions with proper perspectives on worship and called them to: an expansive life of joy, an attitude of prayer, an encompassing sense of thanksgiving, a commitment to the will of God, a reliance on the Spirit, an acceptance of prophecy or preaching, a readiness to evaluate the genuineness of attempts at Christian authenticity, and a holding firm to what is good while eschewing all forms of evil (5:16–21). Then he turned to prayer himself and petitioned the God of peace to make them a unified (spirit, soul, and body), expectant, holy people who were readied for the coming of the Lord. He also requested that they pray for him and that they fully accept each other as part of the family of God (with the early Christian symbol of a holy kiss; cf. Rom 16:16; 1 Cor 16:20; 1 Pet 5:14). He concluded with an affirmation of the grace of Jesus, to which his readers would undoubtedly have added their confirmation.

WORSHIP SUMMARY

First Thessalonians is an important early Christian witness to the close connection between eschatology and holistic worship, since it presupposes the need for trust, love, and hope in God as the basis for all of life. Dependency on God and authentic worship are not, as some contemporary critics think, a failure to achieve maturity or an opiate of the people. Instead the letter sets the world and frail human desires in a proper perspective and leads to a confidence in life. This early letter calls for Christians to embody sanctified or holy living (4:3; 5:23) in the midst of rejection and suffering. It provides a firm confidence for worshipers that the Lord will return to receive God's own into glory.

QUESTIONS

1. Eschatology seems to have been exceedingly significant for Paul in this letter. Is it for you?
2. Is Paul's future expectation just some pie-in-the-sky dream?
3. How does an eternal future affect the way you worship? The way you live?

Second Thessalonians

The Excesses of Eschatology and Punishment for Their Persecutors (1:1–10)

In this brief epistle Paul returns to the subject of eschatology because of the Thessalonians' obvious concerns about it and their on-going experiences of persecution. So, after a very brief introduction, he gave thanks for their faithfulness in the face of hostility. At this point he abandoned the triad of faith, love, and hope (cf. 1 Thess 1:3) and employed only the first two: faith and love (2 Thess 1:3). The apparent reason is that the Thessalonians seemingly had become so engrossed and overwhelmed with eschatological thinking (hope) that some of them had actually ceased to work and became idle in waiting for the appearance of the Lord (3:10–11). Such idleness, Paul knew, did not bode well for them both in the eyes of God and their neighbors, and therefore he had to issue a stern rebuke against such an approach to their future expectations (3:14–15).

His more severe words, however, were directed against their persecutors. The hostility that the Christians experienced, he assured them, would ultimately be reciprocated by divine affliction and judgment upon the persecutors when the Lord Jesus would make his appearance. The believer's task, however, was not to deal the judgment blow. That role belonged to God–and Jesus with his fiery angels (1:5-9). The thought patterns are clearly apocalyptic in nature and are reminiscent of such earlier Jewish works as the Book of Enoch and the Apocalypse of Baruch from the intertestamental period. At the end of time, both living believers and departed saints would stand in awe at the coming of the Lord (1:10).

The Worship Context (1:11-12)

Before moving to a fuller explication of the subject, Paul quickly set this discussion in a worship context by calling the believers to pray that they might truly respond as authentic representatives of their Lord and glorify God in their lives (1:11-12). It is crucial for interpreters of Paul to recognize how strategic the amazing grace of the Lord Jesus Christ was in all of his thinking. He did not recognize himself as a self-made man. He was transformed through his encounter with Jesus. All his thinking then became rooted "in Christ," and his life became molded by responsive prayer.

Eschatological Deceptions (2:1-12)

Paul still needed to care for another issue, which seemingly arose from a fraudulent letter claiming to come from Paul concerning the end (2:2). Accordingly, in 2 Thessalonians he added a typical certification so that they would not be deceived both here and in any future correspondence (3:17). The false letter, however, was for him only another indication of the deception that is current in the world as time moves toward its end. Yet Paul made it clear that the Thessalonian believers were themselves mistaken in supposing the end was imminent.

Rather than attempting to provide them with a timetable concerning the end times (which would have been virtually impossible), he merely noted some vague markers or signs that would suggest the soon coming of the end, such as: a rebellion against God and the coming of an evil leader who would not only demand (as the servant of the devil) not merely political allegiance but also claim divine authority in the world. Nevertheless, believers should not be alarmed or give up their trust in Jesus, because he is in control even of those who are mistaken or are opposed to him. Clearly he ultimately will dispatch all the evil authorities and powers (2:3-12).

The Eschatological Promise and Prayer (2:13-3:18)

Paul's commitment to a proper worship perspective reasserted itself as he promised to pray for the Thessalonians and strongly counseled them to maintain a genuine commitment or stance in relationship to Christ gained through the gospel. Moreover, he reminded them of the sanctifying power of the Holy Spirit in their lives, which would enable them ultimately to receive their intended destiny (glory; *doxes*) in Christ (2:13-15) even though they were currently experiencing persecution. So he concluded the chapter by praying that the Lord Jesus and God would extend divine comfort to them in their suffering and establish them firmly in all their activities (2:16–17).

This book is literally bathed in prayer. Paul closed this little work with a heartfelt request for them also to pray for him in the midst of his traumas so that God would give both him and them patient endurance in trials and a sense of success in the spread of the gospel in spite of the work of evil people (3:1–5). He concluded the epistle by admonishing them pointedly against idleness and warned them to refrain from fellowship with such idle persons, not because they were to be regarded as enemies, but undoubtedly because of the contaminating influence of such people on the Christian community. After his personal certification of the message, he closed this letter, similarly to 1 Thessalonians, by again committing them to the grace of the Lord Jesus Christ (3:18; cf. 1 Thess 5:28).

WORSHIP SUMMARY

This brief epistle is a study in prayer and its significance for all Christians in the face of trials and persecution. It also offers a needed corrective for those who seek to formulate unhealthy futuristic views as the basis for their faith and worship. A wholesome eschatological perspective is essential for authentic worship, but an overemphasis on the subject can lead to substituting speculative activity for genuine Christian life and concern. In this letter Paul sought to weed out such speculation and direct his readers to concentrate on gratitude to God rather than idleness and inappropriate activity.

QUESTIONS

1. How does your view of the future and Christ's return affect the way you pray?
2. Affect your view of the church?
3. Affect your personal relationships?
4. Do you focus on speculations about the future?

14

Personal Letters to Philemon, Timothy, and Titus

Advising Leaders of Strategic Roles and Tasks in the Worshiping Community

In these letters Paul charged leaders to model Christian integrity in life and worship. He challenged Philemon to treat his converted slave as a brother. He instructed his younger associate in the farewell letter of 2 Timothy to develop authentic leaders of worship and community life, to avoid theological arguments, and to be an effective minister and evangelist. He advised Titus on the characteristics of genuine leaders and to confront opponents who disrupted worship and community life in Crete. In the collection of instructions called 1 Timothy, he provided advice to his colleague concerning: confessional worship statements, directions about church officers, relationships with both the community of faith and society, treatment of opponents, and personal exhortations.

Philemon[1]

Philemon is the shortest of the Pauline letters, but its size is scarcely an indication of its significance for the worshiping community of Christ. It models the spirit of Paul, and of his Lord. In it the apostle does not advocate a firebrand type of revolutionary activity for the liberation of slaves, but his advice is hardly less revolutionary in its far-reaching consequences. It is a document that deserves study by all Christians who desire to pattern their lives and worship on the self-giving Jesus.

Introduction to Philemon

This letter undoubtedly comes from the period when Paul was writing to the Colossians and was a prisoner as indicated in that work (Phlm 1; cf. Col 4:10). Timothy is likewise mentioned as a co-writer of this epistle (Phlm 1; Col 1:1). Epaphras, Mark, Aristarchus, Demas, and Luke are listed as companion workers with him (Phlm 23; Col 4:10, 12,14). The churches at that time met in homes. Apparently the home used in Colossae was that of Nympha (Col 4:16). We still speculate on whether or not Philemon was related to that church or alternatively to the nearby church of Laodicea along with Archippus who is mentioned in passing after the statement on Laodicea in the Colossian letter (Phlm 2; Col 4:17). Tychicus, who was one of the envoys that accompanied the Colossian letter (Col 4:7–8), is not mentioned in this epistle, but his companion traveler, Onesimus (Col 4:9), is the focus of this present epistle (Phlm 10–22).

Opening Remarks (1–7)

After the usual literary address to Philemon and the church in his "house" (Phlm 2), along with the typical Christian greeting of "grace" and "peace," Paul opened his remarks with a remembrance prayer of thanksgiving for Philemon, and with a notation concerning that leader's love and faith directed both to the Lord Jesus and to other believers ("saints"). This beginning was strategic because of the delicate nature of the issue with which Paul needed to deal. Obviously, Philemon had evidenced a loving spirit and had been a great support to other Christians, so Paul capitalized on that spirit in his argument (4–7).

Addressing the Problem (8–25)

Onesimus, whose name means "useful," had been a "useless" slave (11). He had run away from the household of Philemon. Subsequently, he had come into contact with Paul and become a Christian (10). Indeed, he had become a "useful" associate of Paul (11), but Paul knew the laws with respect to slaves and so was sending Onesimus back to Philemon, even though he probably would have preferred keeping him as an assistant (12–13). The question was: How should he approach Philemon on this matter? The answer becomes evident in this epistle.

Paul felt quite justified that he could command Philemon to obey him. Instead, he appealed to him on behalf of the powerless Onesimus, who had now become Paul's child in the faith (8–10). Using this approach, he gave Philemon the opportunity to decide for himself. In doing so, he relied on the loving sensitivity of Philemon as a Christian to accept Onesimus as a brother (16). Yet Paul had another arrow in his quiver of logical reasons why Philemon should honor his request. This point was that Philemon owed his very existence as a Christian to Paul who was also his father in the faith. So Paul took the pen from his amanuensis and wrote these words in his own handwriting (19). Moreover, he told Philemon to lay any indebtedness he might have experienced in the loss of Onesimus to Philemon's indebtedness to him (18). Paul finished his argument by assuring Philemon that he was confident in his friend's loyalty to him and of his anticipation in visiting Philemon shortly (21–22).

WORSHIP SUMMARY

In summary, several perspectives become clear and should serve as models for the church in its struggles for authenticity and true worship responses, even today. First, Paul did not try to bypass the law of slavery. Second, he honored Philemon's commitment to Christ and his loving sensitivity as a Christian (4, 7, 20, 21). Third, he testified that authentic transformation can take place even in those whom Christians may not expect it could happen (15). Fourth, he focused on the real nature of indebtedness and the significance of grace extended to Christians, making sure that Philemon did not overlook this big picture (17–19, 25). Fifth, he let Philemon know what he (Paul) wanted his friend to do for the sake of the work of Christ (20). Sixth, he attempted to initiate a quiet revolution, because, when one treats a slave as a brother (16, 20), the end of slavery is in sight. Seventh and finally, he bathed the situation in prayer (4, 6, 22). These perspectives can be applied to many situations in the life and worship of the community of faith, to the end that the grace of the Lord Jesus Christ may be witnessed in Christians (25)!

QUESTIONS

1. How does treating another person as a brother or a sister affect the relationship?
2. Affect your worship?
3. Affect your church?

The Pastoral Epistles[2]

The Pastoral Epistles have been the black hole of New Testament scholarship. In the last two centuries, and especially since F. C. Baur, every conceivable argument has been raised either in support or in opposition to their legitimacy as genuine Pauline letters. It would take countless pages to detail those arguments here; however, since such is not the primary purpose of this work, I will simply refer to the introductions of recent commentaries. (See footnote 2.) I would particularly suggest that the reader consult the long and excellent review of the situation in William Mounce's commentary.[3]

I have chosen to treat the letters in the following order: 2 Timothy, Titus, and 1 Timothy, since it seems to me that the strength of the arguments for them having a direct relationship with Paul proceed in that descending order. In discussing each book I have consistently referred to the author as "Paul," but I leave it completely up to the reader what such a designation will mean to him or her. Nevertheless, whatever the reader should decide on the authorship question, I would suggest that these works should be treated in a manner that they are legitimately canonical. They are among the authoritative writings of Christianity and should so be treated.

Second Timothy

To begin a review of worship in the Pastoral Epistles with 2 Timothy may seem a bit unusual, but this letter is the stellar representative of the Pastorals. Accordingly, I deliberately chose to begin at this point because, if any of the three reflect the genuine perspectives of Paul on worship, this letter is the obvious choice. Second Timothy is like a farewell address, in which Paul called his young associate repeatedly to "remember" what he had learned as a Christian disciple as well as his heritage and his calling. The key advice from Paul, Timothy's supervisor, was for him to look back and to "remember" his commission to ministry through the worship rite of "laying on of hands."

Fanning the Zeal in the Face of Suffering (1:1–12)

Paul also challenged Timothy to become reinvigorated by God's grace so that his zeal for the work of Christ would once again be fanned into the fire of a dynamic life (2 Tim 1:6). Moreover, he was absolutely sure that the awesome divine presence of God in his servant's life would hardly lead to a spirit of timidity or fearfulness. Instead, God's authentic representative should evidence a threefold responsive spirit of power, love, and self-discipline (1:7). These three basic characteristics should be evident in victorious Christian believers and are hardly present in those who succumb to a spirit of defeat.

Accordingly, he reminded Timothy (and any other readers of this letter) not to be ashamed of worshiping and witnessing to the Lord, nor of worrying about the sufferings of Paul (1:8). Instead, he advised Timothy that he himself should be prepared for suffering on behalf of the gospel because, as Paul had indicated in Romans and elsewhere, the gospel may be despised by humans but it is the foundation for authentic worship and power in humanity (1:8; cf., for example, Rom 1:16; 1 Cor 1:18).

In a community culture in which shame and honor were important categories of existence, Paul's counsel is very significant. He clearly anticipated the coming of his own death (2 Tim 4:6). But he was neither afraid of death nor ashamed of his association in life with Christ (1:12). His entire focus on worship and life had changed from his life as a rabbi. The secret of Paul's new confidence was his eschatological perspective. He firmly believed in the coming/appearing of "our Savior Christ Jesus," who had rendered powerless (*katargesantos*) humanity's great fear of "death." In the gospel Christ had revealed the real nature of a Christian's future–namely, both ultimate life and incorruptibility (1:10). Paul's confidence in the gospel had so gripped him that it became the basis for his work as one of Christianity's greatest apostles and teachers. It also became the key factor in his ability to model for Timothy the meaning of ministry. Paul knew in whom he believed and was absolutely certain that God cared for him (1:11–12).

Guard the Faith (1:13–18)

He counseled Timothy, therefore, to copy his relationship with Christ both in terms of faith and love and to guard through the indwelling Holy Spirit the great deposit of faith that he had received from his mentor (1:13–14). Unfortunately, in reflecting on the situation Paul knew that not everyone would be consistent in the commitment to Christ. Many in Asia, like Phygelus and Hermogenes, had abandoned their faith. Nevertheless, a few, such as Onesiphorus's household, had continued to support him (1:15–17).

Leading the Faith Community (2:1–7)

Paul realized the crucial necessity of providing authentic leadership for the worshiping community. Not only did he challenge Timothy to model strong leadership himself, but Paul also advised him to choose and educate other competent leaders for the community of faith. In this process of orientating leaders, Paul provided three helpful illustrations.

First, good leaders should be like purpose-driven soldiers who do not get sidetracked by civilian interests.

Second, they should be like well-trained athletes who consistently follow the rules.

Third, they should be like disciplined farmers who know the sequences of the seasons and therefore are able to receive the just fruits of their labors (2:1–7).

Responding to Jesus (2:8–13)

Paul concluded by reminding Timothy of the strategic role that Christ and his resurrection had in the worshiping community. He did not pen a theological discourse concerning Jesus as the fulfillment of Jewish expectations, but rather a personal worship response by which he lived and worked. Jesus Christ was descended from David and had risen from the dead. In that act Christ unleashed the power of God for Paul personally and for the entire Christian community.

Even though in chains, Paul asserted, just as Luke had concluded in Acts, that the gospel could not be chained (2:8–9; cf. Acts 28:31). Because of the resurrection and the role it plays in our eternal destinies, all Christians are invited to confess with Paul that they can endure hardship and persecution (2 Tim 2:10–13).

Trusting God's Word and Not Human Arguments (2:14–26)

Timothy was warned that not all believers were of the same mindset. A number would tend to argue about the truth. Therefore, Paul instructed Timothy to prepare himself with God to be a faithful interpreter of God's word,[4] and avoid becoming entangled in word disputes because they are like a wild cancer or spreading gangrene in the community (2:14–17).

Indeed, some like Hymenaeus and Philetus actually had argued that the resurrection had already occurred–perhaps an early attempt at existentializing the future event (2:18; cf. a different argument of denying the resurrection in 1 Cor 15:12). Such arguments are a sign of impiety or ungodliness, but they can confuse believers. Therefore, since argument is hardly worship, the goal of the leader is not to argue but to assure believers that God knows those who belong to the Lord (2:19).

In a kind of "connectionistic" thinking, Paul's mind jumped to the difference between sacred and profane (common) vessels, and he compared people to the variety of utensils in a house. When a utensil is purified, it is ready for the appropriate use by the lord of the house (God). So Christians in their lives and worship should shun immature passions and abstain from senseless arguments that lead to quarrels, because they are in fact snares of the devil. Instead, Christian leaders should have pure hearts; adopt the patterns of faith, love, and peace; be patient; and teach others the ways of God with a gentle spirit. Their goal should not be to win arguments but to lead people into authentic repentance and worship (2:20–26).

False Ways in Closing Days (3:1–17)

Paul was convinced that, unfortunately, in the closing days of the world the ways of evil would increase, and people practicing all types of evil would be in evidence (3:1–4; cf. Rom 1:29–31). The reason for evil, as in Romans, is that people choose false worship practices rather than the honoring of God (2 Tim 3:5; cf. Rom 1:18–23). It would be just like in the time of Jannes and Jambres, who, under the devil's direction [Belial], sought to lead the people of Israel into false patterns of life and worship in opposition to Moses (2 Tim 3:8–9).[5]

Instead of yielding to such false ways, Paul offered himself as a model of life and worship for Timothy. In spite of sufferings and persecutions, Paul had remained consistent in his commitment to Christ Jesus; and, consequently, the Lord had rescued him repeatedly. It was clear to Paul that anyone else who would seek to follow Christ would likewise be persecuted, and that deceivers would increasingly flourish (3:10–13). Therefore, Timothy needed to be confirmed in his commitment to what he had been taught, even in his youth (cf. 1:5). The Scripture should become the bedrock of his faith (3:14–15).

The reason for such a reliance on the inspired Scripture was that it is an effective instrument from God: (1) for teaching what is correct, (2) for reproving what is wrong, (3) for setting straight the misguided, and (4) for guiding in the way of righteousness. The purpose of Scripture then is to develop mature people in God who focus their lives in worship and service for others (3:16–17).

Paul's Charge to Timothy (4:1–5)

Having thus outlined his prayerful desire for Timothy's effective leadership in the Christian community, Paul issued a forceful charge to his younger associate, one that could hardly be ignored, since it carried the force of a worship oath before the Judge of the universe (4:1). That charge was that, besides all that Paul had said so far, Timothy's overall task was to be a committed, convincing proclaimer (*keryxon*) of the gospel/word, who called humans to responsibility before God and patiently taught God's truth.

He was called to such a task in the midst of people who had inappropriate perspectives on worship—namely, they desired entertainment, wanted affirming teachers, and waited to hear pleasing stories and fairy tales (4:2–4). By contrast, Paul insisted that Timothy should be dependable, accepting of suffering, faithful in evangelism, and consistent in ministry or service (*diakonian*, 4:5).

Concluding Notes (4:6–22)

Paul drew these intense instructions to a climax with the reminder that he was about to become a worship offering ("poured out as a sacrifice," *spendomai*) for the Lord, but that he was confident that he was an acceptable offering. He detailed his acceptability with three powerful word pictures: an acceptable gladiator for Christ, a finisher in the marathon of life, and a preserver of the faith. He was convinced that God would reward him with the anticipated crown of righteousness. Moreover, Paul had never been an advocate of a private mysticism; instead, his view of worship was corporate. He firmly believed that all faithful Christians would receive the same reward on the great Day of the Lord (4:6–8).

He concluded this wonderful letter of advice to his dear associate with a heart-wrenching request for a visit from Timothy and Mark, and with a renewed warning concerning the opponents of Christ—men such as Alexander, and others, such as Demas, who had turned their backs on the gospel (4:9–16). Reflecting on his past rescues by the Lord, his mind was drawn up to God. Once again he penned a great worship ascription of eternal glory to the Lord (4:17–18).

WORSHIP SUMMARY

This epistle is a wonderful example of a farewell discourse, in which Paul sought to guide his young associate in matters of integrity in worship and ministry. He called Timothy to remember his heritage and avoid the pitfalls of false worship ways and deviant patterns of thinking. Using his own life as a model, he challenged Timothy to worship God with integrity, to choose leaders of authenticity, and to become for them a genuine model of leadership in the church in spite of his youth.

Paul's confidence in the younger Timothy also serves as a fitting example of how supervisors should direct their supervisees in the church. Effective teaching of integrity with God is not done by an insecure instructor, but rather requires a mature model who can personally embody the nature of true worship. This letter is a priceless message for the church and for all Christians. Paul closed this choice message, which has relevance especially for all Christian leaders, with a brief but pointed prayer for the Lord to be with the spirit of his son in the faith and for grace to be visited upon him (4:19–21).

QUESTIONS

1. When you come to the end of your life, as Paul was doing in 2 Timothy, how will you be evaluated?
2. Will you be judged as a model of worship before God?
3. Will you be seen as an example of integrity in life?
4. Will you be considered as having contributed to the work of the church?
5. Or will you be regarded as self-oriented?

Titus

Introduction to Titus

The letter to Titus is an intriguing document, including some sections that are recognizable as being strikingly Pauline in their theological focus (e.g., Titus 2:11–4 and 3:4–7), while other sections could be Pauline but are very general. These sections concern community relationships of the inhabitants of the island of Crete, pertain to a struggling Christian community, and are directed against opponents who seem to be hostile Jewish competitors. The maxim "Cretans are always liars, evil animals, idle gluttons" sets the gloomy context in which Paul recognized that Titus was working (1:12).[6]

It is difficult to fit a mission visit of Paul to Crete into his journeys in the Book of Acts since the only mention of Paul visiting Crete in that book was a brief stop at Fair Havens near Lasea as a prisoner on his way to Rome (cf. Acts 27:7–15). Did Paul visit Crete at another time? With Titus (Titus 1:5)? When did he winter in Nicopolis (3:12)? From other letters we do know of Tychicus (Titus 3:12; cf. Acts 20:4; Col 4:7; Eph 6:21 and especially 2 Tim 4:12) and of Apollos (Titus 3:13; cf. Acts 18:4; 19:1; 1 Cor 1:12; 3:4–6; 4:6; 16:12). Yet a number of questions remain unanswered.

Many scholars today simply lump Titus into the category of the Pastorals and consider all of them to be historically inaccurate and post-Pauline, displaying a later and more developed church organization. Yet each of the Pastoral Epistles is slightly different. While mentioning elders/bishops (Titus 1:5–9), these persons seem to be basically general church leaders. The book does not really seem to have much development in terms of ecclesiastical structure.

Introduction without Thanksgiving (1:1–4)

The book opens with a typical type of Hellenistic identification of the writer, Paul (Titus 1:1–3), that is almost as elaborate as that in Romans 1:1–6. It is as though Paul in both Titus and Romans was seeking to make certain that the readers would recognize not only his relationship to Jesus but also the significance of the awesomeness of Jesus whom Christians worship. He does so, however, without a thanksgiving. Omitting the thanksgiving section in his letters is rather unusual for Paul.[7]

Lacking Leadership (1:5–16)

He turned immediately to rectify an obvious problem in the church: namely, the lack of adequate leadership and its significance for the upheaval in the worshiping community. The lack of authentic leadership in the face of outside pressure to abandon the gospel of the grace of God can be very distressing for a worshiping community. The apostle recognized that reality and wanted the problem corrected immediately.

His advice concerning the appointment of elders/bishops is fairly similar to the instructions in 1 Timothy, but his focus is more stringent. Not only should the leaders be happily married model Christian parents, given to hospitality, honorable, good, truly holy, and self-disciplined; but they must also not be drunkards, arrogant, hot-tempered, violent, or greedy people. Their children should not be recklessly debauched or rebellious (Titus 1:5–8). Wow! Does this list mean that the worshiping community had some leaders who had some, or all, of the negative characteristics? If so, one can easily understand Paul's use of the maxim concerning the beastly Cretans (1:12), which I quoted earlier. They would hardly be imitators of the self-giving Jesus.

What is more, Paul added that the leaders should be people who are firmly grounded in the faith. He stressed that they should hold fast or cling to the faith (*antexomenon*, 1:9). He knew that words were not enough for sustaining the worshiping community. True modeling of authentic faith in life and worship was for him the necessary basis for being able to counteract the arguments of opponents to the Christian gospel.

Next, he attacked the insolent, money-grabbing outsiders who were upsetting the worshiping community with their deceptive teachings on matters of worship, such as Jewish circumcision and myths. Even though they proclaimed to know God, their lives actually revealed that they had corrupt consciences. Their actions were completely despicable. They had to be silenced because the Christians required sound teaching (1:10–16).

Solving Problems through Sound Teaching (2:1–10)

Titus needed to handle some matters immediately through sound teaching (2:1). The first issue related to an effective Christian household (2:2–6). The older men among them were to embody the model of Christian wisdom, discipline, love, and patience. The older women should not be evil gossipers or drunkards. They should be exemplary teachers of reverent living and model for the younger women how to be loving wives and good mothers so that they might evidence the qualities of ideal, chaste Christian women. Paul probably wondered what to say about the younger men and simply summarized the situation by counseling them to "use their heads wisely" (*sophronein*).

Before commenting on slaves, Paul must have realized that he ought to say something about the conduct of his colleague. If Titus' instructions were going to be effective in that situation, then his younger associate would have to model for the worshiping community in his own life what he was teaching them. He had to be a person of integrity. Both his actions and his words would have to be consistent so that all criticism of him would evaporate (2:7–8).

Paul concluded these instructions on the Christian household by reminding the slaves not to be obstinate nor steal from their households, but to be trustworthy and be faithful representatives of the Savior (2:9–10). These household instructions are rather more general than the ones in Ephesians 5:21–6:7 or Colossians 3:18–4:1 (cf. 1 Pet 2:13–3:7), but the perspective is not very different. The point is that family life ought to be modeled on the relationship that the worshiping community has with the Lord.

Worship and Divine Grace (2:11–15)

The text that follows is one of the crucial foundations for authentic worship and life, not only in the present letter to Titus, but in the Pauline corpus. The inspired author indicated that the grace of God is not only crucial for salvation, but also for development in Christian life and worship. God's grace enables believers to reject fraudulent patterns of worship and unholy styles of living.

In their place, Christians are enabled to exemplify godly ways of living, even in a hostile world, because they have an eschatological perspective (a sense of hope) that provides them with the ability to see beyond the current chaotic world to their anticipated future with their God and Savior. In giving himself for us, Jesus Christ freed us from the ways of evil so that we could live and worship him as a cleansed people whose acts of service conform to transformed lives (2:11–14). As a result, Paul instructs Titus to make this message absolutely clear to the believers in Crete and to let none of them misunderstand its import (2:15).

Believers as Citizens (3:1–4)

In the next chapter Paul returned to the issue of their lives in the wider community. He called on Titus to make sure the believers were exemplary citizens in all their relationships, whether it was with political authorities, in business and work activities, or in general relationships with others.

They were to be counseled to avoid quarreling and be cooperative in spirit because they were now transformed people who were not to be like the old maxim applied to Cretans. They had become new people who should have abandoned the old foolish and evil ways of life (3:1–3). Then once again Paul supported his instructions by reference to the transforming work of God in Christ our Savior (3:4).

The Power of Baptism and the Spirit (3:5–15)

Paul carried the argument a step further by instructing Titus to remind them of the foundational significance of their baptism and of the renewing power of the Holy Spirit in their lives, giving them their encompassing hope in Jesus Christ. In typical Pauline fashion, therefore, he linked all three aspects of salvation together (the initial stage of coming to Christ, the living out in holiness of that salvation in the world, and the anticipation of the future eternal life). To make sure the impact of these words was understood, he climaxed the statement of support with what is the equivalent of a worship oath by affirming the certainty of the statement (3:8).

He summarized his advice by instructing Titus to insist that believers make the appropriate applications of this advice to their lives in positive actions and in rejecting contentious arguments and pointless Jewish views on genealogies and issues over the law (3:8–9). He sternly advised Titus to warn those who desired to engage in such controversies that if they persisted in that activity, they should be shunned, since they were perverted people (3:10–11).

The letter concludes with a few greetings and other personal instructions and with a reassertion of the desperate need for believers to evidence transformation in their lives (3:14). He closed the epistle with the worshipful wish for grace to be experienced by all of them (3:15).

WORSHIP SUMMARY

This letter to Titus represents a serious attempt to counter deviant patterns of life and worship within the church. It confronts challenges from outside critics, some of whom seem to have been practicing Jewish forms of worship. The goal of the Pauline writer was to develop leaders in the church who could demonstrate authentic perspectives on worship and life.

QUESTIONS

1. Do you ever wonder if people might evaluate your community as liars, as idle, as gluttons, or as those who act like animals, in the way it was done in Titus?

2. What does it take to have such a categorization?
3. How can Christian worship and life make a difference in such a community?

First Timothy

Introduction to First Timothy

This epistle has caused scholars the greatest hesitation about Pauline authorship. While the first chapter flows in a fairly organized manner, much of the remainder of the letter has been regarded as being a somewhat haphazard collection of materials related to church organization, theological reflection, and community relationships. Some parts of the letter need not be viewed as totally un-Pauline, while other statements seem to reflect opposition to ideas that some skeptics have judged to be akin to gnostic or at least proto-gnostic thought patterns from a later period.

While it is difficult to obtain a consistent picture of the context of the church at Ephesus addressed in the letter (see 1 Tim 1:3), the references to church officers may suggest an ecclesiastical development that many scholars do not see present in other Pauline churches so far described. In spite of these as yet unsolved issues, however, the letter does offer some strategic insights or perspectives that are both significant and useful in considering our subject of worship and life in the Christian community. Whatever one decides concerning authorship, the letter still stands as an important statement about Christians in the early church and is part of our canon. It therefore demands our attention.

Confronting Heresy (1:1–11)

The epistle opens with the usual address of Paul to his recipient, Timothy, followed by the elongated greeting of "grace, mercy, and peace," which is used in the Pauline corpus only in 1 Timothy 1:2 and 2 Timothy 1:2 (cf. 2 John 3). As in Titus, Paul immediately launched into his major concern without pausing to express his usual thanksgiving.

Paul's concern was to make sure that Timothy confronted the opponents and deviants in Ephesus who were confusing and deceiving worshipers with their heretical doctrines (heterodoxy, *heterodidaskalein*) which involved speculative (Jewish?) myths, keeping genealogical records or pedigrees (1 Tim 1:3-4; cf. Titus 1:14), and arguments about the law (1 Tim 1:7-8). Those efforts could hardly lead to a stewardship of life (*oikonomian*) and worship before God. What was required was an authentic fourfold life of love, purity, clear conscience, and faith (1:4–5; cf. the sixfold list at 6:11). The deviants, however, had grossly misunderstood the law's role. It was not to be regarded as a redemptive blessing, as was the gospel, or as a status symbol of acceptance by God, as they presumed. It was to be understood as an instrument of divine warning against corrupt behavior (1:8–11).

Personal Worship and Prophetic Commission (1:12-20)

Having put the deviants in their place, Paul turned to the subject of worship and thanked the Lord for the gracious appointment of him to a divinely commissioned ministry or service (*diakonian*) in spite of the fact that he himself had previously been a blasphemer and persecutor of Christ (1:12-14). In a sense of worshipful ecstasy he confessed his former sinfulness and Christ's merciful salvation, concluding with an exalted ascription of honor and glory to the immortal, invisible God and ending with a forceful "Amen" that reminds one of the awesome praises in Revelation (1:15-17; cf. Rev 5:9-10, 13-14; 7:12).

Paul immediately returned to the subject of the opponents and reminded Timothy that he, too, had been prophetically commissioned to a similar task of being strong in the faith and battling vigorously with apostates such as Hymenaeus and Alexander (cf. 2 Tim 2:17; 4:14), whom Paul had excommunicated from the Christian community so that they would experience the onslaughts of Satan (1 Tim 1:18-20; cf. 1 Cor 5:5).

Household Code and Church Organization Issues (2:1-7)

He next addressed various items, some of which are generally related to household code concerns, and others related to organizational issues. He began with advice concerning the political arena and counseled Timothy to lead the worshiping community to pray and give thanks for authority figures and to live as godly and honorable citizens, obeying the tranquility requirements of the *Pax Romana* (1 Tim 2:1-2).

He set his advice concerning their social responsibilities in an overarching personal and confessional (theological) context of a response directly to God as Savior and to Christ as the Mediator who provided for humanity the effective means of redemption ("ransom," *antilytron*) in God's own timing (*kairos*, 2:3-6).

Women's Roles (2:8-15)

The next passage has become a divisive section on women's roles. It is imperative to notice that these household roles were initiated in a worshipful context of prayer on the part of men (2:8). Women are introduced in terms of modesty and piety, eschewing their contemporary concepts of flamboyancy and allurement. Several problems, however, have been created for modern interpreters besides the usual references to "submission" that I have treated at length in the interpretation of other household codes (especially in Ephesians 5:21-6:9).

These problems are the so-called silence text and the reference to childbearing (1 Tim 2:11-12, 15). Concerning silence (*hesychia*), the same Greek term appears in 2:2, where it is usually translated as living in a "quiet" lifestyle within Roman society. Paul's goal is for Christians to be respectable citizens in the context of their society. Acceptable Christian activity is Paul's contextual concern both in society and before God.

The childbearing text, however, is much more difficult to interpret. Rabbis no doubt had often discussed the implications of the fall and the curse of Eve. (See 1 Tim 2:14; cf. Gen 3:16.) Blaming Eve for humanity's problems was not foreign to their discussions, but one must not forget that Paul in Romans also blamed Adam for the problems in society (Rom 5:12). Early and modern interpreters have sometimes sought to solve this problem of childbearing by speculating that the related curse on the serpent (Gen 2:15) was on Paul's mind as he wrote this. They have suggested that childbearing here refers to the birth of Christ (a kind of proto-evangelium text). Some early Christian scribes even altered the Greek text to conform to that idea. In my readings of the Jewish rabbis, I have learned not to think that any interpretation is impossible; any idea could have been in the mind of Christians who functioned like the Jewish rabbis.

While such an interpretation could be possible, it is at least a stretch! The alternative of women being saved through pregnancy (2:15), however, runs completely counter to the entire New Testament witness. The result is at best a standoff in the meaning and certainly presents a conflict in understanding within the Pauline corpus when compared to Galatians 3:28 and most of the household code texts in the New Testament.[8] At least the passage concludes by returning to the concept of women living and worshiping as authentic people of God (1 Tim 2:15).

Bishops and Deacons (3:1–16)

The next section (3:1–16) deals with the offices of bishop and deacon. Note that chapter 5 appears to describe a consoling office of widow. In contrast to references concerning churches in the other Pauline letters, the structure here does appear to be a little more developed. In the brief statements of Titus, the terms elder(s)/bishop are mentioned, but not deacon, and it does not appear that a developed structure was implied there. The reference to overseers and deacons in Philippians 1:1–2, however, should give pause before hasty conclusions are reached. Similar to Paul's teaching in Titus, the bishop was expected to be happily married, a good parent, honorable, hospitable, a good manager, not a recent convert, and certainly not a drunkard or a violent, arrogant, or a greedy person. A leader thus should be well respected in society and not easily manipulated by the devil (3:6).

The deacons are likewise to be persons in good standing in the community and blameless. The reference to women (*gynaikas*) at 3:11 could either refer to deacons' wives or perhaps even to women deacons, but the use of the term again at 3:12 may argue against the latter interpretation.

Paul expected to join Timothy in Ephesus shortly, but just in case he was delayed he wanted the household of God/the church to act in an exemplary manner with authentic leadership (3:14–15). Yet leadership and authenticity were not ends in themselves. They were aspects of Christians' responses to Christ. So he closed this segment with a magnificent sixfold confession (3:16) concerning the awesome nature of the "mystery" of Christ, who came in the flesh, was vindicated in the Spirit, was beheld by angels, was proclaimed to the nations, was believed in the world, and was received into glory!

Coming Apostasy (4:1–16)

Times were coming when people would apostatize, follow demonic views, and adopt pseudo-worship patterns by denying marriage and forbidding the eating of God-given foods, which, when received with prayerful thanksgiving, are sanctified (4:1–5). Timothy's task as a good minister, therefore, was to teach his people the truth and to dismiss stupid myths. Like a good athlete, he had to set the proper goals and remember that his ultimate hope was in God as the Savior of humanity (4:6–10).

To accomplish his ministry, he needed to be an example of integrity in life and–even though he was young–to lead his people to integrity through the reading of Scripture, through preaching and through instruction. He needed to remember that he had been commissioned through the laying on of hands as a God-endowed proclaimer. His responsibility was to preach to both himself and to his people so that all would experience eternal life (4:11–16).

Church Organization and Relationships (5:1–25)

In the fifth chapter Paul discussed organizational matters and relationships within the church. Everyone should be treated appropriately, as if they were members of a loving family, whether they were old or young, men or women (5:1–2). The church should–on a long term, even lifetime basis–support elderly, caring widows who had no one to care for them. The church should give such widows pastoral duties of praying for others, caring for visitors or strangers, helping the poor or troubled, and modeling the meaning of goodness. This "office" of widowhood in the church was not meant for all widows–only for those who were model Christians and had proved their integrity in life.

Younger widows and others who had not proven their integrity and caring were not to be enrolled in such a permanent position. Paul enjoined them to seek support elsewhere or to remarry. Just as in Jewish tradition, Paul here insisted that any relatives of these widows had the God-given responsibility to care for them so that the church could care for unsupported widows (5:3–16).

In a kind of stream-of-consciousness thinking, Paul returned to elders and their need for support. The church should give "double" honor to those who did their work diligently! Apparently, by this time churches paid their ministers. The matter of payment must have also raised in Paul's mind another issue: the criticism of elders, to which he applied the standard procedure of requiring at least two or three witnesses to bring charges against an elder. The matter was to be handled in a public forum and not secretively. The issue of improper conduct by an elder, in turn, brought to mind the act of commissioning elders. Paul warned Timothy to be careful in laying hands on any person.

This idea evidently brought the issue of alcohol to his mind. Medicinal use of alcohol was quite legitimate (5:23). It should be clear to the reader that in the flow of these disparate thoughts several facts emerge. First, the writing is more like wisdom literature, akin to Proverbs or James, than to deliberative reasoned argument typical of Paul. Second, it appears that the church had reached a stage of development at which leaders were being supported. Third, if the document is not a collection of materials, it is a least a somewhat hastily written document by Paul or someone else who jumped from point to point in reminding the reader of appropriate church procedures.

Slaves and False Teachers (6:1–21)

The sixth chapter continues in the same type of connectional thinking. It begins with household reflections on slave and master relationships. Although one-sided, emphasizing only slaves' responsibilities, the statements would not necessarily be un-Pauline (6:1–2; cf. Eph 6:5–9; Col 3:22–4:1).

The next segment urgently challenges Timothy to teach his people correct doctrine concerning Jesus Christ and to warn them against false teachers (6:3–10) who are arrogant windbags, anxious for argument, hungry for money, and trying to ensnare people into their way of thinking. Such writing would also not be totally foreign to Paul. What is significant is the classic wisdom reminder that we came into the world with nothing and we shall leave the same way, an echo of Ecclesiastes 5:15 and Job 1:21 (cf. Gen 3:19).

In a world that saw the Pharaohs building great tombs filled with costly items for the journey to the next life, such wisdom ran counter to the significance of storing up treasurers on earth. It definitely reflected the perspectives of Jesus concerning things (Matt 6:19–21) and of Paul and others who maintained that resurrection was the key to the future and not transference of status or possessions (cf. 1 Cor 15:42; cf. Jas 5:1–3).

The chapter reaches its climax in a series of exhortations concerning abandoning any practices similar to those of the false teachers. Timothy's duty was to model before others the qualities of righteousness and authenticity, just as Christ did even in front of Pilate. Timothy's task was always to keep mindful in his worship and life the visionary image of the coming of the Lord Jesus. Then, Paul's thoughts once again soared as he reflected on the mystery of Christ and the magnificence of the Sovereign God, the Lord of lords, the immortal, invisible, and totally other one to whom honor and eternal authority belong. Usually when Paul contemplated such a lofty ascription, he added, as he did here, his confessional "Amen" (6:14–16).

He concluded the letter with some additional instructions concerning riches and impious verbal exchanges that give the appearance of wisdom but lack true piety (6:17–21). He closed the letter with a benediction of "grace" upon his associate, assured that the younger leader would follow his advice.

WORSHIP SUMMARY _____

This epistle contains a wealth of advice for Christians in terms of appropriate leadership patterns, lifestyles, avoidance of heterodox views, and of adherence to appropriate worship practices. The thought patterns of the letter (though challenged by some critics) are thoroughly Christian, although the presupposed church structure may be a little more developed toward a patristic-type church than is usually presented in Paul. Accordingly, the reader should remember that various patterns of church structure are present in the New Testament. The general worship concerns are not un-Pauline. The theological confessions expected of the faithful are to be regarded as quite appropriate for such a letter of advice given to an emerging church that was attempting to confront an early Gentile world of loose standards and syncretistic patterns of worship and life. First Timothy can provide significant guidance for churches that are seeking to relate to rationalistic people who have minimal standards.

QUESTIONS

1. What does it take to make an authentic leader in a worshiping community?
2. How do your worship and life conform to the patterns suggested in this Book of 1 Timothy?

15

Hebrews

Worshiping in the Tension Between Assurance and Warning[1]

The preacher of Hebrews presents a picture of Jesus as the Christian's great high priest who beckons the believer to maturity in life and worship even in the face of suffering and adversity, while also warning the follower against turning from the way of salvation and failing to reach the intended reward for the faithful in Christ.

Hebrews is a unique book in the New Testament. It is not a letter like Romans, nor a historical work like Acts, nor an apocalypse like Revelation, nor a Gospel presentation about Jesus like Mark. It most resembles a sermon—a very special sermon that calls the Christian reader to proceed beyond elementary matters of the faith and discover a mature level of Christian life (Heb 6:1). It is exceedingly rich in liturgical implications and is a strategic resource for any who would grow in their understanding of Christian worship.

Introduction to Hebrews

For readers nourished on the works of Paul and John, the Book of Hebrews often offers a rather tough menu to digest. The discussions about covenant, sacrifice, priesthood, tabernacle, and the ancient Jewish cult seem to be rather strange and foreign to contemporary readers. Hebrews contains some very strong passages about "falling away" or apostatizing (cf. 2:11; 3:12; 6:6; 10:26–29). Many Christians do not want to entertain such a possibility, let alone think of it as presented in Hebrews. To add to these matters, the Greek of Hebrews is rather Alexandrian in structure (a kind of neo-classical type), which forces the average New Testament student of *Koine* Greek to return to grammars and lexicons for adequate interpretations. But the committed study of Hebrews can be a very rewarding experience for the reader who would spend time gleaning the valuable worship nuggets from its minefield. The homiletical text itself, as William Johnsson correctly notes, alternates rather systematically between exposition and application.[2]

The original readers of Hebrews faced a bleak, almost hopeless life. Like the Jews, they had to deal with the unpredictable Roman powers. Life appeared much worse for the early Christians at the time when Hebrews was written. Not only did they have problems with Gentile authorities, but the Jews were also hostile to them.

We often say, "Only God knows who wrote Hebrews!" Of course scholars have suggested many names for the preacher—from Apollos to Priscilla. An intelligent guess would be someone associated with the priestly class of Jews who may have lived or worked in Egypt. The writer's ideal messianic model for Jesus is not a Davidic king as it was for Paul (cf. Rom 1:3), but a priestly figure like Melchizedek (cf. Heb 5:6–10; 7:15–22).

Jesus: Superior to the Angels (1:1–14)

Hebrews opens (1:1–4) with one of the highest christological statements in the New Testament (cf. John 1:1–18; Phil 2:5–10; Col 1:15–20; Rev 1:7, 12–16). Angelic sub-figures had become exceedingly important because of the general view that God was remote and transcendent. The people of Israel felt the need for angelic agents to communicate with a God who for them seemed hidden and unconcerned about their plight under the oppressive Roman heel. The point of the argument in chapter 1 concerns the perceived authority ladder involving the relationship between God and humans. One might wonder how helpful and encouraging it might have seemed to the readers to read that they had not yet suffered "to the point of blood" (*haimatos*) or death (Heb 12:4). The opening chapter is crucial in suggesting the answer. In no uncertain terms the writer explained that with the coming of Jesus the authority chain had been radically altered. The old descending authoritative ladder of the Jews, from God to angels and then to humans, had been irrevocably changed. Angels were to be recognized as having little theological hierarchical status in comparison to the awesome Christ who was God's Son (1:5). Indeed, the angels worshiped him (1:6) because the son was *sui generis* with God's self (1:8, 13). If angels worshiped Christ, what did that mean for humans? One can almost sense the refrain, "O come let us adore him," in the background.

Indeed, so radical was the new perception of the authority ladder that the angelic order actually was seen as having been appointed to serve Christians (1:14)! The question then immediately becomes: If the angels were thus dethroned, what did it mean for pagan gods whom the Gentiles worshiped? Paul would have agreed that they were no gods at all (1 Cor 8:4). Such worship would be completely illegitimate for the Christian. Do you see why early Christians refused to put even a pinch of salt on the altar of Caesar?

The Incarnate Christ and the Family of God
(2:1–3:19)

The situation should therefore be clear. In conquering death, Christ brought Christians into the family of God, the true family of Abraham. Moreover, since in the Incarnation Christ shared the same flesh and blood nature as mortal Christians (not angels; cf. Heb 2:16) and had conquered death for them (2:14), Christians ought not to be afraid even of death and its imprisoning chain that usually holds humanity in its power (2:15). Therefore, the preacher announced to his Christian readers that they should pay attention lest they be drawn away from the full implications of Christ's coming (2:1). If they failed, they would receive not God's promised rest (3:11), but rather God's judgment (2:3). It is imperative to understand the implications of this argument. A correct perspective on Christ is essential to adequate worship! Proper worship in turn provides the Christian with the basis for resisting sin and temptation and of gaining the needed resource for living an obedient life (2:18).

All the preacher could do in the light of such a vision of Christ as the perfecter of our faith through suffering (2:9–10) was to respond with all the congregations of God's people in praising God, as he quoted parts of Psalm 22 and Isaiah 8 (Heb 2:12–13). The significance of being identified with God through Christ's holiness completely overwhelmed him with a sense of worshipful gratitude (2:11).

Having seen the guiding power of the Holy Spirit in reflecting on Psalm 95 (Heb 3:7), he employed the Psalm (cf. Heb 3:8–11) as the basis for issuing a stern warning not to yield to a rebellious "unbelieving, evil heart" that could lead them to "withdraw" or apostatize (*apostenai*) from "the living God" (3:12). Moreover, since the preacher realized that the true worshiper is hardly a "lone ranger" in the matter of spiritual development, he challenged his readers to "counsel" (*parakaleite*) one another to faithfulness (3:13), knowing that even the Torah Moses delivered was ultimately intended to serve Christ and his new message for Christians in the days to come (3:5–6). Apostatizing or failing to follow the implications of worshiping Christ can only lead to a failure to receive God's intended "rest," just as the disobedient Israelites failed to gain the promised land and died in the wilderness (3:16–19).

Jesus: The Caring High Priest (4:1–5:14)

The ensuing section pictures Jesus as the caring great high priest who had traversed the vicissitudes of life without sinning. Now this priest calls Christians to his very throne room where they acknowledge him as their Lord and receive his merciful grace (4:14–16). The frailties of the earthly priesthood, such as those of Aaron (5:1–4), hampered earlier patterns of worship, but the case is quite different with the priestly Jesus. He was completely obedient (5:7–8) and is thus able to provide "eternal salvation" to all those who are obedient to him (5:9). He is God's chosen priestly representative in the pattern of Melchizedek (5:10; cf. 7:1–19; and Gen 14:19–20). One of the primary aspects of authentic Christian worship is faithful obedience to God's Son.

Accordingly, Christians are forewarned against being slothful, inattentive, and failing to develop in righteousness (Heb 5:11). Instead of choosing to continue like babies in their faith, they are summoned to a mature Christian life that recognizes the radical differences between the ways of good and evil (5:12–14).

The Cost of Falling Away and the Faithfulness of God (6:1–20)

Christians are not simply to rely on early evidences of a relationship with Christ such as liturgical patterns like baptism, initial experiences of grace, and the coming of the Holy Spirit into their lives. Neither are Christ's followers to regard liturgical cleansings and the laying on of hands to be ultimate. Nor indeed is the initial recognition of being eschatologically oriented by sensing the actual reality both of judgment and eternal reward to be regarded as sufficient (6:2–5). The force of this section is that worship experiences must lead to maturity in life. Failure to accept the call to maturity violates the essential nature of worship itself. This description of persons is so poignant that if these words had appeared in any other context, the average minister would immediately have extracted and employed them as the finest summary of what it means to be a Christian found anywhere in the New Testament. But coming where they do, along with the harsh words indicating the "impossibility" of restoration after "falling away" or consciously departing from God (6:4, 6), they have been shunned by many proclaimers of the gospel. Yet such shunning only indicates the widespread misunderstanding concerning the purpose of Hebrews. Moreover, it highlights the general failure of readers to perceive the fact that there are two statements of "impossibility" in this context (6:4 and 18) rather than just one.[3]

The overall purpose of Hebrews is not only to warn Christians of the seriousness of their worship of Jesus Christ, but also to advise them of the unfailing commitment of God in Christ to provide them with the resource of God's strength and forgiving grace. Hebrews also emphasizes the fact that Christians must rely on the Lord for their support and not simply count on their own human resources. Like an anchor, God will hold God's people stable (6:19) in the vicissitudes of life because God cannot prove untrue to God's nature (6:17–18). God's high priest, Jesus, is absolutely dependable, but human beings are still responsible for their own acts. Liturgical formulas and "sacred actions" of the church such as baptism, the Lord's Supper, and the laying on of hands will never remove the importance of human responsibility.

Jesus: Superior Priest, Covenant-Maker, Redeemer, and Hope
(7:1–10:39)

Having detailed his major thesis that believers must not only understand and worship God's own Son, but also must develop a mature relationship with Christ that moves beyond the early evidences of being a Christian, the preacher turned in the following chapters to bolster his presentation. First, he returned to an important concern and reasserted the absolute superiority of Jesus' priesthood to that of Aaron (chapter 7). Then in chapters 8 and 9 he added that a flawless covenant could only be established by Christ (8:7) who did not sin (4:15) and who, through his unrepeatable sacrifice (9:12), provided for our redemption. His sacrifice and covenant proved that all earlier patterns of worship were merely shadows or imperfect copies (8:5) of God's ultimate plan for the salvation of mortals and for their patterns of appropriate response in worship. Levi, Aaron, and Moses (7:9, 14; 8:5; 9:19) were not inappropriate for their times, but earthly copies of heavenly models are not the same as the divine realities (9:23). They were merely "shadows" or "previews" of what was to come (10:1). Therefore, it goes without much argument that the mere "blood" of animals such as "bulls and goats" in earlier worship practices could hardly take away human sin (10:4). Instead, it took God's action in the very life sacrifice of God's Son, Jesus, to cleanse humanity of sin and open human access to the holiness of God (10:11–22).

Given such a gift of God in Christ Jesus, the preacher directed his Christian readers to some very strategic issues. First, if God did so much for us, should not our worship of God reflect the reality of our eternal hope and evidence our love and good works as an appropriate response (10:23–24)? Second, the preacher had difficulty conceiving of how Christians could willingly neglect meeting together for worship. Did they not realize the eschatological nature of their meetings (10:25)? Moreover, how could they continue to sin deliberately after having experienced the knowledge of the truth? Did they not know that Christ only died "once" for sin and that they were in grave danger of greater judgment when they failed to take his death seriously (9:12; 10:26–27; cf. 6:6–8)? Of course, the preacher fully understood they were being persecuted, suffering public exposure, being imprisoned, and having their property confiscated (10:32–34). But he needed to warn them not to "toss out" (*apobalete*) their confidence (10:35), but rather to realize the significance that God was actually in Christ, and if with him they endured, they could gain their promised inheritance.

Our Responsibility to Faithful Predecessors (11:1–12:29)

Pain and difficulties in life were not something new for God's people. Many faithful servants of God had gone before them—from Abel, to Abraham, to David and Samuel (11:4–32), and on to the many other nameless ones who had been cut apart, stoned, and killed, yet remained faithful (11:33–40). These forebears in the faith were now like a massive support group in an arena. Along with Jesus—their great model—they were watching intently as their successors in the faith were running their own marathons of life (12:1–2).

Christians were not alone in their pilgrimages and needed a reminder that Jesus himself had led the way and was summoning them to accept the disciplines of life, so that they, too, might receive the reward of being designated as legitimate children of God (12:3–11). Reflecting a disciplined life in the face of adversity was, for the preacher of Hebrews, a sign of one who was able authentically to worship God in Christ and had chosen to follow him throughout life.

A Call to Complete the Race (13:1–25)

Summarizing his advice to the Christian marathoners, the preacher called them to reinvigorate their flapping arms and buckling knees, to clear out the impediments of life that blocked their way in completing their race, to learn the real meaning of living in peace and holiness, to avoid the corrupting power of resentment, and to reject accepting the easy choices in life that lead to ruin, as in the case of the pitiful Esau (12:12–17). He reminded them by reference to two mountain scenes that represent two ways in life (12:18–24) that God's final judgment will shake all creation (12:26–27) so that only those who engage in a worship that pleases God will actually be accepted (12:28–29)! The preacher expected true reverence and genuine awe before God. Nothing less would do in the face of God's purging fire!

He closed his sermon with a few general exhortations and a powerful illustration for those who are attracted by a life of comfort. In the context of a camp setting, Christ is likened to the sacrificial animals burned outside the camp to prevent their contaminating the camp. Therefore, the preacher beckoned Christians (those who would follow Christ and enter the eternal city) to join their Savior outside the camp and accept the kind of abuse he experienced (13:10–14). For our benefit he added the imperative that we should offer "our continuing sacrifice of praise to God" through Jesus Christ (13:15)!

WORSHIP SUMMARY

This magnificent homiletical masterpiece is a necessary corrective to simplistic concepts of Christianity and immature examples of worship that seek to avoid suffering and disciplined following of our great high priest. The sermon powerfully challenges Christians to move beyond initial responses of worship to maturity in Christ. It sternly warns believers not to turn their backs on the Lord, nor to reject his summons to follow him even to the point of death. Christ and his faithful martyrs have mapped out the path to peace. They wait to witness later Christians who are consistent in their worship and who are committed to accepting the model of Jesus, even if it means rejection and persecution. True worshipers are confident that the way of their Lord who has passed through the veil to God is the only path that leads to eternal rest. It is the authentic worship "outside the camp" that provides acceptance by the victorious Lord who is enthroned in heaven.

For the preacher, consistent authentic life modeled on the worship of God's awesome son Jesus was the only adequate response to his ultimate sacrifice for us. He concluded his sermon in a climactic doxological benediction with the words: "Glory be to him forever and ever! Amen" (13:21). The faithful worshiper should also assert a confessional, "So let it be!"

QUESTIONS

1. What would going beyond the elementary aspects of worship and faith involve for you and your church?
2. Where are your people in relationship to moving on to maturity?
3. Where are you?

PART IV

Pastoral Concerns for Worshiping Communities

Reflections on the Catholic Epistles

The second segment of epistles contains seven books encompassing three assigned to John, two bearing the name of Peter, and one each from James and Jude. The various authors penned these works with quite distinct goals in mind.

The seven catholic (not addressed to a specific church or individual) epistles differ quite significantly from each other. James is most like wisdom literature. Jude is quite apocalyptic in style and has some sections that appear to have a very close kinship with 2 Peter, so that some dependency appears to be likely. First Peter is an important letter of advice for Christians who sense alienation in the world and are suffering persecution. First John is more like a theological tractate that critiques opposing views on the Incarnation of Jesus and on inauthentic living. Second John is very brief, dealing with opposition as well. Third John is a delightful little letter of concern.

16

James

Pithy Community Instructions for Life and Worship¹

The wisdom of James is a desperately needed message for the church. It calls for integrity in worship and condemns sham Christianity that attempts to separate religious practice from the way believers live their lives.

The Book of James is one of the most practical writings in the Bible. It forms an inspiring collection of intriguing pithy statements, or maxims, that direct the reader to a Christian way of life and worship. In format it resembles the Wisdom literature of the Old Testament and is not unlike some of the sections in the Book of Proverbs.

Introduction to James

Unfortunately for many Protestants, James has often been marginalized because of Luther's caustic judgments concerning its value. Patently, he consigned the book, along with several others, including the book of Jude, to a sub-canonical status wherein it was regarded as appropriate for reading and devotional guidance but not for the formation of Christian doctrine.² In so doing, he missed the strong connection between worship and action in the formulation of correct doctrine.

Prior to Luther, some earlier Christian writers such as Eusebius and Theodore of Mopsuestia questioned its canonical appropriateness. The book is not found in the early Muratorian list of canonically accepted writings. Yet the book was not always so viewed. Among those in the early church who defended its status were Hillary and Augustine. These advocates and to some extent Jerome, in turn, influenced the book's acceptance by the ecumenical councils. The reports of Jerome's acceptance of James, however, seem to have been rather mixed, a fact that seemed to weigh heavily for Luther, who was looking for support against James after his debates with Johann Eck, who used James 2:17–18 against Luther's exposition of Romans 1:16–17 and Galatians 3:11–12. Fortunately for Christians today, the old battle between works of the law and grace has partly subsided in the recognition that the giving of the law by God was an early aspect of God's grace as the Lord sought to lead his people into an understanding of the necessary role of worshipful obedience in a proper relationship to the living God.

James declared himself to be a servant of both God and Jesus, but whether he was the same James who was one of the four bothers of Jesus (cf. Mark 6:3) and one of the "pillars" of the church (cf. Gal 1:19; 2:9) is difficult to be certain. Was he the James to whom the resurrected Lord appeared (1 Cor 15:7) or some other James, such as the son of Alphaeus (Acts 1:13)? Some writers would be tempted to "tie the knot" and identify him as the apparent leader of the Jerusalem church (Acts 15:13) and the brother of Jesus. They may be correct.

As far as the setting is concerned, about all that can be said is that the Greek is quite good, which has led some to think that it could hardly have been written by a Palestinian Jew, but rather by a Hellenist in the Diaspora. Such a view supposes that Galileans could not write good Greek, a position that is no longer generally accepted. About all that can be presumed about the dating is that it was written in the middle of the first century. The question of its delayed canonicity (discussed above) was not so much because of its content but because the early Christians were not sure who wrote it.

The Book of James is a gracious set of directions meant to help God's people in following proper patterns of worship and life. In typical Wisdom fashion, James moved from subject to subject in a kind of stream-of-consciousness thinking that frustrates readers bent on organizing or systematizing his book. I will not try to identify the strands of thinking in James. Instead, I will focus on the matters that pertain to the relationship between worship and life.

The Impossibility of Being Double-minded
(1:1–2:8)

James was absolutely convinced that "wishy-washiness" in worship and life are doomed. Accordingly, he thundered that a "double-minded" or "two-spirited" (*dipsychos*) person is a complete anomaly. Such a person tries to be on both sides of a position and so in life is like a rudderless ship. Even though he or she might seem to honor God in words, such a one should not expect God's approval (Jas 1:6–8). James knew that Christian life was filled with all kinds of trials, yet he wanted believers to be stalwart in their commitments and advised them to accept life with joy (1:2)! Such joy is not self-motivated, but grows out of a worshipful response to the mysterious divine presence in one's life.

Contextually, then, the church is not meant to be merely an assembly (*synagoge,* cf. 2:2) of self-directed or self-willed people who attend some weekly show. Instead, the church is to be a "dispersed" group of worshiping and loving brothers and sisters (cf. 1:16, 19; etc.) who meet together and represent to the world the implications of being called by the name of the Lord (cf. 2:2; 3:9; 5:10), confessing their sins to one another and praying for one another (5:16) to the end that they might keep themselves free from the "staining" perspectives of the world (1:27). The teachers of the church are therefore warned not to enter into their roles lightly, because they will be subject to greater standards of judgment (*krima,* cf. 3:1). James clearly expected his readers to understand the radical nature of the gospel and to respond appropriately as Christian followers of the Lord.

When James suggested that one major goal of his work is the fulfillment of the "royal law" and identified it as loving "your neighbor as yourself" (2:8), he was very close to the perspectives of Jesus (cf. Mark 12:31 and parallels). Moreover, he was absolutely firm in his view that Christians should not make distinctions based on human or worldly attributes such as wealth. Accordingly, he used the church worship experience as his illustration and castigated those who gave preference to the rich in Church meetings and subjected the poor to places of less honor (Jas 2:1–6). He pointedly condemned such church practices as a blasphemy against the very "name by which you are designated" (2:7). Consistency in word and practice was clearly the object of James' work.

Faith and Works (2:9–3:12)

Such consistency was in fact the focus of his statement on faith and works that has been so badly misinterpreted in the history of Protestantism. When James stated that "faith apart from works" is to be judged as "dead" (*nekra*) or totally devoid of significance (2:26), he was merely confirming the necessity of consistency between one's words and one's actions, or between worship statements and activity in life. James was in fact an appropriate corrective to a misunderstanding of Paul's gospel. Thus, for example, he would bring a scathing condemnation on churches whose signs would proclaim that members are faithful Christians yet whose members in reality exhibit lives inconsistent with love and care for others. Worship of the true God in Christ Jesus must evidence itself in a style of life that is consistent with the self-giving Jesus. Otherwise worship is meaningless.

The implications of this message are far-reaching. Notice that James illustrated his thesis by the misuse of the tongue! Do Christians gossip? Do they speak evil of brothers and sisters (4:11)? Such was a crucial concern for James. Do we "bless" (*eulogoumen*) God in worship with our tongues and then also "condemn" or "curse" (*katapometha*) other humans with the same tongues (3:9)? Such activity among Christians violates the very nature of our worship! This manner of inconsistency in worship and life is doomed. James illustrated his reasoning by indicating that sour and good water can not come from the same well or spring, just as olives and grapes do not come from a fig tree (3:11–12).

Self-interest, Jealousy, and Church Fights (3:13–4:8)

James next moved to the electrifying issue of self-interest and jealousy. He contrasted these characteristics with humility and a meek spirit. Meekness and humility are not signs of weakness but of strength (cf. Ps 147:6; Matt 5:5). Scripture designates both Moses and Jesus as being meek (cf. Num 12:3; Matt 11:29). As a Wisdom teacher, James argued that self-interest and jealousy were not the results of worshiping God. They are the results of honoring demonic (*daimoniodes*) and earthly (*epigeios*) orientations (Jas 3:15)!

As though he envisioned the coming multitude of contemporary church wars and disputes, he asked his Christian readers the knotty question: "What is the cause of wars and fusses among you?" (4:1). Notice that he was writing to the Christian churches in the so-called Christian dispersion, using the typology of the Jewish dispersion as his model (1:1). Their terrible state of affairs, he responded, resulted because they did not know how to pray properly (4:3)! So, as did the Old Testament prophets, he castigated the Christians as "adulterers" (*moichalides*) who had little sense of what it actually meant to be Christians. Anyone who patterns himself or herself after the model of the strife-infested world is condemned as an enemy (*echthra*) of God (4:4). The answer to such strife in the church is to "flee" (*pheuxetai*) or to turn away from the devil and to submit (*hypotagete*) to the proper worship of God (4:7). Strife among Christians is a clear indication of an incorrect relationship to God, of sin in their midst, and of the existence of "double-spirited" (*dipsychoi*) people in the church (4:8). Thus, he returned to his opening evaluation of them as being a double-focused people who lacked an understanding of the proper implications of worshiping God (cf. 1:8).

Christian Hope (4:9–5:20)

Instead of submitting to the ways of the world, however, Christians are to be oriented to another world, awaiting the *parousia*, the coming of the Lord (5:7), the great Judge who stands at the door of the future (5:9). Christians find daily direction from the Lord. Whatever they do in their lives they do with the presupposition: "If the Lord wills [or permits (*thelesei*)]" (4:15). This premise should guide all of life. The lives of all Christians are to be lived as worshipful responses to God in Christ Jesus. Therefore, in the midst of suffering, Christians are to "pray"; while in the midst of joy, they are to praise God (5:13). They are also to be concerned and pray for the sick. The leaders of the church are encouraged to visit, pray with, and anoint such sick ones among them (5:14). All believers are to care for those who have "strayed" or "wandered" (*planethe*) from the truth among them (5:19).

WORSHIP SUMMARY

The message of James is a stern call for consistency between verbal profession and authentic activity in living. It is a summons to evidence Christian worship in every day life. It condemns sham Christianity and demands integrity. It is *not* an epistle of "straw," as Luther suggested, but a powerful complement to the messages of both Jesus and Paul. It is a text for the postmodern generation that has rejected rationalistic, formulaic confessions of faith from believers who have failed to embody those confessions practically in their lives. The mysterious awesome God who made divine requirements evident in Jesus expects consistency from believers and not double-mindedness in worship and life. The book is thus a very significant window for the Christian community on the integration of faith and works.

QUESTIONS

1. To what extent does your community of faith follow Luther's dictum that James is an epistle of straw—weak in theology and faith?
2. To what extent do you think your church considers James to be a strong guide for worship concerns?
3. What leads you to these conclusions?

17

Petrine Letters and Jude

*Living Eschatologically as Worshiping Exiles
and Sufferers for Christ[1]*

**In this collection of letters, 1 Peter challenges the readers, who sense
their "homelessness" in the world, to follow in the footsteps of Jesus
in life and worship. Then, in the related works of Jude and 2 Peter,
readers are instructed concerning the horrible end of rebellious pseudo-
worshipers and counseled to defend the faith and adopt the patterns of
authentic worship and life to reach their eternal goal.**

The Petrine letters and Jude are a unique group of works that focus on
how Christians should live and worship in the world with a sense of glorious
anticipation while experiencing temptation, alienation, and suffering.

First Peter

The letter of 1 Peter contains a marvelous message for Christians who
feel anxious, troubled, frightened, and intimidated by forces in society that
seem intent upon squeezing them into a base community mold or inflicting
on them harsh social and economic pressures because of a refusal to conform.
This well-written work was for early Christians a clarion call to those who
considered themselves as being treated like aliens, "homeless," and displaced
people in the world (1:1).

Introduction to First Peter

This letter does not advocate a "pie-in-the-sky Christianity," but rather
issues a summons to follow in the steps of Christ's suffering (2:21). It has often
been likened to a paschal liturgical challenge in which the acceptance of one's

baptism is viewed as a commitment to acknowledge hardship and suffering as an anticipated result of following Christ (4:12). It is one of the New Testament's superb statements on the meaning of authentic life and worship.

Some scholars have argued that the high standard of *Koine* Greek language here could hardly be that of Peter, the fisherman from Galilee, but one should not suppose that all fishermen were "ignorant" in the use of the language of commerce and communications. The statement in Acts 4:13 concerning the "learning" of Peter and John in the presence of the Sanhedrin is a typical view of the *am haeretz* (people of the land) by the Jewish scholarly religious elite. We certainly know that as fishermen they were not among the economically poor or disadvantaged (cf., for example, Mark 1:20); and, therefore, we must be careful in making assumptions concerning their Greek ability. Moreover, apparently Silvanus (Silas, the reporter from the Jerusalem Council and later companion of Paul, cf. Acts 15:32, 40) had some part in this letter (1 Pet 5:12), even though we are not entirely certain whether he was the amanuensis (secretary).

Some Bible students have argued that the dating must be later than the death of Peter under Nero since they think that the context suggests an empire-wide persecution of Christians, such as occurred under Domitian. But the attitude toward the emperor and the state in 2:13–17 is very different from that in Revelation (e.g., Rev 13) and would hardly support such a conjecture. Accordingly, I see no reason for suggesting that anyone other than Peter, the early disciple of Jesus, was the author.

The epistle is a general missive addressed to the churches of Asia Minor—from Pontus and Bithynia in the north, to Asia in the west, and Galatia and Cappadocia in the east (1 Pet 1:1). Since it contains few specific references to particular concerns in the churches, it seems clear that the document was a circular letter written from Rome as greetings were sent from the church in "Babylon," the Christian surrogate name for the capital city of the empire (cf. Rev 14:8; 17:5; 18:2; etc.). Peter mentions Mark (his son in the faith) as being with him there (1 Pet 5:13).

Homeless, but in Christ's Household (1:1–12)

The letter opens by attaching to Christian addressees the familiar Jewish designations of "exiles" and members of the "Diaspora" and by countering their sense of alienation with the specific historical term of the "chosen" (*eklektois*) people of God. Their destiny, sanctification and obedience, as Christians, however, are related to the Triune God (the Father, the Spirit, and Jesus, 1:2). The descriptive order of the Trinity, like that in Revelation 1:4–5, is different from our church confessions because it is prior to the agreed-upon, fixed order after the Council of Chalcedon.

To neutralize their sense of homelessness in society, Peter supplied them with an affirmation of their inheritance in Christ's household (1 Pet 1:3–9). He introduced the assertion by employing the familiar form of Jewish prayers, with a blessing of God similar to those in the Eighteen Benedictions and elsewhere. Peter added the blessing on the Lord Jesus Christ and his worthiness to be so addressed because of the resurrection (1:3). Unlike earthly inheritances, the Christian expectation is that the inheritance is imperishable (cannot rust or rot), undefiled (cannot be stained or polluted), and unfading (will not evaporate) because it is preserved by God in heaven (1:4). As a result, even though Christians are subjected to various forms of buffeting and painful trials, Peter is convinced they can rejoice in their plight because their sufferings strengthen their faith. Moreover, although they cannot see Christ at present, they love him, trust him, and can rejoice in their future salvation, which brings a sense of worshipful praise and glory to Jesus Christ (1:6–9). The apostle (1:1) also reminds them that they should not be surprised by their harsh experiences because their sufferings were predicted by the prophets, whose long-anticipated foresights–and even those of angels–concerning future believers' authentic responses to traumas, have been fulfilled in them though the Holy Spirit (1:10–12).

The Model of Holy Living (1:13–2:3)

Having thus briefly reviewed their context of life, Peter issued a series of strong commands to follow the model of holy living (1:15–16) by getting one's mind in proper order, maintaining a sense of self-control, and fixing one's hope on God's grace in Jesus rather than on the ways of one's former life (1:13–14). When one prays to the Father, one needs to understand that God can judge the integrity of the spirit and the interrelationship of one's worship and actions.

To be redeemed by the precious death (blood) of Jesus means to fear God in confidence while in the hostile world and to eschew the futile ways of society (1:17–21). The authentic life of the believer is patterned on Christ, who glorified God. Authentic life reflects genuine faith and hope and exudes an inner purity, obedience, and love in all things (1:21–22). This type of person has truly been "born anew" (*anagegennemenoi*), not from the seed of the world order, but from the living and eternal word of God. Such a one should not wither in time of trouble (1:23–25).

The mention of new birth raised the specter of the old ways of life, which Christians are unhesitatingly to abandon, such as: nastiness or sheer badness, game-playing or deceitfulness, hypocrisy or masking reality, envy or jealousy, and slander or false accusations (2:1). Contrarily, new birth implies starting life and worship afresh. Like newborn babies, new Christians are to be sustained in a new way by the unadulterated word of God. Salvation is clearly a process that implies a desire to grow in life and in the worship of God (2:2).

Jesus: The Living Stone (2:4–12)

Shifting the image to one that was personal and important to Peter (cf. Matt 16:18), he reminded his readers that Jesus is the living stone, the precious but rejected cornerstone in the edifice of true worship (1 Pet 2:4, 6–8; cf. Isa 28:16; Ps 118:22; Matt 21:42). Our calling as Christians in the spiritual building of God is to come before that living stone and, in imitation, become copies of him.

Indeed, the emphasis in worship is not on a building at all, but rather on a people–a holy and royal priesthood, a specially chosen people, a holy nation–who have an important task of representing light in the midst of darkness (1 Pet 2:9). Even though earlier, as Gentiles, his readers had no role in God's people, Peter firmly asserted that they have become God's authentic representatives through God's mercy (*eleethentes,* 2:10). Therefore, even though in the world they may now be treated like exiles or displaced persons, their task is to live in such a way that when those in their society see their actions they will be led to worship and glorify God (2:11–12).

Household Code (2:13–3:12)

With the shift in focus to Christian responsibilities in the world, Peter turned to the subject of the Hellenistic household codes. While he treated some matters not explicated in Paul, readers are referred to my earlier comments on Ephesians for a fuller discussion on the topic. Peter provided an important triadic insight into relationships of Christians. Since the entire Roman Empire was regarded as Caesar's household, Peter needed to make clear his understanding of relationships within that society. He acknowledged that Christians need to be subject to the orders of creation so that Christians might not be regarded as wrongdoers, but would silence, by their integrity, any false charges that might be leveled at the members of the church (2:13–16).

In this setting he made the startling triadic distinction in the way Christians related to others. Society in general should be "honored" or treated with respect (*timesate*). Other Christians should be "loved" (*agapate*), but God should be "feared" (*phobeisthe*). Then comes the crux of the matter. The emperor should be "honored" (*timate*). It goes without saying that the emperor does not deserve the same type of reverence or *WORSHIP* that belongs to God (2:17)! This distinction was very crucial in the Roman Empire as the emperors increasingly assumed the status of gods.

The local households also had their rules. As indicated in the reflections on Ephesians, the husbands, fathers, and slave owners had the right to establish rules, even severe ones, for their households. Yet in most of the Christian codes, unlike the Hellenistic codes, there were also divine instructions or rules *for* husbands, fathers, and masters. Here, however, the codes are incomplete and do not deal with fathers and children. They actually truncate the advice concerning slaves and masters by focusing only on slaves and their need to be responsible (2:18–20). Obviously, the matter of husbands and wives was foremost in Peter's concern.

Before turning to this important matter, Peter decided to lay a foundation for the discussion by calling his readers to follow in the footprints (or steps) of our model, Christ. Although Christ was perfectly sinless, he both was insulted and suffered an unmerited death. He could have countered the insults and threats with a powerful response, but instead he left the repayments to God (2:21–23). Through his very sufferings, we have experienced divine healing, since he took upon himself our sins (2:24). Our duty is to respond to this incredible mystery of his suffering on our behalf (*hyper,* 2:21) and, like straying sheep, return to our protecting Shepherd (2:25).

With this self-giving model of Christ in mind, Peter turned to the relationship of husbands to wives. He first instructed wives to follow the standard patterns of submission and not draw attention to themselves by outward adornments. He added that by their reverent and chaste behavior Christian wives might be able to lead their non-Christian husbands into a new relationship with God (3:1–5). In this endeavor Peter even cited a somewhat strange example of Sarah's obedience to Abraham. Then he lowered the boom on Christian husbands (3:6). They needed to recognize the frailty of their wives and remember that both members in the marriage were equal in the sight of God. Indeed, if husbands failed to recognize the joint nature of husbands' and wives' stations before God, the husbands would be subject to severe worship consequences–namely, the futility of their prayers with God! Just as in other Christian household codes, the big stick was once again directed at those who perceived themselves to be in charge of human relationships (3:7; cf. Eph 5:25–31; 6:4, 9). Failure to recognize the equality of women and men before God has worship implications of immense proportions. We are all merely human servant-worshipers before God in whom vests the authority of our faith.

Having completed his very sketchy discussion of the household codes, Peter next reviewed general relationships within the Christian community. He was aware that he was dealing with heterogeneous groups of people, and the issue was for them to become truly caring communities of faith. To describe his dream for them, he used five adjectives (3:8), three of which are *hapax legomena,* words used nowhere else in the New Testament. (These three words are denoted by asterisks.) His prayer was that they would evidence a spirit of harmony *(homophones*),* a sense of empathy for each other *(sympatheis*),* a community love for one another *(philadelphoi),* a compassionate attitude for each other *(eusplanchnoi),* and a humility of their minds *(tapeinophones*).* Indeed, his goal for them was to imitate the earlier model of Jesus, who refused to repay evil with evil and blessed others when they insulted him (3:9). In support of his vision for the church, he quoted from a great worship psalm of fear/trust in the Lord (3:10–12; cf. Ps 34:11–16).

Baptismal Exhortations (3:13–18)

In a very intense section, Peter turned back to the hostile context the Christians were living in and set his exhortations for them in the framework of their baptism and their ultimate hope. He questioned them about their fear. In doing so, he was not under any delusion that they were not experiencing pain and suffering (3:14).

Yet he directed them to bottom-line thinking in terms of their relationships with the Lord (3:15), and the fact that Christ had not only provided them with the model for dealing with such traumas, but had also overcome the forces of evil when he died once for all so that we might be brought to God (3:18).

Preaching to Spirits in Prison (3:19)

Peter inserted a statement that has become the subject of significant scholarly debate and strong opinions among Christians—namely, Christ's preaching to the spirits in prison (3:19).[2] The text has unfortunately been linked by many with the reference to preaching to the dead in 4:6. This unfortunate identification by some interpreters has led to a number of theories, such as the view that Christ "descended into hell," preached to the dead there, and allowed people to repent after death.

Several matters must be noted. The first is that the word "spirits" (*pneumasin*) is not used in the New Testament for dead people. The second is that the term often translated at this point in Bibles as "preached" (*ekeruxen*, 3:19) does not here mean to preach the gospel but should be better translated "proclaimed," as in proclaimed victory! Third, the term "went" (*poreutheis*) in 3:19 probably does not mean Christ's activity in any descent into death, but rather to Christ's ascent in the resurrection when all the evil forces were made to recognize that Christ was victorious over evil![3] Indeed, the Old Testament is replete with descriptions of the evil spirits being active in the world. In the strange text of Genesis 6:4, for example, the so-called sons of God pounced on the daughters of men, resulting in the incredible mixture of beings called the *Nephilim*. In the time of Noah everything disintegrated, and humans became as corrupt as the disobedient spirits.

Noah's Symbolism of Baptism (3:20–22)

The mention of Noah raised the issue of the ark and of water, which in Peter's mind was apparently connected to the rite of baptism. In the Noah story, water was in fact destructive, but the concept of being saved from evil suggested to Peter that baptism was the Christian's symbolic promise ("appeal" or "demand," *eperotema*) of victory with God because of Christ's victorious resurrection and the fact that he is now established at the right hand of God with all the principalities and powers subjected to him (3:21–22).

While the argument might seem strange and disconnected to us, it would be perfectly meaningful to a first-century Jew who had been brought up listening to the symbolic logic of the rabbis (cf. Paul's use of the escape of Israel through the Red Sea as a baptism in 1 Cor 10:1–2).

Sin and Death (4:1–6)

Employing the model of Christ once again, Peter raised the question of sin and death. The issue of the death of believers troubled the early Christians, so, just as in Paul's letters to the Thessalonians (cf. 1 Thess 4:13–18), Peter's readers must have wondered whether their end was really any different from that of their pagan neighbors. With respect to sin Peter concluded that those who have "suffered in the flesh have ceased from sin" (1 Pet 4:1). This text can be misunderstood, but it simply means that those who have died are no longer subject to sin.

The point of the text is to remind his readers of their renunciation of sin as Christians and the fact that the pagans are genuinely shocked at Christians' abandonment of their former wild lives. As a result, their former companions in licentious living have visited on these new Christians all sorts of ill treatment (4:2–4). Those earlier companions now despised them, but those pagans are not the ultimate judges of their future. Accordingly, Christians should be confident of the state of believers who had died in the Lord. It is precisely concerning the assurance of Christians' eternal destinies that Peter mentions this important principle–namely, that the gospel had been preached (*euangelisthe*, 4:6; contrast with *ekeruxen* at 3:19) even to those who had since died!

Using Spiritual Gifts (4:7–10)

Peter drew this segment of the argument to a conclusion by reaffirming the immanence of the end and by asserting the call to use the spiritual gifts that God had entrusted to them, including the communication to others of God's will, so that God might be glorified through Jesus.

As though he had been lifted to the very outskirts of heaven in worship, he closed this intense section with an ascription of eternal glory and power to God, and with an anticipated community prayerful response of "Amen" (4:11).

Final Exhortations (4:12–5:14)

In the final section of the letter (4:12–5:14), Peter comes down to earth again and delivers a concluding set of exhortations in three parts: (1) to Christians in the context of suffering (4:12–19), (2) to elders to assume their responsibilities (5:1–4), and (3) to members of the community (5:5–11).[4]

First, while their former companions were shocked by the transformation of the Christians, the Christians were counseled not to be astounded by the coming of "fiery trials" (4:12), since they are really only a prelude to the final cataclysm in which the mysterious glory of Christ will be revealed. In the meantime, the suffering of Christians should be understood as an element of worship, since in suffering the believers are being blessed and the glory of God is actually being revealed (4:12–14). The crucial issue is the reason for one's suffering. It must not be for any evil reasons, such as murder, stealing, or generally being a troublemaker or an evil nuisance (4:15). The glorification of God is the test. Suffering should serve as a stark warning of the impending judgment upon the disobedient that is coming and of the fact that few will escape its consequences (4:16–17). Therefore, even Christians are warned that in their actions they must reject sin and in full commitment entrust themselves to God (4:18–19).

Second, the exhortation to elders provides a superb picture of what Christian leadership entails. Leadership flows out of an authentic worship relationship with the self-giving God in Christ. Peter's instructions do not grow out of a top-down human leadership model, such as that of a chief executive officer, military general, or a legislating bishop commanding obedience from underlings. Peter's model features a collegial senior leader (*sympresbuteros*) to other leaders. Peter spoke as one who had witnessed the self-giving sufferings of Christ, and as one who had learned from the resurrected Christ that the task of a leader is to feed the sheep of Christ (5:1–2; cf. John 21:15–17 and Paul's exhortation in Acts 20:28).

Peter brilliantly summarized the Christian leadership model by means of three antitheses: (1) The *basis* for leadership should not be from some compulsion (*anankastos*) but out of a willing spirit (*exousios*) of divine service. (2) The *motivation* for leadership should not grow out of a desire for personal or economic gain (*aischrokerdos*) but from a genuine zeal (*prothumos*) to serve others. (3) The *style* of the leader should not be one of domineering or lording it over *(katakyrieuontes)* others, but rather one of modeling or exemplifying (*typoi yinomenoi*) for others the proper pattern of Christian living (1 Pet 5:2–3). The promise is that at the *parousia* (the appearing of the Lord), Jesus, the ultimate model leader and shepherd, will provide for his authentic human leaders of the worshiping community the unfading recognition (crown) of acceptable leadership (5;4; cf. 1:4).

The third and final set of exhortations is directed to all members of the Christian community. Picking up the concept of Christian mutuality in subjection from the household codes, Peter instructed the less mature in the faith to respect their elders and for everyone to evidence true humility to one another (5:5). As in all the Christian households, the ultimate authority does not reside in human leaders but in God (5:6).

The mysterious "mighty hand of God" is the basis for a Christian's security and the reason why believers in prayer and worship can throw upon (*epiripsontes*) God all of their pent-up worries and concerns (5:7). The Christian's God is not some *deus absconditus* (a distant, unconcerned God) of Hellenistic thought. God is the caring God we worship. This true God has been made known in Jesus Christ. God's concerns are very real for God's children; however, as Peter warned, we must also treat the presence of the devil as very real. We must firmly resist the evil one who, in mimicking God, is working throughout the world and is behind the suffering of Christians (5:8–9). Yet while the suffering of Christians is real, it is not for believers an eternal reality because beyond the suffering is eternal glory in Christ (5:10). In the interim, however, God in Christ can make us whole (restore us, *katartisei*), support us (*sterixei*), strengthen us (*sthenosei*), and establish our secure foundation (*themeliosei*). Once again Peter's spirit soars to heaven in worship as he recites a powerful ascription to God with another anticipated community response of "Amen" (5:10–11; cf. 4:11). Following a brief set of greetings, he extends the "peace" of Christ to all his dear suffering readers (5:14).

WORSHIP SUMMARY _____

This Epistle of 1 Peter is one of the foundational resources in Christianity for facing suffering and persecution as "exiles" in the world and for understanding the relationship of authentic worship to church leadership principles over against power politics and human management concepts. Christian life is viewed from the perspective of following in the steps of Christ, who alone deserves worship–in contrast to kings and emperors. Jesus' death and resurrection provide the basis for future hope and for worship as the "holy nation" or "people of God." In this letter Peter employs bottom-line thinking for the worshiping community, not in terms of economics, but in terms of eternal life and of relationships with others as his mind soars to encompass the greatness of the exalted Christ.

QUESTIONS _____

1. To what extent does your church think of itself as a community in exile or as aliens in this world?
2. What impact does/would such a view have upon your views of worship?
3. Would you even want to have such a perspective?

Introduction to Jude and Second Peter

The Epistles of 2 Peter and Jude are very different documents than 1 Peter. Moreover, since these two documents are clearly related, it is necessary to make some preliminary remarks concerning them. The second chapter of 2 Peter seems patently to echo the content of Jude and probably is an edited version of Jude. While Jude has been charged with being polemical, that charge is somewhat overstated and seems to apply more to 2 Peter than Jude. Christians may cite a few quotations from these two small books such as: the statement warning against the private interpretation of Scripture (2 Pet 1:20–21), God's perspective on time (3:8), and Jude's magnificent benediction (Jude 24–25). Still, it remains doubtful that most Christians pay a great deal of attention to these books. Furthermore, their references to strange apocalyptic matters detailed in *1 Enoch* and the *Assumption of Moses* (works in the Jewish Pseudepigrapha that virtually no Christians today regard as canonical), have led a number of Christians, such as Luther, to wonder about the level of canonicity of 2 Peter and Jude. Since at least 2 Peter seems to focus on the defense of tradition and both seem to slight the proclamation of the gospel, a number of scholars relegate these books to a period when Christianity had lost its enthusiastic zest and had become primarily involved in the preservation of "the faith."

The authorship question is also quite complex. Although a number of scholars are now prepared to consider that the James mentioned in the letter as Jude's brother (Jude 1:1) was the James who was Jesus' brother (making Jude also Jesus' brother), other possibilities are that he was the brother of another James (James Alphaeus, James the son of Zebedee, or even some James unknown to us). With respect to 2 Peter, there is no difficulty in identifying the person intended to be represented in the salutation, but the question remains: Was Peter still alive when this second epistle was written? One reason for this question is the reference to "all" the Pauline "letters" (*pasais epistolais*) as being a kind of authoritative collection of Scripture. Could such a view have been recognized already in the lifetime of Peter (2 Pet 3:15–16)?

These issues remain somewhat difficult to integrate into some people's views of the nature of the New Testament. While I am here quite prepared to accept the church's decision concerning the canonicity of these books and their contribution to the church's life, worship, and defense of the faith, these introductory concerns will no doubt impinge upon some people's conceptions of these books, as well as their study and use of them. Nevertheless, I consider them to be important sources for providing insight into the early church's perceptions of life and worship.

Jude[5]

The Beloved Faithful (1–11)

Jude is a very brief letter that opens with a reference to those who are loved by God and have been kept safe (*teteremenos*) in Jesus followed by a clear indication that there were some deviants among them (Jude 4). Jude regarded the faithful as those who were among God's "beloved" people, since he uses three expressions of that fact in the first three verses. He summoned them to defend the faith, which had "once for all time" been given to the "holy" (*hagiois*) of humanity, but was being perverted by those who advocated the acceptability of immorality and rejected Jesus as Lord (3–4).

In support of his condemnation of such people, Jude (5–7) reminded them that God actually destroyed the unbelieving people of Israel in the desert even though they earlier had been freed from Egypt (cf. Num 14:20–37), imprisoned disobedient angels (cf. 2 Pet 2:4; 1 Enoch 12:4; also 10:6 and 22:11), and destroyed Sodom and Gomorrah (cf. Gen 19:24). Jude undoubtedly desired these illustrations to serve as warnings about the fires of eternal judgment, because for him evil people were a blight on their society (Jude 7–8). They reminded him of the blasphemous devil who even argued with the archangel Michael in an effort to obtain the body of Moses (cf. the edited ideas in 2 Pet 2:10–11; the image likely came from an early edition of the *Assumption of Moses*). Such people for him should be compared to people like Cain, Balaam, and Korah in the Old Testament and were nothing but ignorant animals, deserving of destruction (Jude 9–11).

Judgment on Unholy Worship (12–25)

Jude's harsh reaction becomes evident because these pseudo-Christians had been joining in the Christian worship services, including their love feasts, and turning them into unholy, immoral escapades (12–13). From Jude's point of view, the patriarch Enoch had already declared that God would bring his vast forces (myriads) of holy ones and deliver judgment on them (cf. 2 Pet 2:17; 1 Enoch 1:9; 18:15–21; 60:8; 93:3). These pseudo-Christians were nothing more than "narcissistic-type," self-centered, loud-mouthed, flattering perverts who were fracturing the church and were neither following the teachings of the apostles nor the leading of the Holy Spirit (Jude 16–19).

Jude calls the genuine believers to establish themselves in an intriguing fourfold pattern of authentic worship by (1) adhering to the "most holy faith" (*hagiotate pistei*), (2) praying in the Spirit, (3) maintaining the way of love, (4) and awaiting the merciful coming of the Lord Jesus to receive them into eternal life (Jude 20–21). He adds a brief mission statement that involves helping the doubters and snatching them out of the judgment flames, showing mercy from a foundation of reverence or fear, and rejecting or hating all things that contaminate human life (22–23).

Jude closed his brief letter with one of the most loved and elevated benedictions of the New Testament, in which he prayed not only for their preservation from moral and spiritual stumbling or "falling" (*aptaistous*) but also for their ultimate joyous and unblemished presentation before God and Jesus Christ. Therefore, to both God and Jesus belong an eternal fourfold ascription of glory, majesty, power, and authority. To this worshipful confession all Christians should agree with their own hearty "Amen!" (24–25).

WORSHIP SUMMARY

The message is so short that it hardly needs a further summation. Those who pervert worship face certain divine punishment. The Christian hope drives believers to obey, pray, stay faithful, and love while waiting for Christ to return. Still, Christians should not become judgmental, but should do everything possible to rescue those who refuse to believe.

QUESTIONS

1. As you reflect on the great concluding benediction of Jude, what type of worship renewal suggestions come to your mind for your personal life? For your church?
2. Does your church follow Jude's fourfold pattern of worship?

Second Peter

Responding to Christ (1:1–11)

This second letter ascribed to Peter is also a general missive, but, in contrast to 1 Peter, it is not even directed to a specified group of churches. It merely opens with a general address to those who shared Peter's faith and standing in

Jesus as "God and Savior." While this significant theological assertion would be affirmed as a worship ascription to Jesus by most early Christians, at least by the later part of the first century, it is a little unusual here and ranks with John's report of Thomas' lofty confession of Jesus as Lord and God (2 Pet 1:1; cf. John 20:28).

What follows is a magnificent statement concerning Peter's view of Christians' worshipful response to the reality of Christ in their lives. Their godliness was based on the knowledge of their calling in Christ to share (*koinonoi*) in his life of glory and goodness (*doxe kai arete*), and on their escape from the world's corruption due to human passions or desires (*epithymia*, 2 Pet 1:3–4; cf. Rom 1: 24–32). Next comes a series of challenges concerning the characteristics Christians should evidence, including faith, high standards of morality, knowledge, self-discipline, community respect, and love. The point is that their lives with Christ should not be useless and unproductive, as was the case for blind or forgetful people who have no idea where they are going or what transformation from sin means (2 Pet 1:5–9). Living and worshiping Christ as our Savior implies earnestly focusing on what it means to be God's chosen people, avoiding the tragedy of moral and spiritual stumbling (*ptaisete*), and being ready to enter Christ's eternal kingdom (1:10–11).

Remembering the Truth (1:12–2:3)

Like a good Hellenistic counselor, Peter next adopted the "reminder" format of farewell addresses by calling his readers to remember the truth that they already knew. Being prepared to die, he challenged them to maintain a strong Christian stance (1:12–15). In support of his authority to give them such advice, he reminded them of one of the great highlights of his own worship experiences with Jesus, the transfiguration, in which he heard the voice of God saying, "This is my beloved Son!" That encounter was no fancy story or myth (*mythois*), and therefore they needed to give special attention to his prophetic declarations (1:16–19; cf. Mark 9:2–13; Matt 17:1–8; Luke 9:28–36) because authentic prophetic insights are not merely human, subjective, private affairs. They are insights supplied by the Holy Spirit and are like the sun breaking into the darkness of night (2 Pet 1:19–21).

The thought of authentic prophecy raised the specter for Peter of false prophets and teachers who were in their midst. Such persons underhandedly presented fraudulent teachings, denied the worship of Jesus as Lord, participated in evil practices, and led Christians away from the truth. From Peter's perspective their doom was assured (2:1–3).

Condemned Persons and Angels (2:4–22)

Peter recalled the message of Jude—or some early source similar to Jude—that detailed the record concerning depraved humans and angels whom God condemned. The wicked angels were imprisoned in the gloomy cells of Tartarus (usually translated in English as "Hell," 2:4; cf. 1 Enoch 10:4–14; 91:15; Jude

6) while earlier corrupt humans were destroyed by a devastating flood in the time of Noah and in a fiery destruction of the cities of Sodom and Gomorrah. Yet in the midst of such cataclysmic judgments, God spared eight people in the family of Noah and rescued Lot from the atomic-like "" fire of Sodom because God knows how to distinguish true worshipers from the immoral and ungodly, even in the context of judgment (2 Pet 2:5–10; cf. Gen 7:7; 19:29; Jude 7).

To make certain that his readers understood the true fallen nature of these pseudo-Christians, Peter detailed their characteristics. Audacious and arrogant, they were not hesitant in their anti-worship activity to scoff at the "glorious ones" (*doxas*), whereas Peter confessed that even the angelic forces (whether good or bad) refrained from charging them with their preposterous blasphemies (*blaspheemountes*) before God. God would deal with them. It was a certainty for Peter!

In matters of morality they were nothing more than dumb, sexually driven animals, even worse than the money-hungry Balaam (2 Pet 2:10–16; cf. Jude 10–12; Num 22:5–7). Peter's description of their pathetic lives would have caused even the Hellenistic moral philosophers to shudder in horror.

These pseudo-Christians were nothing but empty shells of immoral humanity. Their destiny was to be the horrible doom of joining the disobedient in the gloomy pits of darkness (2 Pet 2:17–17; cf. Jude 12–13). Although they apparently had known (*epignosei*) the Lord Jesus and worshiped him as their Savior, they again became enmeshed (*emplakentes*) in sin, with the result that their apostasy left them worse off than if they had never known the way of righteousness (*ten hodon tes dikaiosunes,* 2 Pet 2:20–21). He emphasized their state with the revolting maxim of a dog returning to its puking (2:22).

The Foolishness of Dismissing the Predictions of Prophets and Apostles (3:1–13)

Peter opened the third chapter with a very unusual statement by asserting that this epistle was his second letter (3:1), even though in style, language and content it hardly resembles 1 Peter.[6] In support of his condemnation of the deceivers, the writer reminded his readers of the legitimate "holy" prophets and their predictions concerning the end of time, as well as the apostles' instructions from the Lord. These pseudo-Christians, however, questioned the messages of both because they had observed the death of the ancients and of Christians and nothing seemed to be changed. So they ridiculed the messages, derided the worship of Christians, and mocked the anticipated coming of the Lord (*parousia*). They deliberately dismissed the awesome God who not only made the world, but is also the one who will judge all the ungodly (3:2–7)!

Ignoring God, for Peter, was blatant foolishness. His opponents also assumed that God is subject to human time sequences, such as days or years or even a thousand years. Such conceptualizing was sheer foolishness. Peter assured his readers that simply because God did not act according to any human timetable, this did not reflect a lack of power on God's part, but was an indication of God's patience and a desire that no one should perish. The judgment "Day of the Lord" would certainly come, and it would be unexpected, like the coming of a stealthy robber. It will be a time when all of the present creation will vanish in a divinely initiated, atomic-like cataclysm (3:8–13).

An Upbeat Closing Exhortation (3:14–18)

Second Peter closes with a more upbeat perspective, in which Christians are instructed to be zealous in their anticipation of the end and in the present to live authentic lives of purity and peace, recognizing that the patience of the Lord is actually a sign of their coming salvation, just as Paul in all his complex (!) letters had earlier (!) indicated (3:14–16).

Apparently the undisciplined opponents of Peter at this time were also patently twisting Paul's "hard to understand" (*dysnoeta*) words for their own purposes.[7] So Peter leveled another prediction of the forthcoming condemnation of these false teachers, while at the same time issuing a warning to his readers not to fall prey to their erroneous teachings (3:16–17).

WORSHIP SUMMARY

This epistle, which seems to be considerably later than the Pauline letters and 1 Peter, emphasizes the demented pattern of false worship and its consequences. While the writer issued some brief directives concerning worship and life in the first and third chapters, he focused most of his attention on his opponents and their abysmal lives and pseudo patterns of worship. For such people he had nothing except harsh condemnation.

He closed his work by challenging his readers to mature in both their understanding and worship of Jesus as their Lord and Savior, to whom belongs eternal glory (3:18). In response to this ascription he expected that all Christians would readily confess a concluding "Amen!"

QUESTIONS

1. In viewing your church worship services, to what extent do you think they are syncretistic—combinations of New Testament ideas, nationalism, and social mores?
2. To what extent are you concerned about patterns in your corporate worship experiences?
3. What suggestions would you make for your church? For your own personal life?

18

Johannine Letters

Developing an Orthopractic Community of Worship Amid Internal Conflicts[1]

The Johannine works form an integrated collection that deals with the problems of division in the church, and demands from the worshiping community an integrity of correct theological confession and loving, self-giving practice in life.

The epistles of John form an intriguing collection of works that center on internal controversy within the Johannine community. Each of the three books has a different focus, but each is aimed at terminating the inner upheaval in the church and dealing with the opposition so that the unity desired in the gospel (cf. John 17:20–21) could be achieved. The goal of the collection is both the integrity in believing and worshiping of Jesus as the incarnate Son of God, and of embodying that worship in the Christ-modeled way of love. Thus, the collection, represented primarily by 1 John, asserts the necessary coherence or alignment of orthodoxy and orthopraxy.

Introduction to the Johannine Letters

The three works seem to be interrelated and may even have been delivered to the recipients together. The reason for such a suggestion is that 1 John is not actually a letter, but rather more like a theological paper advocating/defending the positions of the foundational community concerning Jesus and the life of love. The role of 2 John almost seems to serve as an introductory or covering letter for 1 John. One should notice that the only uses of the term "antichrist" in the entire New Testament are used in these first two works with reference to the opponents who have caused a fracture in the writer's missionary community

(1 John 2:18, 22; 4:3; 2 John 7). Then, 3 John could almost function as a companion, friendly missive addressed to Gaius on the matters of integrity in the community as they pertain to love and correct teaching. It includes the identification of Diotrephes as a clear opponent who represented a direct challenge to the writer in the experiences of the community of faith.

These documents probably arose out of the same milieu (or school) as the Gospel of John. In spite of some scholars' arguments to the contrary, the general language and structure of 1 John is sufficiently similar to the gospel to assert a significant commonality. The writer of 2 and 3 John calls himself the "elder," and church tradition has assigned the name of John to these two documents. For ease of discussion, I will at times also use the name "John" for the author, realizing that it does not appear in these epistles. Not much can be said about the recipients of these works, but it is usually presumed, following early tradition, that the community may have been in Asia Minor around Ephesus.[2] Likewise, matters of dating are rather uncertain, but the books probably come from some time in the nineties of the first Christian century.

First John

Introduction to First John

The "letter" of 1 John, as any new Greek student will acknowledge, is rather easy to read. Such an assertion does not mean that the document is easy to interpret. The reason for any difficulty is because of the ways in which the author repeated and connected his theological affirmations or evaluations and at times linked them with practical applications or implications. Statements sometimes do not adhere to one another in what contemporary readers might consider to be direct logical deductions. The elder was wrestling intently with the issue of those former members of the community whose ideas had deviated from his teaching and who had accordingly departed from the group. At the same time the writer wished to reconfirm those who had remained in the fold, anxious for them to evidence a loving integrity. Condemnation and insistence on love were being united in briefly related statements. For us, the result is some redundant and/or missing links. Connecting those links with the historical setting is not always easy because, while we do know what he affirmed, we are not certain that the deviants actually represented the opposite points of view. Such opposite views may simply be the reverse side of a statement. John employed a number of major themes from the Gospel of John, such as the importance of witness, life and death, truth and lying, light and darkness, remaining in a proper relationship, being born of God, and of course the significance of love.[3] The elder developed these themes as elements of a living and worshiping community of faith.

Personal Testimony to Christ and the Authentic Worshiper (1:1–10)

The writer opened his discourse with a testimony asserting personal experiences of the historical Jesus Christ, the Son of God (1 John 1:1–3). The "we" of the testimony undoubtedly refers to the original witnesses, of which he claimed to be one. The reference to "the beginning" picks up the expression from the prologue in the Gospel (John 1:1), but here it probably does not mean the beginning of time, but rather the beginning of their experience with Jesus. The purpose of the letter, he asserted, is to provide the community and himself with a full assurance of joy (1 John 1:4; cf. 2 John 12; 2 John 3; cf. John 15:11; 16:20–24; 17:13). The next verse also reflects the emphasis on the difference between light and darkness from the prologue of the Gospel. Here it is used as a means for introducing the alternative between people who walk in the light and those in the darkness (1 John 1:5; cf. John 1:4–5). The series of conditional sentences that follow define the authentic worshiper as one who does not walk in darkness but in the light, who lives in the truth, who has fellowship with the community, who does not lie but recognizes sin, confesses it and is cleansed from sin by the blood of Jesus, and is forgiven (1 John 1:6–10).

Atonement and Keeping Away from Sin by Walking in Love (2:1–17)

Like a concerned parent, John applied his concern to their integrity and advised them to keep themselves from sin. If they did sin, he assured them that Jesus, their counselor ("paraklete," *parakleton,* cf. John 14:15–16:14), could provide the effective worship atonement (*hilasmos*) for their sins—as well as for those of all people! But the basis for realizing such assurance was nothing other than obedience, which means "walking" in the way Christ walked (1 John 2:1–6; cf. John 15:10, 14).

The concept of walking (*halak*) with God or in his statutes is a fundamental Old Testament idea that does not mean merely keeping rules, but rather living life in worshipful obedience to God (cf. Deut 28:9; Pss 55:14; 81:13; 86:11; 89:15; Prov 20:7; Ezek 18:9; compare in the New Testament Rom 6:4; 2 Cor 5:7; Gal 5:16; 2 John 6; etc.; contrast walking after other gods in Deut 8:19; 2 Pet 2:10; Jude 18). Among those who were said to have walked with God are Enoch, Noah, Abraham, and Hezekiah (Gen 5:24; 6:9; 17:1; 48:15; 2 Kings 20:3; Isa 38:3).

John followed the above statements on obedience by defining the context of obedience as love, which encompassed the commandments of both the Old Testament and the new way of Jesus. Accordingly, the one who loves others belongs to the light, whereas the one who hates others belongs to the blinding darkness (1 John 2:7–11). Convinced that the readers belonged to the light, John used a series of Greek couplets to reason that their sins had been forgiven in Christ and that they were victorious over the evil one (2:12–14). Yet he wanted to make sure that they were among the "overcomers," so he warned them about the wrong kind of love, namely desiring the things of the world, which have no eternal value (2:15–17).

End Times and Antichrists (2:18–29)

The elder turned to the problem that greatly troubled him. He was convinced that the end times were approaching and that a spirit of "antichrist" was infecting the world. Indeed, already many people in the world could be called by that designation (2:18). For this reason some of their members had left their community of faith. John wanted those who were left to remain faithful and to understand the truth. The departure of the deviants was a sign of their lack of genuine membership in the community.

Did the ones who departed their group deny that Jesus is the Christ? We can only surmise the answer. John wanted to make sure that the antichrist spirit did not infect the faithful, because on their confession of Jesus as the Son of God hinged the promise of their eternal life (2:18–25). He was confident they would not yield to a denying spirit because he was convinced that they had received the anointing of the Holy Spirit, which would teach them the truth and help them to remain faithful. He thus concluded this section with the great Johannine imperative of "abiding" or remaining faithful to God in Christ (1 John 2:28; cf. John 15:4–11), who would assure Christians that they are born of God (1 John 2:29; cf. John 3:3–8).

Children of God (3:1–18)

The mention of being born of God led him to define them by the beloved Old Testament designation as "children of God" (1 John 3:1). That relationship meant that the world would not understand their purity in worship, their patterns of life, or their destinies of being like Christ when he would appear in the future because the world did not earlier recognize who Christ was. In Christ's first coming in the flesh he had appeared to take away sin and destroy the works of the devil. So to continue in sin is clearly a violation of God's intended way for humanity. Those who continue in that pattern prove that they belong to the devil (3:4–8). To be born of God, however, means that one lives an authentic worship-filled life of love in Christ and therefore "cannot continue to sin"[4] as do the children of the devil (3:9–10).

Living a life of love means that the Christian is expected to live in a completely different way than the style of the self-centered murderer, Cain, who did not love his brother but instead killed him. Cain's life-orientation was evil. He did not know the meaning of worship and belonged to the world, which actually hates true Christians. To hate one's brother or sister is like being a murderer. Those who hate others have no way to continue to exist as persons destined for eternal life (3:11–15). Loving others does not merely mean saying one loves them. Words are cheap, and worship is pointless if it only consists of personal words. Loving others means being willing to die for them. It means sharing with those in need. Correct words and loving deeds together equal truth (3:16–18). Accordingly, 1 John is not merely about correct theological words (orthodoxy), but it also is about evidencing those words in Christlike actions (orthopraxy)! This combination is what makes Christianity genuine.

Christian Hearts (3:19–4:6)

Just as in the Old Testament God looked at the hearts of people, so in the New Testament and particularly here, the "hearts" (*kardias*) of Christians are the crucial measure of authenticity. God is supreme and knows people's hearts! Our hearts, not our heads, ultimately provide the assurance that we are people of the truth.

Of course, our confessions concerning Jesus are extremely important, but our hearts give us confidence with God. Our lives indicate whether or not we are truly obedient people who please the Lord. Indeed, this obedience from the inner core of a person provides the confirmation of the Holy Spirit in us (3:19–24).

So, Christians are to evaluate people's spirits to determine if they are really from God, because many pseudo-proclaimers are in the world. Those who belong to God are evident in several ways. They are marked as true worshipers: (1) by giving a true confession that Jesus is the incarnate Son of God, (2) by their lives in overcoming the temptations of the world, (3) by recognizing and being recognized as the true people of God, and (4) by knowing the difference between the spirit of truth and the spirit of error (4:1–6).

Godly Love (4:7–21)

To make certain his readers clearly understood his thesis, John returned to the importance of love. Love, he contended, is the key to authenticity because love originated in God. Those who truly love are born of God and know God. God, who is to be identified with love, modeled that love most explicitly by sending his only Son to be the worship sacrifice (*hilasmon*) for our sins so that we might live through him. Therefore, if God loved us, we are, as Jesus said, duty bound to love one another (4:7–11; cf. John 3:16–17; 13:34–35; 15:9, 12–14).

Love is the key to true worship. Since no one has seen God, God's loving example of Jesus is now embodied in those who love (1 John 4:12; cf. John 1:18). Although God has not been seen, the elder reasserted his testimony that the early witnesses had seen the Son of God, the Savior of the world (1 John 4:14; cf. 1:1–3). John was completely confident that those who continue to live in love actually also live in God. Their fears of judgment are, therefore, dissipated because fear and love originate from different realities in life (4:17–18). Those who say they love God and despise others in fact are liars because what one does in the phenomenal realm of the world has extremely serious implications for relations with the eternal realm (4:19–21). Love cannot be pigeonholed with nice statements about loving God and others or by hollow actions such as toying with worship and pseudo-activities of pretended love! Proclaimers of cheap love are, thus, forewarned about the coming judgment.

Confessing and Obeying (5:1–5)

In chapter 5 John drew his important theological statement to a significant climax by summarily reasserting the necessary connection between believing and confessing Jesus as the Christ on the one hand, and loving others and obeying Christ's way on the other hand. Such an embodiment in life is basic to being born of God and of overcoming the world's temptations.

A very significant fact in Greek demands our attention. The only place in the Gospel of John or in the Epistles of John where the noun *pistis* ("faith") is used is at 1 John 5:4. In all the other places the verb *pistuein* ("to believe") is employed. The apparent reason is that by the time these works were written, the community obviously had misinterpreted "faith" as information or head commitment and not as living commitment.

In other words, early Christians were misinterpreting the meaning of Paul and other missionaries. It is not "what you believe" that is crucial. "Whom you worship" and "in whom you put your trust" form the basis of Christianity. So when John used "faith" here, one should *not* suppose that he meant affirming a creed! Believing in Jesus as the Son of God meant for John putting trust in the living incarnate Son of God who directs the life of a Christian through the Holy Spirit (5:5).

Water and Blood (5:6–12)

John moved to a critical point for worship when he identified the coming of Jesus Christ as significant in terms of "water and blood." In its Johannine context, when Jesus died on the cross and was pierced by the soldier, out of the wound flowed "blood and water." The evangelist emphasized the significance of this fact by making what is virtually an oath concerning the legitimacy of that testimony (John 19:34–35). The modern mind that is focused on rational deductions may have difficulty in perceiving the strategic importance of this liturgical symbolism, but water and blood are important symbols in Christian worship.

They undoubtedly point to the rites of baptism and the Lord's Supper as being of significance in the life of Christians. Then the Spirit is added prior to water and blood at 1 John 5:8. Why? The reason is that, without the Spirit, these sacraments/ordinances are merely empty rites or activities of Christians. It is not a minister or a priest who gives significance to the rites, but the Spirit of God, the other "paraklete," whom Jesus promised to send (John 14:16) and whom he gave by breathing on the disciples in their resurrection meeting (John 20:22).

So while human testimony is important, God's testimony in the Spirit provides effective power and eternal life through the life of God's Son. Without divine power there is no life, and worship rites are merely empty shells (1 John 5:9–12).[5]

Belief, Prayer, and Eternal Life (5:13–21)

John moved the discussion to a conclusion by reminding his readers again that active believing is the key to eternal life and the basis for answers to our prayers (5:13–15; cf. John 15:16; 16:23–24). He appended a statement on the seriousness of sin and the importance of Christians in praying for sinners. He added a caveat, however, that there were sins, just as indicated in the Old Testament, that could not be treated through regular worship procedures.

Sins of the "high hand" or deliberated sins were left for God to handle. They were beyond mere human worship patterns of intercessory intervention (1 John 5:16–17).

Just in case the Christians were anxious that they were among the group of such sinners, he reaffirmed their relationship as those who had been born of God. God's power could preserve them while the world was under the powerful spell of the evil one (5:18–19). As John closed with the assurance of Christ's provision of eternal life for them, like a caring father he also balanced his assuring words with a warning for them to avoid idolatry (5:20). Assurance and warning belong together in the gospel proclamation, and John understood the solemn need for that balance.[6]

WORSHIP SUMMARY

This Johannine tractate is a powerful argument for the absolute necessity that words and actions belong together. True orthodoxy presupposes orthopraxy. Love is the key to life and worship. Failure to love is a failure "to walk" as Jesus walked and is condemned. It is in fact a failure to acknowledge him who came "by water and blood," the great symbols of Christian worship. Loving God and loving one's neighbor are the true indications of a person who worships God—namely, one who has been born of God and does not continue to sin. Such a person is directed by the Holy Spirit and has the promise of eternal life.

QUESTIONS

1. If love is actually a key to understanding Christian life and worship, what kind of innovations might you suggest should be made in future worship renewal patterns?
2. How do your worship patterns deal with congregational and personal sin?
3. Have you ever worried about committing an "unforgivable sin"? What did you do about it?

Second John

Second John is a severe letter. As indicated in the introduction to this section on the Johannine letters, 2 John is very short and may have served as the cover letter for 1 John, which is not really a letter at all, but rather a theological discourse.

As with most Greek letters, this one has the "x to y" formula—namely, "the elder to the elect lady and her children." The latter description undoubtedly is a designation for the church to which John was writing. After a rather elongated greeting involving "grace, mercy, and peace," and a reference to both God the Father and Jesus Christ "in truth and love"(2 John 3), the elder plunged immediately into his concern for the church. He first expressed his joy in detecting that "some" of the members/children had been faithful and were observing the proper instructions on love (vv. 4–6). "Many," however, had apparently fallen into the deceptive ways of the world and denied the Incarnation of Jesus. If, as I suggested above, this letter may have served as an introduction to 1 John, then the problem of apostasy would seem to have been quite severe and the reference to such persons as deceivers and antichrist figures would coordinate with the longer letter/discourse (2 John 7; cf. 1 John 2:18–23; 4:1–3).

The letter is short, pointed, and needs no summation except to say that the emphasis in this brief missive is much more emotive and oriented to correct theology/teaching than the fairly carefully nuanced combination of words and practice emphasized in 1 John. The writer was obviously very disturbed at the number of those who had deserted the community of faith and was anxious to plug the leakage by calling for the rest to remain true to correct teaching and not lose their reward for faithfulness. Indeed, he even warned them not to welcome anyone into their midst who deviated from true teaching (2 John 8–10). He concluded by indicating that he hoped to visit them and confront the problem in a face-to-face encounter so that he could help to rebuild their joy. He then closed with a brief greeting from a sister group of Christians (2 John 12–13).

Third John

Third John has a very different feeling from that of its previous counterpart. It has a more irenic spirit, even though it still deals with an upsetting conflict. It also may have accompanied 1 John, but instead of being addressed to the church (the elect lady), it was addressed to Gaius. Apparently Gaius was one of the leaders whom the elder respected and who followed "the truth," probably a hint at the controversy that was taking place in the church (3 John 1, 3–4). He apparently had accepted messengers from John, whereas Diotrephes had not (vv. 5–6, 10).

Diotrephes, the protagonist in the dispute, could well have been the recognized leader of the church (or the deserters?). He not only did not accept messengers from the elder/John, but he excluded them from church meetings (v. 10). He had clearly challenged the elder's authority, even bringing evil charges against him (v. 9). We are not certain whether Diotrephes was the leader of those who had since left the church (cf. 1 John 2:19; 2 John 7), but such is not impossible. The situation obviously had greatly troubled John, but rather than detailing the issues in this letter (v. 13), he preferred to deal with them through a face-to-face encounter in a visit he planned to make to them shortly (v. 14).

The letter contains only a little in the way of information related to worship and life, except to commend the imitation of goodness and the avoidance of evil, which could easily have appeared in the writings of a Greek ethicist (such as Epictetus, for example). The context for the references to God (vv. 6, 11), however, needs to be understood as referring to Christianity, even though Christ is not mentioned. John commended Gaius for following the truth and for evidencing love and service to others (v. 5–8). He also mentioned Demetrius in this letter as an example of integrity (v. 12). We are not certain whether he was an emissary who carried the letter or a colleague of Gaius in the church there. Finally, although the letter did not open with the usual greeting of grace and peace, it closed with a brief greeting and a benediction of peace (v. 15).

WORSHIP SUMMARY

These Johannine works as a whole provide an early example of the fact that disputes do occur in the church and that not all Christians are authentic worshipers or representatives of Jesus Christ. But these works are also testimonies that faithful leaders sought to bring resolutions to the disputes and that words are not the only basis for judging the integrity of Christians. Only when words and actions of Christians are united in embodying the example of Jesus do worshiping believers truly represent God's intentions for sending Christ Jesus into the world to save sinners.

QUESTIONS

1. The Johannine epistles are very harsh on those who lack consistency between worship affirmations, on the one hand, and both their personal lives and divisive actions in the Christian community, on the other. Have you witnessed such patterns in the churches you know?
2. How would you suggest that Christians should deal with such examples?
3. What conditions decide whether a situation can be dealt with by correspondence or must be handled face to face?
4. Has a "Diotrephes" ever troubled your church? What resulted? How could the church have responded more effectively?
5. How does a church disagreement affect its worship?

PART V

Mysterious Cosmic Expectations of the New Worshiping Community

Reflections on the Book of Revelation

19

Revelation[1]

Anticipating Eternal Worship

The New Testament concludes with an awesome presentation of God's ultimate plan for leading God's people to their blessed hope and for dispatching from the world the evil enemies of God. While this mysterious book of Revelation has been the subject of frequent speculative manipulation, it provides a blessing for those who discover through its symbolism its magnificent insights into authentic worship and its directions for life.

The Apocalypse of John, or "Revelation" as it is known in English, is a magnificently designed work whose content reveals the reigning Jesus Christ, God's mysteriously unique messenger, who with God is the victorious conqueror of the evil powers and the hope of suffering believers in the world. The responses of the worshiping community in heaven have reverberated throughout history as the model of what Christian worship should be upon earth. Indeed, the Greek word *proskyneo* ("to worship" or "to bend the knee in obeisance") is used more in Revelation than in any other book in the New Testament. Revelation has inspired countless poets, storytellers, painters, and musicians in their artistic productions that have blessed Christians throughout the ages. One only needs to mention the names of Dante Alighieri, John Bunyan, Albrecht Durer, George Frederick Handel, Paul Hunt, and C. S. Lewis, among many others, to recognize the significant impact those inspired by this book have made on the world.

Introduction to Revelation

The book's symbols, numbers, images, and word pictures have also been the subject of numerous gross speculations, fervent curiosities, constant recalculations of the end of time, and repeated identifications of historical figures from Domitian (the new Nero) to the Pope and Luther, and more recently to Hitler, Saddam Hussein, and various terrorist leaders as the beastly personages represented in its descriptions. Such errant interpretations should not lead Christians who seek a vision of God's hope for the world to abandon the book. Granted, the language and symbols tend to be very strange for contemporary readers, but the book should not be avoided by Christians because of its mysterious presentations.

Unfortunately, many preachers, writers, and interpreters tend to avoid most of Revelation except perhaps the introductory chapter, the letters to the seven churches, and the vision of heaven (Rev 21–22)–either because they do not desire to delve into apocalyptic literature or because they are genuinely skeptical that the book has much to say about the gospel. But the book itself promises a blessing to the Christian worshiping communities where it is read aloud to the hearers, who are instructed to listen and obey its words (Rev 1:3). While Revelation is a written document, it was directed to an oral culture. That is the reason many segments of the book are in hymnic or liturgical form and can be easily recalled.

It would be an understatement to say that authorship of revelation has been debated. The John of Revelation 1:9 has been variously identified as some elder by that name (cf. 3 John 1) or alternatively as some other unknown person. Whatever one may decide on the authorship question, when one does a comparative study of this book with the Gospel by John and the epistles, it quickly becomes evident that this work arose out of the same thought milieu or community of faith as that Gospel, because it emphasizes familiar ideas such as "I am" (e.g., Rev 1:8, 17; 22:13, 16), the "Word" of God (e.g. 19:13), and the "Lamb" (e.g., 5:6; 6:1; 12:11; 13:8; 19:7, 9; 22:1, 3) for Jesus. The concept of witness is significant, as are the ideas of life, water, and light. The antagonism with the Jews is clearly articulated in the designation of the "synagogue of Satan" (2:9; 3:9) reminiscent of Jesus' designation of the Jews as children of their father the devil (John 8:44). I would suggest that the author is clearly a stellar figure related to the late–first-century Johannine community. I have no difficulty referring to him as the apostle John, although I see little to be gained by an extended argument on authorship. I would be strongly opposed to those fresh from the study of Jewish apocalyptic writings who seek to argue that the name "John" is merely a pseudonymous designation for an unknown writer of the second century.

Moreover, I would maintain that the thesis which argues that John's Greek is terrible from illustrations of such phenomena as John's usage of the nominative case with the preposition *apo* ("from") in Revelation 1:4 completely misses the point. Of course the construction could be regarded as bad Greek, and John knew it, as is evident in his two parallel statements in the genitive case that follow concerning the Holy Spirit (seven Spirits) and Jesus Christ related to his Trinitarian formulation. But while the statement is poor Greek, it is superb theology and liturgy when it refers in the nominative case to God (the one who is, who was, and who is to come) and Jesus (the faithful witness, the first born from the dead, and the commander of the kings of the earth). Indeed, notice that both attributions are also triadic statements and liturgically therefore very significant.

Apocalyptic works[2] normally arose in periods of persecution and are "tracts for bad times." Revelation is no exception and was most likely written in the time of Domitian's persecutions. Revelation called the believers to faithfulness and to reliance upon the almighty God in the midst of trouble. Another characteristic of this type of writing is that God is portrayed as supremely powerful. God will ultimately triumph over the enemies. This issue also points to the characteristic of determinism, or the fact that the end is already scheduled in God's over-arching strategy. Since God is transcendent, apocalypses employ secondary figures such as angels and archangels, who wage war with the opposing forces of the devil or Satan, the demons, and human servants of evil–such as political powers. Apocalypses are also esoteric or secretive and use various forms of symbolic language and numbers because they are messages for the in-group or community and are written in such a way that enemies would not understand them. Revelation conforms to these characteristics, the main reason that it is difficult for many today to understand it and easy for others to construct wild speculations from it.

Introductions (1:1–11)

In turning to the text, I have summarized here a number of the ideas that I detailed in my forthcoming commentary. In this present work focusing on worship, I have added many new perspectives.[3] The Book of Revelation opens with three introductions, not merely one, and each has a worship component.

The first introduction is an apocalyptic beginning (Rev 1:1–3), the initial word of which in Greek is *apokalypsis,* which means unveiling or pulling the curtain aside to see beyond the present reality, thus the title "Revelation." The focus of this introduction is on the witness or testimony of Jesus, which is an important element in worship. This statement carries a blessing. The nature of time and its termination is then subjected to the apocalyptic sense of nearness in the divine unveiling (1:3).

The second introduction is epistolary in form and includes the typical familiar greeting of "grace and peace" present in early Christian letters, and always in that order because Christians knew that grace precedes peace. The Trinitarian formulation has already been discussed, but I would add here that the order of "is…was…is to come" for God (1:4, 8) is important. Yet interpreters often miss its significance when comparing it to 4:8, where that order is the one normally assigned to historical reflections ("was...is...is to come"). The contemporaneity ("isness") or immanence of God thus receives priority in speaking of the future and in worship.

That Jesus died and will come again is clear, but for worshipers these facts were placed in the context in which Christians were presently living and struggling. This placement was done to provide them with the knowledge that they had been loosed or freed (*lysanti*) from sins by his blood. As a result, the judgment that is certain to come would not affect them. To this assertion Christians had earlier and now continue to confess their "Amen" because they are members of God's reign and not merely citizens in the past or present kingdoms of a Caesar! Furthermore, they are also priests to God, and they can acknowledge God's sovereignty forever with another "Amen" (1:5-7). So, they proclaim unabashedly in their worship ascriptions to God as "God who is Almighty" (*pantocrator,* an exceedingly exalted term in Greek, 1:8; cf. the song of the Lamb at 15:3). As Revelation progresses, Massyngberde Ford is absolutely correct that the hymnic segments of this book "carry the 'story line' of the Apocalypse." Through them the work gradually moves to a worship crescendo "which becomes the proclamation of the establishment of the Kingdom of God and the enthronement of the Lamb."[4]

The third introduction I designate as an historical introduction, containing material similar to the information in the Gospels or the Book of Acts. In this section John identified himself with three designations: (1) one who shared with them in the reality of suffering, (2) but who also shared in the hope of the kingdom, and (3) who was therefore able to bear trials with patience. The order, of course, is very important because it provides the rationale for enduring suffering and persecution, which John had been experiencing on the prison island of Patmos (1:9). The point of this section is to introduce the messages to the seven churches of Asia given to him in a vision that occurred on "the Lord's day," a designation that by the time of writing the book clearly reflected a liturgical context (1:10). While visions are normally personal, the implications here are undoubtedly intended to be interpreted as having *corporate* liturgical significance.

The Vision of Christ (1:12-20)

The vision of Christ that follows (1:12-20) reminds me of an early experience in my life as a Sunday school student whose teacher was intent upon teaching the Book of Revelation, with his charts, every year of my high school experience. The pictorial representation of Jesus represented by the chart-maker of this chapter was so ghastly that I really doubted the message and the legitimacy of his teaching. I went anyway, however, because of my parents. Yet I was convinced at that point that I would never read the book again. Fortunately, I was rescued later from that decision by a very wise seminary professor. The vision represents various aspects of Jesus' character and role as the leader of the Christian church.

He is pictured as our great priest (the robe and girdle) who functions on behalf of us in the midst of the divine worship sanctuary (1:12–13), but he is also portrayed in the likeness of Daniel's "son of man" (a favorite designation of Jesus) and the Ancient of Days (white hair) who has been around since the beginning of time (1:13–14; cf. Dan 7:13). His ability to see penetrates to the heart of all (flaming eyes), while his stability (bronze feet) is assured and far supersedes the fallen Colossus of Rhodes. The impact of his voice and message are thunderous, and he truly cares for his people as he holds his churches in the palm of his hand. His proclamations (two-edged sword) cut both ways: in grace and judgment. He embodies (shining face) the very radiance of God's self (Rev 1:14–16).

John understood that he had received a "christophany" (a divine vision of Christ). According to Jewish tradition, to see God meant death unless divine grace was extended (the right hand) and/or one heard the familiar words of, "Do not be afraid." The one who died and is alive provided John with that assurance. The vision was one of grace, and here as with any theophany (divine vision) a commission was extended. John was instructed to deliver his visionary insights to the churches (1:17–20). For the early Christians, this awesome picture of Jesus must have inspired great confidence, and led to a captivating sense of worship for John, who is described as falling before the Lord in worship.

Letters to the Seven Churches (2:1–3:22)

This vision prepared Christian readers for the second and third chapters of the book, which contain the revelatory letters to the seven churches. The structures of these letters are parallel, but the messages are different. These differences have sometimes led interpreters to apply them to different periods of time. Their content and formatting, however, suggest that they are to be interpreted as representative churches, or they could even apply to various persons within a church, with the result that it is best to treat them as a unified message providing insights into Christians and church life. Were there more than seven churches in the region? Of course! For example, there were churches in the tri-cities of Colossae, Hierapolis, and Laodicea (cf. Col 4:13–16). The listing of the churches follows something akin to an ancient delivery route from Ephesus, which was the largest city and had recently become the capital of Asia, north to Pergamum, the earlier capital, and then southeast to Laodicea, one of the tri-cities (on the long overland highway from Tarsus in the east) and then back to Ephesus. The other cities are along the route.

The framework of the letters is very carefully designed and in general involves:

1. a commission to the angel or messenger to write to each church;
2. the message including one or more references to the characteristics of Christ identified in the vision of chapter 1;
3. a clarifying statement that Christ is fully aware ("I know") of the works of each church;

4. a description of Christ's concern for the church;
5. one or more references to the church's life and worship practices, reflecting some well-known facts about each city;
6. words of commendation or warning, or both;
7. concluding clarion call for worshipers who have ears to listen and to obey what has been presented and a gracious promise in return for such obedience.

The impression one has of these churches is that their patterns are not unknown to our experience of churches today. Briefly I would categorize each of them as follows:

1. Ephesus is a loyalist type of church that has become protective of its worship and theological traditions, but has lost its fire for Christ and his mission in the world.
2. Smyrna is a persecuted/suffering type of church that needs encouragement in worship and life.
3. Pergamum is the kind of compromising church that requires a clarification of its worship commitments and its basis for membership.
4. Thyatira has many good features, but has become a syncretistic, tolerant church that has allowed worldly patterns to infect its life and worship.
5. Sardis is the type of church that makes a confident outward show of being alive, but is basically going through the routine of church life and worship and actually is more dead than alive.
6. Philadelphia is a struggling, faithful-type church that has an open heart for reaching out, but is buffeted by the world and needs to recognize the assuring presence of Christ.
7. Laodicea is the type of well-endowed institution that may have an understanding of church, but has little commitment to what a true church and worship ought to be like.

The worship of these churches is tested variously: by outside hostility from the enemies of Christ (the synagogue of Satan in Smyrna and Philadelphia, Rev 2:9; 3:9); by heretical proclaimers of infectious immoral and idolatrous worship practices pawned off as being acceptable within Christianity (Pergamum and Thyatira, 2:14, 20); by the anesthetizing affect of repetition and tradition (Ephesus, 2:4); by the withering impact of prosperity and status (Laodicea, 3:17); and by the deadening overconfidence of security (Sardis' fortress mentality, 3:3). Christ "knows" the patterns of life and worship practices in these churches (2:2, 9, 13, 19; 3:1, 8,15) and has a word of warning and/or commendation for each of them. He desires that all of them should be in an authentic worship relationship with him and represent him as vital members of his mission.

The Greek Theater Setting (4:1–5:14)

Chapters 4 and 5 are unique in the New Testament because they function to introduce a stage setting for the dramatic presentation that follows. While some interpreters have suggested that the contextual setting is a Jewish Temple scene, others have sought to find a kinship in Jewish *Merkabah* thinking. Still others have sought to insert a totally unrelated rapture at this point.

A much better framework for understanding these chapters is a Greek theater setting. The throne of God (4:2) here is like the elevated box (*thronos*) where in the Hellenistic theater the "god" sat, oversaw the actions, and acted like a prompter of emotion for the audience (by changing his/her two faces of anger and joy). The twenty-four elders (representing the people of the old and new covenants, 4:4) served as the context or backdrop (scenery/*skene*) for this dramatic presentation of ultimate significance. The fact that these elders were dressed in white is an indication that they have a special divinely designed role. Their falling before God and presenting their golden crowns is a reminder that in the acclamations of Caesar such a practice was regularly followed. Augustus had twelve persons serve in that role, but Domitian in his arrogance doubled that number to twenty-four!

The four living creatures (4:6) represent wild animals (lion), tame animals (ox or bull), humanity (man), and the bird kingdom (eagle). They functioned like the Greek oral chorus, which served in the flat plain or *orchestra* before the stage. The sea of glass (4:6) on which they were positioned was like the valuable tiles that often covered the stone bases of the orchestra and shimmered in the light. Since Greek plays were offered to the gods, the theater contained an altar (*thusiasterion*) in the center of the orchestra, where a sacrifice would be offered for the acceptance of the play (cf. 6:9). The seven torches (4:5) functioned like the stage lights/torches (*lampoi*) lit as an evening play began.

In this divine drama, the hymns in the fourth chapter call the readers to attention and are very instructive. The four living creatures proclaim the threefold holiness of the enthroned God (the *trisagion* or *sanctus*), followed by the declaration or acclamation that God is "the Almighty one" (*ho pantocrator*), far above any Caesar! To that acclamation is added his eternal nature, "the one who was...is...and is to come." Since the living creatures represent creation and not the Christian faith, they interpret time the way the world does–as past, present, and future (4:8)–not the way of divine revelation (cf. 1:4, 8). The twenty-four elders who are representatives of the old and new covenants (the representatives of organized religion and worship), however, provide the responsive insight (antiphone) as they proclaim the worthiness of God to receive a threefold acclamation of "glory, honor, and power." They cast their crowns in worship before God, the Creator of all things. Moreover, they provide the confessional affirmation that all creation is the result of God's will (4:10–11).

But there could be no divine drama without a decipherable script. Of course, a script existed for the drama. It was in the form of a scroll in the hand of God, but the contents could not be exposed because the manuscript was perfectly sealed (seven seals, 5:1). John sadly soon realized that no mere mortal being anywhere could unlock the divine message, but one of the elders advised him that a conqueror, "the Lion of the tribe of Judah," the official "heir of David" had unlocked God's will for humanity. So John waited for the Lion's appearance on the stage of history, but instead of a lion, a "Lamb" emerged who possessed divine power (seven horns) and knowledge (seven eyes). The world expected a conquering lion, but was given a sacrificial lamb! Yet this Lamb appeared strange in that it/he was alive but had been dead (5:6), the symbolic representation of the resurrected Christ!

After the powerful Lamb took the scroll from God, the living creatures and the elders together prostrated themselves before the Lamb and sang a new song of worship and acclamation, proclaiming the Lamb's worthiness in fulfilling the gospel both through his redeeming death for humanity in the entire cosmos (see the fourfold listing of people) and by establishing them as God's special priestly people on earth (5:9–10). The hosts of heaven and the faithful on earth then joined together in a triumphant antiphonal sevenfold worship acclamation of the Lamb for his worthiness (5:11–12). This acclamation was followed by a final fourfold ascription of eternal "blessing, honor, glory, and power" as all of creation acknowledged the unity of the enthroned God and the redeeming Lamb! The preparation for the divine drama was then completed by the confessional "Amen" affirmed both by the four living creatures and the prostrated worship of the twenty-four elders (5:13–14).

The Lamb Breaks the Divine Seals (6:1–8:1)

The first act of this apocalyptic drama involves the breaking of the divine (seven) seals by the Lamb (6:1–8:1). It is initiated on the great stage of history by the summoning of the four horsemen, who represent a picture of the breakdown of world order. The white horse and rider with a bow likely portrays outside destruction through war. The red horse and rider with a sword seems to symbolize annihilation through bloodthirsty violence. The black horse and rider with the scales represents the catastrophic crumbling of economic stability as the poor get poorer (the high cost of basic staples, wheat and barley) while the rich get richer (the unchanged cost of luxuries, oil and wine). The ghastly greenish-yellow colored (*chloros*) horse and rider with the name of "Death and Hades/the Underworld of shades" signifies the various horrible ways of dying and being killed (6:2–8). The sum of worldly effort is thus regarded as leading to purposeless desolation.

A shift occurs with the breaking of the fifth seal, as the focus turns to the altar, where the blood of the martyrs had been offered as they witnessed for the "Word of God" (6:9). The cries that issued from the altar have been repeated throughout history as the faithful have repeatedly questioned, "How long?" Would pain and suffering continue indefinitely? Here the dead ask how long will the "Sovereign One" delay God's judgment and vengeance? The answer that comes is clear: the martyrs are given their symbol of victory (the white robe), but the timing is not in their hands. God's mysterious sovereignty means that timing belongs to God alone (6:10–11). Even Jesus had earlier indicated the same (cf. Mark 13:32). To learn and accept the meaning of God's sovereignty is basic to worship!

In opening the sixth seal, John collapses history and moves immediately to the end of time, as the enemies of God cry out in anguish for rocks and mountains to fall on them and hide them from the terrible consequences of not falling in worship before God earlier. For those who in the past have thought they could program the whole book of Revelation into revealing time sequences for the end (the continuous historical approach to interpretation) the appearance of the end in chapter 6 was a bit frustrating. Their successors (the dispensational interpreters) limited their approach of time sequencing to the letters to the seven churches.[5] Instead of such an approach, readers should understand that Revelation is written in three cycles (three dramatic acts) much like the Gospel of John (the Cana cycle, the festival cycle, and the farewell cycle[6]). At this point in Revelation the first presentation of universal destruction on the world order has been completed, but note that the seventh seal had not yet been opened.

The First Interlude and the Seventh Seal (7:1–8:1)

Before the final seal is broken, everything in the drama is brought to a screeching halt. Something needed to be clarified—the fate of the faithful. So John added this part of his message by inserting an interlude (Rev 7:1–17). He described the faithful in two ways. The first is by reference to sealing the faithful tribes for safekeeping by the living God and listing each tribe as complete in itself with the number of organized religion times the number of fullness (12 x 1000). The twelve tribes, however, are listed in a strange order, indicating that they should *not* be interpreted merely as the people of Israel, but from a different perspective—namely, as symbols of faithful believers. Reuben, who was the eldest, is not mentioned first. The list begins, instead, with Judah, the messianic tribe of David from which Jesus came (7:5). Then Joseph is appropriately listed with two tribes (Manasseh and Joseph for Ephraim) as a traditional replacement for Levi. But Levi is included here! The reason is that Dan has been excluded because in the Old Testament he was regarded as the representative of heretical worship (Gen 49:17; Judg 17:14–20), and in Christian tradition his name was linked with the antichrist figure. The purpose of the message is to assure believers that God knows intimately their number and is responsible for their protection and preservation. This vision, therefore, does not pertain simply to Israel, but to the whole people of God (7:4–8; cf. for perspective the use of 144,000 and its implications for Christianity at 14:1–5; also remember the writer's view of the Jews as the synagogue of Satan in 2:9; 3:9).

In case the reader might become worried about the complete number of the people of God in this first group, another picture was added of God's people being beyond numbering (7:9). This second description is unquestionably a vision of the ultimate heavenly realm. The scene is purposely described in terms of heavenly worship, with all people clothed in the white robes of victory and waving palm branches in their hands, acclaiming both God and the Lamb for "salvation." Then all creation prayerfully adds their sevenfold eternal doxology to God (7:9–12). When the question is raised about who are the white-robed figures, the answer is quickly given that they are the faithful who have come through "great persecution" (7:14), like the martyrs whose blood ran from the altar (cf. 6:9–10). But they have now entered heaven, so that their hunger, thirst, and sorrow have come to an end. The Lamb is in the presence of the throne as the shepherd of the faithful (Rev 7:16–17).

The question then could be raised as to what could be left for the seventh seal? The answer reverberates as dreaded silence (8:1), the most powerful dramatic device on stage, as the audience awaits, with bated breath, the second traumatic act.

The Trumpets (8:2–9:21)

This second act begins with seven trumpeting angels of judgment aligned for their caustic task. Then another angelic figure initiates the judgments by electrifying the scene by hurling a searing incense burner containing the prayers of God's people onto the stage of history. Did Christians in that day (and today!) ever wonder if their prayers were heard? The apocalyptic writer had no doubt about the affirmative answer. As the first four trumpets sounded, the message is obvious: a third of the cosmic structure has come unglued as phenomena akin to the plagues on Egypt, but more severe, are unloosed on the world (Rev 8:7–12; cf. Exod 7:14–12:36). The question is often raised: "Why only a third?" The answer must be: "Just wait! The third act has yet to come." Another question may be posed: "How can all the grass be burned at 8:7 and the grass not be harmed at 9:4?" The answer is that an apocalyptic message is impressionistic writing and one must not ask for Western logic. To do so is to destroy the marvelous nature of apocalyptic imaginary thinking.

The three woes equated with the last three trumpets are introduced (8:13). The fifth trumpet, as with the fifth seal, is different from the previous four and involves a horrible attack by demonic locusts, but not upon plant life as might be expected. The bites of these hideous creatures are judgments and are leveled against humans who have not been protected by the seal of God (9:4; cf. 7:3). The leader of this evil host is none other than the apocalyptic devilish destroyer known as Abaddon or Apollyon (9:11).

The appearance of these demonic creatures is similar to that of weird dragons. Unfortunately, in an effort to contemporize these bewitching figures, some interpreters of Revelation have identified the devilish critters in the fifth and sixth trumpets as futuristic tanks, deadly helicopters, and other modern vehicles or instruments of war. The speculators have likewise sought to identify the country from which the host of enemies in the sixth trumpet originate. Like modern mathematicians, these theorists have multiplied the symbolic numbers "twice myriads times myriads" and have concluded that the only nation with that vast a number of people *today* (!) must be China. The entire picture is thus pathetically historicized, and the apocalyptic impact of the vast array of the satanic servants and enemies of God in the world is sadly lost (9:16).

The important point, however, comes at the end of the chapter (9:20–21), when John makes it clear that no matter whatever judgment might be dispatched on the enemies of God, they refuse to repent of their pathetic *worship* (idolatry) or their *evil moral practices* (from murder to immorality), which are the two basic problems of humanity repeatedly asserted in the New Testament (cf. Acts 15:20, 29; 1 Cor 6:18 and 10:14; Rev 2:14, 20). As Paul indicated in Romans, when the will, the passions, and the mind are turned against God, people would rather seek to conspire and continue in their evil patterns of life than repent of their sins (cf. Rom 1:18–32). By the time one reaches this point in the Book of Revelation, the option of repentance may be offered in the context of punishment; but the option is clearly rejected by false worshipers.

The Second Interlude and the Seventh Trumpet (10:1–11:19)

Before the final trumpet is sounded, John inserts another interlude as a mighty angel possessing the aspects of God issues the seven mighty thunders. But John is not allowed to communicate this mysterious message since God's transcendent wisdom and knowledge are not completely available to humans (Rev 10:1–4). Even when the announcement is made that there would be no further delay in the sounding of the seventh trumpet (10:6–7), the interlude continues with John forced to eat a sweet-bitter scroll of prophecy (10:8–11; cf. Jer 15:16–18; Ezek 3:1–3).

The message that emerges is a crucial attempt by God to bring repentance through a three-and-a-half-year period of testimony by two witnesses, reminiscent of the warnings of doom in the time of Elijah when God shut down the rain, or when God turned the waters to blood in the time of Moses (Rev 11:6; cf. 1 Kgs 17:1; Exod 7:17–19). After the powers of evil finally kill the witnesses, the people, who consider that they had been pestered by God's witnesses, dance and exalt in the fact that they no longer need to listen to the warnings about false worship and life. Their rejoicing soon ends when God raises his witnesses to heaven and responds to the rejection of his warnings with a destruction that amazes all who behold the events. Then and only then do the disobedient finally acknowledge the powerful hand of God in history (11:7–13).

With the victory of God complete, the seventh trumpet sounds. The announcement resounds that the world now belongs to God and Christ, who will reign for ever and ever, a theme magnified in Handel's "Hallelujah Chorus" (11:15). That announcement brings the prostrate worship of the elders once again into focus and their prayerful thanksgiving that the "Almighty" God (*pantokrator*), "the one who is and was," has begun to rule. Notice that the future is finished and the time of the eternal present has finally arrived, as the destroyers of the earth are finally themselves destroyed (11:17–18). The second act is thus completed, but the play is not yet finished. From the open temple of God, the flashing lightning and ear-splitting sounds of the convulsing world signal the next frightening episodes are ready to begin (11:19).

The Great Signs and the Evil Triumvirate (12:1–13:18)

As the Gospel of John has a second beginning at chapter 12 and introduces the third cycle in the second half of the Gospel, so the Book of Revelation also has a second beginning at chapter 12, which introduces the third act in the second half of this book.[7] This second half of Revelation begins with two great signs (*semeia,* a familiar Johannine term) in heaven, which provide the background for understanding the eternal battle between good and evil. Here the message of God's plan for dealing with evil is presented. The first sign is one of a woman representing the people of God, who is/are the subject of attacks from the dragon/devil who represents the other great sign. From the people of God is born the Messiah, but at his birth and during his life the devil sought to destroy him. Yet God protected that child (God's Son) and ultimately caught him to heaven. As a result, in hostile vengeance the devil with renewed vigor sought to destroy the people of God (12:1–6).

The vision glanced back to the divine battle in which the devil had been defeated and which set up his great attack on the people of God. It is important to note that God does not have to fight with the dragon (Satan) directly. He sends an understudy, Michael, which indicates for readers the supreme power of God over evil. But God's power does not mean that humans can take on the devil themselves. In the symbolic incidents that follow, God's preserving power, not their own resources, protects God's people. Whether it is the provision of symbolic wings to escape the dragon's attack or the opening of the earth to swallow the dragon's attempted drowning of God's people (reminiscent of God opening the way through the sea in the time of Moses [Exod 14:1–31]), God is the protector of his people (Rev 12:7–17). The final statement in 12:17 (or 13:1) concerning the figure standing on the sand of the sea probably applies to the dragon, although it could easily apply to the dragon's associate (the beast). It is significant that this symbolic image is a reminder that, in Jewish tradition, the sea is linked with the evil depth (the *tahom*) and thus is the place from which the dragon and his forces arise (cf. the bottomless pit in 9:2 and 20:1; a concept that is related to the creative activity of God in moving over "the deep" in Gen 1:2).

Then in chapter 13 the two other figures of the evil trinity or triumvirate are introduced. The first beast that rises from the sea ("the deep," Rev 13:1) is likely the political power of Rome. Its orientation was associated with idolatry, leading humans to worship the dragon (13:4). The symbolic mixture of seven and ten (supernatural and created completeness) in its designation of heads and crowns is identified as confusion so that readers will understand that the beast's power is almost ultimate but not perfect (13:1). Its one wounded/healed (13:3) head probably refers to the Nero *redivinus* myth in which Domitian was viewed by Christians as the reincarnation of the evil Nero. In contrast to Paul's writing in Romans 13:1–7, the state at this point in history is regarded as in the hands of the devil, unjustly attacking Christians (13:7) and forcing everyone into the ungodly worship of its power (13:8). In response, John does not issue a futile summons to arms against Rome, but provides a clear call to patience or endurance (13:9–10).

The second beast is a false messianic figure, who has the appearance of a lamb but acts like the dragon, and demands that worship be made to the beast (13:11–12). For John that worship could only be the worship of Rome (*Dea Roma*) and its emperor. What made the pattern of such false worship so stringent is that it was linked to economic survival (13:16–17). When political authorities control worship, Christians and all humans face intense pressures to conform. Christians should be constantly aware of the need to advocate religious liberty.

For his readers to be clear on who this false messiah might be, John supplied the key to recognition in the number 666 (13:18). This number when analyzed in John's time would have stood for *Neron Caesar* in Hebrew. To make it more clear, some later scribes who copied the text apparently changed the number to 616, and the result was "Nero Caesar." Since that time the number 666 has been used as a symbol for almost anyone that we can imagine: from Luther to the Pope, from Hitler to Breshnev, to Saddam and many other dictators and terrorists. All one has to do is to have the right system, and a desired identification can be arranged for any name, especially now with computers. I repeat, anyone's name can be made into 666! But for the purposes of our understanding here, the number six, in symbolism, stands between "five" (one form of created completeness) and "seven" (perfection) and has been regarded as the number of evil or the strange and incomplete. Three sixes only raises that number to approximate the Divine. I would only add here that readers should be herewith forewarned that great care must be taken in assigning 666 to any particular contemporary person.

The Lamb and an Overview of Judgment (14:1–20)

With chapter 14, a completely different picture is introduced. In contrast to the dragon and his minions who stand on the shifting sand (12:17), the Lamb and his chosen people are arrayed on the rock of Mount Zion (14:1; cf. Jesus' parable in Matt 7:24–27). Their number is once again 144,000, but this time the people of God are described differently than by reference to tribes. This time they are pictured as the redeemed from the world and as not having been involved in sexual relations with women (14:4). Some of my women friends in academia consider this statement to be obnoxious and very chauvinistic. While I understand their distress, I would remind my readers that the picture is one of an army fully committed to its task of holy war, whose members can be compared to Uriah in the Old Testament story of David, who refused to engage in sexual relations with his wife while committed to battle (2 Sam

11:6–11). An ancient warrior of Israel who was engaged in war took the oath to refrain from civilian pursuits (cf. 2 Tim 2:4), including sexual activities, while involved in battle. The symbolism is not to be taken literally. It means that if one belongs to God's people (is in God's army), that person is committed to eschew evil and focus on God! For John one of those indications is the complete rejection of lying and falsehood (Rev 14:5; cf. 21:8, 27; 22:15). The reason undoubtedly is that John viewed lying as a sign of being a child of the devil, not a true worshiper and servant of God (cf. John 8:44). In Revelation only the true people are marked with the Father's name and can worship God with the new hymn of redemption (Rev 14:3).

The remainder of chapter 14 contains a series of brief vignettes concerning the proclamation of the gospel, the fall of Babylon (Rome), the eternal judgment on those who worship the beast, a repetition of the call for patient endurance, and a blessing on those who die for the Lord. The chapter closes with the picture of the Son of Man and his attending anger bringing judgment, as the reaping sickle of doom sweeps the field of opposition clean and the winepress of God's judgment flows with the blood of God's enemies for a distance akin to that of the length of Israel–John's symbolic context of the historic battlefield area of the fertile crescent (14:14–20).

The Third Act (15:1–16:21)

Chapter 15 opens with another great sign in heaven (15:1; cf. 12:1, 3). This time the portent signals the arrival of the third and final act, with the seven last judgments as the containers of God's wrath are poured out on the earth. The destruction is introduced with a dramatic burst of fire (15:2) in the orchestra plateau and with the united hymn of Moses and the Lamb praising God Almighty. This great confessional hymn is harped and chanted by the victorious children of God as people from all nations come to acknowledge the holiness and ultimate justice of God (15:3–4). Then the heavenly sanctuary is burst open, and one of the four living creatures carries to the seven angels the bowls containing the final horrible plagues for the earth. To ensure that the reader would understand that these angels were divinely dispatched agents of God, John paused to explain that no one could enter the holy sanctuary during this time because of the glorious smoke that filled it–which is reminiscent of the divinely orchestrated cloud both on Sinai at the delivery of the Decalogue and at the dedication of the Solomonic Temple (15:8; cf. Exod 19:16–22; 1 Kgs 8:10–11).

The judgments that followed are once again a reminder of the plagues of Egypt (cf. Exod 7–12), but are far more severe. They include great sores on the people, bloody waters of death, intense atomic-like heat, blinding darkness, and demonic spirits, which all converge on the earth (Rev 16:1–14). Yet while the angel proclaimed God's righteous justice in judgment (16:5–7), those who were judged renewed their curses on God (16:11; cf. the attitude of Pharaoh during the plagues, Exod 7:14; 8:15, 19, 32). Also, the enemies of God assembled in an attempt to do battle with the Almighty, symbolized in the reference to the historic site of Israel's great battles in the Valley of Jezreel and the Mountain (hill) of Meggido (16:16; cf., for example, Judg 5:19; 2 Kgs 9:27; 2 Chr 35:22).

In the Book of Revelation, no one can actually fight God. When the seventh angel enters the scene, a thunderous voice repeats the final words of Jesus from the cross in the Johannine Gospel—"It is Finished!" (Rev 16:17; cf. 21:6; John 19:30). Then the earth's great cataclysm takes place. Babylon (the symbol of the wicked world) is torn apart as islands and mountains disappear into oblivion. But still evil people in their throes of death continue to curse God rather than pray and pay homage to the Lord (Rev 16:18–21). The third act of the play is thus completed.

The Conclusion (17:1–22:21)

Next the Seer of Revelation turns his attention to his two-section conclusion—the final dispatch of evil (chapters 17–20) and the anticipated rewards of the righteous (chapters 21–22). In following this pattern Revelation once again parallels the literary format of the Johannine Gospel—the two sections concluding the Gospel are the stories of Jesus' death and his glorious resurrection (cf. John 18–19 and 20–21).

The End of Evil

The disposal of evil begins with the dramatic termination of Rome, the epitome of a satanic servant in the mind of the writer of Revelation, but she is identified only by means of surrogate names in order to protect the Christian readers. Here, as elsewhere, Rome is identified as Babylon (17:5). Because in worship Rome was viewed as a female goddess (*Dea Roma*), John portrayed her here as a magnificently adorned prostitute drunk, not with wine, but with the blood of Christian martyrs. She had dominion over "many waters" (the ancient Mediterranean world and beyond, Rev 17:1–6). Then, playing off the threefold description of God (1:4, 8), John characterized the beast on which she rode as "one who was, is not and yet ascends from the pit [abyss]" (17:8). This symbol and the one linking the eighth head to an earlier one (17:11) are obvious references to the Nero *redivinius* myth that apparently circulated among the early Christians to the effect that the evil Nero had been reincarnated by the devil in the Emperor Domitian (81–96 C.E.).

When John became awed by the whore's appearance (17:6), he was quickly advised of her corrupt nature. At that point she is precisely identified by the writer's key reference in Revelation to "seven mountains" or hills (a reference hidden deep within the book but for the careful reader a strategic clue, 17:9). Rome's worldwide dominion (ten horns and the fourfold listing of people at 17:15) is purposely articulated before her coming inner self-destruction is predicted (17:16–17). As the revealing servant of God, John knew who actually possessed authority and dominion and who should be worshiped and revered—the Lamb, the Lord of lords and the King of kings

(17:14). Even though the minions of Rome might attack and persecute God's servants (17:13–14), Christians needed to realize that the end of Rome was on the horizon (17:15–18).

Once again referring to Rome in a surrogate manner as Babylon, John issued a moving sevenfold taunt song concerning her forthcoming destruction (18:1–24). In three poetic laments, the things in which people place their trust other than God are dramatically wiped out, and their splendor vanishes before their devotees' eyes (18:9–19). Their items of security become nothing more than meaningless elements in a wasteland (18:2). Indeed, so powerful was one of John's pictorial summons here (18:4) that it became the inspiration for the imprisoned John Bunyan's haunting call for Pilgrim to flee the City of Destruction in his classic novel *The Pilgrim's Progress*. The list of Rome's trading commodities is so encompassing that it reminds one of the vast armada of container ships that today await loading and unloading in such great ports as Singapore. But Rome's list also included the huge number of slaves, which historians suggest could have modestly reached as many as eight million people.[8]

The end of the great Roman Empire was, for John, in sight. In view of its forthcoming destruction, he adds a series of five stark "hallels" or praises to God (19:2, 3, 4, 5, 6) for the termination of such evil and the proclamation of the awesome authority of God in the world. In consequence, the angel who was conducting John announced the coming of the long-anticipated, blessed marriage supper of the Lamb (19:9). Overwhelmed by these events of the future, John fell in worship before the revealing angel, but he was sternly rebuked and reminded that worship belongs only to God (19:10)!

Then heaven opened, and the terminating scenes of evil are unveiled. First, an awesome picture of Jesus riding on a white horse appears. He is also described by nine additional characteristics (total of ten) as: "faithful and righteous"; with penetrating eyes and endowed with many crowns; having a mysterious name and wearing a robe stained in blood; called "the Word of God" and leading the armies of heaven; and empowered with a devastating sharp sword in his mouth and bearing the title King of kings and Lord of lords (19:11–16; cf. the earlier description at 1:12–16). In contrast, the next scene portrays the enemies of God arrayed for battle. Instead of describing a battle, however, John detailed that an angel of God called forth the birds to a feast on the bodies of God's enemies who were killed by the rider on the white horse (19:17–19, 21). The two supporting leaders in the devil's (dragon's) triumvirate are thereupon captured and meet their unwelcome end by being thrown into the terminal lake of fire (19:20).

At this point it was the turn of the devil himself. He is pictured as incarcerated in his own pit (the *tehom*) by a powerful angel, not unlike the angel of the Lord in the Old Testament (cf. for example Gen 6:7–11; Exod 3:2; Judg 6:11–22). On the other hand, the saints of God are blessed for a thousand years (Rev 20:1–4). The concept of the millennium, which is described only in a few verses of Revelation, has been the subject of countless debates, which have been particularly fierce among Christians in the last century and a half. It is as though Satan has succeeded in twisting the focus of these verses that highlight his destruction (20:10) and the believers' victory into a vehicle for frustration and division within churches themselves. When will Christians begin to recognize the symbolism in the Bible? When will interpreters cease fighting over our inspired book and ripping ourselves apart while we should be praising God for God's promise of Satan's ultimate demise? What is clear from our text is the promise of the blessed state of those who experience the first resurrection, because they need not fear the immanent threat of ultimate judgment (20:6). Those, however, who follow Satan may think they can battle with God, but they are herewith warned that even Satan ends up in the eternal flames of the lake of fire (20:7–10).

In the final scenes of judgment, a great white throne emerges on our stage in the hue of God's glory and victory. The throne is so awesome that the entire created order (both earth and sky) dissolves into oblivion (20:11). Before that throne all the previously unredeemed of humanity are summoned from the dead to appear and be judged, not by their mere words, but by what they had actually done with their lives (20:13). All those whose names are not included in the Book of Life (those who were not redeemed nor worshiped the Lord) are then dispatched to their final end (the second death) in the lake of fire. Then and only then is "death" finally terminated in the same eternal pit (20:14–15).

The Glorious Hope

Revelation could easily have ended with the judgment of evil. But without the final two chapters the apocalypse would lose its capstone and its message of hope for a persecuted people. Since the created order will fade away in the judgment (20:11), God promises to supply a new heaven and a new earth, minus the sea or the *tehom* (the dark deep, 21:1). This new creation–the New Jerusalem, a place of "God's peace"–is pictured like a new bride ready for her ultimate wedding. In this new creation pain and death, weeping and mourning will cease to exist (21:2–4). It is a time when "It is finished!" covers all of time past (21:6; cf. John 19:30) and when those who had known the traumas of desert thirst will be blessed with a gracious fountain of freely dispensed water. It is a time and place for experiencing full sonship and daughterhood with God (21:6–7). It is a time when evil is also finished, because all who participated in evil practices–including all liars–have been consigned to the lake of fire and their final death (21:8).

So the stage has been set for John's presentation of the vision of heaven. Of course, for a Jew the scene should be introduced from a mountain, the traditional place of worship and for receiving God's primary revelations (from Sinai to Zion to Carmel to Tabor to Hermon). The holy city, similar to God, is portrayed like a rare jewel (21:11; cf. 4:3). Its dimensions are all defined in terms of the number twelve (the number of God's true people, 21:18–21). But there is no temple in this new city as one might expect, because temples and sanctuaries are really earthly symbols for worship, and God's presence will then be among the redeemed people. Here God and the Lamb are present in their fullness, and direct access for worship of the Divine is now completely available (20:22). What is more, the old sources of light are no longer necessary, because divine light is present and worshipers even present their reflected illumination to the glory of God (20:23–26; 22:5). Moreover, since all evil is gone, including all falsehood, there is no longer any necessity to shut the gates of the city. Only the redeemed (those in the Book of Life) can enter this city (21:27). While we do not conceive of cities as cubes or having walls and gates, we still do build houses with doors and walls/fences with gates. These images are impressionistic and are meant to communicate a new sense of both perfection and openness. The constant refrain of the absence of liars in heaven (21:8, 27; 22:15) is a reminder that John saw a very close link between lying and the devil (John 8:44). True worship of God is violated by lying, and therefore all vices are excluded from the picture of heaven.

To emphasize God's continued care for his people, the scene shifts to the river running directly from the presence of God and the Lamb through the city, with the tree of life (the symbol of eternal life, Rev 22:1–2; cf. Gen 3:22) on both sides of the river. The symbolism is a powerful assertion that there is no impoverished side of this city or "wrong side of the tracks" in heaven. The tree of life is constantly in a state of fruit-bearing or production, so hunger is at an end. The tree brings healing to everyone (Rev 22:2; cf. Ezek 47:12). In addition, since nothing evil will be present, worship will be the natural outflow of God's care. The Lord's people will be able to look directly into the divine face (Rev 22:3–4) without fear (contrast Exod 33:20; Heb 10:31). They belong to God; and, while they will not become divine themselves, they will be nourished by God who will reign forever (Rev 22:5).

The Book of Revelation advances to its conclusion with its sixth and seventh beatitudes (22:7, 12; cf. 1:3; 14:13; 16:15; 19:9; 20:6), and with another warning against improper worship of God's messengers. Worship belongs only to God (22:8). Then, addressing his contemporaries, John reminded them of the necessity of consistency in life and an invitation is issued for readers to "come" and experience the resulting gift of faithfulness (the free water of life, 22:17). The Lord Jesus then offers his promise of his soon return.

WORSHIP SUMMARY

To summarize the worship features of this magnificent work called Revelation would necessitate rewriting this whole chapter, since worship is presupposed in every section. Briefly, however, the reader should remember that God is presented as the "almighty" one who provided for the unveiling of God's mysterious purposes to John through the visions in this book. In response, John felt the necessity repeatedly to fall in worship before Jesus and his messengers, but he was sternly warned to worship only God and God's Son, who are repeatedly the subjects of worship. The visions repeatedly condemn all patterns of false worship, not only in society, but also in the Christian community. The visions call Christians to maintain a consistency in worshiping and praising God, even when forced on point of death to adopt idolatrous worship practices. Martyrdom and persecution are not to be feared, because God will ultimately bring divine victory and will destroy those enemies and false worshipers who refused to acknowledge Jesus. The praise and worship hymns throughout Revelation provide readers with opportunities to join in the worship responses, while the taunt songs serve as clear warnings against idolatrous worship.

As the book reaches its end, we as readers are encouraged to join John in his "Maranatha" prayer, "Come, Lord Jesus!" (22:20) and in his benediction for the "grace of the Lord Jesus" to be with all God's people (22:21). So let us repeatedly respond in our lives with our heartfelt "Maranatha" prayer for our Lord's return and our confident, confessional "Amen!" Let it come to pass!

QUESTIONS

1. To what extent do your worship experiences exemplify the various visions of heavenly worship in the Book of Revelation?
2. Do you think the visions inspire confidence in worship today? Why? Why not? Explain and illustrate you answers.
3. What picture of Jesus Christ do you draw from the Book of Revelation? How do you respond to such a picture?

PART VI

Concluding Reflections on the New Testament Canon and Worship in the Contemporary World

This section draws the book to a conclusion with reflections on the formation of the New Testament as a canon, and with questions on the implications for authentic worship by Christians in the rapidly changing world of the twenty-first century.

A Backward Glimpse at the Cannon

Before turning to a brief summation concerning the impact of our previous reflections from the New Testament upon the worship in our contemporary communities, it is imperative to add a few brief reflections on the term "canonical" that I have used periodically throughout this work.[1] It is derived from the Greek word *kanon,* a Semitic term meaning "reed" that came to imply a measuring reed/rod and thus a "standard" or "ruler for measuring" authenticity.

For the writers of the New Testament, their "canon" or written authority was the Old Testament. It is frequently stated today that the scriptures of the Jews were composed of the Law, the Prophets, and the Writings. But for the Jewish rabbis, the heart of their canon or worship source was the Torah or the Law (the first five books of the Old Testament). From these books they developed their prescriptions, and from these works they formulated their oral implications, which, they argued by reason, also went back to Moses. These implications were then codified in the first century of our era as the *Mishnah* and became the foundation in later centuries for their two *Talmuds*. The interpretations of the Torah "texts" and their implications drawn by the Jewish scholarly elite in the time of Jesus were the focus of many arguments between Jesus and the rabbis, as witnessed in the Gospels.

While it has been recently argued that there was hardly an early three-part canonical division to the Old Testament recognized by the Jews in the first Christian century, it is certainly intriguing to notice that even Luke, a Gentile, was aware of a kind of three-part division to the Scriptures involving Moses, the Prophets, and the Psalms (Luke 24:44).[2] The New Testament writers certainly regarded the Old Testament as an inspired authority and quoted it freely for justification of their ideas (cf., for example, Mark 7:6–8; 11:17; 12:10–11; John 6:45; 10:34–36; Acts 24:14–16; Rom 3:1–20). It was also firmly recommended as the basis for their worship and life (cf., for example, 2 Tim 3:16–17). Moreover, even though the scriptures were transcribed and passed down in various separate scrolls (e.g., the scroll of Isaiah found at Qumran), Jesus himself undoubtedly viewed them in a kind of unity when he referred to the Old Testament as involving the entire record from the blood of Abel in Genesis to the blood of Zechariah in 2 Chronicles, the first and last books of the Hebrew canon, or the Jewish organization for the books.

But what of a New Testament canon? The works of the apostles and their associates were undoubtedly collected very early. Their collections were soon enhanced by the fact that in contrast to the use of individual scrolls by the Jews, the early Christians employed the codex or book (*biblion*) form for the transmission of their written ideas (cf. Rev 1:11). Although it was not practical early to include all of the New Testament works in one codex because of the size, it was possible to the fit the Gospels or the writings of Paul into a single book, which enhanced both their collectibility and preservation. Of course, it is a far cry from our contemporary ability to put an entire library on a compact disk.

One significant factor that hastened the establishment of an official New Testament canon, by forcing Christians in the second century to begin defining which books were to be designated as the authoritative measure of Christian thought and worship, was the emergence of deviant patterns of Christianity. Indeed, the challenger Marcion, who rejected all ideas associated with the Jews and the Old Testament, published the *first* list of books—ones that he regarded as authoritative. They included an expurgated edition of Luke and the ten epistles of Paul, not including the Pastoral letters.

The Muratorian Canon (c. 170–190 C.E.), which is somewhat fragmentary and speculative on matters of authorship and dating, was yet very significant over against Marcion in the identification of the Gospels, Acts, thirteen letters of Paul, Jude, two letters of John, the Apocalypse of John, and the Apocalypse of Peter (not now in our canon) as being the accepted sources for the church.

Other works, such as the Shepherd of Hermas, were regarded as too recent to be from the authoritative apostolic witnesses. By the time of Eusebius, an associate of the great catechetical school in Caesarea (late third and early fourth centuries), several additional books were understood to be fully authoritative in churches, including Hebrews and 1 Peter, as well as some works that had been disputed for authorship or other reasons, such as James, Jude, 2 Peter, 2 and 3 John. But the Apocalypse of Peter was at that point omitted, and anyone who has read it will certainly understand the reason, because of some of its mythological reports about the resurrection of Jesus. In the Easter Letter of Athanasius (367), the twenty-seven books in our canon had been clearly identified. The Council of Carthage (397) declared those works to be the basic standard of Christian faith.[3]

But New Testament canonicity was not dependent merely on church approval. Rather the books were recognized as being the accepted standard or a "canon of faith" long before they were approved by any church council. They were early quoted as the standard in various other writings. So, for example, just as 2 Peter 3:15–16 cited the Pauline letters as authoritative, 1 Clement (end of the first century) quoted substantially from Hebrews and referred to the letter of James. The views of some contemporary scholars who would either suggest that the canon is still open or that the entire idea of canon should be dismissed generally emerge from a sense of skepticism that God could actually have been at work in weak humans and a frail church to provide divine standards for the people of God. But that assertion is a basic affirmation of Christianity. The awesome, almighty God sent the divine Son in human flesh to provide mere humans with the mysterious gift of salvation and called them to respond to new life in Christ. This new life implies the transformation of human worship from the *self* as the center of concern, to *God* as the focus of praise and thanksgiving, and from a self-centered life of indulgence to a self-giving life of service. The foundation and the implications of that new life in Christ are contained in the Christian canon.

The New Testament canon contains four testimonies (Gospels) about who Jesus is. Each has a different focus, but each is a vibrant witness to Jesus, the Son of God, who in his ministry exemplified an authentic model of life and worship and who provided a new relationship for humans with God through his own death and resurrection. The Acts of the Apostles then provides a selected series of vignettes on how early Christians carried the gospel to others and illustrates how worship and life ought to be lived in the new age. The epistles of Paul and others provide insights into concerns and problems that were faced by early Christians in their worship and life (including: patterns of faithfulness to Christ, correct understandings of salvation, directions on moral issues, spiritual gifts, leadership questions, relationships within households and with authorities) as they sought to apply the message of Jesus to living in a world that did not understand what the worship of God in Christ actually meant. Some of the letters offer strategic statements of advice for newly baptized believers, and for counseling in matters of spiritual formation or the facing of persecution and opposition from both within and without their communities of faith. Other works that have been listed as letters are primarily homiletical or theological discourses. The entire twenty-seven–book corpus is brought to a magnificent conclusion by the future-oriented Book of Revelation, which sets out in a dramatic and worshipful combination the anticipated demise of evil and the expected joyous reward of the righteous, who will worship fully in the presence of almighty God.

Throughout the centuries the New Testament canon has given birth to various approaches toward what the texts mean as the standard of authentic Christianity, but it has continually served the people of God as a divinely given guideline for worship and life. God's people, however, have often been tempted to turn away from God and God's way/model for their lives, just as it was in the beginning, in the period of the Judges, and thereafter. They have frequently turned to follow the patterns of the world, to their undoing. In the world people try to deal with their fears and anxieties by establishing their own gods made in the images of their own goals and desires. Even though they should recognize that there is a God, their longings to satisfy their passions, cravings, and care for themselves in the midst of what they experience as an unfriendly cosmos blind them to the mystery of the Divine and lead them to reject the self-giving God in favor of the appeals of the created order (cf. Rom 1:21–22). The one who tempts them to pseudo-solutions gives them pseudo-forms of worship, which cannot help but produce lives that are in fact empty shells of reality, so that their lives become far removed from the standards of God. As a result, the divine guidelines function to judge them rather than offer them hope (cf. Rom 3:19–26; Gal 3:19–24; 5:13; John 16:8–11).

A Worship Glimpse into the Future

As we look to the future, the inventions and innovations of the present provide us with incredible possibilities. But we need to be aware of their dangers and distractions as well. While teaching in the Far East, I became aware of young people text-messaging each other in church services while the "worship" was proceeding; and the pastor or preacher seemed to be completely unaware of what was occurring. The microchip and the computer have changed the way we conduct our lives and communicate with each other. But innovation does not always mean overall improvement. Clearly our great-grandparents could hardly recognize the way we live and travel today. And it will be so for the gap between us and our great-grandchildren, unless the Lord returns in the meantime. The health professions have been revolutionized by new medicines and by innovations such as micro-surgery. The genetic ladder offers an incredible potential for heretofore-unanticipated solutions. But people still become ill and die. Indeed, some of the new disease forms are more virulent and drug resistant than any we knew previously. Despite all the innovations, however, we remain merely frail humans who desperately need God, although some may think humans are now beyond the need for such "a primitive idea."

Authors such as Ray Kurzweil in his *The Age of Spiritual Machines* and such other works force readers today to ask about the potential implications of the transference of mind patterns to machines. What will such a reality mean for the future? The answers are not totally obvious now. But the innovations are both exciting and a little scary. Recent scientific demonstrations are carrying innovations to new horizons–so that one can talk into a phone in English and be heard in French or German in another country, and the French speaker can respond in French and be heard by the English listener in English. The machine is doing the translation for us. Of course, many such innovations are currently at their introductory stage, yet the technology is already in process. But technology is not God, and machines and innovations are basically neutral. Yet their use can be very good and/or very evil, just like the use of the atom!

The New Testament may be an ancient book, but God is not irrelevant; and the divinely ensconced directions provided by the Bible for worship and life under the guidance of the Holy Spirit are not out of date. The questions that confront us, however, are very significant: How will the church respond to the changes that are occurring? Is the God that is worshiped in our churches capable of handling the innovations, or did our conceived God fall asleep ten or fifty or a hundred or a thousand years ago? Is the Christ we perceive that our church worships able to cope with change? Or has our God become a *deus absconditus* (an absentee god) as some people of Israel thought before Jesus came? Is our God so far removed that we need mediators, such as angels and archangels, to relate to God? Where does Jesus actually fit into our lives and worship? Is our Christ actually concerned about us and the world today? In what ways do we actually sense that God is in our worship, and how do we describe what worship is in our setting? Is the God we worship just someone who comes into the picture when we are in trouble or face death? Or, is God really the awesome, mysterious one who confronts us and undoes all our sham and falseness? These reality questions in fact face all of us. The answers that we give are a measure of who the God we worship actually is.

The issues of worship that engage us are likewise very intriguing and need to be pondered. We can begin our reflection with music in our churches, about which there are great differences of opinion. Is integrity of worship to be found in the context of organ music, or in the context of a praise band, or with no instruments at all? Then, is the type of building where we meet crucial to worship? Is the size of the community at worship a measure of genuine worship? Is the order of when the offering is taken foundational to worship? What about my preferences for the accoutrements of worship? How really significant are ritual gowns, incense burners, flags, palm branches, ashes, wine or grape juice, risen bread or unleavened crackers for worship? How important for us in worship is the Bible translation that is used in the reading of Scripture?

These and many other such questions on the surface may seem to be very simplistic, yet for some people they become the keys to worship and the roots of many church disputes.

But let us to move to some other questions. Does the sign outside saying, "We are a welcoming church," actually represent who we are? What would happen if someone in poor clothing or of a different color came in and asked to join? What happens in our minds when we encounter people who are hungry or have AIDS? How do we react when an uninvited person shows up at our class meeting or private party? What is our response when suggestions are made to try something new in our church? How do people who speak in tongues relate to people who do not, and vice versa? How do we and our church deal with issues of immorality? What would be idolatry in our personal and church settings? These questions and many others have been treated in the New Testament. Some of them deal directly with our worship, and some have implications concerning the question that was put to Jesus about, "Who is my neighbor?" Others concern the meaning of Christian integrity and grow out of the kind of God whom we worship.

The fundamental question, however, concerns: "Who is God?" or, "Is the awesome, mysterious God of the New Testament actually relevant to life today?" Perhaps more to the point might be: "What would happen if the incarnate Jesus came into our church and actually touched our lives today?" "How long could we tolerate him?" and, "How would we respond to the presence of such mystery in our midst?" Still another way to put the issue is: "Were the New Testament writers such as Paul just hopeless emotionalists when they broke into praises, thanksgivings, and ascriptions to God in Christ in the midst of their writings and reflections?" Or, to ask the question more personally: "How often do you and I burst into singing about God in the midst of our daily life and work?" Maybe that question can serve to lead us to reflect more intently on whether or not Jesus Christ is really the living Lord of our lives.

My earnest prayer is that the awesome God of peace and complete integrity will be present with you as you continually reflect and renew your responses to the transforming presence of divine mystery in your life and worship! And may God alone receive the glory!

QUESTIONS

1. As you face the future, what kind of God do you worship?
2. What kind of worship goals will you be developing? How will you evaluate them?
3. What worship issues threaten to divide your church? How can the New Testament help you resolve such issues without great damage to the church?
4. How is your worship reflected in your daily life?
5. How many unchurched people know you worship Christ?

Notes

Introduction

[1]See the work of Rudolph Otto, *The Idea of the Holy* (New York: Oxford University Press, [1958] 1917), 8–41.

[2]See for example: David Peterson, *Engaging with God: A Biblical Theology of Worship* (Grand Rapids: Eerdmans, 1992); Paul Bradshaw, *The Search for the Origins of Christian Worship* (New York: Oxford University Press, 1992); Ferdinand Hahn, *The Worship of the Early Church* (Philadelphia: Fortress Press, 1973); Larry Hurtado, *At the Origins of Christian Worship* (Grand Rapids: Eerdmans, 1999); Ralph Martin, *Worship in the Early Church* (Grand Rapids: Eerdmans, 1975). For the Old Testament see Andrew Hill, *Enter His Courts with Praise: Old Testament Worship for the New Testament Church* (Grand Rapids: Baker Book House, 1996), and Walter Brueggemann, *Israel's Praise: Doxology Against Idolatry and Ideology* (Minneapolis: Fortress Press, 1988). See also Robert Webber, ed., *The Biblical Foundations of Christian Worship*, Vol. 1 in *The Complete Library of Christian Worship* (Nashville: Star Song, 1993).

[3]While this author's colleague Andrew Hill does not follow the same pattern as the author does in this work, his perspectives are very important for the use of the Old Testament. See both his work and that of Walter Brueggemann listed in n. 2 above.

[4]For a discussion of various mindsets, see M. Rex Miller's book *The Millennium Matrix* (San Francisco: Jossey-Bass, 2004).

[5]See, for example, Gerald L. Borchert, *John 1–11* and *John 12–21* in *New American Commentary* (Nashville: Broadman & Holman, 1996, 2002) and *Galatians* in *Cornerstone Biblical Commentary* (Wheaton, Ill.: Tyndale House, 2007).

[6]Author's work on "Revelation" is part of a forthcoming commentary on the *New Living Translation* of the Bible to be published shortly by Tyndale House, Wheaton, Ill.

[7]See Karl Barth, *The Knowledge of God and the Service of God* (London: Hodder and Stoughton, 1938).

[8]See Robert E. Webber, *Worship Is a Verb: Eight Principles for Transforming Worship* (Peabody, Mass.: Hendrickson,1992).

Part I: Testifying about Jesus

[1]For further information on the Gospel of Philip, see Gerald L. Borchert, "An Analysis of the Literary Arrangement and Theological Views in the Coptic Gnostic Gospel of Philip," diss., Princeton Theological Seminary, 1967. For a summary of Gnosticism and author's thesis on Gnosticism, see Gerald Borchert, "Insights into the Gnostic Threat to Christianity as Gained through the Gospel of Philip" in *New Dimensions in New Testament Study,* ed. Richard Longenecker and Merrill Tenney (Grand Rapids: Zondervan, 1974), 79–93.

Chapter 1: Matthew

[1]In addition to the commentaries listed in the beginning of this book, for helpful resources on Matthew, see Paul J. Achtemeier, Joel B. Green, and Marianne Meye Thompson, *Introducing the New Testament: Its Literature and Theology* (Grand Rapids: Eerdmans, 2001) and Luke T. Johnson, *The Writings of the New Testament: An Interpretation* (Philadelphia: Fortress Press, 1986).

[2]I will discuss the Sermon on the Mount in more detail later, but for further assistance in interpreting it, see Robert A. Guelich, *The Sermon on the Mount: A Foundation for Understanding* (Waco, Tex.: Word Books, 1982); also see Donald A. Carson, *The Sermon on the Mount* (Grand Rapids: Baker Books, 1978); W. D. Davies, *The Setting of the Sermon on the Mount* (Cambridge, Eng.: Cambridge University Press, 1964); David Lloyd-Jones, *Studies in the Sermon on the Mount*, 2 vols. (Grand Rapids: Eerdmans, 1959–60); John Stott, *Christian Counter-Culture: The Message of the Sermon on the Mount* (Downers Grove, Ill.: InterVarsity Press, 1978) as well as articles in *R&E* 89 (Spring 1992).

[3]Readers should understand that Torah does not merely mean a set of rules but in the best understanding it means a way of life with God.

[4]For references on the Sermon on the Mount see footnote 2. Particularly, see Guelich, *Sermon on the Mount,* 62–118 (from fn. 11).

[5]See Gerald L. Borchert, "1 Corinthians 7:15 and the Church's Historic Misunderstanding of Divorce and Remarriage," *R&E* 96 (1999): 125–29.

[6]See Glenn Stassen's helpful discussion on the sermon in *Just Peacemaking: Transforming Initiatives for Peace and Justice* (Cleveland: Pilgrim Press, 2004).

[7]See the comments of Gerald L. Borchert in, "The Lord of Form and Freedom: A New Testament Perspective on Worship," *R&E* 80 (1983): 5–18. Note also author's comments on Paul's use of *abba* in his Greek letters (e.g., Rom 8:15; Gal 4:6).

Chapter 2: Mark

[1]For various treatments on Mark, see the sources listed at the beginning of this book.

[2]See the discussion in Eusebius, *Historia Ecclesiastica,* 3.39.4, 15.

[3]I discussed my theory of the lost beginning and ending of Mark with the former Cambridge don, C. F. D. Moule, and he was of the same inclination. Norman Perrin's suggestion that the book ended at 16:8 and that the appearance stories in the other Gospels were manufactured in support of a primordial myth is part of his attempt following Bultmann's lead to demythologize the Easter story and remove the historical reality of the resurrection appearances of Jesus. See Perrin, *The Resurrection according to Matthew, Mark and Luke* (Philadelphia: Fortress Press, 1977), 16–28.

[4]See W. Wrede, *The Messianic Secret,* trans. J. C. G. Greig (reprint, London; James Clarke, 1971). For an historical review of the so-called first quest, see Albert Schweitzer, *The Quest for the Historical Jesus,* trans. W. Montgomery (reprint, New York: Macmillan, 1964).

Chapter 3: Luke

[1]For further information on Luke, see the list of commentaries at the beginning of this book

[2]For these matters of introduction, see, for example, John Noland, *Luke 1–9:20* in *WBC* (Dallas: Word Books, 1989–1993), xxvii–xl; I. H. Marshall, *Luke: Historian and Theologian* (Exeter: Paternoster, 1970).

[3]The misleading statement of the heavenly choir on many Christmas cards–that peace is promised to everyone–is drawn from a rather poor translation in the KJV of Luke 2:14.

Chapter 4: John

[1]For further information, see the resources listed at the beginning of this book.

[2]See Gerald Borchert, *John 12–21* in *NAC* (Nashville: Broadman & Holman, 1996, 2002), 369–80.

[3]Ibid., 345–67.

[4]See Rudolf Bultmann, *The Gospel of John* (Philadelphia: Westminster Press, 1971), 11–12.

[5]See, for example, the intriguing work of R. Alan Culpepper, *John, Son of Zebedee: The Life of a Legend* (Columbia, S.C.: University of South Carolina Press, 1994) and his earlier suggestions on *The Johannine School* in SBL Dissertations (Missoula, Mont.: Scholars Press, 1975). See also the revised view of Raymond Brown concerning John in *The Epistles of John* in *AB* (New York: Doubleday, 1982), 30–35, and his *The Community of the Beloved Disciple* (New York: Paulist Press, 1979) 25–91.

[6]See author's comments on the views of Brown, Culpepper, J. Martyn and others in Gerald Borchert, *John 1–11* in *NAC* (Nashville: Broadman & Holman, 1996, 2002), 42–50, 80–94.

[7]See author's comments in ibid., 183–85.

[8]See Bultmann, *The Gospel of John,* vii–x.

[9]For insight into how significant Sabbath was to the rabbis, see *The Mishnah,* trans. H. Danby (London: Oxford University Press, 1933), 100–21.

[10]For a discussion of symbols in John, see Craig Koester, *Symbolism in the Fourth Gospel* (Minneapolis: Fortress Press, 1995).

[11]See, for example, Harold Fisch, ed., *Haggada* (Jerusalem: Koren, 1965).

[12]For the development of the Festival of Tabernacles and the debacle under Alexander Jannaeus, see Borchert, *John 1–11,* 288–91; George MacRae, "The Meaning and Evolution

of the Feast of Tabernacles," *CBQ* (1960): 251–76 and Johannes Pedersen, *Israel: Its Life and Culture* (London: Geoffrey Cumberlege/Oxford University Press, 1940), 418–25. See particularly Josephus, *Antiquities* 13.13.5 (372–76).

[13]See Borchert, *John 1–11*, 295–96.

[14]See Borchert, *John 12–21*, 29–31.

[15]Ibid., 120–25, 131–37, 158–71.

[16]For a description of the Farewell Cycle as a target or bull's-eye, with a series of circular rings from the center (15:1–17) to the outside of the powerful foot-washing act and decisive prayer, see Borchert, *John 12–21*, 73–75.

[17]For a helpful treatment of this section of John, see J. P. Heil, *Blood and Water* (Washington: *CBQ* Monograph Series, 1995).

[18]Those who have concentrated their analysis on the different Greek words for "love" in John 21:15–17 need to study a little more Greek, because *phileo* is used by John interchangeably with *agapao*. See, for example, John 5:20.

Chapter 5: Acts

[1]For further information, see the resources for Acts and for Luke listed at the beginning of this book.

[2]Note the "began" (*erxato*) concerning Luke's previous book at Acts 1:1.

[3]The number 120 is the result of multiplying 12, the number of the tribes, times 10, the number necessary for a synagogue meeting. The use of such symbolic numbers was very significant for the Jews.

[4]The expression "filled with" is a particularly Lucan expression and appears only in one other place in the New Testament (Eph 5:18; see author's comments there). Beyond mentioning "filled with" the Spirit (Luke 1:15, 41, 67; Acts 2:4; 4:8, 31; 9:17; 13:9; etc.), Luke also writes of "filled with" wrath, awe, fear, madness, wonder, wine, indignation, envy (Luke 4:28; 5:26; 6:11; Acts 2:13; 3:10; 5:17; 13:45; 19:29; etc.).

[5]The debate continues whether or not the residents of Qumran were actually monks and if Qumran was even a monastery. See, for example, the report "Qumran–The Pottery Factory," *Biblical Archaeology Review* 32.5 (September–October 2006): 26–32.

[6]Scholars debate the significance of "we" (first-person plural) at this point. The suggestion that "we" does not mean that Luke was with Paul but merely indicates a sea voyage falls flat because other sea voyages in Acts do not follow that pattern (e.g., 13:13; 14:26).

[7]For further information of Philippi see Gerald Borchert, "Philippi," in *ISBE*, ed. Geoffrey Bromiley (Grand Rapids: Eerdmans, 1986), 3.834–36.

[8]For a criticism of the idea that Acts could not reflect Pauline thinking, see Philipp Vielhauer, "On the 'Paulinism' of Acts," reprinted in *The Writings of St. Paul*, ed. Wayne E. Meeks (New York: W. W. Norton, 1972), 166–75. See also Rudolf Bultmann, *Die Stil der paulinischen Predigt und die kynisch-stoiche Diatribe* (Göttingen: Vandenhoeck und Ruprecht, 1910). See also the helpful analysis by N.B. Stonehouse, *The Areopagus Address* (London: Tyndale Press, 1949).

[9]With respect to Paul's pattern of self-support, see author's comments at 1 Corinthians 9:12–18 concerning mission strategy for the worshiping community.

[10]While most vows would last at least thirty days, the Nazarite vow could be done in a minimum of seven days (cf. *Mishnah, Nazir* 3.6). The expenditures included two lambs (a year-old male and a female), a ram, a grain offering, a wine offering, unleavened bread, and, of course, the priest's services.

[11]For a description of the stone warning wall(s) that threatened death to Gentiles who proceeded beyond the marked boundaries, see, for example, Josephus, *Jewish War*, 5.193, 194. In Ephesians 2:14, Paul used the concept of the wall of separation between Jews and Gentiles symbolically to indicate that in Christ there is no longer a dividing wall in worship. It is also one of the reasons for author's suggestion that Luke was probably the amanuensis (scribe) for that letter of Paul. (See author's comments on Ephesians.)

Chapter 6: Romans

[1]For further information on the Epistle to the Romans, see the resources listed at the beginning of this book.

[2]Author is indebted to one of his former Roman Catholic teachers on Romans, Joseph Fitzmyer, for his insights from the Church Fathers on this epistle. Many of his ideas are now available in his commentary on *Romans* in *AB* (New York: Doubleday, 1993).

[3]Paul uses a fascinating Greek expression *ek pisteos eis pistin,* for which some translations are not very helpful (e.g., the RSV has "through faith for faith"). Attention should be paid to the prepositions, because *ek* is the preposition of origin and *eis* signifies direction or goal. Thus, either something such as the KJV rendering "from...to" or the rendering in the *New Living Translation,* that God's working it out was recognized "from start to finish by faith," would be better.

[4]See Gerald Borchert, "Romans, Pastoral Counseling, and the Introspective Conscience of the West," *R&E* 83:1 (Winter 1986): 84.

[5]See Rudolf Bultmann, *Der Stil der paulinischen Predigt und die kynisch-stoiche Diatribe* (Göttingen: Vandenhoeck und Ruprecht, 1910) and the more recent work of S. K. Stowers, *The Diatribe and Paul's Letter to the Romans* (Chico, Calif.: Scholars Press, 1981). While the early view was that the style belonged to Cynic and Stoic preaching or oration, it seems more akin to their early teaching patterns. The style uses shrewd questions and obvious answers (notice, for example: Paul's *me genoito,* "absolutely not" at Rom 3:4 and 6) so that the listener or reader quickly realizes that the opponent has little chance of winning. Resources are brought to bear at crucial times, and the argument is well-designed to win the day.

[6]The use of the genitives for Jesus in both verses 22 and 26 following "faith" can be interpreted either as Jesus' faith or our faith in Jesus. Perhaps Paul was astutely noncommittal at this point, since he did make clear in verses 24 and 25 the necessity of human faith in the salvation process. But he may also have wanted his readers to realize that Jesus was faithful in his role of providing that salvation as well.

[7]Scholars tend to take sides on whether to define the Greek term *hilasterion* here theologically as either "propitiation," or "expiation." Some think that propitiation is too ferocious a term and implies that God is like some pagan god who is angry and demands blood to be satisfied. However one chooses to view the term, God is hardly bloodthirsty. "Blood" here was the way for Paul to make clear that Jesus actually died to take away our guilt.

[8]Perhaps a somewhat apocryphal illustration would help readers at this point. The story goes that two Scottish brother-theologians, who shall remain unnamed here, were walking down the street of the city. A well-meaning Christian engaged in witnessing confronted them: "Brothers, are you saved?" The response from one of the brothers was, "Yes. Partly. And No!" After the shocked look on the face of the witness, the theologian continued: "Yes, I am justified. Partly I am sanctified. And No I am not yet glorified." The point of the story is not to dissuade witnessing, but to be clear on what we are saying. Terms are often confusing, and we need to be clear on what they mean in the context of a discussion.

[9]See Krister Stendahl, "The Apostle Paul and the Introspective Conscience of the West," *Harvard Theological Review* 56 (1963): 199–215; reprinted in *Paul among Jews and Gentiles* (Philadelphia: Fortress Press, 1976), 78–96; J. Christiaan Beker, *Paul the Apostle* (Philadelphia: Fortress Press, 1980), 86, 104–8; E. P. Sanders, *Paul and Palestinian Judaism* (Philadelphia: Fortress Press, 1977), 475–511. Also see author's response in Borchert, "Romans, Pastoral Counseling," 86–88.

[10]For an excellent treatment of these chapters see, Johannes Munck, *Christ and Israel: An Interpretation of Romans 9–11* (Philadelphia: Fortress Press, 1967).

Chapter 7: First Corinthians

[1]For some of the many helpful works on the Corinthian letters, see the list at the beginning of this book.

[2]For helpful discussions on the city of Corinth, see James Blevins, "Introduction to 1 Corinthians," *R&E* 80 (1983): 315–19; Jack Finegan, "Corinth," in *IBD* (Nashville: Abingdon Press, 1962) I: 682–83; J. Murphy-O'Connor, "Corinth," in *ABD* (New York: Doubleday, 1992), I: 1134–39.

[3]Strabo, *Geography,* VIII, 378.

[4]Translators often render the Greek by "servant" to avoid getting into the knotty question of women's roles in the church.

[5]See A. Brassac, "Une inscription de Delphes et la chronologie de Saint Paul," *Revue Biblique,* W.S.X. (1913): 36–53, 207–17.

[6]The Greek word *apostolos* and the Latin *missus,* from which we get the English word "missionary," are clearly similar. In the early church the term implied a very special calling from God in the initial communication of the authentic gospel.

[7]It is not clear whether this Sosthenes was the same ruler of the synagogue in Corinth who was beaten before Gallio after Crispus the former ruler became a Christian. It is intriguing to consider the possibility that this Jewish leader also might have become a Christian after bringing charges against Paul. (See Acts 18:17.)

[8]The Gnostics borrowed these three designations and used them differently. Given their high view of determinism, they viewed themselves as the *pneumatikoi,* who would never lose their salvation because they possessed a divine spark. They identified most Christians as *psychikoi* who had to work hard, be obedient, and might eventually gain eternal rest. The great mass of humanity were regarded as merely fleshly (*sarkinoi*) and were destined for destruction. See, for example, author's comments in Borchert, "Insights into the Gnostic Threat to Christianity as Gained through the Gospel of Philip," in *New Dimensions in New Testament Study,* ed. R.N. Longenecker and M. Tenney (Grand Rapids: Zondervan, 1974), 79–93.

[9]The man was obviously a member of the church, and his father's wife with whom he was living was apparently not a Christian. Otherwise, she also would have been mentioned. (Cf. the problem here with Num 18:7–8.)

[10]Among the forms of discipline were curses such as, "May the Lord swallow you up like Korah" (cf. Num 16:31–33; Jude 11), beatings (cf. 2 Cor 11:25) and shunning in which the community would not talk to the person for about thirty days. (Cf. the covenanters' rules in the *Manual of Discipline* discovered near Qumran.)

[11]For some helpful discussions on the economic and social status of the Corinthian Christians, see Gerd Theissen, *The Social Setting of Pauline Christianity: Essays on Corinth* (Philadelphia: Fortress, 1982).

[12]In one of his dissertations—*Die Stil der paulinischen Predigt und die kynisch-stoiche Diatribe* (Göttingen: Vandenhoeck und Ruprecht, 1910)—Rudolf Bultmann correctly identified, at least to some extent, Paul's kinship in the use of the diatribe method of argument with its multiple uses of questions, but his further assumption that Paul obtained much of his philosophical understanding from that source is to be rejected. For a later study on the diatribe see S. K. Stowers, *The Diatribe and Paul's Letter to the Romans* (Chico, Calif.: Scholars Press, 1981). See author's earlier comments on Romans above.

[13]Compare the first question of the Shorter Catechism, which states that the chief end or purpose of humanity is to "glorify God and to serve him forever."

[14]While I cannot here pursue the matter of divorce and remarriage further, I suggest that you consult my "1 Corinthians 7:15 and the Church's Historic Misunderstanding of Divorce and Remarriage," *R&E* 96 (1999), 125–29, in which I detail the mistranslations of the Hebrew terms for "put away" and "divorce" that have led to countless misinterpretations of situations concerning being bound and being free of the marriage bond in both the Old and New Testaments. I will merely add here that translators of the Bible have created problems in understanding the Jewish concepts of putting the wife out of the house because of some perceived problem in her and issuing her a certificate of divorce. Remember that men were the legal authorities in their homes.

[15]In the New Testament idolatry and immorality are generally linked as the basic sins because whom one honors affects how one lives and acts. Note the prohibition against idolatry and immorality in the decision of the Council of Jerusalem (Acts 15:20, 28–29). In the Book of Revelation both Pergamum and Thyatira are condemned for the combination of idolatry and immorality (Rev 2:14, 20). In the sixth trumpet, humanity refuses to repent of the worship of idols and among other sinful acts the practice of immorality (9:20–21). Paul warns the Corinthians to "flee" (*pheugete*) both immorality and idolatry (1 Cor 6:18; 10:14).

[16]I am indebted to Richard Oster on this matter for his enlightening 1986 paper "Cultural Background to 1 Corinthians 11:4" at the meetings of *Studiorum Novi Testamenti Societas.*

[17]For an interesting contrast in perspective concerning the sharing of food at meals, see the Roman writer Pliny in *The Letters of the Younger Pliny,* trans. Betty Radice (Harmondsorth:

Penguin, 1969), 63–64. See also the comments of Wayne Meeks, *The First Urban Christians* (New Haven: Yale University Press), 67–69.

[18]Paul uses the Greek terms *paralambano* (meaning a true "reception" of the tradition) and *paradidomi* (meaning true passing on of the tradition without alteration) for the rabbinic concepts in order to indicate that he stands firmly in the traditions handed down from Jesus himself. For additional information on the concept of the new obedience in Christianity, see Heikki Raisanen, *Paul and the Law* (Philadelphia: Fortress, 1986), 247; W. D. Davies, *Paul and Rabbinic Judaism* (London: S.P.C.K, 1958), 101, 140, 227ff.

[19]See Strabo, *Geography*, X. 3. 7. See also Livy, *History of Rome*, XXXIX. xv; Plutarch, *Moralia*, 671; Pausanias, *Description of Greece*, II. ii. See also Menander, *Fragments*, 326, and Iamblichus, *The Egyptian Mysteries*, trans. Alexander Wilder (Whitefish, Mont.: Kessinger, 1942), 119–20.

[20]See author's further comments on tradic thinking in connection with 1 Thessalonians 1:3–9.

[21]In his argument of 14:10–11, Paul seeks to make clear the difference between *glossa* ("tongue") and *phonon/aphonon* ("language").

[22]It is crucial to remember that Bacchus/Dionysus was called the god of madness. See Plutarch, *Moralia*, 671. Moreover, Aristophanes spoke of the "tongue of Bacchus" in his modeling of babbling with both wonder and disdain, which was not uncommon among the ancients. See Aristophanes, *Frogs*, 357. Cf. also his poem *Lysistrata*, where the devotee babbles in meaningless words.

[23]See, for example, the book by John Piper and Wayne Grudem, eds., *Recovering Biblical Manhood and Womanhood: A Response to Evangelical Feminism* (Wheaton, Ill.: Crossway Books, 1991).

[24]See Gordon D. Fee, *The First Epistle to the Corinthians* in *NICNT* (Grand Rapids: Eerdmans, 1953), 699–708.

[25]See Gerald L. Borchert, "The Resurrection: 1 Corinthians 15," *R&E* 80 (1983): 401–15.

[26]For a discussion of author's views of the future, please see his essay, Gerald Borchert, "Excursus 33: Questions of Eternity: Where Is the Place? What Is It Like? How Do We Get There?" in *John 12–21* in *NAC*, vol. 25B (Nashville: Broadman & Holman, 2002), 360–67.

[27]See Justin, *Apologia*, 56.

Chapter 8: Second Corinthians

[1]As indicated in the earlier discussion concerning this man, the purpose of Christian discipline is not punitive but redemptive. Here Paul is concerned that the Corinthians convey their love to the man. In the first case, Paul was concerned that Satan's power would bring the man to his senses, but here he wants to make sure that Satan does not get in the midst of the community and cause discontent or a punitive spirit to emerge in the church.

[2]The concept of faith based on the heart, rather than on stone tablets and the rigidity of words, was suggested by the prophets as the sign of the new era. See, for example, Jeremiah 31:31–33; Ezekiel 11:19; 36:26–27. It is important here, however, not to interpret the law in a negative manner, after the style of Marcion, who rejected the Old Testament as emanating from an evil god. His particular point was to separate law and gospel. See, for example, Tertullian, *Against Marcion,* I. 19. For an excellent discussion on Paul's exposition of glory and the law, see David Garland, *2 Corinthians* in *NAC* (Nashville: Broadman & Holman, 1999), 167–202.

[3]See author's discussion on this aspect of worship in Gerald L. Borchert, "The Lord of Form and Freedom: A New Testament Perspective on Worship," *R&E* 80 (1983): 10–11.

[4]See, for example, Plato, *Phaedrus,* 246–49.

[5]For further explanations on Paul's triadic thinking, see author's comments on 1 Cor 13:13 and 1 Thess 1:3–9.

Chapter 9: Galatians

[1]For some helpful works on Galatians, see the list at the beginning of this book.

[2]See Gerald Borchert, "A Key to Pauline Thinking: Galatians 3:23–29," *R&E* 91 (1994):145.

[3]See author's comments in Borchert, "Galatians," the Introduction in *Romans and Galatians* in *Cornerstone Biblical Commentary,* vol. 14 (Wheaton, Ill.:Tyndale House, forthcoming).

[4]See, for example, P. Birnbaum, ed. and trans., *Daily Prayer Book, Ha-Siddur Ha-Shalem* (New York: Hebrew Publishing Company, n.d.), 15–18.

[5]For a discussion of the differences in time between Genesis 15:13 and Exodus 12:40, see how the rabbis dealt with the problem in Longenecker, *Galatians* in *WBC* (Dallas: Word Books, 1990), 133. See also Borchert, "Galatians," sv.

[6]Concerning angelic mediation of the law, see author's discussion in "The Purpose of the Law," in Borchert, "Galatians," sv.

[7]See Borchert, "A Key to Pauline Thinking," 145–51.

[8]Please see author's comments on the subject in Gerald L. Borchert, "The Lord of Form and Freedom," *R&E* 80 (1983): 5–18.

[9]The command to "walk" in Paul is derived from the Hebrew idea of *halak,* which meant "conduct your life with God," as in the case of Abraham or Enoch, who "walked" with God. Unfortunately, among the rabbis the term took a twist and in later arguments the term *halakah* became equated with legal prescriptions, so that in the Talmuds, etc., the contrast was made between materials that were interpretive (*haggadah*) and those that were prescriptive (*halakah*).

Chapter 10: Ephesians

[1]For further information on Ephesians, see the resources listed at the beginning of this book.

[2]See, for example, F. C. Baur, *The Church History of the First Three Centuries,* 2 vols., 3d ed. (London: Williams and Norgate, 1878–79), and id., *Paul the Apostle of Jesus Christ, His Life and Work, His Epistles and His Doctrine,* 2 vols., 2d ed. (London: Williams and Norgate, 1875–1876).

[3]The most comprehensive study on the authorship of Ephesians, in this author's estimation, was done by A. Van Roon, *Authenticity of Ephesians* (Leiden: Brill, 1975). He concluded that Paul wrote Ephesians.

[4]For a fuller discussion of the city, please see G. L. Borchert, "Ephesus," in *ISBE,* rev. ed. (Grand Rapids: Eerdmans, 1982), II. 115–17.

[5]For a complete discussion of these matters, see the work of Hans Jonas, *Gnosis und Spätantiker Geist* (Göttingen: Vandenhoeck und Ruprecht, 1964), or id., *The Gnostic Religion* (Boston: Beacon, 1958). See also Gerald L. Borchert, "An Analysis of the Literary Arrangement and Theological Views in the Coptic Gnostic Gospel of Philip" (Ph.D. dissertation, Princeton Theological Seminary, 1967). For a summary of these views, see Gerald Borchert, "Insights into the Gnostic Threat to Christianity as Gained Through the Gospel of Philip," in *New Dimensions in New Testament Study* (Grand Rapids: Zondervan, 1974), 79–93. For Schlier's work, see his article on *Kephale* ("head") in *TDNT,* III (1965), 673–82. When Heinrich Schlier wrote his first study on Ephesians (*Christus und die Kirche im Epheserbrief*) in 1930, he was seemingly more oriented to a Protestant/Lutheran position; however, by the time he had developed his thinking and wrote his commentary (*Dier Brief an die Epheser*) in 1957–58, he clearly had adopted the Roman Catholic view. See also, among other works, Walter Schmithals, *Gnosticism in Corinth* (Nashville: Abingdon Press, 1971).

[6]See Pamela Scalise and Gerald Borchert, "The Bible and the Spiritual Pilgrimage" in *Becoming Christian,* ed. Bill J. Leonard (Louisville: Westminster/John Knox Press, 1990).

[7]Although some scholars attribute this letter to disciples of Paul, I continue to think that the name Paul stands for the apostle. See the arguments of A. Van Roon in *Authenticity of Ephesians.*

[8]See the works of Sydney Cave, *The Gospel of Paul* (New York: Doubleday, 1929), and Elias Andrews, *The Meaning of Christ for Paul* (New York: Abingdon Press, 1949), 8–16.

[9]The use of the perfect tense *sesosmenoi* ("have been saved") here is significant since it recognizes both the past and the continuing nature of living in Christ.

[10]It is imperative to understand the importance of such "household" terminology because the Roman empire was regarded technically as Caesar's household, and citizens as well as slaves, etc., were all regarded as belonging to Caesar. The emperor was therefore in

control of his domain and the laws of the empire were regarded as aspects of his household (national) codes. Husbands, fathers, and masters were accorded special privileges in this system so that they could establish their own household codes. It is strategic in interpreting the household codes of the New Testament in texts such as Ephesians 5:21–6:9; 1 Timothy 2:1–15; 1 Peter 2:11–20 and 3:1–7 to recognize their nature, but also to understand how they differ from the Hellenistic codes. The differences are what provide the clues to their emphases.

[11]Such a listing here of songs should not be viewed as a complete group of acceptable Christian patterns or styles of singing or of music. They are only meant to be representative of creative patterns for praising God. New forms of praising God should be encouraged as long as the focus is not on ourselves but on the triune God. Narcissism is an ever-present temptation in our culture, and crooning to Jesus often has its focus on the singer rather than on God.

Chapter 11: Philippians

[1]For further information concerning Philippians, see the resources listed at the beginning of this book..

[2]See 1 Clement 5:6.

[3]For further information on the city, see G. L. Borchert, "Philippi," in *ISBE*, rev. ed. (Grand Rapids: Eerdmans, 1986), III. 834–36.

[4]See Ralph Martin, *Carmen Christi: Philippians 2:5–11 in Recent Interpretation and in the Setting of Early Christian Worship* (Cambridge, Eng: Cambridge University Press, 1967).

Chapter 12: Colossians

[1]For further information on Colossians, see the resources listed in the beginning of this book.

[2]See the *Didache* 7. When one visits ancient *mikveh* (washing pools), one is impressed by the effort that the Jews undertook to be sure that the lustration pools provided running water.

Chapter 13: Thessalonian Letters

[1]For further comments on 1 and 2 Thessalonians see the resources listed in the beginning of this book.

[2]For a discussion on the difference between resurrection and immortality, see, for example, O. Cullmann, *Immortality of the Soul or Resurrection of the Dead? The Witness of the New Testament* (London: Epworth Press, 1958).

[3]See author's discussion above in connection with 1 Corinthians 15 and 2 Corinthians 5. For a longer discussion please see Gerald Borchert, "Excursus 33: Questions of Eternity," in *John 12–21* in *NAC* (Nashville: Broadman & Holman, 2002), 360–67. See also Gerald Borchert, "The Resurrection: 1 Corinthians 15," *R&E* 80 (1983): 401–15. Cf. J. A. T. Robinson, "Resurrection in the NT," in *IDB* (Nashville: Abingdon Press, 1962), IV. 45–47.

[4]See Albert Schweitzer, *The Quest of the Historical Jesus: A Critical Study of Its Progress from Reimarus to Wrede* (London: S.C.M., 1954).

[5]For author's earlier views on the Thessalonian letters, see: Gerald Borchert, *Discovering Thessalonians* in *Guidepost Commentaries* (New York: Guideposts, 1986).

[6]For an example of the view that 2 Thessalonians is psuedo-Pauline, see J. A. Bailey, "Who Wrote II Thessalonians?" *NTS* 25 (1978–79): 131–45.

[7]For Paul, the heart was the seat of the will (cf. Rom 1:24). See author's discussion of Paul's psychological views in Gerald Borchert, "Romans, Pastoral Counseling and the Introspective Conscience of the West," *R&E* 83 (1986): 81–92.

Chapter 14: Personal Letters to Philemon, Timothy, and Titus

[1]For further information on this letter see the resources listed in the beginning of this book.

[2]For further information on the varied views concerning the Pastoral Epistles, see the resources listed in the beginning of the book.

[3]See William Mounce, *Pastoral Epistles* in *WBC* (Nashville: Thomas Nelson, 2000).

[4]The KJV rendering of 2 Timothy 2:15 as "rightly dividing the word of truth" has been an unfortunate translation that has led some interpreters "to divide" sections of the Bible,

particularly Revelation, into various time sequences.

⁵Although the Old Testament does not give names to the Egyptian and other opponents or magicians arrayed against Moses, such as in Exodus 7:11–12, Jewish literature provided them with these names. See, for example, the *Damascus Document* (Cairo-CD) 5:18; and the *Targums on Exodus* 1:15; 7:11 and *Numbers* 22:21–22. For further information on the development of these traditions, see Mounce, *Pastoral Epistles,* 549–50.

⁶For a helpful discussion of the Greeks' perspective on the Cretans (Minoans), see the article by Jeremy McInerney, "Did Theseus Slay the Minotaur?: How Myth and Archaeology Inform Each Other," *Biblical Archaeology Review* 32.6 (November–December 2006): 28–43.

⁷The other letter in which Paul patently omitted the thanksgiving section of his letter is Galatians, when he was highly distressed at their abandonment of the grace of God. His omission of the thanksgiving section here is an indication that the problem was a major concern for him.

⁸See author's comments on 1 Corinthians 14:34–36 for the issues concerning the law and that silence text.

Chapter 15: Hebrews

¹For further information on the Book of Hebrews, in addition to the resources listed in the beginning of this book, see the brief survey by Robert H. Gundry, *A Survey of the New Testament,* 3d ed. (Grand Rapids: Zondervan, 1994), 421–30.

²For a further detailing of this alternation see William Johnsson, *Hebrews* in *Knox Preaching Guides* (Atlanta: John Knox Press, 1980), 2.

³See author's comments in Gerald Borchert, *Assurance and Warning* (Nashville: Broadman Press, 1987), 172–79.

Chapter 16: James

¹For further information concerning the Book of James, please consult the resources listed in the beginning of this book.

²For example, Luther's 1522 prefaces to the New Testament books of James and Jude are scathing. See also Ralph Martin, *James* in *WBC* (Waco, Tex.: Word Books, 1988), cv.

Chapter 17: Petrine Letters and Jude

¹For helpful works on the Petrine Epistles and Jude, consult the list of resources at the beginning of this book.

²For the concept of the imprisonment of evil angels, see 1 Enoch 18:12–14; 21:10. Sheol (the place of the dead), however, is not described as a prison. For other discussions on the subject, see: Bo Reicke, *The Disobedient Spirits and Christian Baptism* (Copenhagen: Munksgaard, 946), and W. J. Dalton, *Christ's Proclamation to the Spirits* (Rome: Pontifical Biblical Institute, 1965).

³Concerning the somewhat related matter of preaching to the dead in 1 Peter 4:6, see author's comments in the discussion of that passage.

⁴See Gerald Borchert, "The Conduct of Christians in the Face of the 'Fiery Ordeal,'" *R&E* 79 (1982): 456–57.

⁵For the significance of Jude, besides the bibliographical references listed above and especially the commentary by Richard Baukham, the author recommends the dissertation of his former doctoral student, Kenneth R. Lyle, *Ethical Admonition in the Epistle of Jude* in *Studies in Biblical Literature* (New York: Peter Lang, 1998).

⁶Scholars frequently reflect at this point that the writer was making a bold attempt at giving credence to the legitimacy of his work.

⁷These statements would seem to suggest on face value that 2 Peter was written by a second generation Christian.

Chapter 18: Johannine Letters

¹For further information on the Johannine letters, see the resources listed at the beginning of this book.

²See Irenaeus, *Against Heresies* 3.1.2 and Eusebius, *Ecclesiastical History* 3.1.1. See also G. L. Borchert, "Ephesus," in *ISBE,* rev. ed. (Grand Rapids: Eerdmans, 1982), 2.115–17.

[3]For a discussion of the Johannine themes in the Gospel, see Gerald L. Borchert, "Appendix 1: A Summary of Johannine Theology," in *John 12–21* (Nashville: Broadman & Holman, 2002), 345–67.

[4]The use of the present tenses in 1 John 3:9 should be rendered by the continuous present. Thus the translations of the following expressions in English should be: *hamartian ou poiei* ("does not continue to sin") and *ou dunatai hamartanein* ("cannot continue to sin").

[5]Note: At 5:7–8 the Latin scribes added a Trinitarian statement concerning the Father, the Word, and the Holy Spirit. The Roman Catholic authorities to counteract the careful work of Erasmus fraudulently even constructed a Greek text to support their thesis that this statement was in the original Greek. Erasmus put it in his second edition of the Greek New Testament. Unfortunately, that edition made its way to England and became the basis for the KJV, but such a reading actually disturbs the sequence of the text. The fact that such a reading was removed from later editions of the Erasmian Greek New Testaments and most modern translations is a testimony to the integrity of our New Testaments.

[6]The New Testament is a finely tuned set of works that carefully balances assurances with warnings. For a detailed discussion on this balance, see Gerald L. Borchert, *Assurance and Warning* (Nashville: Broadman Press, 1987).

Chapter 19: Revelation

[1]For further discussions on Revelation, see the resources listed at the beginning of this book.

[2]For further discussion on these characteristics, see Leon Morris, *Apocalyptic* (Grand Rapids: Eerdmans, 1972), 34–67.

[3]For more detail on matters discussed here, please see Gerald Borchert, "Revelation," in the *New Living Translation Study Bible* (Wheaton, Ill.: Tyndale House, forthcoming).

[4]J. Massyngberde Ford, "The Christological Function of the Hymns in Apocalypse of John," *Andrews University Seminary Studies* 56 (1998): 208.

[5]For an excellent discussion of the various methods of interpreting the Book of Revelation, see John P. Newport, *The Lion and the Lamb* (Nashville: Broadman Press, 1988), 79–124.

[6] See author's statements earlier on the Gospel of John, and his commentary noted at that point.

[7]For further information on the structure of the Gospel, see author's comment in the section on the Gospel and his references to the second volume of author's commentary on John there.

[8]See author's comments in Borchert, "Revelation," s.v.

Part VI: Concluding Reflections on theNew Testament Canon and Worship in the Contemporary World

[1]For further information on the subject of the canon, see: Roger Beckwith, *The Old Testament Canon of the New Testament Church and Its Background in Early Judaism* (Grand Rapids: Eerdmans, 1985); F. F. Bruce, *The Canon of Scripture* (Downers Grove, Ill.: InterVarsity Press, 1988); Henry Gamble, *The New Testament Canon: Its Making and Meaning* (Philadelphia: Fortress Press, 1985); Bruce M. Metzger, *The Canon of the New Testament: Its Origin, Development and Significance* (Oxford: Clarendon, 1987); Robert P. Meye, "Canon of the NT," in *ISBE* (Grand Rapids: Eerdmans, 1979), I. 601–6; B. F. Westcott, *The Canon of the New Testament*, 6th ed. (New York: Macmillan, 1889).

[2]While the lines of demarcation were not always clear between the segments, the three-part division of the Jewish authoritative work was also recognized by the Jewish writers such as Josephus, *Contra Apionem*, 1.37–42 and Philo, *On the Contemplative Life*, 3.25.

[3]For complete details on the many lists of the early writers, see, for example, the texts and translations of Daniel J. Theron, *Evidence of Tradition* (Grand Rapids: Baker Book House, 1958), 107–27.

Selected Index

249